MW00803586

NEW ART OF COOKERY

NEW ART OF COOKERY

A SPANISH FRIAR'S KITCHEN NOTEBOOK BY JUAN ALTAMIRAS

VICKY HAYWARD

ROWMAN & LITTLEFIELD
Lanham • Boulder • New York • London

Grateful acknowledgment is made to the following for permission to reprint material. "Blues Castellano," Antonio Gamoneda, c. 1982. "One Meatball," Hy Zaret and Lou Singer, 1940 (renewed) by Oliver Music Publishing. All rights for Oliver Music Publishing Company administered by Music Sales Corporation (ASCAP); worldwide rights for Argosy Music Corp. administered by Helene Blue Musique Ltd.

Cover images: *Nuevo arte de cocina*, 1760, Special Collections Division of the Library of Congress, Washington, DC.

Published by Rowman & Littlefield
A wholly owned subsidiary of The Rowman & Littlefield Publishing Group, Inc.
4501 Forbes Boulevard, Suite 200, Lanham, Maryland 20706
www.rowman.com

Unit A, Whitacre Mews, 26-34 Stannary Street, London SE11 4AB

British Library Cataloguing in Publication Information Available

Library of Congress Cataloging-in-Publication Data
Names: Altamiras, Juan, author. | Hayward, Vicky, translator and coauthor.
Title: New art of cookery : a Spanish friar's kitchen notebook / by Juan Altamiras; [translated, edited, and with new text by] Vicky Hayward.
Other titles: Nuevo arte de cocina, sacado de la escuela de la experiencia económica. English
Description: Lanham : Rowman & Littlefield, [2017] | Translation of: Nuevo arte de cocina, sacado de la escuela de la experiencia económica. | Includes bibliographical references and indexes.
Identifiers: LCCN 2016050011 (print) | LCCN 2016059962 (ebook) | ISBN 9781442279414 (cloth : alk. paper) | ISBN 9781442279421 (Electronic)
Subjects: LCSH: Cooking, Spanish—Early works to 1800. | LCGFT: Cookbooks.
Classification: LCC TX713 .A513 2017 (print) | LCC TX713 (ebook) | DDC 641.5946—dc23
LC record available at https://lccn.loc.gov/2016050011

∞ ™ The paper used in this publication meets the minimum requirements of American National Standard for Information Sciences—Permanence of Paper for Printed Library Materials, ANSI/NISO Z39.48-1992.

Printed in the United States of America

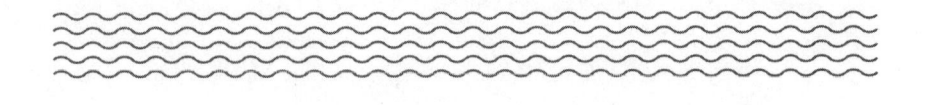

I feel
something marvellous
in the beaten silence:
five human beings
who understand life through the same flavour.

Antonio Gamoneda,
"Taste of Pulses," *Blues Castellano* (1961–1966)

Every era of history brings change in the kitchen and every country or village eats to feed its soul, even before its stomach.

Emilia Pardo Bazán,
The Old Spanish Kitchen (1911)

Cocinero antes que fraile.

Spanish proverb

CONTENTS

PREFACE

I N THE LATE summer of 1745 Juan Altamiras, a Franciscan friar from Aragon, published his recipe notebook, *New Art of Cookery, Drawn from the School of Economic Experience*. I like to imagine him working on it in the kitchen at San Cristóbal, the friars' summer retreat. Built high on a rocky hillside, its vegetable garden laid out in a valley below, it overlooked the wide-horizoned southern Aragonese plains.

Today San Cristóbal stands in ruins. Brambles clamber over fallen stone walls and a spidery fig tree overhangs the path leading to the kitchen garden. Yet the view over the plains has changed little from the one so well known to Altamiras: a patchwork of vineyards, pastures, orchards, and wheat fields, spotted by villages and towns, spreading north towards Zaragoza, the River Ebro and, far beyond, the Pyrenean mountains. Turn south to face the hillside and you can pick out a snow well and hermitage among the boulders rising to sierra peaks; behind those rocky summits lie folded sierras running down to Castile. Travelers to the friary in Altamiras's day came north along a dusty road snaking through river gorges, or they traveled west and south across the plains from Cariñena and Zaragoza. Don Quixote and Sancho Panza had ridden along the very same flat roads to watch the jousting in Barcelona.

Altamiras, a clever man, may have foreseen the success of his little recipe book. His prologue suggests so. It ran through five editions in his lifetime, then, after his death, it took on a life of its own. The slim book grew in size as editors fattened it out with new recipes, but it kept its title, soon a brand, and remarkably it kept reprinting at a time when

French cookery held sway in wealthy Spanish households. Franciscan missionaries also carried copies to Texas, Mexico, Peru, Venezuela, and California where they were traveling north and building missions along the Camino Real. By 1905, a hundred and sixty years after its first publication, *New Art* had run through twenty editions or more.

A long pause followed. Altamiras was largely forgotten and the original slim book became hard to find. Then somebody produced a facsimile edition in 1981. This little string-bound volume was pressed into my hands by Jaime Rodríguez, winemaker, as I was leaving Remelluri, his family wine bodega in the Rioja Alavesa, at the end of a flying visit I made there in the 1990s.

"Read this," he said. "It's important."

One quiet Sunday morning a few weeks later I unknotted the string tying the paper covers and began to read.

Altamiras's cooking drew me in. The aromas of his dishes—braised mutton, fried salt cod with honey, artichokes with cured ham, garlicky chickpea stew, and iced lemonade—hung in the air. His writing, chatty, one-to-one, and witty, yet serious about cooking and designed for hands-on home cooks in humble kitchens, was memorably phrased. The recipes carried a sense of place. Ingredients like borage, artichokes, saffron, and trout sketched out a little known *terroir*. Some dishes seemed to emerge from a time-tunnel, their flavors and techniques evoking the Jewish and Muslim legacy. Others gave a sampling of tastes new to Spain, even to Europe. Low on spices, high on ingenuity, these dishes felt modern. For the time there was a rare balance between meat, fish, and vegetables, given equal importance. Frugal food for the spirit was balanced by the odd festive dish for the soul.

Back then, in the 1990s, when Spanish cooking was untying itself from its past, Altamiras came to feel like a friend. Young chefs' visually dazzling, avant garde haute cuisine was often thrilling, but it was designed for a privileged few. *New Art* was an elegy instead to earthy everyday eating and it revealed friary food as something very different to monastic cooking. Shaped by exchange with neighbors, it was improvised around food gifts and kitchen-garden produce as well as the rhythms of the religious calendar.

Shortly after the turn of the millennium, Altamiras's "calamity and misery of our wretched times," as he called them, reappeared. Hunger and overeating, the *hambre y hartazgo* of Spain's Golden Age, returned to our stuffed and starved world and even knocked at neighbors' doors as the new century progressed: I watched queues lengthen in Madrid's back streets as the hungry waited for food outside convents and churches.

In 2001, I had written to Basque chef Andoni Luis Aduriz, of Mugaritz restaurant, to ask him where he thought the future lay. He replied in a late night e-mail, which I later quoted in an article, "I think in general cooking needs a small revolution. We need to spread a sense of values. We need to ask ourselves questions." His words made my mind turn again to Altamiras. He had wanted to do exactly these same things.

The time seemed right, then, to take *New Art* to a wider readership.

THE MODERN RECIPES

During the work on this book, I have been carried along by the support of many colleagues and food-lovers. My first thanks go to Tom Jaine, editor of the *Oxford Companion to Food*, and Helen Saberi, who gave me the chance to look again at Spanish historic cookbooks. Geraldene Holt urged me on. Gillian Riley, food scholar *extraordinaire*, held a guiding lantern as I headed down unexpected research paths. The work of two distinguished historians, Carlo Ginzburg and Marcelin Defourneaux, suggested how to research and pass on Altamiras's story in a way that would remain true to the spirit of the original (see p. 241). Thanks also to Pilar Garrido of Madrid's Biblioteca Ívan de Vargas and Joaquín San Juan, who helped me find the peace to finish writing.

When I started work on the book's translation I also began to cook a few dishes for friends. To my surprise, they came back for more. In that way, over the next couple of years, I cooked my way through the book and, as I did so, I discovered Altamiras's knack of leaving space for readers to improvise around his guidelines to their own tastes. Claudia Roden encouraged me to reflect that by peopling the book with guest cooks whose modern versions of the original recipes would show their potential. I looked for cooks with whom I thought Altamiras would have enjoyed talking food. Thank you, Claudia, for encouraging me, and thank you to all of the guests for their delicious and inspirational dishes.

Sourcing produce to cook the modern recipes was an essential part of writing the book. Thanks for help with that go to grocers Carlos Pérez Gonzalez and Jesús Marcos Holgado, fishmongers Molino Cadernos and wine merchant José Carlos Ariza, all in Madrid. Kiké Sendón turned up at the door with an armful of fresh borage and cardoon. Butchers L. H. Larratt of Westerham and Daniel Dumkitrache of The Ginger Pig, Hackney; sheep-farmer Sandy Granville of Hebridean Mutton; and Andrew Sharp of Cumbria helped me with guidelines on cooking lamb and mutton. Vicent Peris of Valencia and Christopher Moriarty, from Dublin, shared their knowledge of fishing traditions. Special thanks go to Nora Narro for helping me cook during two years of weekly testing sessions. Kenneth Rimdahl always found something to praise in early testing dinners and brought along wines to taste with them.

Expert home cooks helped out too: Juani Casado of Parla, the Balells Carl family, and Carme Pages (with offal), Cristina Navarro, Cherry Moriarty, a great game cook, loved and missed. Coco de Bunsen, Julia Booth-Clibborn, Cristine MacKie, Tracy Drew, Fraser Leggate, Alison Cathie, and Olivier Auscher read drafts and gave helpful comments. Henrietta Donavon went through the modern recipes with a professional cook's eye. Stephen Hayward, my brother, believed in the book. That meant a lot to me. He pushed me to research everything fully and traveled with me on my first trip to Aragon.

RESEARCHING ALTAMIRAS

Evelyn Powell Jennings, Associate Professor of History at St. Lawrence University, New York State encouraged me to dig into primary sources during a brief conversation in Madrid. It was slow work, but it transformed my understanding of Altamiras and his cookery. As an independent researcher, I am also grateful to bibliographer Juan Delgado Casado of the Biblioteca Nacional de España, librarian Paz Fernández Rodriguez of the Biblioteca del Real Monasterio de San Lorenzo de El Escorial, art historian Carmen Abad of the Universidad de Zaragoza, Isa Bermell for invaluable help, and Hilary Bird for her indexes. Thanks also to Suzanne Staszak-Silva, Kathryn Knigge, and Karen Ackermann of Rowman & Littlefield, as well as Barbara Jarrett, copy editor.

Travels to Altamiras's homeland opened up the research beyond documentary evidence. Don Luis de los Ríos Gracia, Santiago Cabello, and Ángel Baguena deepened my understanding of the Valdejalón's history. José Manuel of Pastelerias Segura, Daroca, shared his family's splendid museum. Carlos Morales of Almonacid, José Manuel Mosteo, and

Roberto del Val of Ricla helped me explore Altamiras's homeland, a frontier territory where many cultures have converged over time. Those were unforgettable days. Thank you to all of them and to José Manuel Mosteo for his skills as an archive researcher.

In 2015, as I was finishing the book, I was introduced to the dynamic team working for La Almunia de Doña Godina's Ayuntamiento. Among them I am especially grateful to mayoress Marta Gracia and José Manuel Latorre Martínez, "Seve," Consejero for Commerce, Tourism, and Social Participation, who wanted to give Juan Altamiras recognition on home ground. They gave the book wholehearted support and extended that through the region. I would also like to thank the Comarca de Valdejalón, in particular Juanjo Moreno, Consejero for Tourism and Environment, and, at the Diputación Provincial de Zaragoza, Bizén Fuster, Delegado for Tourism, Archives, and Libraries.

In 2017, I was honored to receive the Jane Grigson Trust Award for this book. The prize money allows me to start work sooner than hoped on the Archivo Altamiras, to be held at Santo Espíritu del Monte in Gilet, Valencia. It will make available my research references and materials as part of an archive about friary cooking that can grow with new discoveries during the coming years. Hopefully this will encourage other people to take my research further: there is so much fascinating work still to be done.

Finally come the friars. Their grace and humor linger long in the mind. A brief chat with Antonio Esteve, priest of Ibi, Alicante, encouraged me to knock on their doors. Among them I would especially like to name and thank the following friars of the Order of Friars Minor (OFMs): José María Falo Espés, archivist in Valencia, Thomas Herbst, of FISC Canterbury, the late Ángel Martín Fernández, chronicler of the Province of Aragon, Cayetano Sánchez Fuertes of Madrid's Archivo Franciscano Ibero-Oriental, and Philippe Yates, now in New York. Fernando Hueso Iranzo, Javier Pons Silvestre, and José Manuel Sanchis Cantó welcomed me to my first friary lunch and two years later Fernando introduced me to Fray Ángel Ramón Serrano García, who runs the kitchen at Santo Espíritu del Monte near Valencia. He became my final guest cook.

A NOTE ON TRANSLATION

Translating Altamiras's Spanish was a challenge. His writing sounds so close to us, but it is rich in jokes and literary asides, and assumes an understanding of Franciscan thought and the hierarchies of an earlier world. Thanks go to Chris Reid of Queen Mary College, London University, for advice on the eighteenth-century style, and to Horacio García, Francisco Mengual, Cristina Navarro, José Luis Sanahuja, and José Mari Gorrotxategi of Tolosa's Museo de Pastelería for help on particular details. All translations from Spanish are my own except for Bernardo de Sahagún's words.

I have changed very little of the original text. Altamiras's southern Aragonese spellings, like *algarchofas*, remain where he used them in recipe titles. When he had only one word to describe frying, instead of the five or six used in Spanish today, I have kept to his original limited vocabulary. Occasionally I have played with his imagery, but only, I hope, to remain true to his humor. European spelling has been kept for the eighteenth-century text. In this edition the main changes I have introduced came from his invitation to rename dishes: each Spanish recipe title is preceded by a modern English one and the occasional embedded recipe now stands alone. A section with practical advice (pp. 229–40) lays out brief basics for anyone who wishes to recreate Altamiras's recipes.

I would never have dared to take on Altamiras's little book if I had guessed how much he had packed into it. I was able to keep going thanks to Paulita and Angel Sedgwick's generosity. My mother and friends have understood my need for long hours hidden away in libraries. Thank you to them.

I owe much to past and present influences: Elizabeth Russell, who taught me how to cook; Tracey Drew, art historian; Chris Weaver and my brother Stephen Hayward, who always quizzed my thinking; and chef Andoni Luis Aduriz, ever innovative in his culinary thinking.

My final thanks go to everyone at Andrew Nurnberg Associates who helped to make this book happen, in particular Sarah Nundy, Giulia Bernabé, Juliana Galvis, and my agent Charlotte Seymour, who brought editorial vision, tireless enthusiasm, and work to the project. Without their support this book would never have seen the light of day.

Vicky Hayward, Santo Espíritu del Monte, August 2016

INTRODUCTION

THE FRIAR'S TALE

IN THE SUMMER of 1745, the proofs of Juan Altamiras's little book, *New Art of Cookery*, landed on the desk of Don Pascual Sánchez. We know little of Don Pascual, a priest, except that he recommended books for approval by the Inquisition.

His eyebrows must have risen as he flicked through the book. There were no opening notes on table etiquette or carving, no menus or table settings and, at the end of the prologue, his eye picked up a damning swipe at court cookery! Don Pascual recognized some classic dishes by name but, he wondered, was it fitting for an author, even if he was a Franciscan friar, to include so many dishes for the poor—salt cod, turnips, chard? Besides, were the author's jokes about nuns in good taste? Don Pascual had chuckled, but he knew the Inquisition might not.[1]

Perhaps, he thought, he should take a stroll to Madrid's Franciscan friary, San Francisco, on the western edge of town, where he could find out more about the author and see what the friars themselves thought of the book.[2]

When Don Pascual arrived there, the Guardian Father would have sent word to the kitchens. Had anyone heard of Juan Altamiras, a friary cook? Probably nobody knew the name. Don Pascual would have explained he was Aragonese and had spent time at a friary called San Cristóbal, once famed for its austerity and later a summer retreat. Then, perhaps, somebody remembered talk of a lay friar from that small pocket of southern Aragon, a countryman who had won local fame as a highly original cook, preparing many new dishes for fish and vegetables. Goodness knows, San Francisco's kitchen friars might have told Don Pascual, it was not easy to cook for students, preachers and guests, and keep them all happy.

For sure, many of the friars would have recognised the name of San Cristóbal, the hillside retreat above the Aragonese market-town of La Almunia de Doña Godina in southwestern Aragon. News of the town's midsummer flooding fourteen years before had spread far and wide through the friary grapevine. Mountain rivers, swollen by a summer storm, had rushed down to the plains, swept through the town, destroying the walls, damaging hundreds of homes, and submerging the friary. Wine casks burst and floated out of cellars while the townspeople clambered to safety on high ground. When the waters retreated, the friars evacuated the wounded and gave the homeless shelter in cells at the town's friary, San Lorenzo, and San Cristóbal, high in the sierra overlooking the town.[3]

One of the friars who tended to the homeless then, just twenty-two years old at the time, was Raimundo Gómez, a young cook, who later wrote under the pen-name Juan Altamiras.

Today we know much more of Altamiras. The eighth of ten children, he was born in 1709 in La Almunia and christened Raimundo by his parents Catalina and Jacinto. Their marriage agreement reveals they owned enough scattered patches of land, including an olive grove next door to San Lorenzo, to be considered well-off farmers. Catalina was related by marriage to Francisco Asta, a sculptor of some note, who had made an altarpiece for San Lorenzo, and her father was a confectioner. Jacinto's family seem to have held positions of trust in the Consejo that governed the town. Altamiras took vows as a lay friar, then, as a matter of spirituality or humility rather than family poverty. Usually novices did so when they were eighteen. We do not know exactly where Altamiras entered the kitchen, at San Lorenzo or San Cristóbal, but he must have made his mark as a cook quickly for in the 1730s he was sent to San Diego, in Zaragoza. Most likely he followed Fray Francisco Pérez, also born in La Almunia, who became Guardian Father there. Beyond that the book tells us he was in Madrid for the book's publication and, much later, in his fifties, he was back at San Diego as a friary porter. Throughout his life he kept his baptismal name; he used Juan Altamiras only as a pen-name.[4]

Of Altamiras's times we know far more. Social historians have tracked the cycles of failed harvest, famine, and disease in the countryside. Some natural disasters were local.[5] In 1721 came an outbreak of the plague and, the following year, flooding destroyed the irrigation canals of a dozen villages on the Ebro's right bank. In the early 1750s a fire broke out in San Lorenzo and much of it was rebuilt, the work paid for by the townspeople. In 1755 an earthquake reduced Lisbon's old quarter to rubble and shook La Mancha's plains. Voltaire, the French philosopher, was led to question the existence of God. Nature was angry and no amount of processions asking for rain or the saints' protection would settle it down. The Franciscans, or grey friars, knew what these dramas meant on the ground. They fed the poor, they sat with the dying.

Altamiras seemed resigned to the suffering, but he was grumpy about bad management at the top. Aragon's far-flung Mediterranean empire was already a distant memory, but the independent kingdom's economy had ticked over well enough until French-born Philip V, Louis XIV's grandson, brought rebel zones to heel through greater centralization after a war of complex alliances followed his inheritance of the Spanish throne in 1700. By 1711 he had imposed Castilian laws and taxes, its language and currency, weights and measures on Aragon. Worst of all, Philip V squashed the pride of a people whose empire had once included Perpignan, Barcelona, Naples, Valencia, Malta, and Sicily. Decades of slow economic stagnation followed in many rural areas.[6]

But through it all Aragon's capital, Zaragoza, was a lively place to live and work.[7] There were bullfights, a winter season of theater at the Casa de Comedias, celebratory incense and sacred music for fiestas. The city boasted fine gardens and architecture: one of Spain's greatest Muslim castles and palaces, the Aljafería, stood near the cathedral quarter of narrow streets lined with fine urban mansions. Out and about, Altamiras may have known José de Goya, the gilder of the cathedral's new dome, whose son, Francisco, was soon to be an apprentice artist. Other neighbors included confectioners, shoemakers, and the nobles whose palaces lined the Coso, the city's splendid avenue. Among them were the Counts of Fuentes and Counts of Sástago, San Diego's biggest benefactors. Altamiras probably visited their libraries and knew their kitchens.

He had much to learn in this crossroads city where he cooked for the friars' aristocratic patrons as well as college residents. He might chat with market gardeners, snail hunters, innkeepers, food traders, friary guests, and the city's confectioners whose guild met in the neighbouring friary of San Francisco, a hub of the city's cultural life. He might visit its splendid kitchen and wine cellar or listen to choir and organ music in its church.

Yet Altamiras also knew the city's darker side. Cyclical drought brought failed harvests on poor land and, in the winters that followed, the hungry flocked to the cities to live off monastic doles of bread, soups, and gruels. Altamiras was to work with them later in his life, receiving and distributing alms. Meanwhile he wrote wistfully serving meat pie to the friars and the poor. But at heart he was a realist for he knew the real need was to find ways to "miraculously multiply" the friars' soups that fed the hungry and starving who came crowding to the friaries' back doors every day at noon.

When Altamiras had entered San Lorenzo as a young lay novice, he had stepped into a life enriched by many influences. The friary, built in the *mudéjar* style created by earlier Muslim builders, had brick and adobe walls, tiled floors, simple white plasterwork decoration, and lofty brick vaulting.[8] Many of its furnishings, like lattice-doored food cupboards and olive oil urns, were, like those in private kitchens, made to older Muslim designs. So, too, was kitchen equipment: brass spice mortars, ceramic washing-up bowls, and the pots of damp bran where the friars rubbed their hands clean.

For much of the year the kitchen must have been a chilly place. Breakfast followed Laudes, the first prayers after dawn. Lunch followed Sexta, six hours after first light. Supper came before Completas, the final prayers of the day and also the cue for closing the city gates. Then Altamiras would do his accounts, he tells us in the book, noting how many meals he had served, the quantity of spices he had bought, and how many tablecloths he had sent for laundering. Life followed a religious rhythm.[9] There were three meatless Lents, feasting for Christmas, Easter, and other Franciscan saints' days. Even kitchen work might follow religious timing. A couple of Paternosters might time the boiling of an egg or curing of a wound.

Altamiras had always known such a hybrid culture. The name of La Almunia, settled eight centuries earlier by Muslim farmers, came from the Arab word for fertile riverside market garden. For centuries the Muslims had lived here side by side with Christian stockmen and a Jewish community, which made up a quarter of the town's population. Largely self-sufficient, with its own specialized crafts, like tailoring, the town's Jewish population was unusually well integrated into everyday life: the quarter where they lived had no dividing walls, everyone in town shared the same bakers' oven and olive oil mill and there is no documented conflict before the expulsion of the Jews from Spain was decreed in 1492. Equally, while the Muslims moved out of town after the Christians conquered it, retreating to the valley's smaller outlying villages, they kept business interests in La Almunia and the landlords of large estates where they worked as highly skilled tenant farmers were happy to turn a blind eye to their rituals.

Neighbors here were bound by many ties. They ploughed each other's land, lent each other money and, more often, wheat, oil, or wine. They shared the cycles of good and bad harvests. There were quiet conversions. Occasionally their children might marry and, as the centuries passed, members of converted Jewish or Muslim families entered friary or convent life. Some areas of life remained closed to them, such as guilds and professions, but their architecture, dance and song, medicine, language, farming, and cooking skills were absorbed into a porous local culture marked by little conflict and great mutual dependence. Often the Moriscos were the majority of a village population, but their lives folded comfortably into those of the valley's Christian community.[10]

We know from legal squabbling that Christians liked to buy meat from Muslim butchers, some Muslims owned vineyards and drank wine, and everyone had made cheese the Jewish way for hundreds if not a thousand years. This hybrid culture was to endure. In 1585 the courtier Enrique Cock visited Almonacid de la Sierra, close to San Cristóbal friary, and described it as "a large town of the Count of Aranda's Moors."

Long after the expulsion of the Moriscos in 1610 emptied such outlying parishes their culture remained deeply imprinted on local life. All around the landscape in which Altamiras spent his childhood were reminders of their legacy: the old church towers and water fountains built by Muslim masons and their engineers' waterwheels and dams, which, even today, raise river water to irrigate the lush market gardens. Kitchen pots were still made the old way, though they were thrown and fired by new hands. Cooks hung on to good things too: marzipans, aubergine dishes, artichokes, wild asparagus, green garlic, and recipes using the local sweet golden olive oil. All these were among the blessings of Raimundo's childhood, as were the valley's wine, the river's brown trout and eels, and the hams and sausages from the annual family pig-killing.

By the time Altamiras sat down to write he was a well-read cook. Clearly he knew and liked fiction like *Don Quixote* and Lope de Vega's plays, which he may have read as a teenager, but he may not have found cookbooks till he reached Zaragoza. Those he knew best were Spain's two classics, the *Libre del coch*, an early sixteenth-century anthology from the Aragonese empire's court cities—Zaragoza, Barcelona, Valencia, Sicily, and Naples—penned by Maestre Robert, or Ruperto de Nola, and *Arte de Cocina*, a big jumbled book by the veteran Madrid palace cook to the Hapsburgs, Francisco Martinez Montiño. Altamiras liked his bright flavors, but the *Libre del coch*, written about dishes from his own food culture, was the greater influence.[11]

Altamiras also learned through the friary grapevine. Spain's Franciscans, six thousand of them, were citizens of the world who traveled west across its empire in the New World, the Philippines, and as far east as Jerusalem. As they traveled, they carried with them books, maps, the seeds of fruits and vegetables, and livestock. In the New World they planted peaches and vines and fattened wild turkeys. Altamiras may have met returning mission cooks as well as travelers from closer lands.[12] Perhaps a visitor from Florence's Spanish friary taught him how to make breadcrumb noodles. Maybe a French friar taught him how to cook ragout or a Portuguese traveler told him about a cookbook called *Arte de Cozinha*, by Lisbon court cook Domingues Rodriguez, a book structured around meat-eating and lean days. There was a practical idea!

In Altamiras's writing one can also glimpse the styles of Spain's great Franciscan authors: Ramón Llull's pithy proverbs and jokes, Francesc Eiximenis's satirical philosophy, Juan de Pineda's mystic natural ordering of the world and, above all, St. Francis's pacifist vision of an inclusive church, so very different from the harsh dogmatism of the Spanish Inquisition.

Life as a friar, then, behind walls, was in no way closed away from the world; it gave Altamiras precisely the freedom he needed to write the radical little cookbook he published in 1745.

Perhaps Don Pascual Sánchez showed his unbound proofs of *New Art* to the cook at San Francisco friary in Madrid.[13] What would he have made of the two hundred or so recipes? He may have paused at the pumpkin and honey soup, been intrigued by the dishes for kitchen garden produce—useful for the New World too—and by the updating of blancmange and other older court and feast-day dishes.

The friars' approval would have dissolved Don Pascual's last doubts about giving a friar a publishing license under a pen-name. Besides, he had to admit, the recipes for *estofados* made his mouth water. He was tired of the fancy new French cookery at court and in wealthy homes. It was true, this little book still held mysteries for him.[14] Why had the author hidden the identity of his patron, who should have been named on the title page? But that was not his business: the Council of Castile had already licensed the book.[15] Altamiras, he mused, was liked and respected in high places.

In the middle of July, Don Pascual sat down and wrote a note of approval in which he praised the book's compact style. Three weeks later the Inquisition gave its approval for it to be printed. Don Pascual must have breathed a sigh of relief: perhaps they had only read his short report and had not noticed the jokes at the expense of nuns.

By September 1745 the book was bound by Juan Oliveras and on sale at his bookshop just off the Puerta del Sol, at the heart of dusty but bustling Madrid.

Twenty-two years later, in 1767, Altamiras was enjoying an easier life. After some years away, he had returned to San Diego, in Zaragoza, as porter and sacristan. Now he welcomed the friars' patrons and guests, he received alms, attended the poor, decorated the church with flowers, woke the friars, and rang the church bells. He enjoyed the trust placed in him and he appreciated the easier pace of his job. He no longer had to spend the whole day on his feet.[16]

When he looked back on the hot summer of 1745 arranging the book's publication, it must have seemed like another life.[17] Fray Antonio

Luna, then in charge of the Province of Aragon, had given his permission for the journey to Madrid. Some of the writers and university teachers he had known in Zaragoza now held posts in the Royal Library and the Royal Academy and San Diego's patrons also held sway at court. They understood the workings of the King's Household.[18] It all smoothed the way for the book as, too, did Fray Antonio's good name with the Inquisition.

Much had happened in the two decades since *New Art* was first published. Two kings had died. Charles III, a reformer, was on the throne. Juniper Serra had been building missions in the New World and the friars were soon to settle in San Diego before moving north to Los Angeles and San Francisco. On home ground there had been a fire at San Lorenzo, bread riots in Zaragoza and the friars were struggling to balance their kitchen accounts. But renewed economic crisis had brought about another edition of the book.[19]

María Martí, his Barcelona publisher, had written to ask Altamiras for his consent to publish, as she was now obliged to do by law. He was pleased for he had the chance to write to her to say how hc liked to spell his pen-name, as Altamiras, the Aragonese way.[20]

When copies of this new edition, the fifth he had seen, arrived on the mail-coach from Barcelona, he must have smiled. It turned out there were really two editions, one for Barcelona and the other for Castile, each with different local spellings and decorations. But both of them carried his name spelled as he wished: Juan Altamiras.

That is the book that follows here.

NEW ART OF COOKERY, DRAWN FROM THE SCHOOL OF ECONOMIC EXPERIENCE

PROLOGUE

WHEN *I found myself at work in the kitchen, obliged by obedience yet without any Principal to guide me, I vowed straight away that I would write a kitchen notebook when I had learned enough about the subject. For in this way, I thought, anyone lacking kitchen skills when they leave their seminary might learn all they need to know of this craft without needing to ask those questions that reveal ignorance and leave one red-faced with embarrassment.[1]*

To prepare myself, I spoke with friends well-versed in the matter, I studied books and manuscripts, and enlightened myself through knowledge and practise. I hope the book may serve the general good, but especially those readers who are of slender means. For while we must spend money on sustenance, we should not be wasteful. We live in calamitous times that do not allow it and besides, as this handbook would remind you, superfluous spending is blameful among those who have taken the vow of poverty.

Friends and readers, I am not a polished writer. The discordancies of my style are sure to strike you. Forgive me and remember my Craft means I need to write of very diverse foods and their confection. If you find anything of worth here, thank God, author of all good things, and if you find mistakes, blame me alone, yet bear in mind I have written only for God's glory and to help apprentice Cooks who lack kitchen skills.

Now, take note of what follows here.

First and foremost, and here I write not only for Cooks, be consummately clean in your clothes and cookery. Outward cleanliness reflects the soul and neatness reveals a Cook's integrity. Let these be your first concerns for a good and watchful Cook's care in these matters reflects his conscience. Unclean food may upset a delicate stomach or provoke vomiting, even take away life, and it is a wretched matter if the food God gives us threatens rather than sustains us. Bear in mind, too, we Cooks give sustenance to angels and priests, who minister for the Lord and deserve to be well cared for, like earthly princes.

Now Cooks, take note. Keep your kitchens clean, sweep them, and carry out your garbage. Do not be idle in these tasks for they are pertinent and besides, you would be surprised by the pleasure people take in a neat and clean Cook. If you follow this principle you shall find your cooking is never disdained, even by the most refined among feminine tastes. This I have seen with my very own eyes for once I saw a Lady of distinction refuse a Prelate's invitation to take refreshment till she had seen the bearing of the Cook.[2]

Second, assign a place to everything in your Kitchen so you may easily find whatever you need and commit to memory the dishes you shall prepare for a meal, how many mouths they will feed, and how long they take to cook so you may be sure your stews shall not boil dry through the fire's ferocity or your own forgetfulness.

When you are feeding many mouths, for example, three hundred, govern the occasion this way. Cut up the meat rations on the eve of the feast, lay them in their cooking vessels, then, after the bells toll midnight, put your fire in order, prepare all you need for your stews and roasts, and, if you are making pepitorias or offal stews, lay them out on tablecloths so they do not turn sour. Carefully skim off any foam that rises to the top and, once you have seasoned your dishes, set them to one side near the hearth where they can finish cooking over embers. Once the fire is free, cook your rabbit and chicken casseroles, give them a little boil first and then finish them over a gentle fire, feeding the flames if they languish. With all these tasks done, a small fire will suffice for your soupmaking and, if your kitchen is cramped, look for an open field where you can cook. Note this point well for I knew a Cook who failed to do this and who was suffocated by the smoke of his fire.

Thirdly, do not presume of your talents in the kitchen. Take time over your work, for God punishes the careless and self-regarding, and then they do not achieve what they might have done. Do not consider yourself an expert. Man is ennobled by work alone and taste varies as much as individuals, so you can never satisfy everyone. Patience is essential and fairness, too, however tricky the characters for whom you cook. So do not favour some with more or better food. Rather, like San Diego of Alcalá,[3] reserve charity and compassion for the old and sick.

Fourthly, note the weights and measures of foods in the larder and use them well so you may keep others' respect, your own peace of mind and a settled conscience. Take care not to be the keeper of the larder keys and be aware that some Prelates believe Cooks may satisfy many mouths with little food. To them I would say here: who among us is so virtuous that we may feed a crowd with five loaves of bread, as Christ did? So if your provisions fall short for filling many stomachs remember there are only two ways to solve this, a miracle or a trick. The first reflects virtue, the second great roguery. Serving rice or chard stalks instead of meat or stew to keep a Prelate happy is like serving cat for hare, and a Cook's lies can never stay hidden for long. Some may turn a blind eye, but later the Cook will pay, for the traitor who is bought is despised. A wise Cook's virtue lies in balance.

Finally, it falls to you to decide what to cook and for how many, to choose the cooking vessels and provisions. Remember, take just enough broth from the pot to feed those at the table, no more, for in these wretched times we need virtuous cooks who have proven skill in miraculously multiplying the food to hand, and it is better to serve too little rather than too much; yet be wary of anyone who tries to persuade you that, like Saint Francis of Paula, you may sustain a whole religious community on a fig.

Now, let me tell me you how to draw up Kitchen accounts. Take a board with holes in it: thread a string through each one and tie a number on to each string. In this way you may keep a tally of how many lunches you serve, how many people sit down to eat, and the number of guests. Do this at supper, too, for it is simple to pull out the right numbers and tie them on to the strings. Another word of advice: jot down your figures at night when the kitchen is quiet, for then it is very quick to draw up the week's or month's accounts, and bear in mind, you can be asked for them when you least expect it. Take care with the final balance, for it is the most important figure of them all.[4]

I do not mention weights, measures, or other such details here, but, take note, this does not mean they are a matter of taste. Rather, I cannot know how much food you are cooking, or for how many, so it would be foolish for me to give a quantity of spices or ingredients. Instead, take more or less of each one, as you see fit and, as you shall see, I have suggested generous servings, as this is the custom in religious communities.

I have given dishes their everyday names, but, if you do not like them, baptise them anew, and for this I give you a godfather's rights. But if you do that I would be grateful if you mention my name alongside the dish.

Now, having explained all of this, let me make one last thing clear.

I have no interest in exquisite cookery. On that subject, monarchs' cooks have written many books yet their doctrine is as costly as if sung with a silver tongue, so I turn instead to charity's golden voice, pitched for the poor, whether they have taken the vow of poverty or are hard-pressed in the calamity and misery of our wretched times, for surely a Cook singing in any other tone would provoke such a storm of curses and anger that he would find himself sentenced to silence for the rest of his life.

This little work is written as my simple talents allow. I beg you, look well upon it and remember, I write for apprentices, so those who wish to criticise and carp would do better to leave that to the infinite number of fools and meddlers who enjoy sticking their spoons in others' pots. Instead, I would ask you here, overlook my mistakes, note only my good intentions and so, with no more ado, I submit my work to your pleasure.

BOOK ONE

DISHES FOR MEAT-EATING DAYS

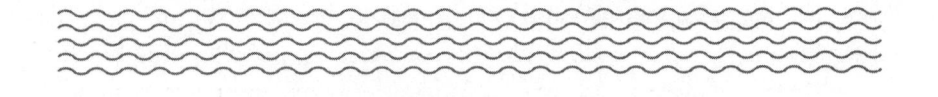

THE SHEPHERDS' TRACK

A RUSTY-RED dirt track zig-zags down from San Cristóbal friary to the village of Alpartir. On the way it runs through almond groves and passes the village cemetery before suddenly swinging north to loop through fruit orchards to Almonacid de la Sierra, the next hillside village.

One cold November morning we made the journey the friars' way, on foot. By the time we reached Almonacid, the weekly food market was in full swing. Farmers were standing by the porch of the church selling green garlic, apples, turnips, and snails from buckets and bags. We bought some muddy turnips and went in search of the old pottery quarter. Up a dusty track we found a beehive kiln, twice the height of a man, where once three dozen kilns had stood. Here medieval potters had fired their *ollas* or cooking pots made from the hillside's red clay.[1] These pots, made at Alpartir and Tobed in Altamiras's time, shaped his meat cookery: slow-cooked casseroles, braised meats, pot roasts, soups, *sopas*, meatballs, and pies.

Many dishes we think of today as Spanish specialities found no place in his book. Don Quixote's *olla podrida*, a pot-au-feu laden with half a dozen types of meat, is absent. So, too, are large spit-roasts or wood-roasted meat joints, too extravagant with firewood for a humble kitchen. More often Altamiras braised or stewed or baked or simmered meat, game, and poultry over his kitchen fire's glowing embers. His tools were simple compared to those of a court kitchen: frying pans, hinged grills, a poker, tongs, a copper pan and cauldron, baking dishes, skimmers, stirring spoons, whisks, pestles and mortars, a cleaver and chopping block, an olive-oil pourer, some wire to mend cracked pots, loose lids, a homemade haybox, and a sharpened cane from the river bed.[2]

What Altamiras lacked in equipment he made up for with flavor. Saffron and pomegranate, lemon and cured ham, fresh mint and white wine, cinnamon and cloves, hazelnuts, parsley, garlic, and tomatoes—these last two used innovatively—gave his food a bright palate of aromas and tastes. Nothing went to waste. For every casseroled leg of grass-fed mutton there was a dish using broth boiled up from the bones.

He opened in style with stews, braised dishes, casseroles, bakemeats, and a family of chopped meat dishes. Perhaps he was keen to snuff out the legend that Franciscan cooks knew only of charity soups.[3] He used browning techniques for flavor, spiced meat subtly the friary way, then braised or boiled it till tender. He would have cooked these dishes for students, guests, or feasts, but on the mission ranches of New Mexico, the Río Grande and California they were to become one-pot meals for the friars.[4]

In his second chapter, Altamiras returned to simpler breakfast soups and creams followed by dishes for special days. Some of these were cooked weekly, on Saturdays, others for Carnival, Holy Week, Christmas, saints' birthdays, or friary gatherings. Shaped by seasonal produce, these dishes spilled over to open a third chapter, this one with an emphasis on local produce and cookery.

Altamiras dedicated his fourth chapter to poultry and game, which were luxurious bought meats in court kitchens, but were given as alms to the friaries, or home-produced. Often a hen coop stood in the kitchen garden.

Finally came his account of a pig-killing, the earliest one to be found in a Spanish cookbook.[5] Written as a finale to the first half of his book, it was also a practical hands-on guide to the work to be done. He dedicated six lines to the salting of the joints, like the hams, but four pages to making the sausages, crackling, cured fat, and soft lard that gave flavor to his dishes year round.

Pigs might be kings in the farmyard, but sheep ruled the land.[6] Spain's wool culture, famed in Europe, gave mutton as a side product:

fifty meat sheep tagged along with every thousand head flock of wool sheep. Revealingly mutton's name, *carnero*, was almost identical to that for meat, *carne*. Much came from wethers, killed at two to three years old, when their meat was full of flavor; this was the gourmet meat of choice.

On that cold winter's day, after walking to Almonacid, we sat down to lunch in the restaurant on the town's square. It was packed with a noisy local crowd. Our first dish came in soup plates: two meatballs as large as oranges were ladled into a shallow puddle of glossy cooking broth in each person's plate. Made with young lamb, beef, and pork rather than mutton, they were in every other way recognizable as Altamiras's meatballs, rewarding in their hidden flavors and satisfying in their simplicity.

CHAPTER I

ON MEAT

L ET US BEGIN *with stews that are made often and balance extrav-agance against scanty spending, for in this way gallants of good taste and others may both find what they need here as I sing out the lessons of this kitchen notebook.*[1]

ESTOFADOS

Spain's fat-bellied cooking pot, the *olla,* gave birth to a large family of dishes, among which Altamiras chose to open with two *estofados.*[2] Slow-cooked over charcoal, his first recipe was sweetened by cinnamon-spiked onion. Today it is more often made with young lamb or beef, easily cas-seroled on top of the stove, although *estofados* are still at their most fla-vorful cooked with mature meats like mutton, venison, partridge, and fighting bull. Let them sit overnight for the flavors to develop.

Lamb or Mutton Stew / Estofado

Cut up leg meat into bits the size of half a walnut shell, and fry them in soft lard in your skillet, then fry fine-cut onion in the fat, add it to the meat in your pot, and e.g. for every pound of meat, add eight ounces of white wine, four garlic cloves, parsley, peppercorns and salt. Pick an onion which fits snugly in the mouth of your pot, spear the onion with cloves and cinnamon shards, sit it in the pot's mouth, but without protruding, and put your esto-fado to cook gently like this, turning it from time to time and uncovering it when cooked to finish seasoning it, but add no more broth. Serve this spooned over bread.

This recipe is good if you are cooking for just a few though it is less useful in a large monastery or convent. The next recipe sheds more light, for these two dishes are as one.

This *estofado*'s cooking time may be adjusted for lamb or mutton, like the other recipes in this chapter (see p. 19). Don't forget to serve the onion with the meat. It's delicious.

2–3 tbsp olive oil or lard, 1.2 kg / 2½ lb braising lamb, hogget or mutton (see p. 235), 1 finely chopped onion, 1 whole skinned onion stuck with 2 cloves and 2 cinnamon shards, ½ bottle dry white wine, 4 crushed garlic cloves, a few stalks of flat-leaf parsley

Warm the oil or lard in a heavy-bottomed frying pan and when it is just bubbling add the seasoned meat to brown in batches, lifting it out into the casserole or pot where you will make the stew. As you transfer the meat let the pan fat and juices drip back into the frying pan. Tip in the chopped onion and, when it is soft and golden, scoop it into the casserole. Now pour the white wine into the frying pan, bubble it away fast to dissolve the crunchy browned bits and pour this over the meat, adding the garlic and parsley stalks. Stir well, submerge your spiced onion, top up with liquid if needed and bring the casserole to a gentle simmer. Cook on top of the stove till the meat is tender: the time may range from 45 minutes for young Spanish lamb to an hour for cubed mature hogget or beef, or 2½ hours for wether mutton (see p. 19). Lift out the parsley stalks, pull the cloves and cinnamon out of the onion, and adjust the seasoning before serving. I like this with pasta or toast rubbed with garlic and olive oil.

Braised Lamb or Mutton with Lemon / Otro Estofado

Prepare the day's meat helpings, sear them over the fire and, as they brown, put them in your large olla *or stewpot. Take cured ham fat, cut it into little dice, fry these till they are opaque, add fine-cut onion and fry it well too. Add all this to your stewpot with spices, a handful of fine-cut parsley and pounded garlic cloves, place the pot over a gentle fire and pour in a little white wine. Seal the pot: cover it with folded paper, weight it down with a little jug of water and seal the paper to your pot with flour and water paste so no vapours are breathed out. When you think your* estofado *has cooked for long enough that the meat will be tender, open up the pot, season it and sharpen the juices with a little citrus juice.*

The sealed braising technique for this *estofado* goes back to the cookery treatises of al-Andalus.[3] The pot, ideally of clay or earthenware, is covered with oiled or dampened folded cooking paper weighted down with a jug of water and is then sealed to the pot's rim by a band of flour and water dough. Once Altamiras opened the pot, he squeezed in lemon juice, which, along with the garlic and cured ham, adds a lovely Mediterranean zing.

2–3 tbsp olive oil, 1.85 kg / 3¾ lb braising lamb or mutton with some bone and fat (e.g., neck), 60 g / 2 oz diced streaky jamón or pancetta (see p. 235), 2 chopped onions, pinches of cinnamon and cloves or oregano to taste, 3 crushed garlic cloves, salt and pepper, 370 ml / 12 fl oz white wine, juice of 1 large lemon or bitter (Seville) orange

Turn on the oven for braising (see p. 230). Heat a little olive oil in a frying pan till it is just bubbling, fry the seasoned meat in it in batches then lift it out into a 2-liter / 3½-pint casserole, letting the fat drip back into the pan. Add the cured ham to the frying pan, so it sweats out its own fat, then add the onions, cover, and sweat till they are soft and glossy, pouring in more oil if needed. Add the wine, bring to a gentle simmer, scoop the pan's contents over the meat and stir in the spices or herbs, salt, and pepper. The casserole should be almost full. Stand it on a grill rack in a roasting pan. Make a folded sheet of greaseproof or cooking paper large enough to cover the casserole, brush both sides with olive oil, press one side on to the stew's surface, and clamp it in place with the casserole's lid. Oven braise, allowing 1½ hours for lamb and another 30–45 minutes for mutton. Skim off the fat after cooking, check the seasoning and squeeze in the lemon or orange juice to taste—it adds a lovely citric twist. Good with baby potatoes, their skins well oiled and salted before you wrap them in a paper parcel for baking during the last half-hour of the cooking time for the meat.

THE SUBTLETIES OF SPICING

Franciscan spicing was set apart by its simplicity and blends with country flavors. So, while aristocratic cooks added exotic hard-edged ginger, caraway, cumin, and mustard to their dishes, Altamiras kept to softer smudges of local saffron plus cinnamon, cloves, and pepper. These he added as a mixed spice, often playing the sweet aromas and flavors off against cured ham, or kitchen-garden parsley, and, less frequently, against bay, or mint.[4] Occasionally he dropped spices altogether, replacing them with tomato, garlic, and lemon, a small practical step, but one that would change the flavors and colors of Spanish cookery.

Fricassee with Pine Kernels and Capers / Gigote Gruesso

Cut up lean leg meat to give fine dice, then chop cured ham fat, warm it in the skillet till the fat melts, add chopped onion and brown your meat with it. Put all this in a stewpot, add salt and spices and cook it till tender. Now add, let us say, two or three pairs of hard-boiled eggs, or however many you see fit, but chop them first, and throw in a handful of parsley and some soaked pine kernels too. Capers are a fine thing in this dish, often called gigote *from Castile, and naturally so, for it originated there.*

Everyday Fricassee with Garlic or Aguardiente / Gigote Comun

Seal lean leg meat over the fire, chop it up with onions, garlic and a handful of parsley, and put this all to cook gently. Sit a jug of water over the mouth of the pot and let everything cook slowly with pepper, salt and just a little water, adding it hot from the jug whenever needed. When the meat is done, dress it. Pound a handful of soaked pine kernels with hard-boiled eggs, add spices and soaked capers—and remember, capers should be soaked before you add them to stews—and serve this meat with just a little broth.

Here is another gigote *for unexpected guests. Take lean leg meat, sear it on the fire, chop it with a little cured ham fat, stir them together quickly in a skillet on a slow fire and, when you reckon they are well done, add salt, spices, a little broth, and a dash of aguardiente; then take your dish to table. There is no faster dish of mutton to cook for guests who appear suddenly: you can hardly throw them out or ask them to move on. It is too late for that, but you can make this dish and it will be ready in half an hour.*

Catalan chef Santi Santamaría re-created this chopped meat fricassee, with venison.[5] I like to serve it as a tapa with roast aubergines, caramelized artichokes (see pp. 197 and 71), and a glass of white wine.

2 tbsp olive oil, 2 finely chopped onions, 3 cloves of garlic (optional), 1 kg / 2 lb finely diced lean lamb or beef or venison, salt, grated nutmeg and cinnamon to taste, 300 ml / 10 fl oz hot meat or chicken broth (see p. 105), a generous handful of snipped flat-leaf parsley, 3 roughly chopped hard-boiled eggs, 100 g / 3½ oz pine kernels, 2–3 tbsp soaked capers

Serves 8 as a tapa or first-course.

Warm the oil in a flameproof casserole, sweat the chopped onion in it, add the garlic, then the seasoned meat of choice. Brown it, spice it, cover with a lid, and braise gently for 15 minutes, shaking the casserole occasionally. Add the hot broth and simmer for another 45 minutes or till tender, depending on your meat. Mash or blend the hard-boiled eggs and pine kernels with a ladleful of cooking juices and stir this thickening back into the meat with the parsley and capers.

FRICASSEE WITH JAMÓN: Throw 120 g / 4 oz streaky jamón or pancetta into your casserole, put it over low heat to seal, then add the meat so it browns in the jamón fat.

QUICK FRICASSEE WITH AGUARDIENTE: Splash 3 tbsp aguardiente into the browned meat before adding the hot broth.

Lamb and Pepper Stew / Pebre

For pebre *prepare your meat servings, brown them in your stewpot and take note of their weight so your other ingredients are in proportion. Pound garlic, salt and peppercorns together in your metal mortar, wash them into the* olla *with water, throw in bay leaves and, for every thirty servings, a pound of olive oil and a cured ham bone. Even a bone with very little meat on it gives a lot of flavour to a stew. Now put it to cook over a gentle fire and, when it is done, dress it with a handful of parsley, pounded hard-boiled eggs thinned with the stew's juice, some sharp citrus juice or, even better, tomatoes. Let all this simmer together for a little while. It is a very good, tasty dish to serve every so often, but take note, the flavours are more intense than in other stews.*

Earlier cookbook writers had made old-fashioned *pebres*, or pepper stews, by boiling their meat, but Altamiras sizzled his in olive oil then braised it gently, switching the spices for tomatoes or lemon juice.[6] The meat turns a crispy brown, the oil crackles and sputters, and the tomato merges with it to give a rich jammy sauce. I like this served with plain mashed potatoes or other roots, like turnips, and a fruity red Somontano wine from Aragon's Pyrenean foothills. You can also make this with lamb shanks, by the way.

1½ kg / 3 lb braising lamb or mutton (see p. 19), 250 ml / 8 fl oz fruity olive oil, 6 chopped garlic cloves, black peppercorns to taste (1–2 dozen), a small wineglass of water, 5 bay leaves, 250 g / 8 oz cured ham-bone (see p. 235), a small handful of snipped flat-leaf parsley, 2 mashed hard-boiled eggs, 400 g / 13 oz skinned and chopped tomatoes, 1 lemon

Brown the seasoned lamb quickly in batches in a little olive oil and, when it is all done, put it in an earthenware casserole with a lid on top to cook slowly for 15–20 minutes (or up to 45 minutes for wether mutton; see p. 232). Pound the garlic and peppercorns in a mortar, wash them onto the meat with the wineglassful of water, add the bay leaves, the rest of the olive oil—cold—and the ham-bone. Arrange everything so it is covered by liquid, cover with a lid and cook, bubbling lazily over low heat, for 1¼ hours for lamb. Open up occasionally to turn everything over and ensure there is no sticking. When the meat is nearly done, take out the ham-bone, cut off any chunks or shreds of meat on it and fork them back into the stew with the parsley, mashed hard-boiled egg, and tomato. Check the seasoning and cook gently for another half hour. Best made a day ahead then warmed through just before serving.

Lampreyed Lamb / Lampreado

This is a good stew to make when you are cooking for many people. Prepare it this way: cut the meat up in bits the size of walnut shells or, if you wish, larger helpings. Chop cured ham fat, melt it in your skillet, fry onion in it, then throw in the meat with a little salt and pepper, and when it is well browned, put it in a stewpot to cook, turning it from time to time, and adding a little water so the meat does not stick. Season your stew with salt and fine spices, and by that I mean cloves and cinnamon, a handful of parsley and a little saffron, and, if you like, you can make a quick sauce of egg yolks stirred up with vinegar and broth from the stew, but do not let the eggs curdle. Pour this into your stew, take care it does not boil, then take it to table.

Gently aromatic, spiced with cloves, cinnamon and saffron, this delicately flavored casserole has nothing to do with older wine stews for cooking river lamprey. But by entitling his recipe this way, Altamiras managed to present it as a respected classic.[7] You can make it with all kinds of meat. Two hundred years later Nancy Johnstone, an English visitor, wrote of a similarly spiced veal stew, "cinnamon and saffron is a heavenly mixture," while at Santo Espíritu de Monte, Fray Ángel makes this with pork. The egg yolk and vinegar thickening enriches the juices, or, for a colorful splash, you can hard-boil the eggs and crumble them over the dish for a "gorse yellow" medieval garnish.

2 tbsp olive oil, 1 chopped onion, 1.2 kg / 2½ lb cubed lamb or mutton, about 250 ml / 8 fl oz warm water, cinnamon and cloves to taste, 3 heaped tbsp chopped flat-leaf parsley, saffron infusion made from 3 dozen threads (see p. 102)

TO FINISH (OPTIONAL): 2 tbsp cream or 3 raw egg yolks (see p. 235) and 1 tbsp sherry vinegar.

Warm the olive oil in a flameproof casserole, sweat the onion in it till soft and golden, add the seasoned lamb or mutton, brown it, pour over half the water, spice it with cinnamon and cloves, stir well, cover and bring to simmering. Cook until the lamb or mutton is tender (see pp. 19 and 32), stir in the parsley and saffron infusion or the egg thickening (see below). The delicate aromas and flavors of this dish are shown off well by plain rice and a chilled white Rueda wine.

TO THICKEN WITH EGGS: Whisk 3 raw egg yolks and a tablespoon of sherry vinegar into a cupful of the hot juices, stir back into the stew just before the end of cooking time.

RAGOUT

I like to imagine San Diego's students spooning up their ragout juices. How hard Altamiras worked to vary their flavors! He gave half a dozen ideas: he seasoned the first one with mint, vinegar, and sweet spices, like an al-Andalus *almorí*, he thickened the second with spiced flour the French way, the third with garlicky fried breadcrumbs like today's Aragonese country stews, and the fourth with a paste of pounded hazelnuts not so different from today's Catalan almond *picadas*.[8] My own favorite, though, is his last-minute larder fallback of sage, bay leaves, and red wine, which led him to a riddle about "simples," the friars' medicinal plants or herbs.[9] Its message to cooks was clear: be adventurous with flavors, but combine them with care.

Lamb or Mutton Ragout / Carne Reogado en Guisado

Put your helpings of meat in a stewpot, season them with salt, pepper and pounded garlic, cut up cured ham fat and onion, make small dice of the fat and melt it in your skillet till it is opaque. Then add the onion, fry it well and add broth to your meat too. Sit the pot in the fire's embers so the ragout cooks slowly and pour in a little hot water from a jugful you warm on top of the pot.

When the meat is cooked dress it this way: take mutton melts, say two or three, or as you see fit, grill and brown them, pound them with garlic and toast soaked in vinegared water and squeezed dry, add a handful of parsley, mint, cloves and cinnamon, all pounded in your mortar and stirred up with four eggs. Wash this into the ragout with broth, then give it all a little simmer.

This is a good dish composed with simple flavours, if cooking may be called composing, yet it is surely true that an accomplished Cook needs to compose well in a simple setting. Use this truth wisely.

"'Everywhere simple or herbal medicines are more prized than composed ones,' Doctor Tirteafuera tells Sancho Panza, 'for there is no danger of erring with simples while anyone may make a mistake with composed medicines.'" (Miguel Cervantes, *Don Quixote Part II*, 1615).

For the basic ragout you need 1½ kg / 3 lb braising lamb or mutton cut into 5 cm / 2 inch cubes, 4 crushed garlic cloves, 3 tbsp olive oil or 60 g / 2 oz jamón fat, melted, 2 chopped onions, about 600 ml / 1 pint hot water or meat stock (see p. 234).

Toss the lamb or mutton with the garlic, season it, and put it in a casserole. Warm the olive oil or melt the jamón fat in a frying pan, sweat the chopped onion in it till soft, and spoon it over the meat. Braise for 15 minutes for lamb or up to 45 minutes for wether or mutton. Pour over enough hot water or stock to cover the meat, bring to a slow simmer and cook on top of the stove or in the oven till the meat is tender, 45 minutes to 1 hour for lamb, or around 2½ hours for wether or hogget, topping up with extra water or stock as you go. Cool, skim off the fat, check the seasoning, and finish with one of the flavorings below.

With Spiced Roux / Otro Modo de Menos Trabajo, Cocida la Cena

Warm two or three spoonfuls of broth in a skillet with a little vinegar and fine spices, by which I mean cloves and cinnamon. Add a handful of flour, stir well till it is toasted then stir this back into the stew and give it a little simmer. This is very tasty yet calls for few provisions.

With Garlic Gravy / Otro Compuesto

Toast bread, soak it in vinegared water. Clean abundant parsley, pound it in your mortar with half a dozen garlic cloves and spices, then add your toasted bread, squeezed dry of water and pound everything together. Wash it all into your ragout with a little of the broth, give it a quick boil, season and serve it.

With Hazelnut Sauce, or Spiced Bread Sauce or Sage, Bay Leaf, and Red Wine / Otro. Idem.

Try to keep a few pine kernels or hazelnuts and eggs in reserve in your kitchen for if a dinner spoils, they shall give you an easy remedy. Pound a fistful of hazelnuts in your mortar, add parsley, garlic and spices and pound them all well with the nuts, stir it then add a small bit of toast or fried bread, soaked and squeezed dry. Add a couple of pairs of raw eggs, stir all this into the ragout and bring it to the boil.

If you have no hazelnuts, you may bind a ragout with toasted bread, spices, eggs and a handful of parsley, but tread carefully with your spices and seasonings. Judge the amounts with care, for remember, cloves and pepper stand out and too many spices imbalance a stew. Cured ham fat and spices alone round out a ragout well, but then you must cook your meat gently with white or red wine, bay leaves and sage.

PARSLEY AND MINT (MAIN RECIPE): Soak a small piece of toast in lightly vinegared water (see p. 234), squeeze it dry and blend it with 2 garlic cloves, 2 raw eggs, large pinches of cinnamon and ground cloves, and a ladleful of cooking juices. Pour this mixture back into the ragout with snipped fresh parsley and mint, and warm through without boiling.

SPICED ROUX: Simmer 125 ml / 4 fl oz stock with 6 cloves, a 4-cm / 1½-inch length of cinnamon stick and 2 tbsp white wine vinegar for 15 minutes in a small covered pan. Infuse off the heat for 30 minutes. Warm 2 tbsp olive oil in a small saucepan, stir in 2 level tsp plain flour, cook to a golden roux, stir in the hot sieved stock, stirring all the time, and return to the ragout to cook for 15 minutes.

GARLIC GRAVY: Blend half a slice of toasted bread (see p. 234) or a small handful of croutons with 2 fat garlic cloves and a ladleful of cooking juices, stir into the cooked ragout, and simmer for 15 minutes.

HAZELNUT SAUCE: Blend 2 dozen toasted skinned small hazelnuts with 3 garlic cloves, a small piece of toasted bread, 1 raw egg, a pinch of cinnamon, and a ladleful of juices. Stir into the ragout with snipped parsley and warm through without boiling.

SPICED BREAD SAUCE: Blend ¼ slice of fried bread soaked in vinegared water and squeezed dry with 2 raw eggs and large pinches of cloves and cinnamon. Stir into the cooked ragout and warm through gently.

SAGE, BAY LEAF, AND RED WINE: Stir 250 ml / 8 fl oz red wine, a dozen shredded fresh sage leaves, and 2 torn or crumbled bay leaves into the ragout and warm through till simmering.

Green Mutton / Carnero Verde

Stews' names are like comedies' titles, expressive, yet trivial, and they rarely shed light on what follows. So, friends and Cooks, pay little heed to titles, even if you are titled in your Craft, for we Cooks must be happy with our own kitchen language. Instead read what follows the title, for there you shall find all there is to learn; remember, the title of a play or dish is of little interest unless, of course, you are a Critic.

For Green Mutton, cut up your meat and put the helpings in your stewpot with salt and pepper. Cut up cured ham fat, chop it into small dice, fry these well in your skillet, add fine-cut onion, fry it too and add everything to the meat. Let this cook over a gentle fire, turn the pot once in a while and after an hour and a half or so add water from a jug warming over the pot's mouth. For a stupendous stew, add abundant parsley, mint and lettuce hearts with soaked chopped pine kernels, spices and a little lemon or bitter orange juice.

Altamiras's wit must have raised a smile. If stews were like comedies, as he proposed, then cookery was an art. Was he, perhaps, hinting to readers that he hoped to do for cookery what Lope de Vega, the great writer—and friend of friars—had done for modern theater? Lope's slim manifesto, *New Art of Writing Comedies* (1609), had argued passionately for a new kind of popular drama, then called comedy, written in everyday street language.[10] Did Altamiras hope his little book *New Art* might stand as a manifesto for modern cookery? Certainly, in this chapter he was radically updating classic court dishes with popular techniques designed to bump up flavor while leaving dishes with their old country feel. Here, for example, old-fashioned boiled sweet yet sour green mutton becomes an herby braised casserole given an edge by a little citrus juice.

1 kg / 2 lb lean braising lamb steaks, 3 tbsp olive oil or 60 g / 2 oz melted jamón fat, 1 chopped onion, 150 ml / 5 fl oz hot water, generous handfuls of snipped mint and parsley, 1–2 shredded small crisp lettuces, juice of ½ lemon, salt and pepper, 2 tbsp toasted pine kernels

Put the seasoned lamb steaks in a flameproof casserole. Warm the olive oil or melt the jamón fat in a heavy frying pan, sweat the onion in it, then tip it and the fat over the lamb. Put the casserole over low heat, shake well, cover with a lid and braise, stirring once in a while, for about 30 minutes. Pour in the hot water little by little when you stir, cover, and leave till the meat is tender and still juicy—say, 45 minutes for lamb or up to 1½ hours for mutton. Add the fresh herbs, lettuce, lemon juice, and pine kernels, adjust the seasoning and leave to sit for 15 minutes for the flavors to blend. This is good with steamed carrot sticks, shredded cabbage, broccoli florets, and new potatoes.

COUNTRY STEWS

Mutton has been replaced by lamb in Spanish kitchens, but it is often casseroled on the bone with some fat left on for flavor. How often we turn our backs on meat cooked this way yet how much we lose: aromatic meat, sticky pan juices, and the pleasure of eating the lamb off the bone. Spain's butchers are experts at cleavering and mixing bone-in cuts. Elsewhere you can ask your butcher to prepare meat this way: once home, clean the splinters off the bone and defat the finished cooking juices. This sounds like a lot of work, but when you sit down to eat it will seem little for what you gain in flavor and aroma.

Lamb Braised with Garlic, Pepper, and Tomato / Guisado a Modo de Prebe

Leg meat is the best for stews. Cut it up the size of walnut shells, put these in your stewpot, add salt and bay leaves. Chop cured ham streaked with fat and lean into small dice, fry these and add them to the meat. Then crush garlic and peppercorns, wash them into the stew and add olive oil, just as I told you in the note for prebe. *Sit your pot in the fire's embers and let your stew cook slowly, adding broth when it is needed, as well as salt and spices. Try your best to add parsley and tomato too, for they make this stew so good you will find yourself licking your fingers—unless, of course, you are a smooth-mannered man.*

We can guess from the finger-licking finish that this was one of Altamiras's favorite dishes. He started the meat slowly in olive oil, a popular technique you still sometimes find in old shepherds' stews,[11] then he threw in streaky cured ham, chopped tomatoes, and a little water, but no spices. Don't be surprised at the amount of olive oil—the end result is quite delicious, a little like a confit.

60 g / 2 oz diced streaky jamón or pancetta, 1.2–1.5 kg / 2½–3 lb mixed cuts of braising lamb or mutton, for example, 1 500–750 g / 1–1½ lb middle neck, 200 g / 7 oz skirt and 500 g / 1 lb chops, shoulder, or leg, with the bone in (see opposite), 1 tsp salt, 5 bay leaves, 2 crushed garlic cloves, 12 pounded peppercorns, 100 ml / 3 ½ fl oz olive oil, 60–90 ml / 2–3 fl oz meat stock, 430 g / 14 oz skinned and chopped tomatoes, a handful of snipped parsley

Sweat the jamón in a large casserole till the fat runs, add the lamb, and toss it with the bay leaves, garlic, and cracked pepper. Pour over the cold olive oil, put the casserole over low heat, let it warm for about 10 minutes, till tiny bubbles rise, and leave to cook for about 1 hour for lamb or up to 2 hours for mutton. Turn it every quarter of an hour. At first the meat's own fat will run out. Towards the end of cooking time—especially that for mutton—you need to keep an eye on the meat as it browns to make sure it does not stick. If it looks like it is doing so, pour in a little hot stock. When the meat is done skim off as much meat fat as you can, add the tomatoes and parsley, adjust the seasoning, and give the finished stew a final simmer. This is rich and filling, good served simply with a green salad (see p. 205).

COSTRADAS: LOCAL TASTES

Spanish *costradas* were a little like early French pâtés or hot baked meat loaves. They started life in court kitchens, but slid sideways into country

MUTTON

"Leg meat is the best for stews." Altamiras cooked mutton from grass-fed sheep *entre dos lanas*, between two shearings. Today's yearling hogget or two-year wethers are not so different from the sheep that gave his mutton, but the recipes in *New Art* are also good cooked with younger lamb or older ewe mutton. Simply adapt the cooking time: it may be 45 minutes for very young lamb, 2 hours for wether mutton, and up to 4 hours slow-cooking for ewe mutton. Sometimes Altamiras started a dish by braising the meat in its own fat (see opposite), a technique good for economic and well-marbled cuts, like neck of lamb. If you cook either mutton or lamb on the bone for full flavor, be sure to skim off any fat that sticks to the foam as the meat begins to simmer and, when it is cooked, cool it and skim any remaining hardened fat off the top with a spoon or kitchen paper.

cooking together with the charcoal braziers on which they were made. In the hands of cooks like Altamiras working on a low budget their expensive sugared pastry crusts were replaced by simpler egg toppings and they took on local tastes, revealing earlier unwritten flavors.[12]

Lamb Costrada with Spiced Omelettes / Costrada de Carne, y Huevos

Sear lean leg meat on the fire, hash it with cured ham fat, onion and a handful of parsley, and put your hash in your stewpot to cook over a gentle fire. Make candied egg thread, as I tell you later in the Chapter on eggs. Season the meat with salt, spices and pine kernels then layer it up with the egg in a pie dish. Bathe the top of the costrada *with cracked and beaten eggs, sprinkle it with sugar and powdered cinnamon, then cook it sitting between hot embers, with more above than below, until it has a good crust. You may serve this cut up like a pie.*

"She broke some eggs into a . . . skillet, and after they were cooked she sprinkled on chopped meat braised with onion, and simultaneously she beat other eggs and poured them on top." So ran a maid's evidence against Clara de Puxmija, a merchant's wife accused by the Inquisition of following a secret Jewish life in the Aragonese town of Teruel in 1486. That a recipe could be damning evidence to the Inquisition may surprise us, but then kitchen customs behind closed doors were one of the few ways a family could express shared faith, and roots together. Clearly layered meat and eggs held such significance: a similar dish was among a small group flagged up as Jewish in a manuscript from al-Andalus. In towns like La Almunia, where there was no conflict between the Jewish quarter and the rest of the population, these were the kind of dishes that filtered into the culinary mainstream. Here, like David Gitlitz and Linda Kay Davidson, who published Clara's story in *A Drizzle of Honey*, their book about Spain's secret Jewish kitchens, I have returned to the thirteenth-century recipe, although I have adapted it to friary taste.[13]

1 tbsp olive oil, 1 finely chopped onion, 750 g / 1½ lb minced lamb or beef, 2 dozen saffron threads (see p. 102), 2 tbsp toasted pine kernels, small handfuls of fresh snipped parsley and mint leaves and a handful of chopped shelled pistachios (optional)

FOR THE OMELETTES: 2 tbsp olive oil, 4 eggs, 3–4 pinches of powdered cinnamon, salt.

Preheat your oven (240°C, 475°F, gas mark 8). Make two 15-cm / 6-in omelettes in a lightly oiled frying pan, using 2 eggs beaten with a couple of pinches of cinnamon for each one. Warm the olive oil, sweat the onion. Knead the meat in a bowl with the roughly cracked or finely pounded pine kernels, parsley, sweated onion, and saffron. Lightly oil a non-stick baking sheet. Divide the meat into 3 equal parts. Spread one part into a round cake the size of your cinnamon omelettes, put it on the baking sheet, scatter over a third of the mint and pistachios and top with an omelette. Repeat these two layers, finishing the costrada with the third layer of meat. Oven-bake for 25–40 minutes, depending on whether you like your meat rare or well done. Serve hot. I like this with green vegetables with an olive oil dressing (see pp. 191–94).

BABY COSTRADAS: Use 7-cm / 2½-in ring cutters to cut the meat and omelettes and cook the costradas for 10–12 minutes (rare) or 15–20 minutes (well done).

Lamb and Sausage Loaf with Garlic and Pine Kernels / Costrada de Otro Modo

Cut up lean leg meat and hash it with streaky cured ham, parsley and some garlic cloves. As I have said you can leave out the garlic, but I add it to many dishes. We poor cooks turn to it a great deal and you can hardly see this as wrong for our country's lamentable state justifies us doing so! So brown the hash in a skillet, put it in your stewpot, cook it with spices and soaked pine kernels, turn it into a large baking dish and add cooked sliced sausage. Crack and stir up some raw eggs: half for the hash and the rest to pour raw over your costrada. Sprinkle sugar and cinnamon over the top, or just cinnamon, then sit your costrada in hot embers and let it bake till the meat sets. This is a very good dish.

Spices were for the rich, garlic for the poor. For Altamiras garlic was also a local crop, part of everyday cookery since his childhood, whether picked fresh as green shoots or taken from a string of bulbs hanging in the friary larder.[14] By the end of the book, he had made use of every Spanish garlic cookery technique we know today: he chopped fresh shoots for his meatballs, he fried sliced garlic in olive oil to give it a nutty flavor and he threw a whole head of garlic into a pot of chickpeas to give it a mellow background flavor. Here, he crushed it raw for pungency in a lamb loaf that you can eat hot or cold as a pâté.

600 g / 1¼ lb coarsely minced lamb or mutton, 75 g / 2½ oz minced streaky jamón, 4 finely chopped garlic cloves (or less or more, as you like), 2 tbsp chopped parsley, 120 g / 4 oz finely diced *longaniza* sausage (see p. 238), 1 heaped tbsp roughly chopped toasted pine kernels, large pinches of ground cloves and cinnamon (see p. 220), 1 beaten egg, sage or bay leaves (optional)

Makes a 1 kg / 2 lb loaf; 8–12 slices.

Warm your oven (170°C, 325°F, gas mark 3). Put the meat, the flavoring ingredients and egg in a large bowl, knead well, season, and press the mixture into a wetted non-stick loaf tin or mold (24 x 10 x 6 cm / 9½ x 4 x 2½ inches). Arrange a few bay or sage leaves on top of the meat, stand the loaf in a spacious roasting tin, put it in the middle of the oven, pour in about 2.5 cm / 1 inch cold water and bake for 50 minutes or until the meat draws away slightly from the edges. When you stick in a skewer, the juices should run transparent. Serve this hot, turned on to a warmed plate, or cooled in the tin and weighted, pouring off the excess fatty juices before you turn it out to serve cold as a pâté. I like this served with an herby rice salad, peppery bundles of watercress tied with chives, and a quince sauce (see p. 94).

Lamb, Artichoke, and Chicken Pie / Otra Costrada

Cut your meat into fine dice. Braise them as if you were making a gigote *then make pastry: take the finest flour, a little white wine, sugar and soft lard or chopped pork fat, and when you have made a dough from these roll part of it out to give a sheet large enough to cover your pie dish. Spread the meat on top and, if you like, add some cooked artichoke hearts and lean partridge or chicken, or capon, then sit your pie in warm embers till the heat sucks up the filling's juices. Roll out another sheet of pastry big enough to cover your pie and lay it over the meat. You can glaze the top snowy white with toasted pounded white sugar and beaten egg whites, but only after baking the pie, for this glaze cooks in no time.*

You may serve this pie to people of distinction, e.g. a Bishop, a Provincial Superior, etc., and it makes a great treat for we poor friars.

Artichokes from the friary kitchen garden gave this pie filling a luscious green juiciness. "A great treat," was how Altamiras described it as food for the poor, a gesture towards the idea that everyone deserved to eat well. How he shaped his pie is not clear. Perhaps he made it as a large flat *empanada*, with a thin layer of filling between piecrusts, or maybe he baked a deep pie with slightly sweet pastry. I have given the main recipe for a large flat *empanada* like those found all around Spain today. Check to see if you have a non-stick baking sheet large enough to fit the pie.

600 g / 1¼ lb minced lamb, 2 tbsp olive oil, 2 finely chopped onions, 3 sliced garlic cloves, 3 tbsp chopped parsley, 12 prepared fresh, pre-served or frozen cooked artichoke hearts (see p. 70), 150 g / 5 oz chicken breasts (or other chicken meat), 250 g / 8 oz flaky or shortcrust pastry (see p. 236)
FOR THE GLAZE: 1 beaten egg yolk.
Makes a 30 x 25 cm / 12 x 10 inch flat empanada.
Put the lamb into a large mixing bowl. Preheat your oven (190°C, 375°F, gas mark 5). Warm the olive oil in a frying pan, sweat the onion and garlic in it, and scoop them into the lamb. Add the parsley, half

the artichoke hearts and seasoning. Divide the pastry in half, rolling each piece out into a rectangle measuring about 30 x 25 cm / 12 x 10 inches. Lay one piece on the non-stick baking sheet (it does not have to fill it entirely). Spoon over the lamb filling, leaving a rim around the edge. Slice the chicken finely across the grain and halve the remaining artichoke hearts. Arrange them on top of the meat, cover with the pastry lid, wetting the edges of the crusts to seal and pinch them together. Bake for 20 minutes, then turn down the oven and bake at 170°C / 325°F / gas mark 3 for another 25 minutes. Check to see if the pie is done with a skewer.

FOR A ROUND DEEP PIE: You need 375 g / 12 oz pastry and a 22.5-cm / 8-inch non-stick spring-form cake pan. Divide the pastry two-thirds and one-third, using the larger piece to make a bottom crust that comes about three-quarters of the way up the sides. Fill the pie, use the smaller piece of pastry to make a lid, put it on top, crimp the edges, and bake for about 40 minutes.

Meatballs / Almondigas de Carnero

Take lean meat and pound it to a hash with a little cured ham fat, parsley leaves, and green garlic shoots. Keep the meat bones and make broth with them, throw in a piece of cured ham fat with rind, let the broth simmer, and skim off the foam which rises on it. Dress your meat with breadcrumbs, cheese, spices, saffron, and raw eggs, as you see fit, knead it in a basin and season it with salt and spices. When your broth is done, strain it into a pot then make your meatballs, but without touching them with your hands, and you may read how in the fifth article of the Chapter where I deal with frogs. Simmer the meatballs in the broth. Prepare a hazelnut sauce as I have told you elsewhere, add this to the broth, give it a little boil and finish it off with a little sharp citrus juice. I should add that I am no lover of meatballs, but they would give me much pleasure cooked this way.

Deeply satisfying in flavor, Altamiras's meatballs are stripped of the modern red tomato sauce with which they are usually cooked. They are still cooked this way near La Almunia at Los 20 Platos, the family restaurant on Almonacid's main plaza where they are made from home-minced meat and served with concentrated cooking broth flavored by whole unskinned garlic cloves. You can thicken the broth with almonds, if you like, as in southern Spain. By the way, don't be put off by the pork fat in the meatball mix—it lubricates the meat beautifully. Two to three large meatballs make a satisfying meal. One makes a good frugal supper.[15]

720 g / 1½ lb minced lamb (or mixed meats, such as pork and beef) per person, 60 g / 2 oz finely diced jamón fat, 2 tbsp ewe's milk or other sharp grated cheese, 4 tbsp fresh breadcrumbs, 1 egg, 60 g / 2 oz toasted pine kernels, 1 heaped tbsp chopped flat-leafed parsley (from about 6 leafy stalks), 6 finely chopped green garlic stalks or 2 large garlic cloves, large pinches of cloves and cinnamon
FOR THE BROTH: 750 ml / 1½ pints meat broth (see pp. 73–75), 2 cloves of garlic in their skin, a saffron infusion made from 2 dozen threads (see p. 102).
FOR THE HAZELNUT THICKENING (OPTIONAL): 75g / 2½ oz skinned small hazelnuts or almonds, 1 raw egg, ½ slice of toasted bread, squeeze of lemon juice.
Makes 8 large, or 2 dozen small meatballs.
Warm the broth with the garlic cloves in a large pan. Knead all the meatball ingredients together well, season the mix, and divide it into even portions to shape like small oranges (about 90 g / 3 oz each) or into smaller modern meatballs. This is done most easily with wetted hands. Lower the meatballs into the simmering broth and cook them, covered, until well done. An orange-sized beef or lamb meatball needs about half an hour, but smaller ones, like golf balls, need 6 minutes. Cut one meatball open to check that it is cooked through, drain them all, reserving the broth, strain it, reduce it to 475 ml / 16 fl oz, add the saffron infusion, and simmer gently for 10 minutes. Serve a little broth into each person's plate, and then ladle in one, two, or a few meatballs.

One meatball,
One meatball,
This here gent wants one meatball.
Hy Zaret and Louis Singer, "One Meatball," 1940

FOUR STUFFED VEGETABLES

Altamiras hollowed out his vegetables for stuffing with a rustic sharpened cane from the river bed. Later cooks extended this family of dishes with local produce whenever a little meat needed to go a long way. Stuffed peaches appeared on Capuchin menus, stuffed plums and aubergines in cooks' kitchen notebooks, and stuffed apples were made in Barcelona's canteens during the Spanish Civil War.[16] Today mixed pork, lamb, and beef are the usual meats for the stuffings, but you can improvise, as Altamiras did, with sausage meat for his cucumbers. I like to serve two or three vegetables and fruit warm in saffron broth: they then take on the simple beauty of a still-life painting.

For the Stuffing and Sauce / Relleno y Salsa o Caldo

STUFFING: 200 g / 7 oz finely minced seasoned lamb or mutton (or pork or beef or a mixture), 30 g / 1 oz fresh breadcrumbs, generous pinches of cinnamon and cloves, 1 tbsp grated mature ewe's milk cheese and 1 beaten egg.

VARIATIONS: You can replace half the lamb with chorizo sausage meat or finely chopped chicken flesh and you can add grated lemon zest, oregano, or thyme.

Makes about 250 g / 8 oz stuffing.

SAFFRON BROTH (OPTIONAL): 600 ml / 1 pint of meat broth (see pp. 73–75), a saffron infusion made with 2 dozen saffron threads (see p. 102), 150 ml / 5 fl oz white wine.

FOR THE HAZELNUT SAUCE (OPTIONAL): 600 ml / 1 pint of meat broth (see pp. 73–75), 3 dozen hazelnuts blended with 1 garlic clove and 15 g / ½ oz bread soaked in water and squeezed dry.

Makes about 750 ml / 1½ pints broth.

Stuffed Onions / Cebollas Rellenas con Carne

Take lean leg meat, hash it as I have told you, put it in a basin with spices, breadcrumbs, salt, pine kernels, a little cheese and raw eggs, e.g. eight for every pound of meat. Knead them in well and season your stuffing. Make broth with the meat bones and a little cured ham fat, and skim the foam off the broth as it simmers. Then stuff your onions, cut out the inside layers with the point of a sharp knife, fill them well with the meat, sit them side by side in a dish and pour broth over them. Cook them like this, make a toasted hazelnut sauce, thicken it with eggs and sharpen it with lemon juice. These are very substantial and tasty.

You can stuff large or small onions this way. Small ones are fiddlier to make, but they look wonderful and make for easier serving and eating.

4–6 large sweet onions, 1 quantity of stuffing (see above), 750 ml / 1½ pints seasoned broth

Skin and slice across the onions' tops and bottoms, cut away the tough outer layers, but be sure to leave the bottom intact, patching it if needed. Carve away the onion's heart so it is hollow like a cup. (I use a potato peeler for this.) Pack in the stuffing (see p. 29). Bring the broth to a gentle boil. Set the onions side by side in a flameproof casserole, pour over the hot broth, put the casserole over a gentle flame or in a fairly hot oven (200°C, 400°F, gas mark 6) and cook the floating onions, rolling them over after half an hour. Finish the broth by straining it and reducing it, then tinting it pale yellow with saffron (see p. 25), or, if you like, thicken it with a creamy pounded hazelnut or almond paste.

Stuffed Lettuces / Lechugas rellenas

Well-grown lettuces are apt for stuffing. Trim them back to their close-packed leaves, wash them well, cook them in boiling water with salt and, when you see they are half-done, lift them out gently. Drain them on a clean board. Make a stuffing and broth, as I said for the onions. Squeeze the lettuces between your palms till no water clings to them. Then take them one by one: hold them the right way up by the stalk, fold back the leaves like petals, and place a large egg of stuffing at the heart of each lettuce. Wrap leaves over the stuffing so they overlap at the top and go on like this, picking leaves attached to the thickest stalk, for then you have no need to tie up your lettuces with string, unlike certain cooks as hidebound as their lettuces. You may play with these like balls, but do not throw them around if you hope to win the day. Sit them in a spacious dish, pour your broth over the top, cook them, make a hazelnut sauce and then make your move: take your lettuces to table.

1 large lettuce, with resistant leaves, 1 quantity of stuffing (see above), 750 ml / 1½ pints seasoned broth or 250 ml / ¼ pint olive oil, and garlic to taste

Wash the lettuce, pull off raggedy bits and bitter outer leaves, then stand it in a pan with a little salt. Pour over boiling water so it is nearly covered. A few minutes later it will open magically like a green rose.

Drain it upside down in a colander and, when it is cool enough to touch, squeeze out the remaining moisture. Set it the right way up in the colander and open up the leaves for stuffing. Place an egg of the stuffing at the heart; around that fold a layer of leaves; flatten another ball of stuffing into a band and plaster it around the broadest part of the leaves; wrap around more leaves. Keep on like this so the lettuce becomes an expanding ball and finish it off with a protective layer of strong outer leaves. I confess that although Altamiras disapproved, I do tie up the lettuce. Now put it to simmer in broth or braise it in garlicky olive oil with a thumb's depth of broth and a little sweet white wine, which draws together the flavors. The lettuce should be done in about 45 minutes and is good turned every quarter of an hour for even cooking.

LETTUCE PACKAGES: In Catalonia leaves are wrapped around stuffing into small packages, or *farcellets*. These are good to make when you are cooking for lots of people.

Stuffed Squash / Calabazas Rellenas

Pick pumpkins as thick as your wrist. Trim a finger from their stalks and crowns and tunnel through them with an unknotted slit reed or cane like those used as drills by cartwrights and coopers. Cut out the hearts this way, stuff the hollows with the chopped and seasoned meat, then sit your stuffed pumpkins in a clay or earthen dish, pour over broth made with the meat bones and simmer the pumpkins for two hours. Be sure to push your stuffing in well so it does not fall out and, when the pumpkins are cooked, make a thickening for the sauce with toasted hazelnuts, a little fried bread soaked and squeezed dry, eggs and spices, all pounded and stirred into the broth. Give the pumpkins a little boil, shake the dish from time to time so the sauce does not stick or burn, then serve them.

4–6 small (500 g / 1 lb) butternut squash, 1 quantity of stuffing (p. 25), about 750 ml / 1½ pints broth

Small organic butternuts "as thick as your wrist" stuff beautifully. Tunnel through them lengthways and fill the hollow with meat—I like it flavored with oregano and lemon zest. Put them in a dish where they fit in a single layer, pour in seasoned broth to come halfway up the sides, roll over the squash from time to time to ensure even cooking for 45–60 minutes, and serve with the strained cooking juices.

Stuffed Cucumbers / Pepinos Rellenos

Pick large cucumbers, trim two or three fingers off the stalks, one and a half off the crowns, skin them and hollow out the hearts with a slit cane, as I have said for pumpkins. Make the stuffing, fill your cucumbers with it, let them cook in broth and make a nut thickening for it. Lean cured ham or sausage meat are good in this, and so is poultry flesh if you care to try it.

4–6 cucumbers, 1 quantity of stuffing (above), 750 ml / 1½ pints saffron broth or hazelnut sauce (see above)

Stubby ridge cucumbers, like Spanish and Turkish ones, keep their shape well when stuffed, they are remarkably juicy and you don't need to salt them since you are cutting out the seeds. Altamiras's mild variation on his stuffing, made with chicken, is especially good in them. Allow around 25 minutes cooking time, rolling over the cucumbers half way through. I like to add a leaf or two of mint to the broth.

Braised Lamb with Pomegranate Juice / Guisado de Carnero con Granada

Prepare your helpings of meat, put them in your olla, *or stewpot, and salt and pepper them. Chop cured ham fat and onion, add them to the pot and put it to braise over a gentle fire. When you see your meat is half done, perhaps a little more, add a hazelnut thickening with all kinds of spices, as described earlier. Then, once your stew is cooked, squeeze in the juice of two or three boiled pomegranates. They will give you a very good, tasty sauce.*

Pomegranates have inspired so much Spanish imagery: the crimson juice symbolized bloodshed to the poets of al-Andalus and to Charles V the leathery skin wrapped around fragile fruit segments represented the protection of his empire for small regions. Muslim cooks had added sour and sweet pomegranate juice to stews, yet few Spanish cooks were to follow their example.[17] This dish, however, is delicious. José Carlos Martín, of El Patio de Goya, La Almunia's flagship restaurant, came up with two versions for it for this book, one made with a leg of young lamb on the bone and the second, for which the recipe is given here, cooked with small steaks cut from the shoulder of locally reared grass-fed hogget. He has added two wonderful touches: a lamb stock made with the meat's roasted bones and a purée of wood-roasted sweet potato.

1.2 kg / 2½ lb mature braising lamb cleaned of fat and cut into small steaks, the lamb's bones, 150 g / 5 oz Iberico pork fat, roughly chopped, 2 roughly chopped onions, 2–3 juicy ripe pomegranates weighing about 750 g / 1½ lb or 250 ml / 8 fl oz pomegranate juice, 500 ml / 16 fl oz defatted lamb stock (see below), 5 cloves, ½ stick cinnamon, and a large pinch of saffron

FOR THE HAZELNUT THICKENING: 4 dozen skinned small hazelnuts, ¼ slice of bread, a little water.

Prepare the meat, leaving on enough fat to make the final meat juicy, and reserve. Warm the oven to 180°C, 350°F, gas mark 4. Roast the bones for 45 minutes, put them covered with unsalted water in a large pan, bring the water to a gentle simmer, and leave for 2 hours. Cool, scrape off any fat and sieve through kitchen paper towel. Put the pork fat into a large casserole, warm till it is transparent and turning gold, add the meat, seal it, salt and pepper lightly, then throw in the onion. Mix it into the meat, turn the temperature to low, and let everything cook like this for about 45 minutes, turning it occasionally. After this time, you should have just a few intense juices. Squeeze the pomegranates, blend the spices with about 475 ml / 16 fl oz stock. Pour the pomegranate juice and stock over the meat and leave to cook for another 1½ hours. When you see the meat is done, though still slightly pink inside, blend the ingredients for the hazelnut thickening and stir into the casserole juices. Cook for a final quarter of an hour. Serve the casserole with a sweet potato purée scattered with jewel-like ruby pomegranate seeds. We drank this with a Garnacha old-vine wine from Calatayud, and it was an excellent match for the slight astringency the pomegranate gives the meat juices.

Mutton or Veal Steaks in White Wine / Lonjas Magras de Carnero, o de Ternera

Cut slices from a leg of mutton or veal. Of the two, veal is the better for this dish. Slice the meat across the grain, salt it and let it sit overnight. When you fry the meat the next day, first sweat cured ham fat till the grease runs out, then lay the fried slices in a clay or earthen dish, add sugar, white wine, bay leaves and cinnamon, cook the meat till it is tender and when you serve it, as you shall see, nobody shall guess whether they are eating mutton or cured ham.

The musky herbed sweet wine sauce served with these meat steaks remained popular right through the nineteenth century. Today, combined with contemporary dishes, it is deliciously different, best set off by plain vegetables.

For 4–6 lean mutton or veal steaks you need half a bottle of medium white wine, 4 bay leaves, a thumb's length of stick cinnamon, 1 tbsp honey, and 2 tbsp olive oil. Simmer the wine with the bay and cinnamon for 10 minutes in a covered pan and stir in the honey. Pan fry the veal steaks in the olive oil, pour over the sauce, and simmer gently, about 10 minutes for escalopes, 20 minutes for steaks. Plain steamed shredded cabbage and couscous or quinoa go well with this.

Lamb Tortillas / Tortillas de Gigote de Carnero

Make your meat into small dice or chop it as you would for gigote, *braise it till it is tender, drain off the cooking liquid, and put the meat in a basin, adding breadcrumbs, sugar, cinnamon and eggs. You can fry these tortillas in soft lard. If you do not want to sweeten them season them with all your spices, but if they are sweetened, then serve them fried with sugar and cinnamon on top.*

These lamb omelettes may have been the inspiration for Spain's potato tortilla. Meat omelettes are much richer, but if you make them like today's *chorizo* tortilla, taking off all the meat's fat, they are very good.[18] I like to serve these as part of a dinner of small plates, for example, along-side mushroom *empanadillas* (see pp. 202–3).

4 tbsp good olive oil, 370 g / 12 oz minced or diced lamb, 3 tbsp fresh breadcrumbs, 4 beaten eggs, a large pinch of cinnamon
Makes 16–20 baby tortillas or one 20-cm / 8-in tortilla.
Warm a tablespoon of the olive oil in a heavy frying pan and pan fry the lamb quickly in it, crushing it with a fork to brown it well. Pour the fat out of the pan, tip the meat on to a paper towel to mop up the fat, put it in a bowl, and stir in the breadcrumbs, eggs, and seasoning. Wipe clean the frying pan. Warm the rest of the oil in it and pan-fry spoonfuls of egg and meat mix to make baby *tortillas* or cook all the mixture at once to make a single large omelette, flipping it on a plate as a support when golden and set underneath.

WITH ROASTED GARLIC AND THYME: Slice off whole garlic heads' tops, set the bulbs on tinfoil, pour over olive oil, roast in a warm oven for 15–20 minutes, cool, then slip the cloves out of their skin, and mash the pulp with bruised thyme leaves. Mix the pulp evenly into the meat with the back of a fork.

BEYOND THE LEG: CHOPS, TAILS, BRAINS, FEET

Altamiras ended his first chapter with ideas for cooking sheep's tails, ribs, brain, and feet. Sheep's tails, docked in springtime, were shepherds' food, once cooked in the open air in the sierra, but they were to become fashionable in turn-of-the-century Madrid in the hands of royal chef Teodoro Bardaji, who was Aragonese by birth. He nicknamed them "mountain asparagus" and cooked them with tomatoes and sweet bell-peppers for King Alfonso XIII.[19] Today you can track down lamb's tails in the countryside. We bought half a dozen from Almonacid's butcher, carried them home, and grilled them the shepherds' way over glowing embers. As the fat melted, dripped down, and fed the leaping flames, we listened to the fire crackling in the dark, then, as it died down and we chewed the tails, the silence was complete.

Lamb Ribs / Costillas de Carnero

Ribs are at their best when the pastures are tall and well-grown, between July and Michaelmas. Take a rack of ribs, check it is well chined, give it blows with the back of your cleaver and grill the ribs on the fire, basting them with feathers dipped in melted ham fat and lemon juice. Sheep's tails are grilled in the same way, and for those who have little appetite, it would be a great kindness if you roll them first in grated breadcrumbs.

One day, exploring the ruins of San Cristóbal, the friars' summer retreat, we met Pedro and Pedro, the elder and younger, pruning almond trees. Nearby thin-cut lamb chops were balanced over a glowing fire of almond prunings. The best lunch, said Pedro the elder, winking at us. We breathed in the sweet smoke and agreed. Outside Spain you can wood-grill ribs or thin-cut chops over a barbecue for something of the same effect. For the chops, ask your butcher to cut one of every two between the bones. Grill or griddle these *vuelta y vuelta*, as the Spanish say, quickly on one side then the other, till well-browned on the outside, rare and pink inside.

Pile them up on a hot plate and serve with green salad, fresh bread, salt flakes, and a glass of good red wine.

Lamb's Brains / Sesos de Carnero

The best way to dress brains is poached in water with salt, cut into small slices, dipped in beaten egg and fried in hot lard or olive oil, and, if you wish, you may serve these with sugar and cinnamon.

Sold as delicacies, peeled of their membranes and nestled protectively in plastic boxes, Spanish lamb's brains need only a quick soaking in vinegared iced water.[20] Then put them in a pan of cold salted water, bring them to a boil, drain, cool till firm, pat dry, divide into lobules, season, and pan-fry quickly in hot olive oil. I like to serve these on hot toast spread with romesco sauce, followed by a plain green salad. In some countries lamb's brains are not always seen as a delicacy and may not be sold peeled of their membranes. Do this carefully. It is not a tricky task.

Lamb's Feet with Tomato, Cheese, and Pine Kernel Sauce / Manos de Carnero

Scald sheep's feet, cut them open and cut out the thread between the toenails. Boil the feet, add salt, lay them in a clay or earthen dish and make a sauce with meat broth, pine kernels, garlic, parsley, tomatoes, grated cheese, a little bread you have soaked in water and squeezed dry, and spices. Pound everything to a paste, thin it with broth to give enough sauce to bathe your feet, simmer them briefly in it and serve them. Later I shall deal with pig's trotters, and let me say here, I shall hide nothing of their preparation from you.

Lamb's feet are an acquired taste, but don't miss out on this recipe's delicious tomato, cheese, and pine kernel purée. It is a little like Catalan *romesco* and is very good with fish or hot new potatoes or green vegetables.

I was finally persuaded to learn to cook lamb's feet because they are so well loved in Madrid. Here are *madrileños'* four golden rules for cooking them. 1. Soak them in very cold water with vinegar for 30 minutes. 2. Start the feet in cold liquid and always simmer them gently. 3. Cook them bone-in to increase the gelatine in the broth. 4. Leave them soaking in their sauce in the fridge for a day or two before rewarming them to serve. Andoni Luis Aduriz, of Michelin-starred Mugaritz restaurant in the Basque Country, adds wine to the cooking broth.

To prepare your lamb's feet, allow 4–6 per person. Tug or cut out the tuft between the toes, called the *ranilla*, singe off any hairs, and then soak the feet in iced water with vinegar. Prepare a large pan of cold salted water or broth with a few bay leaves, put in the feet, and bring to a gentle simmer. When the lamb's feet skin is falling off the bone and the gelatine has softened (check it with a knife), drain, and cool the feet. Pull on your kitchen gloves, peel back the skin and gelatinous flesh, snap the joint, and tease out the long bone. Now submerge the flesh and skin in the prepared sauce in a spacious pan, simmer for 30 minutes, cool, and allow to sit overnight. Transfer to a container with an airtight lid and chill. These keep well for up to 4–5 days. Serve warmed through with bread, spoons, and napkins.

TOMATO, CHEESE, AND PINE KERNEL SAUCE: Whirl together 300 g / 10 oz chopped skinned tomatoes with 15 g / ½ oz fresh breadcrumbs, 75 g / 2½ oz toasted pine kernels, 60 g / 2 oz mature ewe's milk cheese. Blend 6 tbsp lamb's feet broth or water into this thick red purée, season and spice to taste, and add some parsley. You can dilute this with more broth or water if you like.

Makes 500 ml / 12 fl oz sauce.

CHAPTER II

MORE MEAT DISHES

CHURCH BELLS rang out the time of day. Luis Buñuel, the film director, memorably described them tolling for Masses, Vespers, and the Angelus as well as for secular events like gathering storm-clouds or fire in his southern Aragonese hometown, Calanda, in the early 1900s.[1] Bells also marked the hours and days in friary life and handbells called everyone to breakfast, lunch, and supper. Altamiras gave dishes for each of these three friary meals, opening again with a flourish, this time with an original recipe "many people want to know."

Broth Custards / Caldo Helado

Make meat broth, seasoned with salt but not spices. Boil it well, strain off some broth, take off all its fat, let it sit till it is cold, then make this dish with it. Count two egg yolks and an ounce of sugar for every small bowlful and stir them into the broth till the sugar dissolves. If you are making this for just a few people pour it into earthen baking dishes, sit each one over a pot of boiling water and leave till the custards set. Serve these sprinkled with sugar and cinnamon and remember, each one must cook over its own pot of hot water, or you may bake a big dishful between hot embers, with more in the lid than underneath, and serve it like a pie. This is very good and many people want to know how to make it.

You can make these as savory custards with meat, chicken, or other broth and cook them in non-stick molds in a bain marie. I like to tint them leafy green with parsley juice or pale yellow with a saffron infusion.[2]

400 ml / 13 fl oz good meat, poultry or vegetable broth (see p. 234), 4 large beaten eggs and 1 yolk

TO FLAVOR: a large handful of parsley leaves, blended and the juice squeezed out through a sieve, or a saffron infusion made with 16 strands of saffron (see p. 102).

Makes 4 150-ml / 5 fl oz custards.

Preheat the oven (150°C, 300°F, gas mark 2). For parsley custard whizz the broth with the parsley juice till it is tinted green and pour it through a fine sieve. For saffron custard infuse the pounded saffron overnight in a small cupful of hot broth. Lightly beat the broth into the eggs with a knife, sieve to remove clots, pour into four lightly oiled non-stick 150-ml / 5 fl oz molds, set these in a loaf tin or baking dish, pour in cold water to come halfway up the sides, and oven-bake for 30 minutes. A toothpick stuck into the middle of the custards should come out clean. Remove them from the oven, lift them out of the bain marie, cool, and chill. Good served with green leaves and toast moistened with olive oil.

SITTING DOWN TO EAT

As Altamiras turned to everyday friary dishes, he gave us a glimpse of his working day in the kitchen where he served up as well as cooked the food. Dishes were carried into the refectory on a board and passed around for the friars to help themselves. They ate in silence, their sleeves rolled up, their napkins unfolded, seasoning their food with salt and vinegar, and pouring themselves water and wine laid up in the middle of the table. It was considered wasteful to leave food uneaten: soup and vegetable leftovers were kept to serve the poor the next day while fish and meat went back to the kitchen. Hygiene was strict but table manners were not. One 1650 novice's handbook remonstrated, "noses should never be blown with bare hands."[3]

SOUPS

Meat Broth / Caldo de Otro Modo

In the morning, when you have risen, set your feet on the ground and your spirit in God, light a fire in your kitchen workshop and warm pots of water. When the bells chime five or six o'clock you will go to hear Mass and commend

yourself and your doings to God. Then, when you have returned from Church, cut up the servings of meat, put them in a small copper pan or clay or earthen pot. Wash the meat well in some of the water you warmed, and temper it with cold water if it is very hot, so you do not scald the meat, then put it in your soup pot, bring it to the boil and simmer it. Skim off the foam which rises to the top, add salt and a lump of cured ham fat. Season your broth with salt, pepper and saffron, let it cook and pick up a good colour. Keep a little broth to one side in a cup and make a thickening of pounded hazelnuts, spices, hard-boiled eggs and kids' livers or, if you have none of these, just use bread. Stir your thickening into the soup, sit it in a hay basket and, when the heat has faded, skim the fat off the top. Take eggs, counting half an egg for each serving, crack them, whisk them with a chocolate beater, then whisk in a little vinegar to thin any clots and after that add your cupful of lukewarm broth, stirring so no egg coagulates. Now stir this back into the soup.

If you make this for the sick or weak skim the fat off the top and boil the egg, keeping the whites for another dish; mash in the yolk and in this way the soup is better.

Altamiras began work early every day. He would tie on his rope-soled shoes, pad down to the kitchen, sweep the floor, put on his apron, light the fire, fill pots of water from the well or spring, and put them over a hot fire to boil. One pot of water was for washing up and another one for the cook to wash his hands between jobs, but the most important one was for making broth that became the base for various soups and sops. Some were old-fashioned bread soups evolved from early Christian *šúpa*. Others were smooth in what was then the modern style. This seems to have been an everyday recipe, perhaps because it would have been as good cold in summer as hot in winter.[4]

1.4 liters / 2¼ pints meat broth skimmed of its fat (see p. 74), 60 g / 2 oz calves' or lambs' livers, few drops of olive oil

TO THICKEN: 3 dozen small skinned hazelnuts, generous pinches of cinnamon and ground black pepper, 2 hard-boiled eggs, salt, a saffron infusion made with 2 dozen threads (see p. 102), 1 raw egg whisked with 2 tsp white wine vinegar.

Warm the broth in a large serving pot. Sear the livers in olive oil, blend to a pink paste with the hazelnuts, spices, and hard-boiled eggs, stir in a ladleful or two of hot broth to make a thin cream, pour back into the potful of broth, season, and simmer for 15 minutes. Finally whisk in the saffron infusion, the egg, and vinegar, and cook the soup for a few more minutes without boiling it. I like this served with croûtons scattered on top and a glass of red wine.

Country Ham, Artichoke and Bread Soup / Sopa

Cut slices from a good loaf of bread and toast them. Chop lean ham, cut little slices of fried liver, chop parsley and hard-boiled eggs, but leave a few yolks whole, and then assemble your soup. Make a bed of toast, scatter over liver, ham, eggs and parsley, then a little grated cheese, powdered cloves and cinnamon; make another layer of toast on top then another of flavourings. Now make a hazelnut sauce with meat broth, let it cook in a small pan, stirring well so it cannot burn, season and spice it and pour half over the sops. Leave them to sit so they drink up the broth. Then lift your sops off the fire, pour over the rest of the broth and lay the halved egg yolks on top, tucked in between the cooked artichoke hearts. You may finish cooking your soup between hot embers or toast the top, and you may add cracked and stirred eggs. But remember, if you do this, you need no hard-boiled eggs. This is a very good soup, but there are more to follow.

Cured ham, cheese, liver, artichokes, and a hazelnut-thickened broth give a gorgeous rustic depth of flavor to this second layered bread soup. A few tips. One, your loaf needs to be two to three days old. Two, take care when toasting or frying your bread—frying in olive oil is often preferred today (see p. 234)—since even a small piece of burned or scorched bread leeches bitterness right through the soup. Finally, hold back a little broth in case you need to moisten the finished soup. Before buying or measuring ingredients, choose a big flameproof bowl or cast iron casserole in which to make it. I have lightened the original recipe, as friary cooks did later on, so the soup has just one layer of bread.[5]

olive oil for brushing the soup bowl, 1.4 liters / 2½ pints defatted broth (see p. 234), 4–6 very thinly cut slices of day-old bread fried in olive oil, 2 hard-boiled eggs, 100 g / 3½ oz fried chopped streaky jamón or pancetta, 250 g / 8 oz chopped artichoke hearts and stalks, a handful of snipped parsley, 100 g / 3½ oz mature ewe's milk cheese, large pinches of ground cloves and cinnamon, 250 g / 8 oz calf's or lamb's liver, seared and cut into thin ribbons (optional), 6 artichoke hearts (see p. 71)

FOR THE HAZELNUT PASTE: 3 dozen toasted hazelnuts blended with 1/2 slice of bread, 3 garlic cloves, salt.

OPTIONAL TOPPING: 2 raw beaten eggs and 105 g / 3½ oz grated sheep's milk cheese.

Brush a large flameproof soup bowl or casserole with olive oil. Warm the broth in a pan, season it and blend a ladleful with the hazelnut paste, stir this thickening back into the soup, then add the chopped bits and pieces: egg whites (reserve the yolks), fried jamón, chopped artichokes, and snipped parsley. Stir in the grated cheese and spices too and simmer gently for 10 minutes. Make a tight-fitting bed of fried bread on the bottom of the bowl, sprinkle with a little salt, pour over soup to cover, and warm gently till it is absorbed. Now pour over the rest of the soup and warm through till simmering. If you are adding the liver, sear the ribbons quickly and add to the soup for the last few minutes, to avoid toughening. Float the remaining fried bread and halved egg yolks on top of the soup. You can also pour over the optional egg and cheese topping and grill it till golden and bubbling. This makes a good one-dish meal served with salad, bread, cheese, and fruit.

Aragonese Cheese and Liver Soup / Sopa Común

Take a good loaf, toast large thin slices on the fire or in a dish between hot embers. Watch your toast so it does not singe then grate cheese and cooked liver, and assemble your soup. Make layers of toast in a soup bowl, with liver, cheese, cloves, cinnamon and chopped parsley between them, till your bowl is full, pound and make a hazelnut sauce thinned with broth from the stewpot, cook it and pour half over the sops so they are well soaked. Put them over the fire, let them simmer, lift them off, pour over the rest of your sauce and leave it till the top has toasted. This makes a very good meal that you may serve to anyone who comes to eat with you.

Aragon's rustic horned cattle gave calf's liver and cheese at a time when these were rare luxuries in most of Spain. Over a century earlier Francisco Martínez Montiño, veteran Madrid court cook, had given a very similar recipe, identifying it with Aragon, then an independent kingdom.[6] Today this is rarely made. It is rich and good if you like the flavor of liver, but be aware that grating it takes time.

300 g / 10 oz calf's liver, 1 tbsp wine vinegar, 100 g / 3½ oz grated ewe's milk cheese, 1 liter / 1¾ pints good meat broth (see p. 234), 100 g / 3½ oz bread, 2 tbsp olive oil, a little extra grated cheese

The best modern version of this recipe that I know is given by José Manuel Porquet in *Eating in Huesca*. He does not add in a hazelnut sauce. He washes the liver carefully with a little vinegar in the water, simmers it till just cooked through, for about 10 minutes, then grates it. This takes time, especially if you grate the liver finely, which will give you a smoother soup. Mix the liver with the cheese, scoop them into a large pan and add meat broth, stirring till you have the right consistency. Cook for about 10 minutes. Adjust the seasoning. Slice the bread, fry it in the olive oil, and lay in individual soup bowls. Pour over the soup, sprinkle with a little grated cheese, and toast quickly in the oven.

SOUP FOR A GRANDEE

Playfully Altamiras piled this soup high in the court style, throwing in luxurious meats and perching a roast capon on the top.[7] It is the book's only concession to deliberately opulent court cookery, prepared perhaps for the friars' patrons who came to San Diego. Among them were a couple of grandees, the Count of Sastago and the friars' neighbor and patron, Joaquín Pignatelli, Count of Fuentes, one of whose forebears had founded San Diego, where Altamiras cooked. His family were great patrons of the arts. One younger brother, Ramón, for example, was a lifelong supporter of Francisco de Goya, who learned to paint in the Pignatellis' palace, a stone's throw from Altamiras's kitchen. Joaquín, the eldest brother, is the most likely mystery patron of Altamiras's book since his father-in-law was the head of Madrid's household and kitchen in 1745.

Game, Sausage, and Bread Soup / Otra Sopa

Slice and toast bread, as I have said. Then fry some liver, cook capon and partridge breasts and sausage in meat broth. Take a little of your best cured ham fat, sliced and soaked to remove the salt, and some small birds and hard-boiled eggs. Assemble your soup, throw in sweet things like sugar and cinnamon or comfits as you go, bathe the sops with broth spiced with cloves, cinnamon and saffron. Let the sops simmer to drink up the broth, crack open and beat eggs, pour them over the top, let them soak in and lay on more comfits and artichoke hearts.

If you wish you may sit a roasted capon or hen on top. Spit and roast it till it is good and brown: then spear a lump of fatty cured ham wrapped in paper on the spit, feed the fire below so it melts the fat, which drips down and bastes your bird, then paint it with egg with a handful of feathers till gilded all over. Toast your soup till the crust is golden and sit the bird on top, breast down. This is good enough to serve to a Spanish Grandee.

From a cook's point of view this soup is memorable for its mix of game, chicken, sausages, liver, ham, artichokes, spices, and comfits, for which the quince paste stands in well. This is a lightened version close to Castilian bread soups.

You need 1.4 liters / 2½ pints partridge or other game broth, 6–8 very thin slices of bread fried in olive oil, 5 chopped cooked sausages, 250 g / 8 oz coarsely grated calf's or lamb's liver, 125 g / 4 oz fried diced streaky jamón or pancetta, 6–12 halved artichoke hearts (fresh, frozen, or preserved), 125 g / 4 oz diced quince paste.

Warm the seasoned broth, adding bay leaves, parsley stalks, celery, carrot, and an onion with cloves for extra flavor, and simmer for 30 minutes. Make a jigsaw of the fried bread to cover the bottom of your soup bowl, reserving a couple of slices. Strain the broth, return to the pan, add the sausages and fried cured ham, simmer for 10 minutes, and pour the broth and bits and pieces over the fried bread. Drop the diced quince paste and artichoke hearts into the soup, float the reserved fried bread and seared liver on top, warm through and ladle into serving bowls.

BREAKFAST IN A BOWL

Altamiras named his breakfast creams after the deep round bowls, or *escudillas*, in which they were served. In the friaries these were sometimes plain white bowls, or they might be elegantly painted and enameled, or, like ceramics fragments found at San Cristóbal in Alpartir, painted blue and white.[8] The breakfast creams, like his morning soups, were energizing and easy to eat, as good for young friars doing physical work as for older ones short on teeth. Today the savory soups make good one-dish meals and the sweet creams are comforting puddings.

Green Soup with Meat / Burete

Let us talk of breakfast burete *for meat-eating days. Take four ounces of cheese for forty bowlfuls of soup. Chop bread and boiled green vegetables, like chard and lettuce with lungs, a handful of parsley and sorrel, put them in a pot where you will make the soup, add pepper, saffron, cloves and cinnamon. Then season your broth with salt, pepper and enough saffron to give it a good colour, pour it over the greens and put the pot on the fire. Let your soup boil, make fresh breadcrumbs and add them to your* burete *so it is thick enough for your stirring spoon to stand up in it. Let it cook then stand it in a hay basket so it sweats, and set aside a little of the soup in a clay or earthen dish so it is tepid, stir up fifty eggs for every hundred bowlfuls, beat them into your lukewarm soup and as you pour it into your pot stir well so the egg does not cook to threads.*

My very first friary lunch was at Nuestra Señora de Los Ángeles in Ruzafa, a buzzy quarter in Valencia, and it opened with a soup cooked by Reyes Busto Morcillo, who had been making lunch for the friars for twenty years. The friars came and went, but Reyes had stayed, adapting to the friary style: after lunch she told me how she cooked on a shoestring budget, saving money by buying her vegetables direct from market gardeners. She served us casseroled rabbit, a green salad, and oranges, with red wine and coffee to drink. Later we sat down together with a copy of *New Art* and she chose two recipes to cook for this book (see also p. 88). Here, then, is Reyes's version of *burete* made with three greens, sent to me in a letter, entitled "My Personal Composition." The thickening with uncooked eggs is optional.[9]

250 g / 8 oz chopped chicken flesh, 3 handfuls of sliced chard stalks (about 500 g / 1 lb), ½ coarsely shredded lettuce, a small handful of shredded sorrel or spinach (60 g / 2 oz), 4 tbsp olive oil, 3 leafy stalks of parsley and 2 mint sprigs, a thumb's length of cinnamon quill, 1 clove, 125 g / 4 oz ewe's milk cheese, 1.75 liters / 2½ pints chicken or meat broth (see p. 234), a saffron infusion made with 3 dozen saffron threads (see p. 102), 300 g / 10 oz good white bread, 3 raw eggs (optional)

When you have prepared the chopped chicken and shredded vegetables, warm the olive oil in a big soup pan and sweat first the seasoned chicken, then the greens, stirring well. Throw in the snipped parsley and mint, the pounded or ground spices and cheese, pour in the broth, cook for another 5 minutes, stir in the saffron infusion, the bread torn into bits and the beaten egg, which may break into threads—this does not really matter. Simmer gently for a final 10 minutes.

Angel's Blancmange / Escudilla de Ángel

Take eight pounds of rice, twenty of milk, six of sugar, six dozen eggs and two ounces of cinnamon. Pound half an ounce of the cinnamon with half a pound of sugar. Put the rest of the cinnamon to infuse in a pot of warmed water covered with folded paper. Make sure your rice is good and clean: rinse it in warm water, refreshing once or twice, or as many times as needed to wash it. Let the rice dry, grind it and pass it through a flour sieve. In hot weather spread the rice-flour on tablecloths and check your milk is not sour: boil it in a clean skillet and watch closely that it does not curdle as it boils. This I tell you so you do not risk a nasty surprise. Put your rice-flour in a little clay or earthen dish, stir in enough milk to make a cream and put it with the rest of the milk in a large pot where you will make the blancmange. Add the sugar, put the pot on the fire, add half the eggs with their whites, the other half without them, and keep stirring with your wooden spoon. Do not stop for a moment till your eggs have thickened the cream, watch the blancmange carefully and check to see the taste of rice-flour has cooked away.

All this I have set down in great detail for there is a lot of trouble and work in this dish. When you serve it add one part of meat broth to every four of blancmange and sprinkle the top with sugar and cinnamon. Your broth should be made with good meat and ham, but neither fatty nor rancid, and unspiced.

Altamiras complained of the work for no other dish, but then he had to wash and grind the rice, pound the sugar and scald the milk before flexing his arm to beat the lumps out of his blancmange. It must have been a relief, then, that he cooked it only occasionally, on *días grandes*, monastic holy days. Today, of course, kitchen blenders or ready-made rice flour make light work of this. I like to stick to the original flavors of cane sugar and goat's milk, and I use rice.[10]

2 liters / 3.5 pints goat's milk, 2 thumb-length cinnamon sticks, 90 g / 3 oz paella or pudding rice, 2 whole eggs, 120 g / 4 oz cane sugar (or to taste), a saffron infusion made with 12 strands, or cinnamon infusion (see pp. 102 and 220), or shot of coffee (optional)

Warm the milk with the cinnamon sticks, bring to a boil and infuse off the heat for at least 30 minutes or overnight. Put the cold milk and rice in a pan and simmer, covered, till the grains are very soft all the way through, about 40 minutes. Do not hurry this: the rice needs to be soft at the heart of the grains, or the final cream cannot be smooth. Reduce the heat so the cream is only just simmering, dissolve the sugar to taste, then add the beaten eggs and saffron infusion, stirring all the time, without boiling, for 10 minutes. Remove from the heat, blend to a smooth cream, sieve and chill in small pots, cups, or ramekins. Good served with thin ginger snaps or dark chocolate biscuits.

Squash and Honey Soup / Escudilla de Calabaza con Leche, Caldo de Carne y Miel

Blancmange makes a good breakfast, but is costly, and this dish is as good for the same price. Skin pumpkins, boil them with salt, and rub them through a clean linen cloth to catch the threads. Put your pumpkin flesh in a pillow case and hang it up overnight so its liquor drips out, and the next morning take milk, measure for measure, and eight pounds of honey for every sixteen pints of milk. Let the honey melt in the milk over a slow fire, stir so it does not stick and cook it till it thickens. Add one part of meat broth to every four of pumpkin, but remember, be sure your broth has as little fat as can be, for otherwise droplets rise to the top of a dish, and are off-putting, especially on rice.

This easily made soup of squash and honey captures Altamiras's fondness for dishes that were, at one and the same time, low-fuss, naturally sweet, and full of taste. You can make it by eye.

Guideline quantities are 370 g / 12 oz boiled and puréed skinned butternut squash, 600 ml / 1 liter / 1¾ pints mild chicken or beef broth, 250 ml / 8 fl oz creamy milk, 2–3 tbsp honey. I like to add the zest of a grated lemon, orange, or lime over the top. First warm through the butternut purée in your soup pan over gentle heat for 5 minutes to drive out excess moisture then stir in the broth, milk, and honey to make a smooth cream. Season to taste and serve hot or chilled.

SATURDAY FOODS

Spanish eating fascinated eighteenth-century travelers to Spain. They loved hot chocolate and iced drinks, but kept their distance from other flavors, like pungent garlic and offal. Yet they watched fascinated as markets did a brisk Saturday trade in blood, trotters, heads, livers, hearts and lungs, chitterlings, and tripe (though rarely kidneys). Historian Eloy Terron traced these so-called Saturday foods back to war-torn medieval Castile where the papacy allowed "innards, blood and extremities" to replace costly fish on Saturday, the seventh day of the week, a meatless day elsewhere.[11] Whatever the reasons for the custom it stuck, as did the taste for offal, and by Altamiras's lifetime Saturday foods were also sold in Aragon. Here Altamiras gave three dishes, as his pick of Saturday food. If you know a discerning whole beast butcher you can try them; they are still thought of as gourmet eating in Spain.

Pig's Trotters, Three Ways /
Pies de Puerco Rellenos

Take well-singed trotters, soak them all night, the next day give them a good boil, lay them on a board to cut out the bones and do your best to stop the meat falling into little pieces. If it does, then dip it in a flour and egg batter or some grated breadcrumbs. Put the skillet on the fire with lard or olive oil to fry your trotters and cover them with a lid for the fat spits fiercely. You may serve these with sugar and cinnamon or dress them with a sauce made with trotter broth, hazelnuts, parsley and spices.

When I looked for a modern version of Altamiras's fried battered trotters the closest recipe I could find came from the Poor Clare nuns of Tudela, Navarre, just half an hour's drive from Altamiras's home town. They wrote it up for a best-selling 1990s anthology of Poor Clare cookery entitled *Cocina Monacal*. For their recipe they mix boned and chopped trotter chunks with a flour and egg batter and shallow-fry large tablespoonfuls in olive oil. Finally they sugar their little fritters, just as Altamiras did. But the truth is that all trotter recipes start with the laborious work of boiling them—unless you happen to live near a butcher offering specialities, who sells them parboiled. If you are going to do it yourself, ask your butcher to halve the trotters lengthways for you. At home, singe off any hairs, soak the trotters in iced water for an hour to drain out any last drop of blood, scald them quickly in boiling water, drain, return them to the pan, cover with fresh salted water, throw in a couple of peeled carrots and onions, and bring to the boil. Open the window so the steam can fly out and simmer for 2½–3 hours. You can use a pressure cooker, but Spanish trotter-lovers say the result is not as good. Pour the stock through a sieve lined with kitchen paper into a large bowl, cool the trotters in it, cover, and chill.

When the time comes to bone the trotters, put on rubber gloves for a good grip. Wrestle out the long central bone, the top knuckle and the small toe bones till you have a few large (or a handful of smaller) chunks of boneless meat and lip-sticking gelatine. Try to avoid the meat falling apart, but don't worry if it does. Wrap the meat chunks in tinfoil and chill. They can then be used within a couple of days to make Altamiras's fritters, best served with a garlic *ajo* (see pp. 157–58). Keep the stock for sauces (see p. 61).

Lamb or Kid Pepitoria / Pepitoria

Pepitoria is usually made with a lamb's or kid's livers and lights. Give the lights a little boil in water with salt and sear the livers on the fire or send them to the baker's oven to roast. Cut out the piping and gristle, then chop the livers and lights and fry them. Warm lard or olive oil, throw in a little onion as they fry, and let the livers finish frying like this. Turn them into a clay or earthen dish and make a hazelnut picada *pounded with garlic, spices and fried bread, and thin it with a little water seasoned with salt. Add chopped hard-boiled eggs, a handful of parsley and pine kernels, pour your sauce over your* pepitoria *and let it simmer a little while.*

Once *pepitorias* of lamb's, kid's, or chicken's liver and lungs were cooked on market-days, or whenever livestock was slaughtered. Today they are usually made with boned chicken flesh, but Aragonese cookbooks sometimes include the old recipe and I have adapted that here to chicken livers. You can also throw in wing-tips, feet, the heart, and other bits and pieces, or chicken breast, as in other recipes.[12]

2 tbsp olive oil, 1 small onion, 500 g / 1 lb thickly chunked chicken or calf's liver, 2 hard-boiled eggs, 30 g / 1 oz toasted pine kernels (see p. 236), a small handful of chopped flat-leaf parsley

FOR THE HAZELNUT THICKENING: 30 skinned small hazelnuts, 1 garlic clove, 30g / 1 oz fried bread (see p. 234), 250 ml / 8 fl oz water.

Serves 4–6 as a first course.

Warm the oil and sweat the onion in it until golden and soft. Blend the thickening ingredients—hazelnuts, garlic, and fried bread—with a hand blender, slowly adding the water to give a thin creamy sauce. Season to taste. Cut the liver into large chunks, toss it quickly with the onion to seal it, pour the sauce over the top, and cook gently for 5–10 minutes, till you see that the liver is nearly done. Fold in the chopped hard-boiled egg, pine kernels, and parsley. I like this served in small quantities with *picatostes*, or fried bread triangles, as a richly flavored first course.

Fried Blood / Sangre de Cordero, o Cabrito

Before you kill your lamb or kid, prepare plenty of onion. Skin and slice it, add salt and pepper, then after the slaughter, stir it into the blood. Baked in the bread oven this is very tasty, and it is good eaten cold, or, if you do not want to leave the kitchen, roast it in a little olive oil or soft pork lard in front of the fire. Another way is to throw spoonfuls of blood into a skillet of hot olive oil to fry like fritters. Serve these with pepper and salt.

Fried blood may sound ghoulish, but it is a popular tapa right around Spain with many gourmets who, on the other hand, would not usually eat kidneys. It is mild in flavor, cooked tossed with a mass of soft golden onion sweated in olive oil. Here are guideline quantities: 750 g / 1½ lb onion, 1 kg / 2¼ lb of baked blood, 250 ml / 8 fl oz olive oil, seasoning to taste, and one or two pinches of oregano. A few Málaga raisins soaked in water or wine make a good addition too.[13]

Yo no sé si guisa bien	I don't know
o si guisa mal tu madre;	If your mother cooks well
solo sé que a mí me fríe	Or not, but I do know this,
divinamente la sangre.	When she fries my blood it's divine.

Luis Mompeón Ferruz

SEASONS AND FEAST DAYS

A friary feast might celebrate a provincial gathering or be part of a larger town or village fiesta. Country celebrations would include dawn choirs, ribbon-and-stick dances, cockfights, and perhaps, at the end of the day, a bite of cheese with a glass of wine. Some fiestas had an important practical purpose: animals were blessed on San Antón, in January, and processions on San Sebastián's day aimed to keep the plague at bay. In the big cities, a friary fiesta might be a formal affair, the patrons invited for iced drinks and, sometimes, a feastday meat dish. Kitchen accounts at San Diego reveal half a dozen or so calves were bought and fattened every year, so we know veal was a favorite fiesta food.[14]

Pot-Roast Rose Veal / Ternera Asada

Cut your veal into pieces that weigh half a pound, more or less, and put them to roast slowly over hot embers in a clay or earthen dish, with more embers on top. Have ready a little bowl of melted cured ham fat seasoned with crushed garlic, parsley, pepper, lemon juice, salt and a measure of water, and as the veal roasts, baste it with this liquor. Veal is very tasty done like this, but if it has a lot of fat on it, then roast it as it is. When it is half-done drain off the juices, add a little cured ham fat and white wine or aguardiente, *and finish it off like this, and if you have no cured ham fat, you may use good olive oil instead.*

Altamiras was a practiced hand at cooking rosy veal on the bone, dissolving its brown roasting crusts into the pot juices with wine or grape spirit. "The best veal is aged six weeks to two months," ran the 1835 cookbook *La Cuynera Catalana*, "because if it is younger it has no taste and if it is older it is not tender; it is best from May to September." Perhaps Altamiras first cooked this recipe in La Almunia, where cattle grazed nearby at Alfamen. Weaned young to release their mother's milk for cheesemaking, calves were run down from the mountains in spring to graze on lowland pastures till their grass dried up in the summer months.[15]

For each person you need a 500 g / 1 lb chunk of veal shank on the bone. You also need, for 4–6 servings, 4 tbsp olive oil, 2–3 tbsp finely chopped garlic, a small handful of chopped flat-leaf parsley, 2 tbsp lemon juice, a pinch of thyme leaves, 2 tbsp white wine or *aguardiente* (see p. 234), and about 250 ml / 8 fl oz water

Preheat the oven (180°C, 350°F, gas mark 4). Warm the olive oil in a large flameproof casserole, brown the seasoned veal in it, add the garlic, parsley, lemon juice, and thyme, toss well, cover, and put in the oven to pot-roast. After about 40 minutes, lifting the lid every so often to see how the meat is getting on, splash in the white wine or *aguardiente*, swirling it around to dissolve the crunchy brown deposits. Cook for another 45 minutes, taking the odd look to see the meat is not sticking or burning, and test with a skewer for tenderness. Remove from the oven, pour off the juices, skim the fat off them, and splash in a little wine or water to make a sauce for the meat. A little quince jelly is good stirred in for extra flavor. I like this with spinach and bakers' potatoes (see pp. 192 and 237).

Rabbit Casserole with Peppercorns, Capers, and Lime / Conejos en Prebe

The best way to cook rabbits is in pepper sauce. Skin them, sear them on the fire, cut them up, put them in a pot or clay casserole, add fresh olive oil, crushed parsley, garlic and peppercorns and leave them to braise slowly. When you see they are half cooked, then add hot water, bay leaves, cloves and cinnamon. Capers are good in this too, and green lemon or lime slices are even better. This is the most popular of all our pepper stews.

Rabbit, wild or reared for the table, has given so many popular Spanish dishes. Paella, from Valencia's marshlands, is the best known, but there are dozens of others: such as southern *tojunto*, a Gitano stew of rabbit and green peppers; Catalan rabbit with pears; and this little known peppery Aragonese stew. Some cooks would have made this with homegrown spicy red *guindilla* peppers, the cheapest option, but Altamiras stuck to peppercorns. I adapted a modern version I found in Éliane Thibaut Comelade's *Catalan Cuisine*, an excellent book on home cooking.

150 ml / 5 fl oz olive oil, 1.5–2 kg / 3–4 lb cleaned and jointed rabbit, half a dozen stalks of flat-leaf parsley, 6 sliced fat garlic cloves, 12 peppercorns, salt, 370 ml / 12 fl oz hot water, a large pinch of cinnamon, 4 bay leaves, 3 tbsp capers (soaked if brined or salted, see p. 235), 4 cloves, 1 sliced untreated lime or lemon blanched for 10 minutes

Warm a tablespoon or two of the olive oil in a large flameproof casserole and brown the seasoned rabbit joints in batches. Put them all back in together, pour over the remaining olive oil, stir in the parsley stalks, sliced garlic, and seasoning to taste, bring to a gentle simmer, and cook for 15 minutes. Pour in the hot water, add the cinnamon, bay leaves, capers, powdered cloves, and blanched lime or lemon slices, and cook for 20–25 minutes for farm-reared rabbit or 1½–2 hours for wild rabbit. Remove the lime slices and bay leaves, and check the seasoning before serving. I like this served with rice, roots, or bread for mopping up the juices and a full-bodied white or young red wine.

Rabbit in Hazelnut Sauce / Gazapos en guisado

Take skinned young rabbits, cut them up, chop cured ham fat into small dice and melt them in your skillet. Fry the rabbits, powdered with salt, then put them in a cooking pot to braise slowly. Pound toasted hazelnuts with a little bread, wetted and squeezed dry, garlic, parsley and spices and pour this over your rabbits, but do not let your sauce be too thick. This is very tasty, and another way is to fry young rabbits in cured ham fat or soft lard with spices and finish them off in aguardiente *or white wine.*

While wild rabbit was tough but flavorful, farmed young rabbits, or *gazapos*, were tender, best when grazed on herbs. In his *Book of the Secrets of Agriculture* Miquel Agustí, a Catalan prior, had explained how to give them flavor by rearing them in high-walled meadows planted with juniper, thyme, gorse, wild parsley, and chicory.[16] Such rabbits were costly at market, but the friars reared their own. Everyday farmed rabbit is also very good cooked like this, served with spring vegetables and a fruity red Mediterranean wine, like a Jumilla, Priorato or Bullas.

3 tbsp olive oil, 1.5–2 kg / 3–4 lb cleaned and jointed farmed rabbit, 60 g / 2 oz jamón fat or pancetta, 300 ml / 10 fl oz hot water, 2 tbsp snipped flat-leaf parsley

FOR THE SAUCE: 2 dozen toasted skinned small hazelnuts, ¼ slice good bread, large pinches of nutmeg and cinnamon, freshly ground black pepper, 2 fat garlic cloves.

Warm the olive oil in a large flameproof casserole. Season the rabbit pieces and fry them in batches till golden brown, removing them as they are done. Throw in the diced jamón fat, turn down the heat, cover with a lid, and render the fat gently without scorching it. Put the rabbit pieces back in the casserole, pour in the hot water, stir, cover tightly, and keep the rabbit cooking at a gentle bubble over low heat for 30–45 minutes, topping up with more hot water if needed. Blend the thickening ingredients, stir them into the cooking juices, adding more water if needed, check the seasoning, sprinkle with parsley, and serve.

CARNAL CARNIVAL

Carnival, the year's biggest food fiesta, ended the winter, offering everyone three days of street revelry and fleshy pleasures before the butchers and brothels closed shop for Lent. The friars did not join in the masked street revelry, but we know they enjoyed the odd Carnival dish like these ham rashers.[17]

Ham Rashers, Three Ways / Lonjas de Tocino

Ham rashers must have no rancid flesh or fat on them. So choose good ones, soak them overnight and if you are serving them with chickpeas, leave them lying in the same water. When the salt has soaked away dry the rashers with a cloth, fry them in soft lard or olive oil, and dress them in an earthenware dish with white wine, sugar and cinnamon. Cook them like that and serve them with more sugar and cinnamon on top.

Rashers are good without sugar too. Fry them, add water, cinnamon and bay leaves and finish them with a little vinegar. There are other ways to cook them, too, but remember, rashers must always be soaked properly to wash them free of salt. They are delicious roasted in front of the fire in a pie dish with parsley, olive oil and a few grains of dried verjuice or slices of lemon. Other people like them fried, though these are not for watery or wishy-washy characters, but bear in mind, above all, however you cook them, they must be well soaked so they are neither hard nor salty.

Altamiras gave readers three ideas for cooking the thick-cut cured ham rashers he laid down in salt-filled urns after the pig-killing. The one below was also given by Fray Sever de Olot, a Catalan friar who wrote a recipe notebook just over forty years later, giving serving advice for many recipes, like this one, which he described as food for Carnival. Spiced lentils, chickpea stew, mashed roots, braised celery, and cardoon go well with it.

Four to six well-soaked dried ham rashers or fresh gammon steaks, their rind trimmed, 3–4 tbsp olive oil for frying, 1 tbsp wine vinegar, ½ bottle of medium white wine, 1–2 tsp brown sugar or honey, a couple of pinches of powdered cinnamon

Warm a moderate oven (180°C, 350°F, gas mark 4). Trim the ham or gammon rind with kitchen scissors and cut into the fat at right angles every couple of inches. Warm the olive oil in a frying pan, brown the rashers or steaks on both sides, lift them on to a baking dish, cover, and keep warm. Pour the wine vinegar into the frying pan, bubble to dissolve the crispy browned bits, add the wine, warm through, stir in the sugar or honey and cinnamon, reduce to a light syrup, season, and pour over the ham. Bake for 20–30 minutes or till the rashers or steaks are cooked through.

WITH BAY LEAVES AND WINE VINEGAR: Warm 370 ml / 12 fl oz water or light stock with 2 tbsp white wine vinegar and 3–4 bay leaves and pour over the meat before baking.

WITH PARSLEY, OLIVE OIL, AND VERJUICE: Sprinkle 4 tbsp flat-leaf parsley, 4 tbsp fruity olive oil, and a tbsp of verjuice (see p. 239), or the chopped flesh of a lemon, over the browned rashers, season, and roast as above.

Pork Sausages or Loin in Spiced White Wine / Longaniza o Solomo

Sausages or loin are done like this: fry the meat, put it in a clay or earthen casserole, cover it with white wine or aguardiente, *add bay leaves and cinnamon, cover it with a close-fitting lid so the flavours do not fade, and you will be left with just a little liquid. This is very tasty.*

Longaniza sausages are still the most popular flavor of Carnival in Aragon, where they are given to children as a school fiesta snack on Lardy Thursday. Here they are fried then cooked in spiced wine. Serve with poached spiced apple slices, baked red cabbage, and potatoes for a homely modern feast.

For every dozen sausages—thin or fat chipolatas or *longanizas*—you need a half-bottle of white wine, 4 bay leaves, a thumb's length of cinnamon stick, and seasoning. Warm the wine with the bay and cinnamon in a lidded pan for 10 minutes, remove from the heat, and leave to infuse for half an hour. Brown the sausages in a little olive oil, lift them into a baking dish where they fit comfortably, pour over the wine, cover, and bake in a warm oven for 15–20 minutes. Serve with a glass of the same white wine in which you cooked the sausages.

Por Pascua garrovillas como,	For Easter I eat carob twigs,
y por carnestolendas longaniza.	And for Carnival sausage.

Lope de Vega, *Rhymes Human and Divine*
of the Licentiate Tomé de Burguillo, 1634

ROASTING LAMB'S HEADS

"It's a great dish!" exclaimed Mexican-born artist Miguel Condé. "You can't leave it out!" I was planning to do so. Roast lamb's head seemed one of *New Art*'s few dishes too antique for modern tastes. Not so, claimed Miguel: in the 1960s he had eaten an unforgettable roast lamb's head in Calanda, Buñuel's birthplace, after the Holy Week drumming. Was it then, I wondered, a Holy Week dish? Still-life paintings suggested so. Often a woolly lamb's head sits next to a sacrificial Easter lamb. Goya had also painted a sheep's head alongside glistening dark lumps of meat. Such paintings were hints. But it was Fray Sever de Olot's notebook that solved the mystery; he tagged this recipe as funeral food.[18] What better reminder of mortality might there be than a skull facing us on a plate—and what was more appropriate to Holy Week than funeral food?

Lamb's Head with Ham, Garlic, and Parsley / Una Cabeza de Cordero

Cut your lamb's head in half, lift open the nostrils, one at a time, and peer up them to see if the head is dirty. Wash it well and once it is good and clean dress it: sprinkle it with parsley, pounded garlic, pepper and salt, lay over a mouthful of thin-sliced streaky cured ham, tie it up with linen thread, wrap it in paper and then roast it till the bones are tender—but remember, these are not for eating.

"Exquisite and unforgettable," is how food writer Darío Vidal Llisterri describes roast lamb's head in his food memoir *Blue Thistle Flower*. Helpfully he explains why. "You taste all the different flavors of a lamb and perceive all its aromas, yet they stay separate." By this he meant the brain, the tongue, and the cheek meat. I invited over Miguel Condé's family to try my first experimental lamb's heads roasted in oiled greaseproof paper. They came out edible but nothing to write home about, though Max, eight years old, the youngest family member, was happy to go home with a jawbone for his natural history cabinet.

Finally, it was Luis Ángel Muñoz, a young baker in Almonacid, in Altamiras's home valley, who showed me why roasted heads are considered by many gourmets to be the choicest cut of lamb. He roasts them for home cooks who bring them to him, laid cut side up on a bed of sliced potatoes (see p. 237) with a couple of garlic cloves thrown in. Luis Ángel roasts them till the brain is just set, turns the heads over and keeps roasting them for another hour and a half, the juices dripping on to the potatoes below. I have tried this method, adding Altamiras's ham slice over the brains to stop them from drying up, and it is very good indeed, as it gives the cheeks, tongues, and brains their own time each and lets the cheeks roast till they are brown and crispy. Eating a head roasted this way, I finally understood Miguel, Darío Vidal Llisterri and all the Spanish home cooks who take their roasting trays up to bakers on a Sunday morning.

Lamb's Head with Hazelnut Sauce / Otra Cabeza

Roast your head with cured ham, parsley, crushed garlic and peppercorns, salt, verjuice or sour grapes and, in season, lemon or sharp orange juice. Wrap your head in a fold of paper rubbed with lard, then pound hazelnuts with parsley and a clove of garlic, stir in two egg yolks and cook these in a spoonful of lard in a little clay or earthen dish to give you a smooth sauce. Open up the head, pour in the sauce, tie the two halves together with a long piece of thread so it may not come loose, fasten the head to your spit on the fire and brown it slowly. When it has finished roasting you can brush it with breadcrumbs and egg yolks, and spice the sauce, or leave it plain and sprinkle the head with sugar and cinnamon.

A HARE CIVET

"Hares die of old age contemplating Spaniards eat rabbits," wrote Alexander Dumas, the French novelist, after a short trip to Spain in the 1840s. Richard Ford, the English traveler, thought differently. He found and ate Spanish hare, calling it "the glory of edible quadrupeds," but then he visited all kinds of taverns up and down the land. Dumas ended up concluding that the Spanish were superstitious about eating hare and he may have been right: a century later Miguel Delibes, the Castilian writer, penned a short story about a village chasing out a hare they believed to embody the devil. Or was the real problem the fear of being served cat for hare? The trick was a popular one and was feared since it was believed that eating a cat's brain would send you mad. The trick lingered on. Navarrese food writer Vicente Sarobe Pueyo wrote up eating civet in a country restaurant as late as the 1960s, and, when he asked for the hare's head, could only extract one reply, "Miaow! Miaow!"[19]

Hare in White Wine / Liebre Guisada Sin Agua

Skin the hare, cut it up, steep the pieces in white wine, brown them in soft lard and put them in your stewpot. Add two pounded garlic cloves, salt, the soaking wine and fine-cut onion fried in the skillet fat. But do not add saffron. Put the pot over a gentle fire, let the hare cook for a couple of hours and you will have a little but very good rich sauce.

Altamiras skinned his own hares, which were probably given to the friars by local hunters. He called this recipe hare "without water," but you can also think of it as a white wine civet. It is good cooked one day to eat the next, served with lots of napkins, so people can chew the meat off the fiddly bones. If you want a richer dish add the blood and liver. I have also made this with rabbit, lighter but good.

You need a skinned hare, with liver and blood, a bottle of medium dry white wine, 4 tbsp olive oil, 1 large onion, a few chopped garlic cloves, grated nutmeg, 1 cinnamon stick

First joint your hare. Bend the front legs till the shoulder bone protrudes, slicing cleanly behind it, open the hind legs till you hear the joints crack and cut through them. Open the stomach sacs, pour off the blood into a bowl, add a little vinegar to stop the blood clotting, and put the liver in there too. Cut out the heart and kidneys and keep. Put the hare joints in a large bowl, dividing the saddle into two or three servings (I do this with poultry scissors). Pour over the wine and leave for 4–6 hours or, better still, overnight.

Warm your oven (180°C, 350°F, gas mark 4). Take the hare joints out of the wine, pat them dry, warm half the olive oil in a large flameproof casserole, and seal the hare joints evenly, browning them in batches, then removing them. Add the chopped onion and garlic to the remaining oil, adding more if needed, and sweat till soft. Put back the hare joints, season, and pour over the wine, making sure the thicker joints are well covered. Add the spices, bring to a simmer, cover tightly, and oven-braise till the hare is tender, about 2½–3 hours, opening up from time to time to top up with wine if the casserole is drying up. If you are adding the blood and liver, pour off the cooking juices into a small pan, cool, blend with the blood and liver, warm through without boiling, and pour back over the hare before serving. Good with mashed potatoes and a rich smooth red wine from Toro in Castile.

Braised Veal / Ternera Estofada

Take lean veal and cut it up the size of walnut shells. Melt cured ham fat in your skillet, fry the veal in it and put it in your stewpot. Fry fine-cut onion in the skillet fat, add it to the meat, pour over white wine and add two cloves of

WINE

"Skin the hare, cut it up, steep the pieces in white wine. . . ." Unlike some other religious orders the Franciscans rarely planted their own vineyards,[1] but they were practiced cellarmen who matured young wines given to them as alms or bought from local wine-makers. Aragonese wines were kept in barrels, but much Spanish white wine for drinking and cooking was aged in tall earthenware vats. Cooks generally used white wine, but the friars ate their meals with watered wine. Today's closest equivalents for cooking are full-bodied varietal whites while the new Aragonese red Garnachas, intense and spicy, especially when made from old vines, make good drinking with Altamiras's big, earthy, garlicky flavors.

NOTE

1. Francisco José Alfaro Pérez, "El Convento de Santa Catalina en los siglos XVII y XVIII," in *Tierra de Conventos*, 80, 86. *Disposición, "reparar un tonel y reparar la cuba pequeña"*; "to repair a barrel and repair the small cask." Accounts 1761. Ex-cat, ACPV.

garlic pounded with salt, spices, parsley and bay leaves. Then put your pot over a gentle fire, cover it with paper to keep it simmering, and cover that with a little jug of water. Make a flour and water dough, seal the rim of the pot and jug with it so it does not exhale its vapours, and leave it to cook for two hours. Like this you will have only a few juices, but they will be good and tasty.

Altamiras's second veal recipe—see p. 48 for a pot-roast—was a traditional *estofado*. Soon to be ousted from Spanish menus by French *fricando*,[20] it survived in popular kitchens. Today it is cooked with young beef, often with peas or baby carrots thrown in to add color. I prefer it like this, spiced but otherwise plain.

4 tbsp olive oil or 60 g / 2 oz diced jamón fat or pancetta, 1.25 kg / 2½ lb stewing beef or pink veal (e.g., breast or rump), salt and pepper, 1 finely chopped onion, just over half a bottle of white wine, 2 fat garlic

cloves, 4 bay leaves, a handful of flat-leaf parsley, generous pinches of cinnamon and cloves, a saffron infusion (see p. 102)

Turn on the oven to heat for braising (see p. 232). Bear in mind the temperature will depend on the cooking method and pot you are using. Warm the olive oil or melt the cured ham fat in a frying pan, seal the seasoned meat in batches, brown it, and remove it to your earthenware or other ovenproof casserole or pot. Sweat the onion in the pan fat, scoop it on to the meat, pour over the warmed white wine, add the garlic, bay leaf, and spices. Seal the pot with olive-oiled cooking paper pressed down on the stew's surface and clamp it in place with the pot's lid (see p. 9). Put in the oven for 1½–2 hours to cook until very tender, checking that the casserole does not dry up. Check the seasoning and add the saffron infusion. This is very good with green beans tossed with flaked almonds or dressed with onion oil (see p. 194).

A FEAST FROM THE BREAD OVEN

A friary oven might be either a rustic affair dug out of a hillside or a city-center brick beehive oven where anyone in the neighborhood could pay to bake bread. On feast days the ovens were as busy as on weekly or fortnightly baking days. A fast-burning fire would be lit, the embers would be shoveled to one side and large joints of meat would be pushed into the back of the oven for roasting at high heat. When they were done smaller dishes—large pies, custards, sweetbreads and pasties—would be baked at lower heat to make full use of the oven's fading warmth. The next four recipes seem to be such feast-day food. We know, from a later friary lunch menu for St. Francis's Day, that meat dishes might be grouped like this, with sweet courses or pastries between them as well as a roast to end the meal.[21]

Roast Suckling Pig with Rice / Lechoncito de leche con arroz

Shave off your piglet's hairs, cut open its belly, clean out the stomach and rub it with parsley, ground peppercorns, salt and garlic. Let it roast in front of the fire, or between hot embers, or carry it out to the bread oven to roast. Boil some rice in seasoned water and when you have roasted your pig, add the rice, then leave the dish in the fire's warmth, but not so the heat toasts the rice, for it would give anyone a stomach ache, as raw rice does too.

Think of Spanish roast suckling pig and Botín, Madrid's legendary wood-roasting restaurant, comes to mind, conjuring up the sweet aroma of holm-oak smoke and mythical visits by fictional characters from Ernest Hemingway's and Grahame Greene's novels. A wood-fired oven stood here by 1725 and master-roasters still fire up today's oven, rebuilt a century ago, early every morning. One of them, Pino, invited me in to watch: he propped holm-oak logs over the previous day's glowing embers, splashed them with liquid lard till they burst into tall flames then pushed half a dozen seasoned suckling pigs deep into the oven. That same day Carlos González, whose family has owned Botín for two generations, suggested an experiment. We would roast a piglet Altamiras's way, adding boiled rice, and invite friends to have it for lunch with us. When the day came, six of us sat down to feast. First came Botín's fried boned pig's trotters (see pp. 45–46), then the piglet itself, its crackling as crisp as filo pastry, with the rice sopping up the rich juices. Surprising as the combination may sound, it went beautifully with the meat. Good suckling pig like this is very hard to cook at home for, as casual as a plateful of piglet may look, the meat needs immaculate sourcing—Botín's come from Segovia—and the roasting requires a very skilled hand. Besides, there is something about the experience of visiting a wood-roasting restaurant that makes one appreciate the idea of eating meat only as an occasional luxury, like this, as a feast.

Crumb Custard / Plato de Huevos, y Leche con Dulce

Grate bread, toast it, and when it is well browned, take two bowls of milk, four ounces of sugar and two pairs of beaten eggs for every dishful of custard. Stir all this well and bake it in front of the fire, with embers in the lid, so the top browns well, and serve this with sugar and cinnamon, and it may be served on lean or meatless days too.

Altamiras's crunchy breadcrumbs make this pudding delicious. Today cooks have swapped them for soft sweet cake crumbs in a pudding called *pan de Jumilla*, but it is not as good, I think. You can warm the milk with a vanilla pod or flavor it with a little almond or orange flower extract.[22]

200 g / 7 oz coarsely grated oven-toasted breadcrumbs (see p. 234), 120 g / 4 oz sugar, 5 eggs, 1 liter / 1¾ pints full cream milk, coarsely grated cinnamon, and sugar

TO FLAVOR (OPTIONAL): grated orange zest and vanilla, almond or orange flower extract.

Preheat the oven to 180°C, 350°F, gas mark 4. Oven-toast the breadcrumbs (see p. 234). Set a lightly oiled 1-liter / 1½-pint shallow-sided baking dish in a roasting pan. Whisk the sugar, eggs, and milk, stir in the cooled breadcrumbs and pour the custard into the baking dish. Stand it in a roasting pan, put it on a shelf in the oven, then pour water into the seated pan to come halfway up the side of the dish. Bake till a skewer or toothpick stuck into the custard comes out clean, about an hour. I like this served at room temperature with a small jugful of sieved tart fresh raspberry purée.

Sweet Tongued Pastries / Para Añadir un Plato con Lenguas de Ternera

Boil your tongues and skin them with a knife. Shell a pound of almonds, pound them with eight ounces of sugar, half a dozen hard-boiled eggs and the tongues, and shape this paste into small cakes or pasties. Bake them in the oven or fry them in a skillet, or make one good large pie, and to every pound of almonds add three or four ounces of butter. Be sure your almonds are not old, for rancid ones will spoil the flavour, and if you have no cow's butter, then use soft lard.

This almond paste makes fine food for nightingales for it keeps well in a covered pot, though Niggardly Men may have purses and stomachs too delicate to allow little birds to carry it off. Yet there are other Gentlemen, Señores, *who are happy to share with nightingales,* Ruiseñores, *and they are as graceful as song-birds in voice, manner and bearing.*

This tongue marzipan is unexpectedly delicious. Altamiras may have baked it for St. Francis's Day just as patissiers today make marzipan saints' bones for All Saints' Day. The friars had long been nicknamed nightingales, an image referring to the sweet-tongued beauty of their utterance, which contemporaries compared to that of troubadors or minstrels.[23] The image echoed down the centuries and was picked up by Federico García Lorca. One calf's tongue gives a lot of marzipan, so when I make this I usually freeze half a batch. It turns out best in small pies, which keep the filling soft, and are good served at Christmas paired with hot sweet mulled wine.

1–2 calf's tongues, total weight about 1.2 kg / 2½ lb, 500 g / 1 lb skinned almonds, 6 hard-boiled egg yolks, 120 g / 4 oz softened butter, about 12 oz / 370 g brown sugar

Makes 1.75 kg / 3½ lb tongue marzipan (a half-quantity fills 4 dozen empanadillas).

Soak the scrubbed tongue in cold water with a little vinegar for an hour. Put it in a large pan of salted water, bring it to a quick simmer, drain and start again, this time letting it simmer in salted water for 2–2½ hours, turning it once or twice. When the tongue is cooked, you should be able to tug off its white vinyl-like skin quite easily with a sharp knife. Drain, cool, skin, and trim it while warm and damp, cool, chop it roughly, and blend it with almonds, hard-boiled egg yolks, butter, and brown sugar. Chill. I like this best in *empanadilla* pastries (see p. 202) baked at 190°C, 375°F, gas mark 4 for about 15 minutes. The filling, sealed inside the pastry, stays soft and velvety.

Ya en la tarde caída	And in the fallen night
quería ser mi voz.	I wished to be my voice.
Ruiseñor.	A Nightingale.

Federico García Lorca,
"Cancioncilla del primer deseo," *Canciones*, 1921–1924

Braised Calf's or Ox's Cheeks, Three Ways / Cabeza de Ternera en Guisado

Scald your head in a cauldron of boiling water. Plunge it in, lift it out and skin it. Boil it in water with salt, halve it, cut out the brains and tongue to keep for other dishes, and place the cheek meat in a roasting dish with cured pig's jowl cut into little dice, parsley and pepper. Carry this out to roast in the bread oven or, if you want to stay in the kitchen, sit it close to the fire in hot embers, and tomatoes or slices of lemon are very good in this too.

You may also boil the head with salt in the water. Sit it in a big dish, bathe it with white wine, crushed garlic, pounded peppercorns, cloves and cinnamon and, when it is done, and just a little liquor is left, season it with salt, halve the head and take it to table. There are other ways for heads and cheeks. You may spread a halved boiled head with lard and breadcrumbs and toast it, or serve it white, boiled with pepper, a little vinegar and parsley stalks. Another way is to fry cured ham cut in dice with fine-cut onion, add wine, vinegar, a little sugar, cinnamon and plenty of spices, simmer this, pour it all over the head, and then it will all disappear down your own throat.

Altamiras butchered his own calf's cheeks. Today butchers do the work for us, dividing them into the small inner cushion, or *tapa*, and the shaggier outer *carrillera*, a cut which has made a spectacular comeback in Spain in the hands of young chefs. One of my favorite places to eat them is La Musa de Espronceda, in Lavapiés, where Antonio Amago creates delicious dishes from deliberately humble ingredients. Many of Altamiras's favorite foods appear on the menu: pumpkin, tomato, cabbage, beef or pig's cheeks, good meat broths, and bread. His parents' values, he says, are his greatest influence. Antonio's mother was a cook before the years of economic affluence and his guiding idea is to create food that allows customers and friends to eat well, affordably, with a glass or two of wine. He adds pig's trotter broth to this dish (see pp. 45–46) to give the sauce body. Cheeks vary in size considerably so remember to vary the cooking time accordingly.

4–6 trimmed calf's cheeks (weighing about 250–300 g / 8–10 oz each), flour, 4 tbsp extra-virgin olive oil, 1 large skinned and chopped carrot, 1 large trimmed and chopped leek, about ¾ bottle of a medium dry white wine, 750 ml / 1½ pints pig's trotter's broth

Choose a large pan or casserole in which the cheeks fit comfortably. Season then flour them. Warm the olive oil and, when hot and bubbling, throw in the cheeks to brown them. Remove, toss the carrots in the oil, add the leeks after a few minutes, pour in the white wine, put back the cheeks, and warm till the wine comes to a simmer. Leave to cook for 5 minutes, pour in the pig's trotter broth, so the cheeks are well covered, and bring back to a gentle simmer, skimming off the foam as it rises to the top. After an hour remove the cheeks and blend the cooking liquid to a thickened sauce. Return the cheeks to the pan and simmer till tender, around another 15–20 minutes for the weight given above.

CONTINUING ON THE PREVIOUS SUBJECT

I N HIS THIRD chapter Altamiras turned to local cooking. He opened with feasting food for shepherds and friars alike: a trio of dishes for a whole slaughtered lamb.

A FEASTDAY LAMB: THREE DISHES

PLUCK PIE / COSTRADA DE ASSADURILLAS

Wrap three or four plucks in caul. Roast, pound and spice them, add lemon juice and six ounces of sugar, half a dozen hard-boiled eggs, or more, as you see fit, two slices of cooked beef and some ground toasted almonds in their skins, for they give the pie a good flavour. Make a fine pie crust with yolks, soft lard, a little sugar and white wine, knead it well so it stretches (and, remember, if it does not stretch, as often happens, it needs more kneading). Now assemble your pie: roll out your dough to make a large sheet, grease your pie dish with lard, lay a bottom crust on it, then put the pluck beaten with eight eggs and half a pound of sugar on that, put another crust on top, take your pie to the bread oven, bake it and dust the top with powdered sugar.

This pie is good made with veal or any other good meat or fish. Among them sturgeon is the best of all and if you cut fillets from it close to the head, sliced like ham rashers, nobody will guess they are eating fish.

When Moroccan-born chef Noreddine Lamaghaizi Zouhai read *New Art* he kept returning to this pie. He told me the trio of dishes here reminded him of those his mother makes for Morocco's three-day Feast of the Lamb. Her pie is called a *bstilla,* but its ingredients are very much like those Altamiras threw into his deep-dish filling. Perhaps his recipe was a simplified version of an older layered dish? Noreddine, chef at Valencia's Dukala restaurant, which serves fine Moroccan cuisine, makes user-friendly baby *bstillas*, easy to time and serve, while maître Juan Pérez Palmer suggests matching the rich offal flavors with a Mediterranean Monastrell wine from Jumilla, in Murcia.

500 g / 1lb packet of brik or filo pastry sheets, 60 g / 2 oz melted butter

FOR THE MEAT FILLING: 500 g / 1 lb lamb's or kid's pluck or, if not available, heart and liver, 5 tbsp olive oil, 2 grated onions, chopped fresh parsley and mint, 1 tsp ground cinnamon, ½ tsp ground pepper, 1 tsp ground ginger, ½ tsp ras-el-hanout or large pinch of ground cloves.

FOR THE EGG FILLING: 30 g / 1 oz unsalted butter, 6 eggs, ½ tsp pounded cumin seeds.

FOR THE ALMOND FILLING: a handful of almonds in their skins, 175 ml / 6 fl oz olive oil, 1 tsp ground cinnamon, 1 tsp cane sugar (or to taste).

Makes 6–8 baby 11-cm / 4.5-in pies.

To shape the pies, you need a shallow non-stick tartlet mold or ring about 10 cm / 4 in. in diameter. Prepare the pie fillings. Trim the pluck, or heart and liver, of its membrane and cut it into small dice. Warm the olive oil in a frying pan, sweat the grated onion, add the seasoned diced pluck, toss to seal evenly, stir in the herbs and spices. Cool. Make the egg filling: melt the butter in a non-stick pan, scramble the eggs in it with the cumin and a pinch of salt, and turn it into a bowl to cool. Make the almond filling: put the unskinned nuts in a heavy bottomed frying pan, cover them with cold olive oil and warm gently till the almonds cook crisp and golden inside (the oil becomes wonderfully almondy and you can keep it for another dish). Drain and roughly chop the cooled almonds, add cinnamon, and sugar to taste.

For each pie take one and a half sheets of filo pastry out of their wrapping. Working quickly, brush the sheets with melted butter on both sides, and line the mold with the half sheet, pressing it into the corners then letting the edges hang over the side. Cover with a thin layer of almond filling, then with a second half-sheet of buttered pastry laid at right-angles to the first one. Spoon over meat thinly and fold in the top two loose corners of pastry to cover it. Finally, spoon over a layer of spiced scrambled eggs and fold in the remaining loose pastry corners to cover. Lay the last buttered half-sheet of pastry on top and turn the pie upside down out of its mold into your hand so you can fold in the loose corners, as if making a packet. Turn it back over so the top is the smooth side. Make all the pies this way and chill them, wrapped in cling film, till you want to bake them. You can also freeze them.

Preheat the oven (250°C, 500°F, gas mark 9). Lay out the pies on a baking sheet and cook for 10 minutes, then reduce the temperature to 200°C, 400°F, gas mark 6 for a further 10 minutes, raising it at the end if the pastry is not golden. These pies are intense in flavor, though not fatty, and are good served following a light soup with salad to follow.

LAMB'S TESTICLES / CRIADILLAS DE CORDEROS

Friends and Cooks, I write bashfully here of testicles for while I may joke, others are skilled in bawdy innuendo, and I have no desire to give them cause for brazen laughter. So here I shall tell you briefly what I know, hoping it does not offend your ears. Lambs' testicles are at their best in April or May. Open them, lift off their membranes, inner and outer, simmer them in water with salt, drain them, heat olive oil and when it is very hot fry them. Leave them to drain, beat egg yolks, have ready a dusting of flour and salt, dip them in these and fry them again, and serve them with sugar and cinnamon. This dish is a great treat.

Was Altamiras really so bashful? One wonders. Today lamb's testicles, sold skinned and filleted to order, are still "a great treat" in Spain. To prepare them yourself, nick the shiny tight-fitting outer skins with a sharp knife point, tug them off like socks, pull away the inner membranes and slice the testicles quite thickly with a very sharp knife. Dip these fillets in olive oil, season, and fry them in a gently warmed non-stick frying pan. Serve on toast with grilled mushrooms, a romesco sauce, and salad leaves.

POT-ROAST LAMB OR KID / CORDERO O CABRITO ASADO

Cut up your kid or lamb to give half pound servings, or whatever weight you like, put them in a clay or earthen dish and sit it between hot embers, turning it every so often, and when the joints have roasted a while, throw in cured ham fat cut up in little dice, a handful of pounded parsley, a few crushed garlic cloves and some green lemon or lime juice. Baste the meat with these as it roasts and, if you have no cured ham fat, add white wine, aguardiente *or fresh olive oil with two spoonfuls of lard, for it helps make the meat tender. If it is fatty then it needs none of this. And remember, roast meat, like snow, waits for no man, so serve it straight away. Leave it to sit and it is lost.*

Until modern times most traditional Spanish roast kid or lamb was pot-roasted like this to help deal with the toughness of the meat.[1] Ask the butcher to cleaver the leg, with bone and fat, into 120 g / 4 oz servings. Warm your oven (180°C, 350°F, gas mark 4). Put the seasoned meat into an earthenware or clay roasting pot without any additional fat and pot-roast it for about 20 minutes so that it seals in its own fat. The rest of the ingredients—the cured ham, garlic, and citrus juice—can be judged by eye. I use about a handful of diced streaky cured ham, 3 or 4 cloves of sliced garlic, and the juice of a lemon or lime, plus a handful of snipped parsley leaves. Toss well with the meat and return to the oven for about half an hour, making sure the meat does not stick or burn. Now remove the dish, spoon off the fat, splash in a little white wine, check the seasoning, and return to the oven for a final 10–20 minutes, depending on the age of your lamb or kid. Delicious with oven-baked potatoes or turnips (see p. 199).

BARLEY: FOODS OF CHILDHOOD

Friary manners might be refined, wrote Francesc Eiximenis in his *Customs of Eating and Drinking* in the fourteenth century, but simple foods were best. "I advise you to return to those foods that nourished your childhood," said a doctor, one of his characters, lecturing a fat friar. Then he listed them: "barley bread, onions, garlic, a little cured ham fat."[2] The flavors of onion, garlic, and ham fat run right through *New Art*, but barley, the grain of the poor, appears only once in the book, in this pottage. Altamiras was clearly surprised to discover doctors considered it brain food. Cooked like this, with almond milk, the pottage makes a delicious chilled modern summer pudding.

Barley and Almond Milk Cream / Escudilla de Farro

This dish, like some others, is rarely cooked in the Order of Our Father Saint Francis, but it may not be left out for it is made in other monasteries. Once I was offered it and it is cooked with barley, but no matter, for I have seen it served to the sick every day.

Take coarsely ground barley, shake it to remove the chaff, sift it, wash it in warm water three times then boil it in meat broth till it thickens a little. Pound skinned almonds in your metal mortar—just a few are enough to whiten the barley—and add them. Pound this well, put it in a napkin, squeeze it tight so the husk is left behind then put the cream back in the pot, sweeten it and simmer it briefly or it may turn brown. If you cook your barley in almond milk alone, as is often done, it stays very white, though it is nourishing. To make four bowlfuls of this dish boil four ounces of barley in water or broth and use the same weight of almonds and sugar.

How strange it is that a food may be shared by donkeys and wise men, and be given as a reward to the studious yet they say it nourishes and refreshes the brain.

Today's cracked barley, or barley couscous, sometimes called *malhūtn*, is not so different from Altimiras's coarsely ground barley and it works well in this cream. Cook 180 g / 6 oz precooked cracked barley or barley couscous, following packet instructions. When it has cooked, at room temperature stir in cane sugar to taste with a few drops of orange-flower extract and 250 ml / 8 fl oz home-made almond milk (see p. 142). Have a little extra almond milk on hand in case the final cream is too thick. Scatter over rose petals, pomegranate seeds, or shredded mint leaves for a casually beautiful pudding.

SANCHO'S SUPPER

Don Quixote's sidekick, Sancho Panza, was Altamiras's kind of hero. Whenever he had a chance he piped up for everyman. Better to be "a modest little friar of any religious order than a brave knight errant," he told Don Quixote as they set out on their road adventures. Later, as they rode through Aragon, he spoke up again after a quacky doctor prescribed him courtly cooking. "If by chance I'm served up palace food," he replied, "then my stomach turns queasy or I'm sickened." As he spoke, he put his mouth where his words were, tucking into "*salpicón* of beef and onion and some boiled calf's feet." How Altamiras must have chuckled as he wrote up Sancho's supper.[3]

Calf's Feet Fritters / Manos de Ternera

Take calf's feet, boil up a small cauldron of water, duck the feet into it one by one, scrape them with a knife to shave off any hairs, pull out the petty-toes then boil the feet in fresh water with salt, and dress them. They are good boned, coated in egg and breadcrumbs and fried, and served dusted with sugar and cinnamon, or you may simmer them whole in a hazelnut or pine kernel sauce flavoured with garlic, cheese and parsley. Then give them a last little simmer and serve them.

Relished for their chunky gelatinous meat, calf's hoofs were the priciest feet or trotters on Spanish butchers' stalls.[4] In the New World, where cattle ranching flourished on a scale unthinkable in Europe, they are still highly rated and recently they have made the journey back to Spanish kitchens. My Madrid-based Peruvian friend Nora immediately recognized these fritters fried just as Altamiras describes in hot, golden, bubbling olive oil. Sancho, no doubt, would have gulped them down.

Beef Salpicón / Salpicón de Baca

A salpicón *makes a good light supper or it ends a meal well if you have no salad. Chop lean cured ham, twice its weight of beef and a little onion. Arrange the salpicón on a ceramic dish, dress it with oil, pepper and salt, lay onion rings on top then add a little sharp citrus juice, and there you have a very good dish.*

In Altamiras's home valley beef *salpicón* was served this way, at the end of old-fashioned country meals. Today you can still make it as he describes, salting the onion first to take out some of its fierceness (see p. 213). There are memorable New World recipes for this too. In her book entitled *A Mouthful of Angels* Rosalia Loreto López gives a punchy Mexican convent *salpicón*. She marinates the beef raw in bitter orange juice with a pinch of salt, poaches it in water, shreds, and tosses it in olive oil with sliced green olives, parsley, and chopped preserved green chilli peppers. Delicious, though not for the faint-hearted.[5]

Rice in Stock and Pine-Kernel Milk / Arroz de Grassa

Rice cooked in meat broth is very good though you must be sure your broth is salted, not spiced. Wash your rice in warm water, dry it then cook it in the broth. For every pound of raw rice, take a pound of sugar, pine-kernel milk made with three ounces of kernels, and a cinnamon infusion made with one ounce of cinnamon for every eight pounds of rice and sugar. Then add half a dozen egg yolks, thinned with a little more broth, to every pound of cooked rice and serve it sprinkled with sugar and cinnamon, and you will see, when people taste this, they often think the rice has been cooked in milk.

Courtly medieval white rices, both sweet and savory, were going out of fashion in the eighteenth century, but Altamiras needed to note the recipe since it was a sweet treat on certain monastic feast days. Curiously, at the same time, these dishes were being adapted in the New World where they became popular made with coconut milk, a safe alternative to fresh milks and cheaper than nut milks.[6] Among such sweet white rices Columbia's *arroz con coco* is a good example. However, I like to treat this more as a Valencian *arroz meloso*, or moist savory rice, served with toasted pine kernels or flaked almonds.

½ teacupful cinnamon infusion, 90 g / 3 oz pine kernels, about 150 ml / 5 fl oz cold water, 1.4 liters / 2½ pints seasoned broth skimmed free of all fat, 500 g / 1 lb rice—ideally Bomba (see p. 238), or, failing that, Arborio, pinch of sugar, 2 egg yolks (optional)

TO SERVE: toasted pine kernels or flaked almonds, powdered cinnamon.

Make the cinnamon infusion (see pp. 191–92). Blend the pine kernels and cold water to give a thin white milk. In a large flameproof casserole, ideally an earthenware or clay one, bring the seasoned broth and cinnamon infusion to a boil. Add the rice, boil it for 15 minutes, lower to simmering, check the seasoning, and keep cooking for about 7 minutes or until the rice is *al dente*. Stir in the pine-kernel milk carefully with a fork towards the end of cooking time. Remove the casserole from the heat and, if you like, stir in the egg yolks. Scatter the pine kernels or flaked almonds over the top and leave to sit for 5 minutes. Good with a floral Verdejo white wine.

BABY PURPLE ARTICHOKES

Altamiras loved artichokes and he clearly had a plentiful supply. His dishes (see also pp. 191–92) made good use of them at every moment of the growing cycle, from tiny and tender to larger and tougher. The Romans had been the first to domesticate artichokes from the wild and they probably did so in the Ebro Valley, but the purple-tinged baby ones Altamiras cooked were the legacy of Muslim farmers' seed selection. A star of today's market garden crops, locally cooked with their velvety *rijos* or stalks attached, they are cropped in spring and autumn to avoid the fluffy choke provoked by summer heat.

If you are buying fresh baby purple artichokes, a dozen will weigh around a kilo and a half (3 lb). If you cannot find them fresh, then you can fall back on frozen or preserved ones: they are not as good, but they are often fairly priced and not bad eating. As a rule of thumb, a dozen frozen or preserved large artichoke hearts weigh about 500 g / 1 lb.

PREPARING FRESH WHOLE OR QUARTERED BABY ARTI-CHOKES: Pull off the tough outer leaves, pare the skin off the stalks and lower bulbs with a stainless steel knife or vegetable peeler, slice across the tough dark green leaf tops, and leave only tender pale green leaves below. Dig out any hairy choke with a teaspoon, taking care you do not dig into the heart below. Rub a cut lemon over each artichoke, drop it into a bowl of cold water with parsley in it (the lemon and parsley help to stop the artichoke darkening), and quarter it just before cooking. For some recipes you can parboil artichokes before preparing them, which speeds up this preparation.

PREPARING HEARTS: If an artichoke's leaves are too tough to cook whole, skin the stalks and lower bulbs, cut across the top of the hearts and pull off all the leaves so you are left only with the hearts with their stalk attached. These are absolutely delicious.

Stuffed Artichokes / Algarchofas Rellenas

Pull off the artichokes' outer leaves, give them a little boil in water with salt, drain them on a board so all the water runs out, then prepare a stuffing as for lettuce or other everyday stuffed dishes. Push your stuffing down between the leaves and place a ball of it at the artichokes' hearts, and if they look as though they might come apart, whisk egg white and dip them in it before you cook them. Cook these like stuffed lettuces and pumpkins, adding a hazelnut sauce.

Surprisingly easy to make, these can be kept warm well in the oven bathed in broth or hazelnut sauce (see p. 16).

12 baby artichokes, 2 quantities of lamb stuffing or dumpling dough (see pp. 25 and 75), 750 ml / 1¾ pints chicken or vegetable stock, ½ bottle of dry white wine, hazelnut thickening (see p. 16), optional

Parboil whole prepared artichokes (see above), scraping out any choke and stripping off the very tough outer leaves. Take about 60 g

/ 2 oz seasoned stuffing for each artichoke. First fill the hollow hearts then make a space between outer leaves all the way around and put in a narrow band of stuffing. Put the artichokes in a pan, cover with the broth and wine, season, and simmer gently for 20–30 minutes, rolling them over to cook evenly. You can thicken the broth with a pounded hazelnut sauce if you like (see p. 16). Good with wild rice and radicchio salad.

Artichoke Hearts Fried with Cured Ham / Algarchofas con Tocino Magro

Pull off all the artichokes' leaves till you are left with the hearts. Cut them in half, simmer them quickly in water with salt and drain them well. Then take lean ham rashers, fry them in your skillet, add the artichokes and cook them in the melted fat.

This is a memorable combination if you are lucky enough to have fresh artichoke hearts, a few slices of Iberico ham, and a sweet olive oil. But this dish is also good cooked with preserved artichoke hearts, as in many Spanish restaurants.

Count 4 parboiled artichoke hearts (see p. 70), a couple of tablespoonfuls of olive oil and a good slice of jamón for each person. Fry the ham gently and quickly in the olive oil, taking care not to burn it, add the artichoke hearts, and cook over low heat, shaking the pan, for 10 minutes. This is good made in an earthenware dish like a *cazuela* that effortlessly gives you the right kind of low cooking temperatures.

Artichokes in Caramel Glaze / Algarchofas con Dulce

Take off the artichokes' tough outer leaves, make cuts in the stems so they can sop up your flavourings, trim and drop them quickly into cold water. Scald them; boil them with salt. To dress them, cut cured ham into fine dice, fry these with chopped onion, throw them in with the drained cooked artichokes, add sugar as you see fit and stir all this quickly over a gentle fire. Nuns are used to cooking artichokes this way, but such sweetness is not to everyone's taste, even when it comes from a convent.

French cook and chemist Edouard de Pomiane wrote up a recipe very much like this one in the 1930s, calling it "Jewish artichokes."[7] Since

CURED HAM

"Cut up cured ham fat in small dice, melt these in your skillet." In his childhood, Altamiras would have known the hams cured from black-footed pigs that grazed on acorns in the sierra behind La Almunia. Later, as a friary cook he did the work of the pig-killing himself, salting hams, stuffing sausages, curing chunks of fat and making fresh soft lard for the friary larder (see p. 110). Their subtle flavor, so different from bacon's harsh twang, runs right through his cooking. Most of these products can be found in specialist food shops today, but one that is good to make easily at home is soft lard: warm diced cured Iberico fat—or off-cuts of the fat from its rind—very slowly in a heavy-based pan, watching carefully as it turns opaque, then begins to melt. Check that there is absolutely no burning or browning. Alternatively, for fat for frying at higher temperatures, sweat diced streaky air-dried ham—Serrano, Italian *pancetta*, or French *lardons* will all do well—in olive oil until it picks up the cured ham flavor.

he had studied Jewish cuisine, which may be a clue to the origins of Altamiras's recipe, I have adapted the recipe to Pomiane's method since it allows you to adjust the sweetness to your tastes.

12 prepared raw artichoke hearts (see p. 70) or 500 g / 1 lb frozen artichoke hearts, 1–2 tbsp cane sugar, large pinch of salt, 4 tbsp olive oil, 1 finely chopped large sweet onion, 60 g / 2 oz diced streaky cured jamón or pancetta, 3 tbsp water

Simmer the artichoke hearts in just enough water to cover, with the sugar, salt, and a tablespoonful of olive oil. After 5 minutes remove the artichokes and boil the syrup down to about 90 ml / 3 fl oz, so you have just enough caramelized syrup to coat each artichoke. Meanwhile warm the rest of the olive oil in a frying pan, sweat the onion, add the jamón, toss the artichoke hearts with them, pour in the syrup, and cook gently so the artichokes can absorb the flavors. Check the seasoning and serve.

Pot-Roast Artichokes / Algarchofas Assadas

Pull off the artichokes' outer leaves till you have only tender inner ones, trim the tops and make cuts in the stems so they can absorb your flavourings. Then fry cured ham, with fat and lean on it, throw it into a pot with the artichokes with a little salt, a handful of pounded parsley, a few green garlic shoots and a dusting of pepper. Sit the pot over hot embers, with more in the lid, and shake it once or twice as the artichokes cook. They may seem tough on the outside, but when you cut them open you will find them tender inside. This is a good dish for lean days too, when you can cook them with olive oil and fried garlic.

When you first open up this pot of artichokes the outer leaves will appear leathery, as Altamiras warned readers, but inside you will find them lovely and tender.

6 tbsp olive oil, 120 g / 4 oz cubed streaky jamón or pancetta, 4 chopped fresh green garlic stems or 2 sliced garlic cloves, 12 prepared small purple artichokes, halved lengthways, a few stalks of flat-leaf parsley
Preheat the oven (170°C, 325°F, gas mark 3). Warm the olive oil in a flameproof casserole—earthenware is best to keep the temperatures low—and add the jamón, garlic and halved artichokes. Toss well, season and put the casserole in the oven, tightly covered, for 40 minutes, checking to see that there is no sticking. Stir in the snipped parsley leaves for the last 5 minutes of cooking time. Serve with a jug or bottle of olive oil so each person can pour on a little extra, as they like.

BREAKING BREAD: DUMPLINGS AND NOODLES

The friars treated bread with reverence. They begged wheat, barley, rye, and baked loaves and sometimes received grains as rent in kind from tenants.[8] Breadcrumbs were as valued too: they were swept from the refectory table with a palm-leaf brush and recycled in cooked dishes. Here crumbs fresh and dried are recycled to become the main ingredient in two ingenious hot dishes. The dumplings bring with them the story of a remarkable family.

Carnival Dumplings / Rellenos de Pan, y Grassa

Take broth from a stewpot in which you have cooked meat. Grate bread and cheese: one part of cheese for every six of bread, then add spices, parsley, mint, lettuce hearts boiled in water with salt and, for every dozen dumplings the size of walnuts, half a dozen raw eggs. Bind your dough with broth and mould it into dumplings in a chocolate cup with a spoon, wetted from time to time, for in this way dumplings turn out well and are untouched by human hand. If you wish you can add chopped capon breasts, or lean boiled cured ham or beef, for these are good in this, then cook your dumplings like meat-balls, though they need less time.

A chance encounter led me to the Lechal family in Castellote, a village in the most isolated area of Aragon's Maestrazgo sierra. In the 1940s Miguela Lechal, a widow, the grandmother of the current owner, opened a modest lodging-house for mineworkers here. Miguela served homely meals, but she never forgot to make feastday dishes like her mother's dumplings for Carnival, a clandestine fiesta during Franco's dictatorship. "She did not call them Carnival dumplings," her grandson Mariano wrote to me, "but local people knew she served them and what they meant." Miguela's lodging-house has now become the Hostal Castellote where Mariano's wife still cooks the dumplings and other traditional feastday dishes (see p. 201). When I visited them we discovered that, while they did not know Altamiras's book, their dumplings are almost identical to those of *New Art*.[9] Mariano later wrote to me to explain why they cherish such cookery, as the art of "transforming humble food into a dish that gathers the whole family round the table, so simplicity becomes a fiesta."

1 pork rib, 1 pig's trotter, ¼ boiling hen, 2 cooking chorizos, 1 chunk of ham bone, 1 beef bone, a little piece of cured ham fat, 1 lamb shank, ¼ trimmed green cabbage, 200 g / 7 oz chickpeas soaked overnight, 4 liters / 7 pints water, 2 tsp salt

FOR THE DUMPLINGS: 100 ml / 4 fl oz olive oil, 6 chopped garlic cloves, 300 g / 10 oz of finely chopped carnival meats (chicken breast, jamón, cured loin of pork, longaniza, and fresh cooking chorizo), 500 g / 16 oz yesterday's bread cut into tiny pieces, 4 eggs, salt, pepper, 150 g / 5 oz grated cheese, chopped leaves from a stalk of flat-leafed parsley.

Makes about 2 dozen dumplings and 2 liters / 3.5 pints of broth.

Choose a very large pan where all the broth ingredients fit comforta-bly and can be left to bubble away happily for 2 hours, covered, without boiling over. Strain the broth when cool. Pick the different meats off the bones, throwing away the skin, fat, and gristle. Skin the chorizo. Keep the chickpeas and cabbage that do not go into the dumplings—they are great tossed quickly in olive oil sweated first with sliced garlic and then with spinach leaves.

To make the dumplings, warm a little of the olive oil to sweat the garlic, add the chopped meats to brown them, scoop both into a large mixing bowl, and stir in the breadcrumbs soaked in hot stock and squeezed dry. Knead in the beaten eggs, seasoning, cheese, and parsley. Check the balance of tastes, rub your palms with a little olive oil, and shape into dumplings the size of a round plum. Warm the rest of the olive oil in a deep frying pan and, when it is bubbling, throw in the dumplings to brown them. Put the broth in a large pan, warm to a gentle simmer, add the dumplings with tongs or a straining spoon, and simmer for 30 minutes. Serve them in a puddle of strained hot broth in warmed soup plates. Good with a young red Garnacha wine. These are filling enough to make a one-dish meal, opened by olives (see p. 216), and rounded off by a fruit ragout (see p. 187).

Jueves Lardero, las pellas al puchero.
Lardy Thursday, dumplings in the pot.

Aragonese rhyming proverb

Breadcrumb Noodles / Fideos Gruessos

Grate bread and cheese. Take one part of cheese to six of bread, add spices, sugar and cinnamon and enough raw eggs to give a soft dough. Bind this with meat broth. Place a small cauldron of broth over a gentle flame then press the dough through the holes of your large skimming spoon with a wooden spoon or spatula, so the small noodles fall into the boiling broth and, as they cook, you can watch them curve like round spoon ends. Put them on serving plates and sprinkle them with sugar and cinnamon.

Make these breadcrumb noodles thin and they curve like horseshoes. Make them fat and they work as well though they may not curve. A potato ricer, sometimes called a German noodle or spaetzle maker, is handy for preparing them, or you can roll them easily, like little cheroots, between oiled palms. I like these served plain with cheese, pepper, and olive oil, as a first course.[10]

175 g / 6 oz very fine dried natural breadcrumbs, 1 heaped tbsp finely grated sharp ewe's milk cheese, ½ tsp each of ground cinnamon

and cloves, salt and pepper, 2 tsps olive oil, 2 medium eggs, about 1 tbsp chicken broth

TO COOK: 1 liter / 1¾ pints chicken broth.

Makes 4–6 first-course servings.

Pass any coarse breadcrumbs through a coffee-grinder till very fine and evenly textured. Mix all the dry ingredients and seasonings in a food processor, add enough broth to give a soft but compact dough, wrap it in cling film and rest it for 30 minutes. Press the dough through a potato ricer to give little heaps of noodles on a sheet of non-stick cooking parchment. Dry for 10 minutes; cover with cooking film if you leave them for any longer before cooking them. Bring the broth to a fast boil. Drop in the noodles, bring back to a boil, and simmer for about 4 minutes, checking that one is done before straining them all. Serve dry or in the broth, like a soup. Reserve the strained broth for other dishes, even if you are not serving the noodles in it.

> *Del pan y del cerdo se aprovecha todo.*
> Of the pig and bread, nothing goes to waste.
>
> Traditional Spanish proverb

TWO COUNTRY DISHES

Lungs in Hot Vinaigrette / Liviano Gustoso

Cook lungs in your meat pot: wash them, first hang the windpipe over the side of the pot then boil them, take them out, cut them up in little dice and dress them. Pound four cloves of garlic with a dusting of pepper, wash them out of the mortar with good vinegar and pour it over the lungs with a little fresh olive oil and salt, and stir all this over a gentle fire. This is a very good dish to excite the appetite.

In Altamiras's day lungs were thought to be good for those in need of lung power, so perhaps he served them to the preachers at San Diego. Today they are considered gourmet food. Indeed, many Spaniards prefer them to kidneys. Manolo, an offalmonger in my local Madrid market, used to insist on chopping them up into little cubes for me, but I found the squeals of the air as it rushed out of the lung's piping in the pot so unnerving that I took up Altamiras's way of blanching them whole, dangling the windpipe over the saucepan's rim so the air rushes out silently. I blanche the garlic to soften the shock of its flavor.[11]

2 pairs of lamb's lungs, weighing around 370 g / 12 oz, ½ small head of blanched garlic, 2 tbsp mild white wine vinegar, a generous handful of snipped parsley, 2 tbsp olive oil

Serves 4–6 as a tapa.

Simmer the whole lungs and unskinned garlic in salted water for 5 minutes, leaving the windpipe hanging over the edge of the saucepan. Their meat will become firm, shrink, and take on the look of cooked kidneys. Drain, dry, and chop the lungs, cutting out the piping. Pop the garlic flesh out of its skin and mash it with the vinegar, parsley, and salt. Heat the olive oil in a frying pan, season the chopped lung, toss it in the oil for 4–5 minutes, and stir in the vinegar dressing. This makes a good first course with bread to mop up the juices.

Cow, or Beef, in White Wine / Baca en Guisado

Cut lean meat from the leg of a well-fattened cow. Early in the day put it to cook in your stewpot. Cool it and cut it up in bits the size of walnut shells. Melt cured ham fat in your skillet, fry the meat in it and, once it is well browned, put it to braise this way: fry fine-cut onion in the skillet fat, add it to the meat, throw in spices, pounded garlic, a little white wine and a handful of parsley, and put all this to cook. Cover the pot with paper, stick it to the rim with a flour and water dough and sit a jug of water over the pot's mouth. Leave this to cook slowly, uncovering the stew half an hour before you wish to serve it and, take note, if you can find cow's meat to make this, it is tastier than veal.

Dionisio Pérez discovered this old-fashioned "stewed cow" being cooked high in the Pyrenean mountains in the 1920s.[12] Pérez, a journalist with inquisitive tastebuds, wrote up many such overlooked dishes in his 1929 *Guide to Good Spanish Eating*. The book opened with a patriotic blast against French cuisine—reflecting general long-held anti-French sentiment in Spain—but later chapters shed interesting perspectives on the history of Spanish food, underlining the influence of medieval Aragon's food cultures, which enriched themselves through exchange between its courts in Barcelona, Valencia, Naples, Zaragoza, and Sicily.[13]

4 tbsp olive oil, 90 g / 3 oz finely diced streaky jamón, 1.25 kg / 2½ lb trimmed braising or stewing beef (e.g., chuck or blade steak), cut into

large cubes or small steaks, 1 chopped onion, 3 finely chopped garlic cloves, a 2.5-cm / 1-in length of cinnamon stick, 6 whole cloves, a few fresh parsley stalks, a bottle of dry white wine (or more if necessary), a small handful of snipped flat-leaf parsley

Turn on the oven to heat for braising (see p. 232). The temperature will depend on the method and pot you are using. Heat the olive oil gently in a non-stick frying pan, add the streaky jamón, and fry it gently so the fat melts. Brown the seasoned beef in the fat, removing it to an ovenproof casserole, ideally of earthenware or clay. Lower the heat under the frying pan, add the onion and garlic, sweat them till soft in the pan fat, and scoop them on to the meat. Pour enough wine over to nearly cover the meat, stir in the cinnamon, and seal the casserole with oiled folded greaseproof or cooking paper (see p. 9). Bring to a gentle simmer and cook in the oven for 1½–2 hours, checking every so often and topping up with more wine or stock if the stew dries out. Stir in the parsley for the last 10 minutes of cooking time and check the seasoning. Pérez ate this with ash-baked onions from the hearth, skinned and served with olive oil, salt, and vinegar, or you can try Altamiras's onion wedges with crunchy breadcrumbs (see p. 185).

THE HUNGRY TRAVELER

Few travel writers captured Spanish life on the road as well as Richard Ford, the English diarist. His *Handbook*, first published exactly one hundred years after Altamiras's cookbook, echoed earlier travelers' observations: he described eating mutton stews cooked over charcoal, drinking from wineskins at tavern tables, and slaking summer thirst with iced water sold on hot city streets. But Ford, like other travelers, also had a list of complaints, which ranged from garlic to high prices and fleas.[14] Those who were invited to stay at a Franciscan friary as they journeyed knew they were lucky. Guests were given their own cell with clean sheets and, on arrival, they had their feet washed and were served an extra large portion of food. Here Altamiras linked up a recipe for travelers to take with them on the road to another for unexpected guests.

A Ham in Spiced White Wine / Pernil Cocido con Vino Blanco

Chop the trotter off the ham then soak it overnight in water, boil it for an hour and a half, sit it in a cooking dish, bathe it in white wine. Throw in

cinnamon shards, half a dozen cloves and bay leaves, and, if you wish to cook this in a sweet sauce, add a pound of sugar. You may drain off the cooking liquor so the ham is good for travelling or serve it with its liquor.

Think of Spanish boiled ham and Galicia's steaming rustic platefuls of ham, cabbage, and potatoes may come to mind. But in Altamiras's day hams were luxury food reserved for weddings or special guests. Those he cooked may have come from the black-footed pigs that roamed in the southern Aragonese sierras, grazing on holm-oak acorns.[15] I have adapted the original to take on board some modern culinary ideas from Grange Farm, a sustainable farm on the North Yorkshire Moors.

a whole unsmoked ham, about 1.25-kg / 2½-lb, 1 bottle of good fruity white wine, 2 large cinnamon sticks, 8 cloves, 8 bay leaves, 4 tbsp unrefined brown cane sugar

Preheat your oven (180°C, 350°F, gas mark 4). Wash the ham and stand it on a rack in a baking or roasting tin. Pour 2.5 cm / 1 inch of water into the tin. Now cover the ham with doubled strong foil wrapped over the edges of the tin to seal tightly and put it to roast, allowing ¾ hour per kilo. Warm the wine with the spices and bay leaves, but no salt, for 15 minutes and leave to infuse. At the end of roasting time, take out the ham, open it up, cutting off any skin or rind, put it in a large pan, pour over the spiced wine, and put it back in the oven for another 30 minutes, basting from time to time. Check that the ham is done by inserting a skewer into the center, transfer the joint to a roasting tin, and put it in the oven to crisp the skin. Pour the cooking liquid into a pan, skim off the fat, reduce the remaining pan-juices to a syrupy liquor, season, and pour into a warmed jug. Slice the ham thickly and serve on a heated dish with the wine sauce. I like this with a squash ragout (p. 184) and green beans (p. 194).

"What a good cooking aroma . . . ! Unless I'm mistaken, that's not the smell of country thyme and rushes, but the whiff of ham rashers, and that means a liberal and generous wedding feast."

Miguel Cervantes, *Don Quixote*,
Part II, 1615 (Camacho's wedding feast)

Flattened Meatballs / Almondigas Repentinas

Hash lean meat as for meatballs, throw in a little cured ham and for every half pound of hash add four eggs, a few grated breadcrumbs, sugar and

cinnamon, but no spices. Make meatballs, put the skillet on the fire with some good lard in it, make it very hot for frying, flatten your meatballs with a spatula, pick them up and put them in the skillet. Fry them well on one side and then on the other and put them on plates. Serve them with sugar and cinnamon on top to unexpected guests.

I first came upon cinnamon-spiced meatballs served with almond milk gravy in an old Menorcan cookbook. These ones are flattened, a little like chubby miniature burgers, but they are just as good in a Mediterranean almond milk gravy, which I have added here.

500 g / 1 lb lean minced beef, lamb or pork, 125 g / 4 oz finely chopped streaky jamón or pancetta, 2 eggs, 3 tbsp dried breadcrumbs, ½ tsp cinnamon, about 120 ml / 4 fl oz olive oil

FOR FRYING AND THE ALMOND MILK GRAVY: Stir 250 ml / 8 fl oz home-made almond milk (see pp. 213–14) into the pan juices.

Makes 32 small meatballs.

Knead together the meatball ingredients, season to taste, shape with oiled hands to the size you want—anything between a whole walnut shell and a small orange—flatten lightly with a spatula on a wooden board and pan-fry to taste. I like these well browned but still juicy inside, served on mashed potatoes whipped up with olive oil and the almond milk gravy poured on top. You can finish this off with a little extra powdered cinnamon too.

CHAPTER IV

ON FOWL

POULTRY AND GAME

MIGUEL DELIBES, the great Castilian novelist, reflected on his passion for hunting by noting that a Franciscan spirit restrained him from killing large soft-eyed game. The dishes Altamiras gave here for game seem guided by the same spirit: there are plenty of recipes for small birds, but not a single one for boar or venison.[1]

However, he did give over a dozen imaginative ideas for chickens and hens, which were luxury bought meats at court. Clearly the friars were good poultry farmers. Sometimes they reared a pig too and Altamiras rounded off this chapter with a breathless account of a pig-killing and sausage-making, the first to be published in a Spanish cookbook.

QUAIL

Quail in a Breadcrumb Jacket / Codornices Assadas

Roast the quails this way. Pluck and clean them, tie them to the spit and have ready a little clay or earthen dish to warm some soft lard with an egg yolk, salt, breadcrumbs and a dusting of pepper for each brace of quail. Stir this mixture well, brush it over your birds with a handful of feathers and turn them over the fire till they roast to a ruddy gold, and you can cook tender chickens, young partridges, a boiled hen or capon the same way too.

Quail were too humble for court cooks, but ideal for a friary kitchen near the wheat plains. They are still hunted there by farmers as they scuttle through the stubble in late summer.[2]

In Aragon today they are usually cooked in *escabeches*, but Altamiras spit-roasted young birds with a recipe reminiscent of earlier Muslim dishes. I like to marinate the quail first. Simple as this dish may sound, it needs a careful eye for detail to keep the crust on.

8–12 farmed quails, a few thyme sprigs, 4 sliced garlic cloves, salt and pepper, ½ bottle white wine, 300 g / 10 oz fresh coarse breadcrumbs, 4 egg whites, plateful of plain flour, 8–12 egg yolks beaten with 5 tbsp melted quality cured ham fat (ideally Ibérico)

Rub the quails inside and out with thyme, garlic, salt, and pepper, then marinate them overnight in the white wine. Dry them and tie together the legs. Toast the breadcrumbs in a warm oven for about 10 minutes, tossing them so they crisp evenly. Cool them, blend or crush to fine crumbs, and season. Paint the quails with egg white, let it dry for 10 minutes, pat on a flour coating, working it well into the awkward corners, then paint over that with the egg yolk beaten with melted ham fat. Roll the birds in the breadcrumbs and chill for 15 minutes. Preheat a hot oven (220°C, 425°F, gas mark 7). Oven-roast the quail for just over a quarter of an hour—the exact time will depend on their weight. I like these quail served with garlicky *ajo* (see p. 157) and napkins for eating with your hands.

"For my home I need little furniture . . . a print of the Virgin Mary, a table, five chairs, a frying pan, a wineskin, and a guitar, and a spit and a candle. . . . Everything else is superfluous."

Francisco de Goya in a letter to
his friend Martin Zapater, July 1780

Quail Casseroled in Wine / Codornices en Guisados

Cut cured ham fat into dice, fry them till their fat runs, lift them out of the skillet, put in the quails and brown them in the fat. Then put them in a cooking pot. Throw onion into the skillet to fry in the fat, add it to the quails with pounded parsley, a little white wine and spices. Cook these quail slowly and they will turn out very well simply because they are cooked in wine rather than water.

This is a simple casserole made delicious by a characterful white wine like a Verdejo, Garnacha, or Albariño. Again, the recipe works well made with farmed birds.

8–12 farmed quails, 4 tbsp olive oil, a couple of large chopped onions, a handful of chopped diced jamón and another of snipped flat-leaf parsley, half a bottle of dry white wine, small pinches each of powdered cinnamon and cloves

Choose a flameproof casserole in which the quails fit comfortably. Warm the olive oil in it, brown the birds in the oil, take them out, add the chopped onion and diced jamón, and a little extra oil if needed. Sweat the onion till it is soft, pour in the white wine, add the spices and seasoning to taste, then lay the quails on their side in the casserole so the wine comes halfway up them. Simmer for 10 minutes, turn the birds over and cook for another 10 minutes on the other side. Check the seasoning when the birds are done and stir in the parsley. These are good with mashed roots and a salad of green leaves and shoots.

WILD TURKEY

Fray Bernadino de Sahagún quoted Mexicans' praise for wild turkey in his censored *General History of the Things of New Spain* (1544–1570). "It leads the meats . . . some turkeys are smoky, some quite black, some like crow feathers, glistening, some white. . . ." In the New World, both south and north, the turkeys were caught by expert local hunters and fattened up in mission farms' adobe corrals. Only when ranching took off did such wild meats become less valuable to the friars. Meanwhile, back in Spain turkey had long been a tender farmyard bird, so when here Altamiras dropped in a medieval recipe for tough peacock, adapted it to turkey and followed on with more game recipes, he was probably thinking of mission cooks learning how to handle wild birds in the New World.[3]

Roast Turkey with Soursweet Lemon Sauce / Pabos Assados

This is the simplest way. When they are plucked, drawn and clean, hang them for two nights in the cool evening air then simmer them in your stewpot till they are half-done and tie them on the spit, fastening them on well. Brush them with soft lard, dust them with salt and pepper, nail cloves into the breast and leg, wrap them in paper tied on with string and roast them over a gentle fire till they are well done. Now make a sauce: warm the broth with a little sugar and lemon juice, spice it with cinnamon, pepper and salt, and this is good with all kinds of roasts and for the sick: most people like it since soursweet flavours are so tasty.

This recipe, originally for peacocks, appeared in Ruperto de Nola's *Libre del coch* (see p. xx). They were often kept by medieval monasteries, not just for their beauty, but also as guard birds which spied down from rooftops and chased away intruders, before ending up in a pot at the end of their life. The sweet and sour lemon sauce is delicious and equally good with turkey joints.

1 medium-sized turkey, about 2.7–3.6 kg / 6–8 lb, 2 tbsp soft lard, 12 cloves

FOR THE LEMON SAUCE: 2 tbsp olive oil, 60g / 2 oz sugar, juice and zest of 1 lemon, 250 ml / 8 fl oz water, 5 cm / 2 inch cinnamon quill.

Warm the oven (200°C, 400°F, gas mark 6). Season the turkey, lard it, stud the skin and flesh evenly with cloves, piercing the skin, and tie the legs together. Roast on a rack for 30 minutes, then turn the oven down to 180°C, 350°F, gas mark 4, and leave for 1¾ hours. Now remove the turkey from the oven, check that it is cooked through by sticking a skewer into the flesh inside the leg and cover it with foil to keep it warm while you make the sauce. Pour off the roasting juices into a small bowl, skim off, and discard the fat. Warm the olive oil in a small, heavy-bottomed pan, melt the sugar in it and, as it turns golden, add the lemon juice, zest, and cinnamon quill. Simmer to give a light syrup, stir in the water and defatted roasting juices, season to taste, reduce to a sauce, and strain into a heated jug to serve with the turkey, pulling out the cloves before carving the bird. I like this with couscous and spinach (see p. 192).

PARTRIDGE

Vivieron felices y comieron perdices. "They lived happily ever after and ate partridges." So runs the ending of many Spanish fairy tales. But how were partridges cooked? In most recipe books we find them soberly braised in winy juices though greater fame was won by an elaborate dish written up by French gastronome Auguste Escoffier. He believed pheasant or partridge "a la Alcántara," featuring foie, truffles, and Port wine, came from a Spanish friary cookbook carried home by a Napoleonic general. But food historians, looking at the dish's ingredients and matching them up with the story of the Napoleonic retreat at the end of the Peninsula War, suggest the recipe and book came from Sâo Pedro de Alcántara, a convent in Lisbon's Barrio Alto famed both for its cooking and library. Altamiras's partridges are, by comparison, simple, though that does not mean they are any less delicious.[4]

Partridge Casseroled in Wine / Perdices en Guisados

Pluck and clean your partridges, sear them on the fire or seal them in a skillet then put them in a small stewpot with fried cured ham cut up in dice, onion, parsley and spices, two cloves of crushed garlic and a little white wine, and cover this tight with a jug of water and, even better, seal the jug to the pot with a flour and water dough if you have it. Let your partridges cook on a gentle fire and, when they are done, stir up some egg yolks, pour them on top and serve them. This is a good dish for those who do not care for partridges in pepper sauce.

In the last fifty years Spain's red-legged partridges have retreated to high sierras and private estates to avoid the hunters who now drive into isolated areas once visited only on foot. But recipes to tenderize a wild bird can also be made with farmed partridges or even partridge breasts. If your bird comes with its liver and heart, keep them to fry as a delicious snack on toast.

6 partridges, 4 tbsp olive oil, 2 chopped onions, 4 sliced garlic cloves, 500 ml / ¾ pint white wine, 175 ml / 6 fl oz hot water
1 partridge per person for a main dish, half a bird for a first course.
Clean and season the partridges. Tie up their legs. Warm the olive oil gently in a flameproof casserole—an earthenware or clay one is best—where the partridges can fit in a single layer. Brown them, remove them from the casserole, add the onions, cover and sweat, add the garlic, toss, pour in the wine and water, then put back the partridges, lying on their sides so one leg and breast are submerged. Bring to a gentle simmer, cover, and cook till tender, turning every 20 minutes. Allow about 1 hour's casseroling for farmed birds and 1½ hours for wild ones. Add extra liquid if needed to keep the birds half covered, then let it reduce at the end of cooking time. Steamed shredded green cabbage and *patatas a la panadera* (see p. 237) go well with this.

Partridges in Pepper Sauce / Perdices en Prebe

Partridges are usually dressed like this, in a pepper sauce. Clean them well, sear them on the fire, sit them in a clay or earthen casserole and add parsley, salt, peppercorns, bay leaves, lemon or orange slices, fresh olive oil and a little water. Leave them to cook dressed like this, and add a little crushed garlic. If you have no oranges or lemons, you can throw in olives, but first take out their stones or add capers. When the birds are done lift the pot off the fire, take an egg yolk for each partridge and stir it into the cooking liquor to give a tasty little sauce. These birds are best served whole.

A modern version of these slow-cooked partridges in citric peppery juices appears in an anthology entitled *A History of Cooking in Albacete and its Best Recipes*. The author, Andrés Gómez Flores, learned the dish in southern Castile from a country cook unaware of its source. Don't be put off by the amount of olive oil: this is almost like a confit. But do go easy on the peppercorns. One traveler, Norberto Caimo, commented that he, like other travelers, found partridges "spoiled by the quantity of pepper with which they had been seasoned."[5]

4–6 partridges, about 120 ml / 4 fl oz fruity olive oil, 3 bay leaves, 2 tsp peppercorns or to taste, 3 lemon slices, 3 pounded garlic cloves, handful of snipped flat-leaf parsley, 3 egg yolks (optional)

Clean and season the partridges, and tie up the legs. Brown them in a little of the olive oil, put them in a flameproof casserole where they fit comfortably on their sides, throw in the bay leaf, peppercorns, lemon, garlic, and the rest of the olive oil, add water to cover the bird and simmer slowly, with the lid on, for 1–2 hours. The birds should be tender and cooked through, the liquid reduced to a small amount of a slightly separated olive-oil sauce, and the parsley added towards the end of cooking time. You can thicken the sauce with egg yolk, but it is not really needed. Try this with roast pumpkin cubes to squash into the sauce and couscous or quinoa.

Partridges with Sardines / Perdices Assadas con Sardinas

Take your partridges, well cleaned and plucked, put two salted sardines inside each one, make sure they do not stick out, rub the birds with good soft lard, or, if you have none, brush them with melted ham fat. Take tomatoes sin cutis:

blacken their skins on the fire's embers, or if you have no tomatoes, you can use lime or bitter orange juice, a dusting of pepper, salt and a little parsley. Now roast the birds in a pot, sitting in embers and with more in the lid, and, when they are done, pull out the sardines. Then serve the partridges, which will keep the salty smack of sardines' flavour. Indeed, some may prefer sardines to partridges and either way you will end up with plenty of stuffed bellies.

When I discovered Emilia Pardo Bazán (see p. 172) had given a recipe for this dish, I was fascinated to see if it would work. So I stuffed the birds with salted anchovies rather than sardines, squashing them into the pot juices with the roasted tomatoes. When we sat down to eat, a little skeptical, we found the briny anchovies had merged with the fruity tomato and gamy roasting juices to give a gorgeously intense sauce. But one or two food writers have taken this dish instead as a nod to the Carnavalesque fleshy pleasures and the famous Lenten food fight from the *Book of Good Love*, a bawdy poem by a cleric, the Archpriest of Hita. His Lenten battle between meat and fish, ending Carnaval's sensual fun, opened with a salted sardine, a humble hero, knocking a partridge on the head.[6]

Mas vale en convento las sardinas saladas,
E fazer a Dios servicio con las dueñas onradas,
Que perder la mi alma con perdices assadas
E fincar escarnida con otras deserradas.

Salted convent sardines that serve God
And honest ladies are worth more to me
Than losing my soul to roast partridge
And scorn in the company of straying men.

Archpriest of Hita, *Book of Good Love*, 1330–1343

A FRIARY CHRISTMAS

For the friars, Christmas began with the pig-killing, followed by midnight mass on Christmas Eve. The church would blaze with candles while carol singing, cribs and tableaux, often with real animals, would help to make the nativity story real for the worshippers. Shepherds might come down from the countryside, leaving their flocks outside church, to dance in the aisles with a lamb in their arms. Some years Altamiras might roast a turkey for Christmas lunch, but if the harvest had failed and there was no grain to fatten farmyard birds, then he would cook more simply. For as shepherd Jorge Puyó Navarro later remembered of his childhood, in a bad year the poor celebrated with little more than "bread, wine and sardines roasted on the fire's embers or ashes."[7]

Roast Turkey with Cardoons and Lettuce / Pabo Assado con Verdura

Take a good fat turkey, pluck and clean it well, cut off the wing-tips and neck, pull its feet back towards the Pope's nose to make a nice neat shape, scald it then dress it this way. Put a little fried cured ham fat, boiled lettuce hearts and cardoon, pepper and salt in the turkey. Sit it comfortably in a spacious baking dish, bathe it well with melted soft lard, salt and pepper it and carry it out to the bread oven to roast. Be watchful, turn it once or twice as it roasts, and when you see it is done, sprinkle it with a dishful of good white wine, put your bird back in the oven and roast it till the flesh is tender. Take out the cardoon and lettuce, lay them in the roasting juices with one or two cured ham rashers and put your bird back in the oven. When you serve it dust it with cinnamon and you will see by then, the greens and turkey are as good as each other.

My studies of friary archives began at Nuestra Señora de Los Ángeles in Valencia where the friars invited me to have lunch with them on a cold wintry day. Afterwards, in the spacious kitchen off the dining room, I sat down for a long chat with the cook, Reyes (see p. 42), who chose two dishes to re-create for the book (see p. 41). This one makes an original Mediterranean Christmas lunch. If you have no cardoon, then celery stands in well.

1 medium turkey, weighing about 2.7–3.6 kg / 6–8 lb, 2 tbsp olive oil, 4 slices of streaky cured ham, 6 lettuce hearts, 300 g / 10 oz blanched cardoon (see p. 202) or celery stalks, a handful of hazelnuts, 1 bottle of good white wine

Put the turkey into a pot of salted cold water, simmer it for 25 minutes and leave it to cool in its broth. Dry the turkey and reserve the cooking broth. Warm your oven (200°C, 400°F, gas mark 6). Season the turkey, set it on a rack in a shallow-sided roasting dish or pan, rub it with olive oil, tie up the legs, lay the cured streaky ham slices over the top, and ladle over a little turkey broth. Roast for 20 minutes. Test with a skewer to see if the thick flesh inside the thigh is nearly done. If not, return the bird to the oven for another 10–15 minutes. Remove and carve the bird. Arrange the green vegetables and cured ham rashers around the turkey, pour over another 300 ml / 10 fl oz broth and oven-roast for 10 minutes. Blend the hazelnuts with the white wine, season, pour the mixture over the turkey and return it to the oven for a final 10 minutes. The turkey's skin should be golden brown, the sauce bubbling, the vegetables tender. A young red Rioja or Ribera del Duero wine, both made with the Tempranillo grape, or one of Cariñena's Garnachas, will go well with this.

THE HEN COOP

"And still the main hen-coops, in farms' and monks' hatcheries, are more in the power of men than women," wrote Gabriel Alonso de Herrera in *General Agriculture*, a sixteenth-century farming guide. Often coops were built in the friars' kitchen gardens; one stands in the center of the vegetable terraces at San Cristóbal.[8] February was the month to start hatching chicks, wrote Herrera; the first chickens might be killed in July. By the autumn they would have grown into dark-fleshed braising fowl and by mid-winter they would be fat boiling hens. Soon after that the annual cycle began again. Only the hens' smoothest white eggs were picked for hatching. Altamiras gave so many recipes for chicken that we can guess he had a plentiful supply: we know there were up to six dozen chickens at San Diego, in Zaragoza, so outnumbering the friars by nearly four to one.

Roast Chicken / Pollos Assados

Make sure your chickens are well plucked and cleaned. Trim off their wing-tips, necks and anything superfluous, chop up cured ham fat and put it inside the birds with pepper, salt, a little pounded parsley and tomatoes, which are good in this dish when they are in season. Take a fold of paper rubbed with soft lard, and wrap the birds separately, tying them up with a thread; and take note, the paper should be sprinkled with pepper, salt and parsley. Then roast your birds between embers and, as you shall see, they are very tasty.

The soft lard rubbed over this chicken gives it a beautifully crispy skin while the ripe tomatoes and cured ham fat give it sunny flavors. Warm the oven (200°C, 400°F, gas mark 6). Fork finely chopped parsley, salt, and pepper into a big dob of soft lard and rub it over the chicken, inside and out. Put a small handful of diced streaky jamón or pancetta and another one of ripe cherry tomatoes inside the bird, tie up its legs, and put it, lying on one side, on a rack in a roasting pan. Roast it on one side for 20 minutes, turn it on to the other side for the same time and finish it on its back, breast up, in the same way. You may need to lengthen these times for a large chicken. Carve and keep the bird warm while you scoop out the tomato and ham, pour off and defat the roasting juices, then mash the tomatoes and ham into them. Check the seasoning. Serve the juices hot in a jug with a big green salad to follow. Noodles or bakers' potatoes (see p. 237) go well with this.

Chicken with Liver and Wine Gravy / Pollos Guisados

Take cleaned and well-plucked chickens. Melt soft lard in your skillet and brown the birds in it or, if you have no lard, then use cured ham fat. Put the birds in the pot where you are going to cook them, and fry a little finely chopped onion in the fat left in the skillet; throw this over the chickens with spices, pepper, cloves and cinnamon, but do not add saffron, for adding it to a dark sauce is as wasteful as leaving a candle burning in daylight. Add a little salt and a measure of white wine and spices, put the pot over a gentle flame, sit a jug of water on top, seal the jug to the pot with flour and water dough and in this way none of the cooking vapours and goodness are lost. Let your chickens simmer for an hour, sear their livers on the fire and mash them with garlic to make a paste to stir into the stew's juices. Season, cover again, give the stew a little boil and then this gravy is even better than a hazelnut sauce.

Liver-thickened gravies like this one can be traced back to al-Andalus's medieval cookery treatises. Today they are most often found with lamb stews, or *calderetas*, though chicken livers' sweet richness is especially good, I think.[9] For a fat farmhouse chicken you need about half a bottle of good white wine, a finely chopped large onion, a heaped teaspoon of powdered cinnamon, a clove or two of garlic and seasoning. If the chicken does not come with its livers, you can usually buy them separately.

Warm the olive oil or ham fat in a large flameproof casserole, season and brown the chicken joints in it, take them out then sweat the onion in the casserole till soft. Return the chicken to the casserole, pour in white wine to cover, add the spices, press a folded sheet of oiled grease-proof paper down on the stew's surface (see p. 9), and clamp it down with the casserole lid. Simmer for about 40 minutes, opening up once in a while to check that all is going well. Sear the livers in a little olive oil, blend to a smooth paste with the garlic and a ladleful or two of cooking juices, stir into the stew, season to taste, and give it a final brief simmer. So much richness is well balanced by rice or mashed potatoes and a green salad to follow.

Chicken Liver Pepitoria / Pepitoria de Menudillos de Pollos

When you have chicken wing-tips, gizzards, livers and necks to cook, cut them up, wash them and let them drain. Melt cured ham fat in a cazuela, *fry the bits and pieces, put them in your cooking vessel, then fry fine-cut onion in the same fat, pound garlic cloves with peppercorns, salt, cloves, cinnamon and parsley and add them too. Make a hazelnut sauce as I have told you elsewhere, simmer it quickly, add a little sharp citrus juice, and pour it over the chicken. Now you have the notes for making another dish, delicious to some people.*

Altamiras's chicken *pepitoria* was a very different dish to the one we know today, cooked with skinned breast flesh. His was designed to use the bits and pieces, from necks to wingtips, that were left over after several birds were killed. For a balance of flavor and flesh I use half skinned chicken wings or breast, and half livers.[10] This is a rich dish, so good served with plain bread to mop up the juices.

2 tbsp olive oil, 30 g / 1 oz diced jamón or pancetta, 370 g / 12 oz chicken, either boned flesh or trimmed chicken wings, cut into small bits, 370 g / 12 oz trimmed and chopped chicken livers, 2 chopped onions

FOR THE HAZELNUT SAUCE: 250 ml / 8 fl oz chicken broth, 2.5 cm /1 inch of stick cinnamon, 6 cloves, 3 peppercorns, a dozen hazelnuts, a small piece of moistened bread pressed dry in your fist, 1–3 garlic cloves, lemon juice or vinegar to taste, 1 tbsp snipped flat-leaf parsley.

Serves 4–6 as a first course.

Make the sauce. Simmer the broth and spices for 20 minutes, drain and blend the infusion with the hazelnuts, garlic, lemon juice and seasoning to taste, and stir in the parsley. Warm the oil in a frying pan, brown the jamón, add the seasoned chicken bits, fry for about 10 minutes, till nearly done, and put them in a flameproof casserole. Sear the livers in the frying pan and add them to the casserole. Finally sweat the onion, adding extra oil if needed, scoop it into the casserole, pour the sauce over the chicken and simmer for just 5 minutes. Slightly caramelized or plummy New World wines go well with this rich dish.

Stuffed Poussins with Spiced Lamb Stuffing and Hazelnut Sauce / Pollos Rellenos

Chop meat as you would to stuff lettuces or make meatballs, cook it with spices, parsley and salt, bind it with raw eggs and stir it up very well. Cut off the chickens' wing-tips and necks, stuff the cavity, cross the birds' feet so your stuffing cannot spill out, then roast the birds in a clay or earthen casserole, adding a little fresh soft lard. If you want to serve them with a sauce then make a hazelnut picada, *thin it with broth and thicken it with eggs, as you have read elsewhere.*

Altamiras's fragrant spiced lamb stuffing and nut sauce are a lovely combination with roast chicken though I prefer to make this with poussins cut in half to reveal the stuffing. The nut sauce, which pops up frequently throughout the book, is perhaps a legacy from earlier Muslim cooking. "Then take almonds and peeled and pounded nuts, breadcrumbs and pepper and beat all this with six eggs," ran one thirteenth-century recipe for hen, capon, or goose in *Matters of the Table*. The author, Ibn Razīn al-Tuğībī, an Arab scholar, wrote his book nostalgically after going into exile in North Africa.

2–3 poussins, about 500–750 g / 1–1½ lb each, 2 tbsp olive oil

FOR THE STUFFING: 1 quantity of lamb meatball or stuffing mixture (see pp. 9, 74–75), cinnamon to taste.

FOR THE HAZELNUT SAUCE: ½ quantity hazelnut sauce made with 300 ml / 10 fl oz chicken broth (see pp. 105–6, 135).

Warm your oven (180°C, 350°F, gas mark 4). Season the poussins inside and out, stuff them, tie up the legs, and fasten the skin flap well with a couple of toothpicks. Warm the olive oil in a casserole, brown the poussins, cover the casserole tightly, put it in the oven, and pot-roast, turning the birds once or twice for half an hour. Meanwhile make the hazelnut sauce. Transfer the birds to a hot serving dish, cut them open with poultry scissors and serve the sauce in a heated jug with the poussins. Good with baked courgettes or marrow.

Poussins with Wine and Saffron / Pollos Lampreados

Put well-plucked and cleaned chickens in a pot. Cut cured ham fat into dice, melt them in a skillet, add fine-cut onion and spices, two pounded garlic cloves and a little white wine. Add all this to the chicken, let it cook for an hour, shake the pot from time to time, season your stew with salt and a little saffron for colour, and finish it off with sharp citrus juice, parsley and toasted flour.

The very first historical cook I knew, Cristine MacKie, wrote of the Caribbean's mosaic of food cultures taken there by cooks from different continents. When she read this recipe she immediately picked up on the toasted flour finish, a technique she recognized from the islands. It may have been taken there by Portuguese or Spanish settlers, who had arrived there in 1498, soon followed by friars.[11] Used this way the flour is much more than a thickening: it also lends toasted colors and flavors to the dish. Here is Cristine's modern interpretation of it.

30 g / 1 oz cured lard, 150 g / 6 oz finely chopped onion, 3 garlic cloves, 3 tbsp olive oil, 60 g / 2 oz unsalted butter, 30 g /1 oz diced cured jamón or pancetta, 2–4 trussed poussins, about 500–750 g / 1–1½ lb each, a handful of finely chopped flat-leaf parsley, 4 sprigs of thyme, 1 bottle of white wine, 1 tbsp flour, a saffron infusion made with 2 dozen threads (see p. 102), ¼ lemon

Sweat the diced cured lard in a heavy-based pan, taking care it does not scorch. Remove any burned fragments, add the onion and stir, cover and sweat till soft, adding the garlic towards the end. Warm the oil and butter in a flameproof casserole, throw in the diced cured ham or pancetta, then the seasoned poussins, browning them all over. Stir in the garlic and onions, the herbs and wine, lay the poussins on one side in the liquid and simmer for 10 minutes, then turn them on to the other side and cook for the same time again. Sprinkle the flour through a sieve into a non-stick frying pan, toast it to a rich chestnut brown, turn it into a cup, and whisk in a little of the poussin's cooking juices. Stir back into the casserole, cook for a final 5 minutes, and then squeeze over the juice of the lemon quarter. Place the poussin whole or halved on a hot dish and serve it with the sauce strained over the top. I like this served with a glass of lemony Albariño wine from Galicia.

DUCK

Quince and duck make a great autumnal marriage. Altamiras roasted wild duck, he tells us, but we know it was not by choice. Farmyard duck rearing had ended abruptly when the Moriscos were sent into exile, taking with them their skills as poultry farmers and the tradition was not revived by agricultural reformers till the end of the eighteenth century.[12] Meanwhile cooks fell back on wild duck, or *ánades*, catching them in river marshes and carrying them home in a bag to plump up in the farmyard.

Duck with Quince Sauce / Ánades con Membrillos

Serve roast wild duck with a quince sauce: skin quinces, halve them, cut them in thin slices. Then cut up cured ham fat in small dice, fry them till opaque and, when the fat runs, add fine-cut onion, then cook the quinces till they are soft, season them with spices and cinnamon, add a little wine, vinegar, sugar and broth from the stewpot. Roast your duck with cured ham fat, arrange them on toasted slices of bread and pour the sauce over them. This sauce is good for other plump birds too, say curlews or sandgrouse or tender hares, and if you like, you can dress a leg of mutton or cow with it.

If you make this with wild duck cook just the breasts and put the rest of the bird to good use in other ways. You can render down the skin to give a potful of fat to fry potatoes, boil up the carcass for broth, and braise the legs to make an Andalusian duck rice.

1–2 wild duck, each weighing about 1–1.5 kg / 2–3 lb, or 4–6 skinned whole or filleted duck breasts
FOR THE SAUCE: 200 ml / 7 fl oz white or red wine, 200 ml / 7 fl oz good chicken or ham stock, 1 tbsp honey, 1 tbsp white wine vinegar, a thumb's length of stick cinnamon, a few nutmeg shavings, 6 peppercorns, 2 tbsp good olive oil or melted cured ham fat, 1 chopped onion, 500 g / 1 lb fresh quince, peeled and thinly sliced, or two 150 g / 5 oz jars of preserved quince pieces, 1 lemon.
Makes 500 ml / ¾ pint sauce.
Check over your duck: pull out feather stubs, dig out shot fragments, wipe the skin clean, and rub it with plenty of salt. Warm your oven well in advance (200°C, 400°F, gas mark 6). Season the duck's cavity, prick its skin, sear it all over in a frying pan to sweat out excess fat, set it in a game rack or lie it breast-down on the rack of a roasting pan and roast for

35–40 minutes, turning half way through. Rest for 15 minutes and keep warm. To serve the duck, carve along the breastbone, down and around on each side to lift off the breasts, and cut off any tough skin (you can render this down later to give you a jar of duck fat).

Make the sauce while the duck is roasting. Simmer the wine, broth, honey, and wine vinegar with the spices for 15 minutes. In a frying pan sweat the onion in the olive oil or melted ham fat, add the sliced quince, cook for 15 minutes, stir in the spiced honeyed wine and broth. Simmer for another 15 minutes or till the quince is soft. Squeeze in lemon juice and seasoning to taste. You can blend or sieve this, but I prefer it pulpy. Serve the duck on hot plates with the warm sauce, fried bread triangles, and a good Ribera del Duero wine.

Duck for Wayfarers / Ánades para Caminantes

Duck are often tough and time can run short when you dress them for travellers. Cook them like this: pluck and draw them, singe them, for a little down is always left behind, and fasten them on the spit. Fry cured ham, pour the melted fat into a little clay or earthen dish and add pounded garlic cloves, salt, pepper and bitter lemon juice or verjuice. Brush this liquor over your duck with a handful of feathers, letting the birds roast slowly as the cooking liquor soaks into the skin. When you see that they are done warm a little pot of aguardiente *and sprinkle it over your birds, for however tough their flesh, it will make it tender, and so your dish is done, and in this way your travellers or pilgrims may move on quickly.*

Who were Altamiras's wayfarers? Perhaps they were pilgrims on their way to the shrine of the Virgen del Pilar in Zaragoza or in Calatorao, near La Almunia, where lepers and disabled people flocked in the hope of a miraculous cure. Often such travelers brought with them foods they foraged or bought on the road as gifts for the friary kitchen. I have adapted the recipe to duck breasts or fillets, skinned to make way for the ham fat in Altamiras's basting liquor.[13]

For 4–6 skinned duck breasts or fillets, about 370 g / 12 oz per person, you need 1 fat garlic clove, ½ tsp salt, juice of 1 lemon, 60 g / 2 oz cured lard, 3 tbsp grape spirit

Crush the garlic and salt in a mortar and stir in the lemon juice. Sweat the diced cured lard in a small non-stick pan, taking care it does not scorch, remove any burned fragments, and stir the fat into the seasoned lemon juice. Warm a large heavy frying pan. Brush the duck breasts with the basting liquor and sear them till they are rare on the inside. Meanwhile warm the grape spirit in a small pan and pour it over the duck. Take care as it may burst briefly into flames. Good served with shredded steamed white or green cabbage and Altamiras's minty mushroom stew (see p. 195).

THE FRIARY MELTING POT

Born in a valley where the food cultures of different faiths were equally valued, Altamiras saw the cooking of his valley belonging to one shared melting pot. So while earlier Iberian cookbook writers had titled this dish Morisco, he dropped the tag.[14] But through local lore and hearsay he would have known of the Moriscos' skills in herbal medicine, making ointments, cordials, potions, and spells for curing the sick.[15] That in turn had meant they were expert foragers with great depth of knowledge of medicinal wild ingredients: for example, fennel seeds, borage, asparagus root, mint, sorrel and, as here, bitter greens, characteristic of Morisco cooking.

Chicken or Hen with Sorrel or Wild Greens / Gallinas con acederas

Roast a hen and cut it up in quarters. Cut a little cured ham fat into very small dice, fry these in a big skillet till the fat melts, fry the quartered hen in it and add a fine-cut onion. Let your hen cook slowly, add broth, wine and vinegar, and if you have a little fresh soft lard, add it, and spices too. You may add chopped greens, and bitter greens of any kind, like sorrel, are very good in this, but do not add eggs, for this dish should be slightly sour.

Sorrel makes sauces murky green, but it gives this one a marvelous tang. Curiously Michel Guérard, the great French chef who came up with *nouvelle cuisine*, gave a similar modern recipe for chicken with wine vinegar and sorrel.

3 tbsp olive oil, 1 jointed chicken weighing about 1.5 kg / 3 lb, 1 chopped onion, 2 tbsp diced jamón or pancetta, 5 tbsp white wine vinegar, 250 ml / 8 fl oz mixed chicken broth and white wine, 4 tbsp white wine for the sauce, a large handful of wild or cultivated sorrel leaves or other foraged leaves

Warm the olive oil in a flameproof casserole, brown the seasoned chicken joints in it, add the onion and jamón and braise for 20 minutes. Spoon off all except a tablespoon of fat, add the white wine vinegar, and cook briefly, then add the broth. Check the seasoning, stir well, and cook for another 10–20 minutes, throwing in your well-washed bitter greens for the last few minutes of cooking time.

FOR A BOILING HEN: Cover the hen with salted cold water in a large pot, add bay leaves and an onion stuck with cloves, bring to a gentle simmer, and cook for about 1 hour. Cool in the cooking broth. Remove. Dry the hen well, joint and skin it, and continue as above.

STUFFED SQUAB

Once, at San Antonio de Padua, a convent in the small Basque town of Durango, I was invited behind the high walls enclosing the kitchen garden. Rows of weeded green beans, onions, and carrots ran down as far as the eye could see. There was a compost heap, too, but the pigeon house standing next to it was deserted. Sister María Ester, who was showing me around, explained it had been full of life till the 1960s: the squab had given valued meat and the birds' droppings gave fertilizer for the vegetable beds. Cheap chicken and chemical fertilizer, which arrived in the 1960s, changed that. Now a younger generation of farmers are turning back to rearing squab. Perhaps the old pigeon houses, like the one in Durango, which stand empty, the paint peeling away, will find new uses in the years to come.[16]

Roast Squab or Pigeonneaux with Spiced Meat Stuffing / Pichones, o pollos rellenos

To stuff and roast these, fry cured ham fat with onion, add hashed meat to the skillet, brown it well and stir in raw eggs till they are dry and scrambled. Turn all this onto a wooden board, chop it once more with some parsley, turn it into a clay or earthen casserole, add spices and bind it with raw eggs. Be sure your birds are well cleaned and trimmed of their necks and wing-tips: stuff them, lop off the Pope's nose, cross the birds' feet so the stuffing does not fall out and take a fold of paper rubbed with soft lard and dusted with salt and pepper, and wrap each one, then roast the birds close to the fire, in gentle heat, but not over the flames, turning them once in a while, and in an hour and a half they shall be done.

This is a lovely dish for fat-breasted squab or pigeonneaux. I like to pot-roast them and serve them cut in half to show the stuffing, with spiced couscous and a mellow red wine.

2 farmed squab or pigonneaux, each weighing about 500 g / 1lb, salt and pepper, a large dob of good quality lard, about ½ bottle of wine or equivalent of water

FOR THE STUFFING: 3 tbsp olive oil, 250 g / 8 oz chopped onion, 250 g / 8 oz finely minced lamb, veal, or pork (or a mix), 1 tsp freshly ground cinnamon, a handful of chopped flat-leaf parsley, 1 egg, a few soft breadcrumbs.

Warm the oven (170°C, 320°C, gas mark 3). Make the stuffing. Warm the olive oil in a large frying pan, sweat the onion, add the seasoned meat, squashing it with a fork to brown it, stir in the spices and parsley. Cool, then stir in the egg and breadcrumbs and check the seasoning. Spoon the stuffing into the squab, tie their legs with string, season the skins, and brown them in the lard in a heavy frying pan. Now lie them on one side in a large flameproof casserole, pour in the wine or water and pot-roast in the oven, covered with a lid, for 30–45 minutes, turning the birds to sit on their other side half way through and splashing in a little more liquid if you see them sticking.

Gilded Cinnamoned Chicken / Gallina Dorada

Take a well-fattened hen, cut off its feet, wing tips and neck, clean it well and boil it in your stewpot for meat. When it is tender, fasten it on the spit. Now wrap a little lump of cured ham fat in paper, spear it on the point of the spit, set fire to the paper and hold the spit upright so the melted fat drips down all over the hen. Crack open four eggs, beat their yolks, paint them on your hot hen and, as it roasts, add sugar and cinnamon, or just cinnamon. You may serve the broth first as a soup spiced with cinnamon and take it to table before your gilded hen. This is a good dish for capons or other birds too.

Some food writers have claimed that the so-called "gilded hens" found in medieval Spanish courtly cookbooks can be traced back to Santa María de Casbas, an Aragonese convent where blue-blooded nuns and their cooks—some of whom were Muslim and Morisco—won fame for their spit-roast hens brushed with an egg yolk, milk, cinnamon, flour, and sugar batter.[17] In fact such gilded hens were roasted right around Europe, but they did linger long in Spanish kitchens. Altamiras simplified the recipe, glazing the birds with cinnamon and egg, and I have done so again, but I have kept the fragrant cinnamon.

4–6 chicken thighs, 1 thumb's length of stick cinnamon
FOR THE GLAZE: 1 tbsp soft lard, 1 beaten egg yolk, 1 tsp crushed brown cane sugar.

Warm your oven (200°C, 400°F, gas mark 6). Whizz the cinnamon in a coffee or spice grinder to crack it. Place the chicken thighs on a large piece of extra-strong tinfoil, either non-stick or lightly oiled, press the cinnamon into both sides of the chicken. Enclose this parcel within a second sheet of tinfoil, the two tightly sealed, and oven-bake for 20 minutes. Meanwhile mix the soft lard, yolk, and cane sugar. Open up the chicken, pour off any roasting juices and reserve, brush one side of the joints with the glaze, put them back in a hot oven to crisp, then turn them over, and glaze the other side in the same way. This is good served with spiced rice moistened by the defatted roasting juices, Altamiras's spinach with raisins (see p. 192), and a flowery Garnacha or Chardonnay white wine.

Chicken or Rabbit Pies / Pasteles de Pollos, o Gazapos

Clean and cut up chickens or fat young rabbits, stew them gently with a little fried cured ham fat, onion, parsley, two shredded lettuces, four garlic cloves, spices and a little white wine. Make a pastry dough with warm water, salt and other ingredients in proportion to your flour, as I have said elsewhere: say, four ounces of soft lard and four eggs for four chickens. Knead your dough till it stretches, cut it into pieces and roll them out so each one is big enough to cover a cazuelita, or small pie dish. Pour a little of the cooking liquid over the chicken or rabbit in each dish, lay on your pastry lids and crimp your pies or make any other figures you like to decorate the middle of the pies. Then take these to bake in the bread oven. Half way through brush the top of the pies with feathers dipped in beaten egg and put them back in the oven. This is a good note for the thrifty: four chickens leave eight people happy.

Small straight-sided *cazuelitas* make great individual pie dishes. Altamiras's quantities at the end, half a chicken per person, suggest that even if his chickens were skinny, he dished up generous portions. The lettuce is good in this, but be sure you do not include any bitter outer leaves.

3 tbsp olive oil, 30 g / 2 oz diced jamón or pancetta, 370 g / 12 oz chicken or rabbit flesh, 200 g / 7 oz chopped onion, 1 tsp salt, 4 sliced garlic cloves, 300 ml / ½ pint white wine, 150 ml / 5 fl oz chicken or rabbit stock, peppercorns, cinnamon, a large handful of chopped flat-leaf parsley, 1 shredded lettuce, 370 g / 12 oz pastry (see p. 152), beaten egg yolks for glazing

Makes six 16 cm / 5½ in pies.

Preheat your oven (200°C, 400°F, gas mark 6). Warm the olive oil in a flameproof casserole, fry the jamón gently in it, add the seasoned rabbit or chicken, and fry till golden-brown. Scoop it out onto a plate. Now add the onion to the casserole and sweat it till soft and golden, add the garlic, sweat it briefly, put back in the chicken or rabbit pieces, cover tightly, and cook gently for 10 minutes. Pour over the white wine, stock, and spices, check the seasoning, and simmer everything for another 15 minutes, stirring in the parsley and lettuce a few minutes before the end of cooking time. Divide the pie filling between the dishes. Roll out the pastry, cut out circles large enough to cover the pie dishes, leaving an extra inch (2.5 cm) all around to fold under, and make a thick crimped or pinched rim. Bake the pies for 20–25 minutes, brushing them with beaten egg yolk 10 minutes before the end of baking time. I like this following a first-course of turnip cubes and chard (see pp. 199 and 189).

Drunk Poussins / Pollas de Leche en Abreviatura

Take well-fattened milk-fed chickens, pluck and clean them and cut them into quarters. In your skillet sweat diced lean and fat cured ham and, as the fat melts, fry the chickens in it. Measure two soup bowls of white wine for every four birds, charge it well with cinnamon, pour it over the chickens and let them simmer briefly. You may serve the broth as a soup before the chicken and this is good for guests whose travels call them to move on briskly.

Milk-fed chickens, wrote Alonso de Herrera in his *General Agriculture*, were a tender luxury "for high-born gentlemen." Altamiras seems to have taken them for granted, perhaps because the friars received them in payment for preaching or hearing confession or in thanks for attending the sick.[18] Poussins or coquelets stand in well here.

4–6 poussins, 1 tbsp olive oil, 60 g / 2 oz diced jamón or pancetta, 175 ml / 6 fl oz white wine, and a thumb's-length of stick cinnamon

Warm the olive oil in a large casserole. Season the poussins and tie up the legs. Sweat the jamón or pancetta in the oil, add the poussins and brown them, pour over the wine, and throw in the cinnamon. Simmer gently for about 25 minutes on the stove or in the oven, check the seasoning, and serve with rice.

Saffroned Roast Chicken / Pollas y Capones Assados

When you have plucked, cleaned and jointed your capons or pullets as I have told you, make holes in the bird's skin near the Pope's nose where you can tuck in the capon's legs, for which you must crack the legs at the joints. Then roast the birds in a clay or earthen casserole with a little good soft lard. This keeps sweet and fresh right around the year if you add clear water to it every twelve days, or, better still, refresh the water every eight days so the lard will not turn rancid. Such lard is good for dressing roast poultry and meat and you can flavour it with parsley, two cloves of crushed garlic, a dusting of pepper, salt and saffron. If you are roasting capons, remember they may be tough, so simmer them first in the stewpot and have ready a little well-dressed gigote *to serve with them. Serve them beak up, and add a spoonful of* gigote *to each plate.*

Garlicky saffroned soft lard gives a wonderfully golden crisp skin and flavor to a roast capon, pullet, or farmhouse chicken. Capons are still popular for Christmas in northern Spain although a large chicken stands in well.[19] Lard the bird well before roasting so the flavors rubbed inside have a chance to penetrate the flesh.

1.5 kg / 3 lb free-range chicken (or pullet or capon), 3 heaped tbsp best quality soft lard

FOR THE SEASONED LARD: 3 cloves of garlic pounded or blended with a small handful of snipped flat-leaf parsley, 2 dozen threads of saffron.

Tie up the chicken's legs. Pound all the lard seasonings—the garlic cloves, saffron, parsley, plus seasoning—to a paste, fork them into the soft lard, and rub it over the chicken, inside and out, then put the bird in a large, shallow-sided earthenware or clay pot or roasting dish and leave it in a cool place for the flavors to penetrate. Warm the oven (200°C, 400°F, gas mark 6) and roast the chicken, starting it lying on one side,

SAFFRON

"Season your stew with salt and a little saffron for colour. . . ." For Altamiras saffron was a local crop: it was given to the friars as alms. Place-names still mark many of the scattered patches where it grew, like El Zafrana, a small square of dry, poor lowlands on the plains outside La Almunia.[1] As Aragonese growing has waned, despite the saffron's extraordinary quality, it has become more difficult to find. La Mancha's is a good replacement for flavor and color in Altamiras's broths, sauces, rices, and soft lard although Aragonese organic saffron is the more fragrant. For the best taste and color, add it to simmering liquid 10 minutes before the end of cooking time, avoiding a heavy boil. Locally, it is used as an infusion: pour just-off-the-boil water, stock, or wine on to saffron threads and leave the color and flavor to deepen for up to 48 hours, then add the liquid to your dish before cooking finishes.

NOTE

1. Aragonese saffron-growing: Asso, *Historia*, 78, 93–94, 113. Saffron as alms: Encarna Jarque Martínez, "Los Franciscanos, Las Clarisas y El Pueblo de Cariñena," in *Tierra de Conventos: Santa Catalina y San Cristóbal de Cariñena (siglos XV–XIX),* ed. Encarna Jarque Martínez (Institución Fernando el Católico, Zaragoza, 2010), 166. Today saffron is still grown commercially at Monreal del Campo.

and turning it onto the other side after 20 minutes, then finally sitting it on its back. When it is done, remove it to keep warm, defat the roasting juices, splash a little water or wine into the dish to dissolve the roasting crusts, simmer to dissolve, and pour the juices into a hot jug to pass with the chicken. This is good with a mellow red wine like a Valdepeñas.

Little Chicken Dumplings / Almondiguillas de Ave

Take the breast flesh of well-fattened birds, boil up the rest of their carcases for broth. Pound the breast flesh well, and the ovary fat of a good fresh hen in the same way. Have ready the crumb of a white loaf soaked in water and squeezed dry, mix it with two egg yolks and the flesh, hash it all again, put it in a dish, adding two raw eggs, and season with salt and cinnamon. Have ready the cooking broth, boiled without any vegetables and strained, put it in a clay or earthenware casserole, then make little dumplings no bigger than the top of your thumb, throw them into the broth, simmer them for three-quarters of an hour and add a little lime juice or verjuice. These are for the infirm; they should have no sauce with them.

Altamiras enriched his dumplings for the sick with hens' ovary fat, or *enjundia*, believed to have medicinal powers. Today, long after that belief died away, *enjundia* remains a compliment for the deep nourishing spirit to be found in great writing, painting, or music. The dumplings are delicious simple food, good served in their strained broth or dry with olive oil, grated cheese, and pepper.[20]

½ chicken breast (about 325 g / 11 oz), 90 g / 3 oz fresh breadcrumbs, 2 egg yolks, 1 tsp powdered cinnamon

TO COOK: 750 ml / 1¼ pints chicken broth (see p. 234), a squeeze of lemon or lime juice.

Makes about 24 dumplings.

Put all the dumpling ingredients in a food processor, blend, and season to taste. Oil your hands, or two teaspoons, and shape the dough into dumplings about the size of a golf ball. Bring the seasoned broth to the boil in a large pan, squeeze in the lime juice, lower in the dumplings with tongs or a slotted spoon, and poach them for 15 minutes. Cut open one of the dumplings to check they are cooked through. Strain the broth and sit the pan off the heat with the dumplings keeping warm in it.

CARTERS AND MULETEERS

Spain's mule caravans crept slowly along the roads like "a train of camels in the desert," wrote Washington Irving in his *Tales of the Alhambra*, a book which explored the romance of everyday Spanish life for travelers.[21] Alongside the heavily laden mules rumbled ox-drawn carts stacked high with loads of rope, wineskins, timber, dried fish, and barrels of wine or grape spirit. The carters, or *carreteros*, were famed for their bravery: at night, after cooking a roadside supper, they would sleep on top of their loads to protect them. Sometimes they gave the friars lifts on short or long journeys. Of them Cervantes wrote, "their music is in their mortar, their sauce is hunger."[22] Altamiras did not hesitate to learn from them.

Carters' Chicken with Poor Men's Sauce / Pollos de Carretero con Salsa de Pobres

This is a swift and tasty way for chickens. Fry quartered, well-plucked and cleaned chickens in melted cured ham fat or olive oil. Boil water with salt in a puchero, *crush garlic with pounded peppercorns, verjuice and saffron, swill them into the boiling water and thicken it with a handful of bread-crumbs. Lay your fried chickens in a dish, pour the sauce over them, give them a little simmer and shake the dish so the chicken does not stick. When time is short this is very good, for the sauce rounds out the chicken, makes it tender and tasty, and it is ready to eat from the dish in half an hour.*

This peppery sauce, tinted yellow by saffron and given bite by verjuice, is mentioned by many travelers well into the twentieth century. If you make it with saffron and green or red peppercorns, to soften the bite, you will come up with a surprisingly modern dish.

3 tbsp olive oil, 6 skinned chicken thighs, 3 fat garlic cloves, about 2 tsp peppercorns, 250 ml / 8 fl oz hot water, a handful of fresh bread-crumbs, a few drops of sherry vinegar or lemon juice to taste, a saffron infusion made with 3 dozen threads (see p. 102)

Warm the olive oil in a wide-bottomed flameproof casserole in which the chicken fits in one layer. Brown the seasoned chicken in the olive oil. Pound the garlic and peppercorns, stir in the measured hot water, add the breadcrumbs, vinegar or lemon juice—or verjuice if you can find it, and season to taste. Simmer for 5 minutes, press through a sieve with a wooden spoon over the chicken and cook for 15 minutes, stirring in the saffron infusion towards the end of cooking time. This dish is best made a day ahead and left to sit to allow the flavors to develop. It is good served with ribbon pasta and a tomato and onion salad.

COOKING FOR THE SICK

Medicinal thinking shaped much of Altamiras's cookery. He skimmed fat off his meat broths. He made dumplings without touching them by hand. He blanched beans and home-grown greens to kill bugs and bacteria. But his received medicinal thinking was very different to our own; his were derived from ancient Christian and Muslim beliefs that a balance of the body's four humors—earth, air, fire, and water—was the basis of health. From this came the idea that certain foods—for example, frogs, lungs, green almonds, and candied eggs—were medicinal.[23] Sometimes, though, the theory of the humours led him to foods that are familiar today. For instance, a good hen or chicken soup was considered one of the best possible foods to balance the humors. As one Spanish proverb put it, "*Olla con gallina, la mejor medicina.*" A hen in the pot, the best medicine we've got.

Chicken or Hen Essence for the Infirm / Sustancia para Enfermos

Sick people often eat little so their food needs to give them lots of nourishment. To make a dish of essence for them take a quarter of a good hen, a dozen chickpeas and a knuckle of lamb. Boil these up well together. Pick off the hen's flesh and pound it in your metal mortar. Have ready bread soaked in broth and squeezed dry, pound it with the meats and add this back into your broth. Strain everything through a clean cloth into a small pot, warm it on the fire and season it with salt and a little saffron. Serve this to the Sick, stirring it up with a little spoon, for even when you strain it, the flesh may settle, and remember broths and essences may spoil, especially on hot Summer days, when they need to be freshly made, so then make half the quantities twice over. If you wish to add fresh egg yolks, boil them slightly, beat them in a dish then stir them into the broth.

You need little saffron to tint chicken broth primrose yellow. Altamiras probably added it for medicinal reasons, but a cup of hot clear broth, refreshingly thin, pale yellow and with a sprig of mint floating in it, makes luxurious everyday eating. In summer you can also chill a good broth and serve it jellied to eat with a teaspoon.

½ chicken (or boiling fowl if available), 1 knuckle of lamb or 600 g / 1¼ lb lamb flank, 24 soaked dried chickpeas, 2.5 liters / 5 pints water, salt, 30 g / 1 oz fresh breadcrumbs (optional), a saffron infusion made with 2 dozen threads (see p. 102)
Makes about 2 l / 3½ pints clear soup or 2.8 l / 5 pints thickened soup.
Put the chicken, lamb, chickpeas, and water in a large pot, add salt to taste, cover, and simmer for 2½ hours. Cool, defat, and strain, reserving

all the flavoring ingredients, and pick the chicken and lamb flesh off the bones. You can blend the chicken and lamb flesh, broth-soaked breadcrumbs, and chickpeas back into the soup, together with the saffron infusion, or you can serve it thin with mint and a lemon wedge and reserve the meat for making croquettes. Serve hot or chilled.

SANTO ESPÍRITU DE GILET CHICKEN SOUP: Fray Ángel flavors his chicken broth with baby turnips, leeks, celery, onion, tomatoes, and apples (no garlic), then purées them all into the soup, except for the pungent turnips. Finally, he says, he "always, always" adds plenty of chopped mint. I like to make a large panful of this soup in winter and keep it in the fridge as quick food heated through in a few minutes.

Roast Mutton with Cloves / Una Pierna de Carne Asada

Take a good leg of mutton, give it blows with the back of your cleaver and cut off its hoof. Make ready a fold of paper, bathe it with melted soft lard, sprinkle it with salt and dust it with pepper. Spike your meat with half a dozen cloves, make knife stabs deep into the meat and pour in green lemon, lime or bitter orange juice. Then wrap your leg in paper, fasten it on the spit and let it roast slowly. This is a very good dish, and some people will think you have poached the meat rather than roasting it.

This recipe is the only one Altamiras gives for a big spit-roast meat joint.[24] Firewood's expense, meat's toughness, and the laboriousness of turning the spit by hand meant that only small cuts of meat and birds, often game, were spit-roasted in everyday kitchens. This modern version, using wrapped roasting, like the original, comes from Ivan Baker, an expert in cooking over fire and hot coals. He made it with shoulder of lamb; most of the preparation time goes into stripping out the fat. "This requires patience and concentration," Ivan wrote to me. "Do not hurry it as it is almost all the preparation you need. Use a sharp pointed blade to get right in between the layers of muscle." Today the fat can be as much as a quarter of the meat, even a third. Keep going: the end effect, juicy and lean and fragrant, is worth it.

1 leg or shoulder of lamb or hogget or roasting mutton, with the fat removed (see above), 3 cloves of garlic, skinned and quartered lengthways, 3 tbsp of thick honey, 12 cloves, ½ tsp salt, 1 glass of red wine, lemon or lime juice (optional)

Remove all the lamb's or mutton's fat, as described above. Try to hold the meat together, but if it separates into two or three bits, reassemble them in their natural shape. Warm a hot oven (220°C, 425°F, gas mark 7). Cut two pieces of extra-strong foil, ideally non-stick, one large enough to encircle the joint and the second bigger, to make a complete sealed envelope. Lay the larger piece of foil, then the smaller one on top of it, in a large roasting tin. Set the lamb on it. Make incisions in the meat with a sharp knife point, insert the garlic and cloves in them, sprinkle the lamb with salt and rub it all over with honey. Pour over the red wine. Now seal up the foil packets, leaving space around the top of the lamb. Be very careful not to puncture the foil.

Roast the lamb in the middle of the oven for 20 minutes, reduce the heat (190°C, 375°F, gas mark 5), and keep roasting till tender, allowing about 30 minutes for each half kilo, plus an extra 30 minutes, depending on your taste and the age of the lamb or mutton. Rest for 15–20 minutes before pulling out the cloves and carving. The result should be very succulent meat with a cup or two of rich juices. Squeeze the lemon or lime juice into it if you like and check you have pulled out the cloves. Ivan serves this with creamy mashed potatoes. I have also tried it with hot curly endive (see p. 205), a juicy and garlicky accompaniment.

THE PIG-KILLING

"There are so many ways, and things, and particularities to tell of pigs and their marinades, that one would never finish if one wrote of them all . . . there is no other animal from which so many delicacies may be made."

Gabriel Alonso de Herrera, *General Agriculture,* 1513[25]

The pig-killing, or *matanza*, was a challenge for any friary cook. Altamiras went into buying the spices, washing the pigs' guts, making sausages, and rendering soft lard, all traditionally women's work, in great detail, but he dealt with more familiar men's work, like butchering and salting, in just a sentence or two.[26] Some festive details he left out altogether: barbecuing the pig's tail, drying the bladder for a drumskin, and stewing the pig's liver for a celebratory supper at the end of the day. He would have enjoyed these as treats at childhood family pig-killings; but those happy memories would have brought with them darker ones. After the great flood of 1731 swept all before it, including the town's livestock— its horses, mules, goats, hens, chickens, pigeons and, of course, pigs— Altamiras's family must have lost their livelihood, their stocks of olive oil and wine, and maybe even their home. Perhaps that is why they seem to have been among those who "went to other places," as La Almunia's parish priest put it. They simply disappear from the parish records. Altamiras left soon afterwards too. His life and cooking were to become caught up in Zaragoza's cosmopolitan cross-currents. New ideas from the wider world were to season his dishes, his repertoire grew as he cooked daily for students and guests, and finally, some ten years later, with his reputation well established, he was able to write and publish his kitchen notebook.

How to Dress a Pig, from the Killing to Hanging the Hams and Sausages: Of Special Use for Nuns / Modo de Componer un Lechón Desde que se Deguella, hasta Colgarse: Servirá en Especial para Religiosas

First, you must know all the provisions you need, in particular the spices and flavourings: six strings of onions, half a pound of pepper, four ounces of cinnamon, one and a half of cloves, one and a half pounds of hazelnuts, one of pine kernels, another of anise seed, two handfuls of oregano for aromatising the water to wash your sausage skins, a little thyme, fennel and a dozen bitter oranges. Rub salt, cinnamon and cloves through a flour sieve together with some salt.

Put an eight-gallon cauldron of water on the fire to boil so you have plenty ready following the pig-killing. Choose a large earthenware bowl, throw in a handful of salt ready to catch the pig's blood as it spurts out, and, as it does, stir all the time without a pause, so it may not congeal. Cut out the pig's veins, lay them on a linen cloth and have ready a big basket lined with a thick wool cloth on which to lay the washed guts. Be sure you have string to hand for tying up the blood puddings and longaniza *sausages, and have ready a second basket lined with cloth on which you can lie the fat for the blood puddings. Wash the warm guts in tepid water, refreshing it till it runs clear, and add a little flour to the last bowlful before you leave the guts to steep in water aromatised with oregano. Then have ready two big pots: one for the guts for the blood puddings and the other for the sausages. Leave them to steep and add hot water to keep the skins soft, especially just before you are going to stuff them.*

Black Pudding with Onion / Morcillas de Cebolla

Prepare the onions for black pudding the day before your pig-killing: skin them, trim them, boil them in water with salt, chop and drain them on a wooden board. Then take a very clean linen bag, put the onion inside and leave it hanging in the cool night air.

The blood puddings should be made as soon as the pig is killed: chop up the fat and offal for them, make very small pieces, place them in a large clay or earthen casserole, add the onion, salt, half or a little less of the peppercorns, cinnamon and cloves, all the pine kernels, soaked and dried, half the cleaned and toasted anise seed, and all the skinned and toasted hazelnuts. Then pour over the pig's blood, stirring everything so it may not turn rancid. Fry a little of this pudding, check it for spices and salt and, when it is well seasoned, stuff the guts with it and leave the puddings floating in water so they do not burst, adding them to your cauldron filled with lukewarm water. When they are all ready put them in to simmer, well spaced, skimming off the foam with great care, and prick them with a needle stuck into a fennel stalk so they do not burst. When you see they are cooked, lift them out of the water by the threads that tie them, lay them on a cloth you have laid out on the table, and dry them gently with another cloth. Strain and keep the fat which runs out of the puddings for it is good for making crackling bread and frying breadcrumbs.

Longaniza Sausages / Longanizas

To make longaniza, *chop the pig's flesh finely on a well-washed board. Warm a pan of white wine with some anise seed in it, give it a little simmer, cover it close so it does not lose its vapours, add your remaining spices and salt. Stir your chopped meat into this marinade, taste it for seasoning and keep it hot on the fire. Wash your funnels for stuffing sausages before you make your* longanizas *and take care they are not too long. Tie them up, spread them on a table, pat them dry with a cloth and, if the weather is damp, hang them to dry in a good draught. Leave them to cure like this.*

Offal Sausages / Salchichas, o Longaniza Basta

These are made with the lungs, tongue, heart, kidneys, and scraps you gather up from the slaughter-table. Chop them finely and add pepper and salt. Tie them up like blood puddings, but you need not boil them for they cure as they hang.

Lard / Derretido

Cut up the pig's fat and jowls into little bits and put them in a copper pan, skillet or a clay or earthen casserole. Pour a couple of dishfuls of water over them so the fat does not burn as you render it. As the water warms and the fat melts, pour it off the top, straining it into your lard basin, throw a quartered pippin into the basin and take it to a cool place where it may last well all year round. If you refresh this water every eight days, your lard shall stay as good as the day it was made. This melted lard we call derretido.

How to Salt Cuts / Salar las Piezas

Rub fine salt into the pig's joints and other cuts, especially the trotters, pack the hooves well with salt, and stack them, one leaning against the other, so the liquid runs off and drains away. Remember, flitches need lighter salting. After eight days have passed you may hang your cuts and joints for curing.

Scratchings Sweetbread / Chicharrones del Derretido

Make sweetbread with your scratchings. Break them into little bits in a clay or earthenware dish, knead them into your bread dough, shape it into small flat loaves, and lay them on wafers for baking. Sprinkle these with sugar and cinnamon and they are splendid brushed with egg yolk. Carry these out to the bread oven to bake, watching they do not burn.

Let me add here, of course, that if your pig is very large, then judge your other ingredients by eye, using as much of each as you see fit.

BOOK TWO

LEAN DAYS
AND FASTING

THE FRIARS' SPRING

THE HILLSIDE friary of San Cristóbal grew around a mountain spring, which still bubbles up in a pool of pure cold water in a sheltered cave. The spring never runs dry and it feeds a smaller water tap further down the hill, close to the ruined friary kitchen. Altamiras would have come here early in the day to draw water to soak salt cod, to cook beans, and wash kitchen-garden produce.

More often than not the cooking water was for meatless food.[1] The friars respected three winter Lents: first Advent, then a voluntary "blessed" Lent after Epiphany, and finally the Lent we know before Easter. During these three months of *ayuno*, or fasting, there was just one meal a day, a lunch of fish, vegetables, pulses, grains, and fruit. The sick might also eat eggs. Breakfast was liquid, perhaps a soup or cream, and supper was a vegetarian snack called a collation. The rest of the year there were three days of meatless eating or lean days a week and, besides that, the friars never ate meat for supper and they enjoyed celebratory meatless dishes for the eves of certain fiestas. It was a tall order, even for the most experienced cook.[2]

To these meatless dishes, the most original of his book's recipes, Altamiras dedicated the second half of his book. He came up with a varied repertoire by pulling together shepherds' and market gardeners' cookery, confectioners' and guilds' sweet things, monastic dishes and, we may guess, the food he ate in childhood. There are fewer reworked cookery book recipes here and more notes from everyday life, even a romantic daydream.

One thing is clear. Altamiras had no time for lean-day luxuries. Turtle broth, crayfish, seagulls, otters, and river shrimp didn't find the space in his repertoire they did in other religious cookbooks.[3] Nor do we find hot drinking chocolate, served at the royal Jeronimo monastery, San Lorenzo de El Escorial, near Madrid, where the monks had a resident chocolate maker who delivered foaming cupfuls to the monks' cells every morning.[4]

Instead he shaped a repertoire of simple eating. "Beautiful delicacies should not be served, only those which allow us to maintain ourselves," was how mystic writer Juan de Pineda had defined the style.[5]

But this did not mean the friars could not eat well.[6] Quite the opposite. For an experimental cook like Altamiras, meatless cookery was a chance to come up with "new art" learned outside cookbooks, from other friars, carters, tavern, or home cooks. We find a mix of friary and feast-day classics, new dishes for ingredients from far afield and lots of local country cooking, probably shared by word-of-mouth or observed in others' kitchens. In this half of the book, one newly published recipe follows another.

At first glance the food here is simple: salt cod with tomatoes, chickpea pottage, stuffed onions, fried turnips, green beans, garlic mayonnaise, dishes unflavored by expensive spices, but given subtle or bright tastes by local saffron, aromatized oils, onion *sofrito,* and fried tomato. Wine flowed generously in his dishes.[7] "Drinking temperately is good for man," friary philosopher Francesc Eiximenis had written. "It makes him happy." Olive oil, which replaced meat fats and butter, flowed, too.[8] Bread accompanied meals and fruit ended them, except on feast days, when rice pudding or another home-made sweet might be served.[9] Glancing through this repertoire, we can glimpse all the main elements of what we now call the Mediterranean diet, which was shaped not only by the produce at hand, but also by the religious year, the friars' ideas about healthy eating, and popular cooking techniques.

This second meatless half of the book opens humbly with salt cod then follows on with the finest fish—eel, sturgeon, sea-bass, and tuna—before turning to trout, other river-fish, frogs, and snails. Most of these Altamiras matched with fresh flavors like citrus and kitchen-garden greenery. On to his fish chapter, the longest in the book, Altamiras tacked eggs, which he cooked in everything from tortillas, models for later potato ones, to a sweet foam.

Next came a short chapter comprised of lean-day soups, sweet things for feast days, and vegetarian suppers, then his final long chapter on the friars' vegetable dishes or *yerbas*. Here, more than anywhere, he seemed to draw on the produce of his home valley. How hard Altamiras worked to make it taste good! Yet even he sighed about boiled borage and carrots. He closed with the most everyday food, chickpeas and beans, which are still convent and friary specialities, a delicious festive almond milk blanc-mange and spiced or herby table olives.

A gifted storyteller, Altamiras ended on a high note. He knew his slushy sweet iced drinks were winners and he used them to open a short final chapter. How he must have chuckled as he stirred his tangy lemonade.[10] For in the hot summer months, while royal cooks sweated over roasting spits in palace kitchens, he churned heavenly chilled drinks in his icebox to serve to his fellow friars on their breezy hillside.[11]

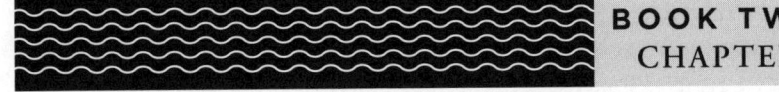

CHAPTER I

ON SALT COD

ALTAMIRAS WAS a skilled fish cook. He knew how to deal with eel, sturgeon, and salmon, the finest river fish served on the tables of the wealthy. But he chose to open the second half of his book with salt cod. Realism came before refinement. Salt cod cost a fraction of the price of other fish,[1] it was a good traveler, ideal for land-locked kitchens, and friary cooks served it so often they needed recipes to ring the changes.

Clearly, though, he also liked salt cod. Perhaps it was its briny smack evoking distant oceans, or the alchemy of restoring it from desiccated to fleshy form, or the freedom of devising dishes without the need to follow a rulebook.

For Altamiras was the first cookery writer in Spain to publish recipes for salt cod.[2] They are a small group (see also pp. 163 and 176), just over a dozen, but they sketch out the flavors and techniques around which a huge repertoire would grow. He matched his salt cod or *abadejo*[3] with tomato, onion, honey, and parsley. His combinations were to have a remarkable resonance. Take just one, his chickpea *potaje* with salt cod heads, garlic, and greens (see p. 209). Today it is one of Spain's best loved Lenten dishes, but Altamiras still has something new to teach us about bringing on the flavor by adding the salt cod unsoaked.

Salt cod's very success in the hands of popular cooks was to change its place in the Spanish kitchen. "At this point you may think it is of little substance," wrote Altamiras. As late as the 1920s Dionisio Pérez could still write of "merciful salt cod . . . on the table of the poor."[4] But in the following decades, as the early salt cod, dry as cardboard, was ousted by flexible, partially dried salt cod, it escalated to gourmet prices. Now it lands on our plate at around the same cost as wild salmon or eel.

How, then, can we make the most of Altamiras's salt cod recipes? He probably cooked lightly cured golden salt cod, quick to soak and good eaten raw, but hard to find outside eastern Mediterranean Spain.[5] But there are alternatives. Caribbean saltfish is good in dumplings, omelettes, and chickpea stews; fresh or home-salted cod[6] work well in most other dishes (see p. 238); and a few deserve thick fillets of the best delicatessen *bacalao*. Alternatively, you can cook these recipes with other fresh fish, as Altamiras would have loved to do himself. In other words, improvization still carries the day. For details of soaking salt cod see p. 238.

FRUGALITY: THE ANGEL'S COOKING

Sometimes the friars swopped simple for frugal food. Altamiras chose to open the second half of this book with such cookery, perhaps to show-case how poor food could "outdo in taste and delicacy the exquisite things and tasty sauces of kings' and princes' tables," as it did when the angels cooked.[7] Earthly cooks, though, needed the right recipes to do that. Altamiras gave four of them here.

Baked Salt Cod and Breadcrumb Pie / Abadejo

Since it is my hope to teach you everything you need to know, I thought I would open with salt cod. At this point you may think it is of little substance so here, then, is an artful way to make it tasty. Cut up the fish, wash it well, lay it out in a glass dish till it is full, scatter over skinned garlic, breadcrumbs and abundant parsley, lay more salt cod on top and, when you have fitted it all in the dish, pour over fresh olive oil, water to cover, and add a little salt. Then put your dressed cod to cook over a slow fire, covering it tightly so the fish drinks up the broth. Serve this with just a little of the cooking liquor.

This recipe evolved into gourmet eating like so many other Spanish classics that began life as frugal food—paella, for example.[8] A tavern cook from Cádiz, Carmen Sanchez, revamped this dish in the 1880s, sealing in the salt cod's moisture with an outer crust of crisp dried crumbs. Writer Benito Pérez Galdos ate her succulent version and passed on the recipe to Ángel Muro, who put it in print. I have adapted

Carmen's idea to small crumb pies, which cook quickly, evenly, and are easy to serve.

4–6 servings of soaked salt cod fillet (dry weight each about 150 g / 5 oz) or fresh cod, about 2 tbsp olive oil

FOR THE CRUST: 30 g / 1 oz coarsely grated fresh breadcrumbs, 1 very finely chopped garlic clove, about 2 tbsp finely snipped parsley for each portion of fish.

Warm the olive oil in a heavy-based non-stick frying pan. Pat the salt cod fillets dry with kitchen paper and put them to cook skin down in the pan, without turning them, until the skin lifts off easily. This should take no more than 2 minutes. Remove the fish from the pan, cool, and lift off the skins. Heat a moderately hot oven (190°C, 375°F, gas mark 5) to toast the breadcrumbs with the garlic, a teaspoon or two of the parsley, and a pinch of salt for 10 minutes. Cool. Brush the skinned fillets with olive oil on both sides and put them, well spaced, on a low-sided, preferably non-stick roasting or baking sheet. Scatter over the parsley, quite thickly, then the toasted breadcrumbs, press these into the sides of the fillets and roast quickly for 7–10 minutes, depending on the fish's thickness, checking with a knife-point to see that the center is done. I like this served with tomato vinaigrette, a green salad, and a bottle of chilled *fino* sherry.

Salt Cod with Lime / Abadejo Ordinario

Temper your salt cod. Put the salt cod in water, bring it to the boil, drain the pieces on a wooden board, bathe them in olive oil, lay them in a dish and add parsley, seasoned water, fried onions, a handful of flour, spices and a little sharp citrus juice. Then give your seasoned fish a little boil, adding salt. And take note of the following: when I call for sharp citrus juice, I mean lime or bitter orange and, if you have neither of these, then vinegar or verjuice will do, but remember, nothing sour is good in a dish with cheese or milk in it.

One of the best ways to cook old-fashioned dried salt cod on the bone is to poach it on the top of the stove. The timing is easy to judge and the salt cod turns out beautifully moist, without any fat, making it very good with sauces or these lemony fried onions.

4 tbsp olive oil, 2 large onions thinly sliced into rings, small pinches of pounded cinnamon and cloves, about 1 tbsp lemon juice, 1 heaped

tbsp finely snipped flat-leaf parsley, 4–6 servings of soaked salt cod, dry weight each 150 g / 5 oz

Warm the olive oil in a frying pan, sweat the thinly sliced onion rings in it, covered, till floppy but not caramelized. Pour off any surplus oil, season and spice the onions, splash in lemon juice to taste, and throw in the parsley. Leave to sit while you poach the salt cod on the bone in salted simmering water for about 7–10 minutes—the timing will depend on the thickness of the salt cod pieces. Drain well and serve with the lemony onion spooned over the top. Good following Altamiras's spinach dish (see p. 192).

SOFRITO

When Altamiras explained how to make onion *sofrito* he gave a very brief method, but he went straight to the point on technique: first he sweated the onion in olive oil, then he added water to finish the cooking by poaching. In the Catalan style he also suggested adding flavorings, tomato, and parsley, which bring a lovely fresh edge to the sweet onion although in other dishes sweet white wine, like Moscatel, soaked raisins, dried thyme, oregano, and bay leaves work well too. This is best made one day to eat the next. Today it is a key element in many dishes.

Salt Cod and Onion Sofrito / Abadejo de Otro Modo

Temper and simmer your salt cod. Fry abundant onion. Pound garlic, peppercorns and saffron in your metal mortar, pour in a little water, swill all this into the fried onion, add salt and put it all in a clay or earthen casserole on the fire to cook gently. Then spoon this over your salt cod, add a little tomato juice or verjuice, whichever is in season, and a handful of parsley, and serve.

4–6 servings of soaked salt cod, preferably thick-cut square steaks, dry weight each about 150 g / 5 oz, a little olive oil

FOR THE SOFRITO: 6 tbsp good olive oil, about 1.15 kg / 2½ lb finely chopped sweet onions, 6 tbsp water, 2 tbsp saffron infusion made with 2 dozen threads saffron (see p. 102), 1 tbsp tomato juice or verjuice, a small handful of snipped flat-leaf parsley.

Makes about 500 ml / ¾ pint.

Make the *sofrito*. Warm the olive oil gently in a large frying pan or *cazuela*, add the onions, toss well, and cook slowly for about 30 minutes

ONION SOFRITO

"Fry abundant onion. Pound garlic, peppercorns and saffron in your metal mortar, pour in a little water, swill all this into the fried onion. . . ." Altamiras's description of how to make onion *sofrito* was limited by his frying vocabulary, but he did pinpoint the two stages of making one well: first sweating the onion in olive oil then cooking it in water. The second key to success is patience to cook it down to a thick, jammy, sweet *sofrito*. You can grate or finely chop the onion, according to your recipe, but make sure you cook it gently so it does not caramelize. Making *sofrito* is a time-consuming procedure, which takes at least an hour, but it can be made in large quantities well ahead of time and then either chilled or frozen.

over gentle heat with a lid on top to avoid browning. When the onions are well softened and the water they release has cooked away, add the measured water and a pinch or two of salt, and simmer gently for another half an hour or more till the *sofrito* reduces to a thick compote. Stir from time to time to ensure there is no sticking or browning. Spoon off surplus oil, stir in the saffron infusion, tomato, and parsley, lift this *sofrito* off the heat and leave for the flavors to blend till you are ready to cook. Warm the oven (200°C, 400°F, gas mark 6). Seal the salt cod on both sides in the minimum of olive oil, ideally in a non-stick pan, transfer the fillets to a baking dish or small individual *cazuelitas*, spoon the onion *sofrito* over the top and finish them in a warm oven till a sharp knife pushed into the flesh reveals the center is done, about 7 minutes in all. Good served with tomato salad.

Salt Cod with Garlic and Parsley Sauce / Otro Abadejo Diferente

Temper your salt cod. Give it a little boil, skim off any foam then drain away the water. Toast bread, soak it in vinegared water, squeeze it dry and pound it with garlic, spices and a good handful of parsley. Warm olive oil with garlic and make a sauce with this oil, the spiced breadcrumbs and a little cold water. Pour all this over the salt cod, put it on the fire, simmer it and add salt. This gives a very good sauce, as you will see, and nobody will guess whether it is made from nuts or something else.

Built around economic ingredients, this is one of *New Art*'s best recipes for home-salted cod fillets (see p. 238).

4–6 servings of soaked salt cod, each 150 g / 5 oz dry weight, 120 ml / 4 fl oz water

FOR THE SAUCE: 3 tbsp olive oil warmed with 2 skinned and sliced garlic cloves, 60 g / 2 oz dampened toasted bread, 400 ml / 13 fl oz water (or fish broth), a small handful of snipped flat-leaf parsley, small pinches of cinnamon and cloves.

Skin the salt cod servings and pull out as many bones as you can. Preheat the oven (200°C, 400°F, gas mark 6). Lay the salt cod in a single layer in a lightly oiled ovenproof dish. Make the sauce: warm the olive oil with the sliced garlic, and when it has softened blend it with the dampened toasted bread, squeezed dry, parsley and spices, dilute all this with water, season to taste, and warm through in a small pan. Pour the sauce over the fish and oven-bake for about 20 minutes. I like this with a plate of vegetables beforehand or on the side: chard, carrots tossed in parsleyed olive oil, and potatoes baked in their skins.

SALT COD: THE TASTE OF HOLY WEEK

Food in Holy Week was meatless, but it brought with it an explosion of flavor. After weeks of beans and vegetables there would be fresh fish and blancmange in wealthy homes, salt cod and sweet dumplings in poorer ones. Sold whole as a butterflied fish by traveling muleteers, salt cod needed two days' soaking time,[9] ideally dangled in a river or stream. Little dumplings were made first with off-cuts and the thin edges of the fish, then, after the full soaking, fat salt cod fillets were served with honey or parsley sauce.

Salt Cod Dumplings / Almondiguillas de Abadejo

Simmer your salt cod in water with salt, drain it, take out the bones, mince your fish finely and add raw eggs, breadcrumbs, spices, parsley, mint and a little grated cheese, as you see fit. Then make little balls from the paste into

rissoles and fry them in olive oil. Put a panful of water to boil, add seasoning and olive oil fried with garlic to flavour it, then poach your fried fishballs. Make a hazelnut thickening for the sauce: pound the nuts with breadcrumbs soaked in water and squeezed dry, add a little vinegar and some fish broth, pour this over the rissoles and leave the sauce to simmer.

The breadcrumb thickening of these salt cod dumplings is usually replaced by mashed potatoes or béchamel in modern recipes. But the crumbs give a lovely light spongy texture, especially if the dumplings are cooked just before eating. Leftovers can be kept in the fridge and reheated though the dumplings lose some of their lightness. Caribbean salt fish works well in these.

150 g / 5 oz soaked salt cod, 2 beaten eggs, 250 g / 10 oz yesterday's bread torn into tiny pieces or roughly grated, 2 tbsp finely chopped parsley, a dozen threads of pounded saffron, 1 heaped tbsp finely chopped mint leaves, 90 g / 3 oz finely grated mature ewe's milk or other sharp cheese, olive oil for shallow-frying, about 600 ml / 1 pint water or fish broth, 4 sliced cloves of garlic
Makes 18 dumplings.
Dry the soaked salt cod and pull the flesh into flakes. Put them in a large mixing bowl and add the lightly beaten eggs, bread, all the flavorings, and a pinch or two of salt. You should have a moist mixture that just holds together as dumplings. Oil your hands to shape the dough into little balls about the size of walnuts in their shells. Heat a good thumb's depth of olive oil in a deep frying pan and fry three or four dumplings at a time, rolling them over, so they are a deep golden brown. Drain on kitchen paper. Warm the water or broth with the sliced garlic in a deep saucepan or frying pan, add salt, settle the water at a fast simmer, and lower in the dumplings to cook gently for about 25 minutes. Serve them in large plates in a puddle of their own broth or dry, with a bowlful of garlic *ajo* (see p. 157) or fresh tomato sauce.

Salt Cod with Honey Sauce / Abadejo Frito con Miel

Temper your salt cod and drain it. Make a batter: for every ten servings of fish take a small dish of honey, your finest flour and a little water. Put a skillet on the fire, make the oil very hot, and always remember to do this when you are frying, except for lean meat, of which I spoke earlier when we dealt with meat cookery. Dip your salt cod in the batter and fry it in the oil. This is good to make for those who have a sweet tooth or you can make it with an egg and saffron batter, but then you should add no honey.

Cooks' instincts may reveal untold stories. When Moroccan-born chef Noureddine Lameghaizi of Valencia's Dukala restaurant (see p. 64) recreated this dish, he separated out the honey in a saffroned sauce, returning to styles from the Muslim centuries when golden salt cod was cured along Spain's Mediterranean coast and honey sauces were popular. Some Catalans, however, argue the dish was dreamed up later at Poblet, a Cistercian monastery south of Barcelona.[10] Whichever, this version is delicious and the flavor match of the salt fish and sweet honey is wonderful.

8–12 1-in / 2.5-cm cubes of salt cod, soaked, olive oil for shallow-frying

FOR THE TEMPURA BATTER: 1 egg, 90 g / 3 oz plain flour, 50 g / 2 oz cornflour, 200 ml / 7 fl oz iced water.

FOR THE HONEY SAUCE: 2 tbsp olive oil, 1 grated sweet onion, 2 dozen Malaga raisins, soaked in warm water and seeded, 120 ml / 4 fl oz thyme, orange-flower or rosemary honey, 2 teacupfuls of water, 1 teacupful saffron infusion made with a dozen saffron strands (see p. 102), 2 level tsp cornflour (optional), 4 tbsp toasted flaked almonds.

Makes 4–6 first-course servings.

Soak the salt cod for 12 hours, change the water, and soak for 4 hours more. Skin the pieces, bone them as well as you can, and pat them dry. Whisk together all the ingredients for the tempura batter and chill it. Make the sauce. Warm the olive oil, sweat the grated onion in it till soft and golden, add the soaked raisins, honey, and water, and simmer for 10 minutes. Stir the cornflour into the saffron infusion, and add this to the reduced sauce along with the toasted flaked almonds. Season to taste. Dip each salt cod square into the tempura (tongs make this easy) and shallow-fry them, one or two at a time, for 4 minutes each, turning them halfway through. Drain on kitchen paper towel and serve on hot plates with a little pool of honey sauce.

Salt Cod in a Green Sauce / Abadejo en Otra Forma

Take the day's salt cod servings, wash and dry them and lay them in a cooking dish where they sit comfortably. Warm seasoned water in a small pot, add

garlic, parsley and spices, pour the liquid over your fish and shake the dish so the seasonings spread over the bottom. Put this over a gentle fire so the fish cooks as you shake it from side to side. Remember to use a large dish and first cook together the flavouring ingredients, except for the olive oil, which you fry separately with some garlic before adding it to your fish. Finish it off with a little simmer, then squeeze in some lemon juice. Bream is very good cooked this way too.

The technique for emulsifying salt cod's cooking juices with its own gelatinous plasma is often said to have been born on the fishing boats. It gives one of the best known among Basque sauces, turned green by a handful of finely chopped parsley. Here Altamiras uses the shaking or *meneado* of the cooking pot that defines the technique. Perhaps, then, it was not born on fishing boats, but from landlocked ingenuity or accident and became popular among the fishermen who relied heavily on salt cod while at sea. Here is an excellent modern recipe from Oskar and the late Victor Lanziego, brothers from a San Sebastian family of chefs who have shared cookery wisdom with me since the 1980s. You need a flat-based earthenware or clay *cazuela* to give the low temperatures required for a sauce to emulsify well.[11] One good trick for pulling this off is to throw in a couple of soaked salt cod tails, which are packed with the gelatinous plasma.

4–6 servings of best-quality salt cod fillet, dry weight each 175 g / 6 oz (see p. 238), 1–2 salt cod tails, about 6 tbsp mild extra-virgin olive oil, ½ finely chopped onion, 1 clove chopped garlic, a little finely chopped parsley

"Buy the very best salt cod available," Oskar wrote to me. "Soak it in cold water in the fridge for 48 hours. Change the water three times for thick fillets. Drain and dry them, and check the taste. If you are using salt cod tails, rinse and soak them with the fillets. Choose a large flat-bottomed earthenware dish where the salt cod fits comfortably. Pour in enough olive oil to cover the bottom of the dish and sweat the chopped onion and garlic in it. Lower the heat almost as far as you can, put in the salt cod, skin down, adding a little salt if needed. Tiny bubbles should rise in the oil. Cook very gently for about 5 minutes, turn the fish over, cook the other side in the same way and when it is done add the parsley. Take it off the heat and put it on a marble slab or other smooth surface where you can spin and jig the earthenware dish between your palms, one way and the other—this is known as the *meneado*—till the fish skin's plasma is drawn out to thicken the oil into an opaque sauce. Reheat and serve." Good with a classic wine from the Rioja Alta, for example, Remelluri.

. . . y llámanme Bacallao	. . . and they call me Bacalao,
primo hermano del pescado	the first cousin of that fish
abadejo, que en Vizcaya	called Abadejo, which in Bilbao,
dicen que es muy buen hidalgo.	they say, is very noble.

Francisco de Quevedo, *Entremés*, one-act play

TOMATOES: TASTE AND APPETITE

The Franciscans took quickly to tomatoes, perhaps because they knew them from their missions in Mexico and they rated them highly as food for the sick. It's no surprise, then, that the first documented appearance of tomatoes being eaten in Spain, in the summer of 1608, is at the Hospital de la Sangre, a Seville women's hospital funded by lay Franciscans.[12] We do not know how the tomatoes purchased there were prepared, but perhaps as an appetizing relish for the sick, as in a later friary manuscript (see below). By comparison courtly tomato sauces were dense and sugared. Altamiras did something else again, adding the little red fruit sparingly as a savory seasoning alongside garlic, onion, and parsley in olive oil. Simple, perhaps, but daring in its own way, it was an idea that transformed modern Spanish cookery.

Salt Cod with Tomato and Orange / Otro Guisado de Abadejo

Lay your salt cod servings in a ceramic cooking vessel and add raw garlic cloves, salt, pepper, saffron, olive oil, parsley, tomato and some little bits of orange. Pour a little water over your fish then put it to cook. This is a very good dish and remember, everything calls for a little tasty sauce but not a jumble of flavours, which spoils any dish.

Bitter oranges grow in Andalusian city streets and still flavor the south's Spanish salt cod salad, called *remojón*, as well as a fish soup from Cadiz.[13]

Altamiras added tomato and saffron too, so coming up with a magical triangle of flavors.

4–6 servings of soaked salt cod fillet, dry weight each about 150 g / 5 oz, or fresh cod fillet

FOR THE SAUCE: 2 skinned tomatoes, 1 bitter or sweet orange skinned of peel and pith (see p. 144), 2 garlic cloves, 2 tbsp snipped parsley, about 4 tbsp olive oil, a saffron infusion made with 2 dozen threads (see p. 102).

Lay the salt cod servings, skin-side down, in a single layer in a lightly oiled ovenproof dish. Preheat a hot oven (200°C, 400°F, gas mark 6). Chop the skinned tomatoes, orange flesh, skinned garlic and parsley, separately then together. Warm the olive oil, toss the tomato and orange mixture in it, remove from the heat, stir in the saffron infusion, and season to taste. Spoon this over the fish and oven-bake till it is just done, about 7–10 minutes. Good as a main course following pasta or cracked wheat tossed with fresh herbs and moistened with a little olive oil.

A TOMATO RELISH: Joan Bagués, a Franciscan friar who cooked at Gerona's hospital in the late eighteenth century, gave a sauce "to animate the appetite" in his 1770s notebook: wood-roasted ripe tomatoes, chopped and mixed with finely chopped garlic, parsley and onion, salt, pepper, and vinegar. This is great served with fish, meat, rice, or oven-roasted vegetables.

A MODERN FRIARY COOK

Fray Ángel Ramón Serrano is the only Franciscan friar in Spain who runs a working kitchen. A vocational cook, convinced that food preparation is an important part of the friars' lives, he spent eight years teaching at Santo Espíritu de Monte, a medieval friary close to Valencia, before moving sideways into kitchen work there. Today he cooks for around two dozen people a day, not only the friars, but also guests at the friars' *hospedería*. Near the kitchen are a hen house and, further away, a black-footed pig snuffling around close to lemon trees. On Sundays the poor come for cooked food. What makes Ángel's work so exciting is his knack for turning "plain ingredients into something exquisite" through mastery of popular techniques and melting-pot flavors.

Salt Cod Confit with Tomato / Abadejo con Tomate

Cut your salt cod into servings. Wash them well, simmer them in water, skim any foam off the top and drain the fish on a wooden board. Fry onion with abundant tomato then assemble the dish: make a first layer of salt cod in a wide glass dish, cover it with the onion and tomato, parsley, pepper and pounded garlic, and continue like this, with artful capework,[14] *till the dish is full. Bathe the fish in water, let it simmer briefly then add salt, but no other spices, for tomato alone replaces them well. This is delicious and later I shall tell you how you may preserve your tomatoes so they last all year.*

This is a perfect example of Fray Ángel's style, in which everyday ingredients are transformed through popular techniques, in this case those of olive oil confits from La Mancha, where he grew up.

4–6 servings of soaked salt cod fillet (dry weight each about 150 g / 5 oz), a whole bulb of skinned garlic cloves, olive oil to cover the fish, 500 g / 1lb finely chopped or grated fresh ripe tomatoes (or, out of season, quality preserved tomatoes), 2 finely chopped onions, 2 finely chopped green peppers, the pulped paste of a dried cooking pepper (optional), 1 level tsp plain pimentón, not smoked or spicy-hot, 3 chopped hard-boiled eggs

Ángel soaks his salt cod in cold water in the fridge for only a day, without changing the water. Put the soaked and dried fillets into a casserole, ideally a clay or earthenware *cazuela* just large enough to fit them, add the skinned garlic cloves, cover with olive oil, and warm for about 10 minutes till little bubbles rise from the fish, the sign that it is beginning to cook. Don't worry about using a lot of oil: some goes back into the dish and the rest, aromatized with garlic and salt cod, is very good for frying fish. Remove from the heat and leave to sit for 45 minutes. (An earthenware dish will hold the warmth, but you may need to put other casseroles back on the heat briefly after 7–8 minutes, to hold the cooking temperature.) Lift the fish out on to a board, leaving the fillets intact if possible.

Pull off the skin, chop it finely, and put it into a large heavy-based pan or *cazuela* with 3 tablespoonfuls of the confit oil. Warm together over low heat, stirring all the time till the skins almost dissolve and their gelatine leeches out into the oil. Leave to settle. Add the chopped onions and peppers to the oil and sweat gently, for about 25 minutes, till well cooked.

Decant the rest of the confit's olive oil, leaving behind the garlic and white fatty liquid released by the salt cod during cooking. Mash or pound the garlic and gelatine in a bowl or mortar, stir in the pimentón, and a trickle of water if the paste is very thick. Add the chopped or grated tomatoes to the sweated onions and peppers, bring to a simmer, stir in the mashed garlic and gelatin, and the dried pepper flesh, if you are using it, and cook to evaporate surplus liquid. Add a pinch of sugar to bring out the tomato's sweetness if the final sauce is in any way acidic. Turn off the heat, add the salt cod, and leave it sitting in the sauce long enough to warm through, shaking the pan gently and allowing the cod to fall naturally into large flakes or pieces. Finally scatter the hard-boiled egg over the top. This is rich, intensely flavored and very satisfying.

THE FRIARS FRY: A KITCHEN FIGHT

Altamiras made up many of his own kitchen rules for few friary thinkers had turned their thoughts to cooking rather than eating the right way.[15] One of his favorite ideas was frying fish without flour so the oil could be recycled and any leftovers be preserved in vinegar without the flour clouding the liquid (see pp. 150–51). But Carmelite cooks on a visit to San Cristobal disagreed, words were exchanged, and a fight broke out. The spat rumbled on and fifty years later a Carmelite cook issued a "Warning" against Altamiras in his own kitchen notebook, an interesting comment on the extent of *New Art*'s influence.[16] Today Altamiras would be delighted: recycling olive oil for frying has become a common denominator of home and restaurant cooking in Spain.

Fried Salt Cod in Pepper Sauce / Abadejo con Prebe

I had not intended to add this final note on salt cod here until I remembered an episode that took place in the Sierra de Alpartir. Two Cooks who were of as little substance as their salt cod, yet presumptuous about their knowledge, told me I was wrong to temper the fish in warm water and that I should dredge it directly with flour for frying. Imagine! You might ask me, is that not a good idea? I would reply by saying that while such floury extravagance might be fit for Carnival, neither flour nor oil should be squandered in Lent or on lean days for then it cannot be used again. Rather, I would say, ignore Cooks who wear Carnival masks and hand out advice unfitting for those who have taken the vow of poverty. They waste flour in such a way that it cannot be used again and that, I say, does more harm than good.

Read on here, instead, for as you shall see, I do not dismiss flour altogether.

Wash your salt cod, temper it in warm water with a little salt, skim off any foam, pick off putrefied flesh, and always start this way when you cook salt cod, skimming the foam off the simmering water as often as needed. Leave your fish to drain on a wooden board, put your skillet on the fire, warm your oil in it, fry your fish then lay it in a cooking dish, skin up, for it is easier to serve like this. Pour a little of the frying oil into a pot and scatter in a handful of flour, or however much you need. Now, this truly is a fine idea!

Put the pot on the fire, stir till the flour turns brown then spoon it over your salt cod. In this way the fish shall turn out as though it had been floured, yet without spoiling the oil, which can be used again, e.g., for eggs and vegetables on lean days. For remember, oil spotted with flour cannot be used again. But if you fry your salt cod as I say, you can use the oil again, as if it was fresh and, take note, temper your fish first so you are sure it's clean.

Now, take bay leaves, crushed garlic, peppercorns, saffron and salt, add a little water and swill the seasonings over the salt cod in its dish with some sharp orange juice or, if there is none, vinegar stands in well, as I have mentioned. Bathe the fish in this liquid, put it on the fire to cook, then let it simmer for a little bit, and season it. Parsley is very good with any fish, but especially with salt cod.

Some food writers have suggested this was one of the earliest tavern recipes for salt cod; the peppery sauce would have made customers thirsty for a drink.

4–6 servings of soaked salt cod, dry weight each about 150 g / 5 oz, 2 tbsp olive oil

FOR THE SAUCE: a teacupful of water, 12 peppercorns pounded with 4 garlic cloves, 1 tbsp lemon juice, 3 tbsp parsley, 2 bay leaves, salt, 1 tsp flour, a saffron infusion made with 2 dozen strands (see p. 102).

Dry the soaked cod well. Simmer all the ingredients for the sauce except for the flour and saffron infusion. Warm the olive oil for frying the fish, ideally in a non-stick frying pan. Fry the salt cod skin side down for just 2 minutes and lift it into a baking dish. Sprinkle a teaspoon of flour into the oil in the pan and cook, stirring quickly, to a golden roux. Pour in the hot broth, little by little, to make a smooth sauce, stir in the saffron infusion, pour the sauce over the fish, and simmer for a final 3–4 minutes. This is good with green beans and a Chardonnay white wine.

Tres españoles, cuatro opiniones.   Three Spaniards, four opinions.

Spanish proverb

CHAPTER II

ON FISH AND EGGS

S AN DIEGO, where Altamiras cooked in Zaragoza, was a ten minute walk away from the Río Ebro, known by fishermen as the river of life and death. When it flooded it washed away crops and livestock, but for most of the year it gave life: fish, sold in the streets of the cities and towns, and water, which irrigated the valley's market gardens and fields. In spring the fishermen punted out in flat-bottomed boats to net salmon, shad, and lamprey, but the year's prize catch was silver eel, which swam downriver in autumn.[1] Bad weather gave good fishing. As the eels blundered through muddy water the fishermen transfixed them in pools of lantern light and speared them. Smaller eels that swam in the rivers behind La Almunia gave good eating too. Often they were caught alive and kept in ponds to sell or eat when a feastday came around.[2]

EEL: THE FRESHEST FISH

Roast or Griddled Eel / Anguila Assada

Be sure your eel is well washed: trim two fingers from the head and four from the tail, dry the eel with a cloth and wipe it so it does not taste of mud, cut it into pieces and lay them on bay leaves or, if you have none, lay them on split dried reeds. I should add here, all fish, or at least most of them, are good cooked over a fire this way.

Eels are still popular gourmet food in the Albufera marshes and rice fields south of Valencia. Once they were wood-roasted for the summer fiestas in El Palmar, the fishermen's village, but today's smaller wild or farmed eels are griddled on a flat-top metal *plancha*.[3] The skin is rubbed with coarse salt, the flesh slashed to the bone every inch or so, and the eel curled in a ring on the griddle under an upside-down plate. The skin quickly turns crunchy, but the eel stays on the *plancha* for about a quarter of an hour till a knife reveals the flesh next to the bone is cooked through. This is good served with bread and a glass of chilled white wine.

Rice with Eel / Anguila con Arroz

Boil rice with spices then add your eels. If they are fat, throw them in when the rice is half-cooked, if they are small, add them with a handful of parsley at the end. They make very good eating dressed this way.

The earliest popular rice dishes, like paella, began life as everyday food in the rice fields, and were cooked with whatever came to hand: home-grown vegetables, wild eels, and game-like rabbits, even water rat. This eel rice probably began life in such a hand-to-mouth way, perhaps in Villa de Zuera on the Río Gallego, north of Zaragoza, where a friary stood close to rice fields that were finally drained in the 1740s to end persistent outbreaks of malaria.[4]

a 500 g / 1 lb cleaned eel chopped into 2.5-cm / 1-in lengths, 4 tbsp olive oil, about 1.75 liters / 3 pints hot fish broth or water, 400 g / 13 oz paella rice, preferably Bomba variety, a thumb's length of cinnamon stick, a saffron infusion made with 3 dozen threads (see p. 102), 2 handfuls of snipped flat-leaf parsley, freshly ground black pepper

Crisp the eels' skin in a lick of olive oil. Warm the fish broth or water. Heat the oil in a large flameproof casserole dish—an earthenware one is ideal—and toss the rice in it. Pour over the hot fish broth or water, throw in the cinnamon and salt, bring to a fast boil, and cook for 15 minutes. If the rice sticks, top up with more boiling water. When you see it is nearly done, but not quite cooked, stir in the saffron infusion, drop in the eel pieces, combine evenly with a fork, and simmer slowly for 5 minutes. Remove from the heat, cover with a cloth, and leave to sit for a further 5 minutes till the rice finishes absorbing the liquid and the eel is done.

Eel or Monkfish in Hazelnut Sauce /
Anguilas en Guisado con Salsa

Here is the most popular dish for eels. Once they are slit open and their bellies emptied, cut them up in pieces, say two fingers thick, or as you like, then wash and lay them in a clay or earthen casserole. Add fried garlic, a handful of fine-cut parsley, pepper, saffron, cloves and cinnamon, but take care with the cloves, for they are so ardent in flavour. Add a little water and salt, and put the eels to cook. Make a pine kernel or hazelnut thickening: pound the nuts with damp bread, soaked then squeezed dry; if you are using hazelnuts toast them first and toast the bread, and add a couple of cloves of garlic, or as much as you like, roasting it for a less pungent sauce. Pound all this together, strain in the eels' cooking liquor and stir to make a sauce, pour it over the eels and give them a little simmer, shake and jig your dish from side to side so the sauce does not stick. These eels are very good without any sauce too, served just with their cooking liquor.

Today Valencian *all-i-pebre*, not so very different to this, is thought of as a luxurious dish. Its broth is liquid, while Altamiras's sauce is creamier.[5] I make this with monkfish tail.

about 250 ml / ¼ pint fish broth, 6 peppercorns, 4 cloves, a cinnamon shard, pinch of salt, 3 sliced garlic cloves sweated in 2 tbsp olive oil, 2 eels (each about 500 g / 1 lb) or 1 monkfish tail, about 750 g / 1½ lb, cut across the bone into large bite-size chunks, a handful of snipped parsley, a cup of saffron infusion made with 2 dozen threads (see p. 102)
FOR THE HAZELNUT THICKENING (OPTIONAL): 20 skinned and toasted hazelnuts blended with 30g / 1 oz fresh toasted breadcrumbs and 3 skinned garlic cloves.
Warm the fish broth with the spices, a pinch of salt, and the garlic slices sweated in the olive oil. Simmer together for 30 minutes. Slip in the fish, add water if needed to cover, lower the broth to a gentle simmer, and cook the fish very quickly for small eel or a couple of minutes longer for monkfish. As soon as the fish is done lift it out on to a serving dish. Now stir the saffron infusion into the broth, blend in the hazelnut thickening to give a creamy sauce, lay the fish chunks in it, and warm through gently. Good with green beans (see p. 194) and mashed roots.

STURGEON: FISH FOR A FEW

Sturgeon rarely made its way up the Río Ebro, where dams blocked its swimming path, but Altamiras clearly knew how to cook it. In Andalusia, where the Río Guadalquivir gave plentiful sturgeon, it swam far inland till the nineteenth century.[6] Today in the Granadan sierras it is farmed for its caviar. The flesh is sold direct to a small group of chefs,[7] one of whom, Brazilian-born Diego Gallegos, is an expert sturgeon cook. He calls it a generous fish, one of a kind, meaty, and rich in oils. When you cannot find it he suggests salmon, bream, even grouper as an alternative.

Poached Sturgeon / Sollo

To serve sturgeon in good taste, lop off its head so it does not offend anyone, then make an infusion with diluted wine, vinegar and salt. Lay fresh cow's milk butter on top of the fish, add spices and plenty of herbs, such as parsley, a little fennel and oregano. Cook the fish in this infusion, turn it into a sauce with pounded toasted bread, and, in this way, your poor mortified sturgeon shall make good eating.

Oregano, fennel, and parsley give a lovely herbiness to this infusion. Measure a half-half mix of wine and water to cover your fish, simmer them with the pounded fennel, oregano, and parsley for 20 minutes and leave to sit overnight or for at least 4 hours for the flavors to develop. Warm through the infusion in a flameproof dish where your fish—fillets, slices, or whole—fits easily. Put it in gently, cook it with small dobs of butter on top, lift it out when it is done, and keep it warm on a covered hot serving dish. Reduce the cooking liquid to a few juices, whisk in extra butter or olive oil and serve them in a small heated jug to pass with the fish. Good with ribbon pasta, a green salad and, to drink, the same white wine you used for the infusion.

Marinated Wood-Grilled Fish Steaks / Sollo Assado

Take oregano, salt and garlic, crush them in your mortar, wash them into a clay pot with vinegar, put a lid on it and add white wine and some whole cloves, but no other spices, only salt. It should be a little bitter. Put the sturgeon slices in this adobo, *pour over some good fresh olive oil and when you put the fish on the fire, baste it with the oil and marinade, or with butter.*

You can chop this up like a gigote, and it will be as white as capon, but nonetheless it will be gigote.

This intriguingly astringent marinade, perfumed with cloves, is also good for barbecued or grilled swordfish, or albacore tuna. To make it, crush two fat cloves of garlic with half a teaspoon of salt and a sprinkling of oregano. Wash out the mortar with a little wine vinegar into a small pan with 250 ml / 8 fl oz white wine. Add three whole cloves. Bring to a boil, then leave to cool. Pour it over the fish and leave for an hour or two before grilling or marinating it. A salad of sliced orange and thinly shaved fennel balance the tart marinade well.[8]

Sturgeon Fishballs / Almondiguillas de Sollo

Chop raw sturgeon very finely. Add eggs, breadcrumbs, pepper, cloves and cinnamon. Have ready hot chickpea broth. Make your fish balls, adding a little chopped greenery to them, cook and thicken the broth with beaten egg yolks. Serve them like this.

I met Michelin-starred chef Diego Gallegos when he was cooking in the Granada sierras. Since then he has moved closer to the coast and set up a unique restaurant, called Sollo, dedicated to sturgeon cookery. He also has an organic kitchen garden and a hydroponics system supplying a small freshwater fish farm. Diego looked over all the sturgeon recipes before choosing to re-create this one, drawn by its inventive originality to which he added two new elements: a powdered sun-dried tomato skin and a rich chicken broth. You can prepare these fishballs easily ahead of time, but poach them at the last minute if you want them to stay spongy and light.

600 g / 1¼ lb fresh sturgeon or other fish (see above), 120 g / 4 oz onion, 30 g / 1 oz shallot, chopped fresh parsley, 3 eggs, 90 g / 3 oz flour, cloves, cinnamon

FOR THE CHICKEN BROTH: 2 chicken carcasses, a little olive oil, a slug of brandy, a glassful of red and another of white wine, about 750 ml / 1¼ pints water, cinnamon, pepper, cloves, marjoram, tarragon, thyme.

Makes about 2 dozen fishballs.

Blend all the fishball ingredients, season the mix to taste, and chill for 4 hours. Make the chicken broth: brown the carcasses in olive oil in a frying pan, pour over the brandy, toss well, transfer the carcasses to a large pan, pour over the wines and water, add the spices and herbs, and simmer for 30 minutes. Strain the broth into a pan wide enough to cook half a dozen or so fishballs at once. Bring it slowly to a simmering point. Meanwhile, oil your hands, make little balls of the mix (about 30 g / 1 oz) and roll them in the sun-dried tomato skin if you are using it (see below). Drop in half a dozen fishballs and cook them for 15 minutes. Cook them all this way, keeping the cooked ones warm, and serve in a puddle of strained broth in heated deep plates.

FOR THE SUN-DRIED TOMATO SKIN (OPTIONAL): 1 whole chicken skin oven-roasted till crispy and mopped dry of any remaining surface fat, 10 g (about 4) sun-dried tomatoes, a pinch of fine salt, 2 g (about 2 level tsp) smoked pimentón paprika. Blend everything to a fine loose powder and use to coat the fish balls, previously painted with olive oil. Dry for 5 minutes in a warm oven before cooking.

Fish with an Egg Crust / Costrada de Sollo

Brown the sturgeon flesh in good butter or olive oil in your skillet, leave it in one piece, cool it, season it with spices, cinnamon, a little lemon juice and pounded sugar, brush the top with cracked and well stirred eggs and finish cooking it over a gentle fire. Usually this is as good as any meat costrada.

Cristina Navarro, a Valencian artist, grew up eating fish every lunchtime of her Mediterranean childhood. She is a wonderful instinctive cook so I asked her to update this *costrada*, keeping Altamiras's flavors, but evolving the textures and ingredients: her fish is chunked not minced, lemon zest replaces juice, naturally sweet onion *sofrito* replaces sugar, and saffron and crushed pink peppercorns add color to the egg crust. Pack the fish quite closely into a dish in which the beaten eggs cover it well. A flat, low-sided earthenware *cazuela* is perfect.

1 tsp olive oil, about 1 kg / 2 lb total weight of fish fillets (e.g., hake, salmon, salt cod), 1 tbsp parsley very finely chopped with 1 garlic clove, finely grated zest of ½ lemon, 1 tsp coarsely grated cinnamon, 250 ml / 8 fl oz onion sofrito (see pp. 120–21), 12 pink peppercorns, 4–6 eggs, 6 saffron strands, a small handful of fresh breadcrumbs (optional)

Warm the olive oil in a heavy non-stick frying pan, add the fish, and seal it for about 30 seconds on each side, just long enough to be able to remove the bones and skin. Divide the fish into even nuggets, about

2.5-cm / 1-in square, arrange them over the bottom of the lightly oiled dish and sprinkle with a little parsley, garlic, lemon zest, cinnamon, and salt. Warm a slow oven (150°C, 300°F, gas mark 2). Heat the *sofrito*, check its seasoning and spoon it around the fish. Beat the eggs till they begin to foam, stir in the pounded pink peppercorns and a pinch or two of salt, pour the egg quickly over the fish, and sprinkle the saffron stigmas on top. Bake for about 10 minutes, checking that the fish is done with the point of a sharp knife. This makes a good light lunch or supper, accompanied by a green salad dressed with lemon juice rather than vinegar.

Fish Cakes / Pastelillos de Sollo

Chop raw sturgeon finely. Take cracked eggs, e.g. half a dozen, or as many as you need for your fish, stir them and add them to the sturgeon, season it with spices and citrus juice, salt and olive oil. Add flour, sieved and pounded sugar, a little olive oil or lard, some hard-boiled yolks, more salt, and knead everything together with a little white wine. Shape the dough into some small cakes, fry them in your skillet, shake powdered sugar on top, serve these hot, and then you shall see they are a fine thing.

Saffron is wonderful in these fish cakes: its flavor and color really stand out. You can make up the cakes ahead of time and then quickly fry them just before eating. I keep in the tiniest pinch of sugar.[9]

500 g / 1 lb firm white fish, 2 beaten eggs, 100 g / 3½ oz finely ground fresh breadcrumbs, a dozen pounded saffron threads, 1 juiced lemon or lime, a pinch of sugar, 3 mashed hard-boiled egg yolks, 1 tbsp white wine
FOR FRYING: plain flour or dry breadcrumbs, olive oil for shallow-frying.
Makes 8 cakes.
Chop the fish very finely by hand, mix in all the other ingredients evenly, season to taste, and chill for 2 hours. Pour off any liquid that runs out. Take portions of the fish paste, about 90 g / 3 oz each, lightly oil your hands, and shape each portion into a cake. Chill them until you want to cook them. Just before frying, coat them with seasoned flour or breadcrumbs. Shallow-fry in bubbling hot olive oil. I like these served with fried onions with crispy breadcrumbs, chard in tempura, and fried turnips (see pp. 185–86, 190, 199).

SEA BASS: THE SEA WOLF

The chattiness of Altamiras's writing makes us feel close to him yet occasionally he reveals how differently he understood the world. Here he wrote of sea bass and sturgeon, believing, like naturalists of the time, that they were members of the mythical wolf-fish family described in Spain's dictionary.[10] Today the myth of the wolf-fish family is long gone, but it lingers on in the French and Catalan cooks' names for sea bass, *loup de mer* or *llobarro*, literally the sea wolf. Old recipes for sea bass like this one have lingered too, though today the fish is more often than not filleted rather than whole and lies on a bed of potatoes and tomatoes.

Roast Sea Bass / Lobo de Mar Assado

Once in a while, we come across the sea wolf in the Kingdom of Aragon. It looks like shad, and as we eat it little we treat it like sturgeon and the best way to dress it is to roast it. Cut it up, lay the pieces on bay leaves in a spacious cooking dish, fry some garlic and put it on top of the fish. Have ready a dishful of citrus juice with fine-cut parsley, garlic and pepper stirred into it and brush this over the bass with a bunch of parsley as you roast it between hot embers, with more in the lid of the dish than below. Turn your fish over once, brush it with more citrus juice and, when it is cooked, take it to table.

Ask the fishmonger to gut the bass for you and leave it whole or fillet it, as you wish. Wipe any fine scales off whole fish. Preheat the oven to 250°F, 500°C, gas mark 9. Mix the juice of two lemons with a crushed garlic clove, salt, pepper, and snipped parsley, and pour it over both sides of the fish. Warm a wineglassful of olive oil with 3 or 4 sliced garlic cloves and pour that over the fish too. Choose a shallow-sided baking dish or roasting pan, oil it lightly, make a single layer of thinly sliced potatoes in it, season, lay sliced tomatoes on top, season again, then set the fish on top in the middle. Cover with foil and oven-roast, allowing about 25 minutes for a whole bass weighing a kilo. For fillets, roast the potatoes for 10 minutes before laying the fillets on top and returning to the oven for a further 10 minutes. This makes delicious celebration food with a glass of brut Cava.

SEAFISH: TUNA, BREAM, SALMON, SARDINES

Salt Tuna

After eel and sturgeon, the most prized fish of the time, Altamiras grouped blue fish, suggesting how desirable its rich and fatty flesh was for the friars. Salt tuna came first. Today its metallic tang is still scattered sparingly through traditional feast-day dishes like *xato*, a Catalan salad of curly endive with salt tuna flakes,[11] and *coca de San Juan*, a flatbread baked at midsummer. Better known today are salt-tuna delicacies like pressed and cured fillet, or *mojama*, and the fatty loin, *tonyina de sorra*.[12] On home ground, where these are produced, they are simply sliced and eaten with olive oil, bread, salted almonds, and olives—all old foods from the old sea. Most of the dishes originally designed for salt tuna are now made with fresh albacore or blue-fin tuna, although salting the fish adds flavor to some and is essential for *salpicón* salad. Below Vicent Peris, a *tonyiner*, or tuna curer, explains how you can do that at home.

Tuna and Onion in White Wine

Lay your tuna in clean running water for two days to wash away the salt, then cut it into bits the size of walnut shells, put them in a pot of water and bring it to the boil to scald the tuna. Drain it and give it a little simmer in fresh water, and, if it is still salty, leave it to steep in clean water with a handful of onion stems or a little rye straw, for these draw out the salt. Now drain and cool the tuna, coat it with flour, fry it and put it to cook with abundant fried onion, white wine and spices. Let these simmer together in a pot over a gentle fire, stir the fish carefully from time to time so it does not break up, then finish seasoning it. The flour that coated the fish for frying gives a little very good sauce and, when you serve this, you will see some people won't know if it is meat or fish.

A very popular dish, usually now cooked with fresh tuna, this is good made with a Chardonnay or another decent wine that you can also drink alongside it. I like to add back in the old pinches of spices, but I do not add flour. You can make the onion *sofrito* ahead of time (see p. 121), which then makes this a very quick dish to cook at the last minute.[13]

2 tbsp olive oil, 1.15 kg / 2½ lb of fresh white albacore or red tuna cut into bite-sized chunks, 450 ml onion sofrito (see p. 140), 250 ml / 8 fl oz white wine, pinches of powdered cinnamon and cloves

Warm the olive oil in a flameproof casserole and fry the tuna for just a minute or two till golden. Add the prepared onion *sofrito*, stir in the white wine, bring to a gentle simmer, and leave to cook till juicy, about 5–8 minutes, adding the spices right at the end so they keep their sweet aromas. I like this preceded by a tomato gazpacho soup and followed by a salad and fruit.

Tuna Fishcakes with Raisins / Costrada de Atún

Take lean tuna and a little fatty belly flesh and chop them finely together, just as you would chop lean meat with cured ham fat. Take a little cow's milk butter and warm it in a cazuela, *and if you have no butter then use olive oil, for we poor must spend only as our pockets allow. Put the* cazuela *on the fire and when it is hot, seal the chopped fish and season it with spices, cinnamon, lemon juice, raisins and four ounces of sugar, or as much as you see fit. Add raw eggs, shape a* costrada, *add salt too and, if you like, glaze the top with cracked stirred eggs, then toast this gently with embers below it and in the lid above it.*

Altamiras added raisins to chopped fresh or salt tuna, or a mix of the two, to give delicious fishcakes. Make his large loaf if you need to feed many mouths, but it is easier to cook small cakes to each person's taste. You need to start salting the fish and aromatizing the oil a day ahead— the extra time is well worth the effort. Since the fishcakes are lean they will emerge crumbly, but if need be you can bind them with a few dried breadcrumbs.

2 tbsp fruity olive oil, 90 g / 3 oz soaked and seeded raisins or sultanas, 1 tsp lemon zest, a small handful of shredded fresh mint leaves, 2 finely chopped hard-boiled eggs, 500 g / 1 lb thinly sliced fresh red or albacore tuna or bonito, a dozen saffron threads pounded to a powder, dried breadcrumbs (optional), olive oil for pan-frying

Makes 16 baby fishcakes.

Pour the warmed oil over the soaked raisins, lemon zest, and half the mint leaves. Leave to sit overnight. Cut the membrane off the tuna and slice the fish in half. Salt one half for 10–12 hours or overnight (see below). The following day soak the salted tuna till mildly briny, about 2 hours; dry well. Chop the salted and fresh tuna very finely with a sharp knife, put the mix in a bowl, stir evenly, add the aromatized oil with its flavorings, the rest of the fresh mint, the egg, and seasoning. If the mix is not well bound because it is too dry, you can throw in a little beaten egg. Now shape this mix into evenly sized fishcakes, each weighing about 45 g / 1½ oz. Try frying one to see if it crumbles too much, in which case add breadcrumbs to bind. Pan fry the fishcakes quickly in a very little hot olive oil and serve straight away. Good with a lemony mayonnaise and hot couscous.

Tuna Salpicón / Salpicón de Atun

Salt tuna loin is very good once it has been soaked. Give it a little boil, cut fat fingers from the thick lean flesh and dress the rest, with onion, as a salpicón. *Lay the fingers around the edge of a serving plate, put the* salpicón *in the middle, the raw onion slices on top, and add olive oil, vinegar, powdered pepper. For this* salpicón *tuna is the best fish.*

In Valencia's central market dried cured fish—baby tope shark, octopus, dogfish, and smooth hound—are strung up on a washing line above the stall of Vicent Peris, one of the Mediterranean's finest *tonyiners* or tuna curers. Once they could be seen hanging like this outside fishermen's houses; now you find them only outside the odd coastal restaurant. Vicent came up with this delicious modern *salpicón* with easily home-salted albacore or blue-fine tuna. He takes the harshness out of the onion with salt and vinegar, adds color and texture with diced sweet red pepper, and finishes the dressing with pepper and lemon juice.[14]

For each person you need 120 g / 4 oz fresh loin of red or albacore tuna, preferably a mix of lean fillet and belly marbled with fat, about 3–4 handfuls of best quality coarse sea salt or rock mineral salt, 60 g / 2 oz onion, ¼ sweet red pepper, ½ lemon, 1 tbsp wine vinegar, 1 sweet green pepper, trimmed and diced, fruity olive oil, 1 lemon
Serves 4–6 as a first course.
Cut the tuna into 120 g / 4 oz fillets, lay them on a bed of salt in a non-reactive dish, sprinkle with more salt, and leave to sit for 8–10 hours. Wash off the salt and leave the fish to soak in cold water, for 2 hours, changing the water after an hour. To test that the saltiness is to

your taste, nip off a small piece and check it. If it is not ready, return the tuna to soak for a little longer. When it is ready, cut the fish into fingers, skin the onions, slice them into thin rings, and salt them for 10 minutes. Wash off the salt and juices, squeeze dry, drip vinegar over them, leave for 5 minutes, and wipe clean again. Trim and dice the sweet peppers finely. Spoon the onion over the center of a large flat dish, lay the diced sweet pepper on top, arrange the tuna fingers around the edge, drip over olive oil, squeeze over lemon juice, and finish with freshly ground black pepper. Good served with a chilled white wine.

CHRISTMAS BREAM

In mid-winter, when red bream is buffeted by rough, cold seas, its flesh becomes rich in oils. Today lorry drivers speed it inland overnight for Christmas, but in Altamiras's time muleteers had a long hard ride from the fishing ports in search of high prices far from the sea. José María Busca Isusi, the great Basque food writer, told the story of one such muleteer who reached Aragon in time to sell his bream on Christmas Eve.[15] When he reached a friary the porter came out to ask the price he wanted for his fish: "*Hoy onza por onza!*" Today ounce for ounce, one of gold for one of fish. Clearly the friars got no discount for the muleteer's story ended wryly, "*El besugo mata mulo y gana mulo.*" Bream kills and wins a mule.

Roasted Red Bream or Snapper / Besugo Asado

This is the finest fish we know in the Lands of Aragon. Once it is gutted and scaled, wash it, dry it with a clean cloth, lay it on bay leaves in a spacious dish and put fried garlic on top, then season it, put a lid on top and roast it with hot embers below and above it, on the lid. Have ready a little dishful of lime or lemon juice seasoned with chopped garlic, pepper, parsley and salt, drip this liquor over the fish with a handful of feathers or parsley, and brush first one side of the fish then the other with the liquor as it roasts.

Slash the skin and flesh of the red bream every few inches on both sides. Juice a lemon, add garlic, pepper, parsley and salt, pour the juice over the fish, and leave to marinate for 20 minutes. Roast at 170°C, 350°F, gas mark 6. Spanish cooks say bream is done when its eyes run liquid, or you can time it by weight, about 10–15 minutes on each side for a fish weighing 1.3–1.6 kg (2lb 10 oz / 3¼ lb). This is very good served with *patatas a la panadera* (see p. 237).

Red Bream or Snapper in Orange Escabeche / Escabeche de Besugo

Scale your bream, wash them well, let them dry. If you want them whole you can fry them like that, and if you want them in pieces cut them up first, but either way take off the heads, for you can make another dish with these, and your fish are no worse for being beheaded. But do not cheat with the heads, for then you are a man of no substance, little better than an empty bream head. So fry your fish, let it cool, take bitter orange juice as sharp as a mother-in-law's tongue, extend it with a pint of vinegar and double that volume with water. Add a little salt and some peppercorns, a touch of cloves and some saffron, and warm all this in a clay pot but do not let it boil. Take it off the fire hot, season it and leave it to cool. Lay the bream, close-packed, in this escabeche. *You may serve some warm: lift out the quantity you need with a little* adobo, *but add nothing else to it, for the fish releases the frying oil it absorbed, and in this way your fish shall be preserved for quite some time.*

This bream was a favorite of later friary cooks who copied out Altamiras's recipes in their own notebooks. They made it with other fish, too, like salt cod, trout, sardines, and Mediterranean rock fish. Midwinter bitter orange lends it a delicious citrus tang.[16] You can serve it hot, with a little pungent green olive oil poured over the top or it is very good chilled in its jellied juices for a day or two so the flesh absorbs the *escabeche's* flavors.

1 whole red bream, weighing about 1.5 kg / 3 lb, gutted and boned, but skin on, about 6 tbsp olive oil

FOR THE ESCABECHE: juice of 8–12 bitter oranges or of 6 oranges, 2 lemons and a dash of sherry vinegar (about 370 ml / 12 fl oz juice), 370 ml / 12 fl oz mild white wine or cider vinegar, 300 ml / 10 fl oz water, 12 peppercorns, 2 cloves, 1–2 tbsp honey (or 60 g / 2 oz sugar), a pinch of thyme or oregano tied in a muslin bag.

Simmer all the *escabeche* ingredients with salt to taste for 10–15 minutes. Cool. Clean the fish, but leave on the skin, gently wiping off its scales. Warm the olive oil in a large frying pan, fry the bream gently for 5 minutes on each side and lift into a non-reactive dish. Pour over the

BITTER ORANGE

"So fry your fish, let it cool, then take bitter orange juice as sharp as a mother-in-law's tongue." Orange trees were first planted in friary patios for the medicinal value of their fruit, from which cooks made *naranjada*, a healthy breakfast jam.[1] But Altamiras also used bitter oranges' juice to add a sharp edge to tomato sauce, poached fish, mutton stews, and bream escabeche (see p. 143). Ripening oranges were left on the tree and picked only when they were needed during the winter. Today they have a briefer season, but you can freeze the juice for year-round use or replace it with sweet orange juice with a squeeze of lemon and a splash of orange-flower water, which is distilled from bitter orange blossom.

Note

1. Covarrubias defined *naranjada* as an orange preserve. *Tesoro*, 773.

cooled *escabeche* so it covers the fish, check the seasoning, cover the dish with a tight tin-foil lid, and leave it in the fridge. To serve, remove the skin and bones, arrange the fillets on a serving plate, and surround them with the jellied orange *escabeche*. A salad of thinly sliced cucumber and radish goes well with this. Marinate the cucumber and radish in white wine vinegar for half an hour, rinse, dry, and lightly salt before serving.

Salmon and Onion Sofrito / Salmon

Fresh salmon is best boiled and served with a little fresh olive oil and sharp citrus juice or fried onion and salt. Salted salmon needs soaking in clean running water for a full day and night, like tuna, then scouring with new esparto grass before cooking. Such cleanliness, though learned, not natural, is enough to make you a fine cook. Serve this salmon with a dusting of pepper and a jug of fresh olive oil.

Fresh spring salmon was a luxury, so Altamiras fell back on salted salmon at half the price.[17] He served it with an olive oil and lemon juice dressing or an onion *sofrito* (see pp. 120–21). Both these ways of eating fresh salmon are good; the pairing with onion *sofrito* is the more original.

500 ml / ¾ pint onion *sofrito* (see p. 120–21), 150 ml / 5 fl oz sweet white wine (e.g., Moscatel), 4–6 thick salmon steaks or escalopes, 2 tsp salt, parsley stalks, bay leaves, a slice of lemon

Warm through the onion *sofrito* with the sweet white wine, letting it cook down so any extra liquid bubbles away. Spoon the *sofrito* over the bottom of a large serving dish and keep warm. Poach the salmon steaks if you like, using the method for trout (p. 146), drain them well on kitchen paper, lay them on the *sofrito*, and shine them up with a little olive oil. Good at room temperature with freshly boiled hot new potatoes.

SARDINES

Over a hundred new recipes were added to the sixth edition of *New Art*, which was published in Barcelona, in August 1770, after Altamiras's death. Most were drawn from earlier court cookery books and had nothing to do with Altamiras's style, but two of them, written up in his chatty way, were true to his simple but deft country cooking. This is the first of those two recipes: spiced, parsleyed sardines baked in a paper box. The second one is a baked custard (see p. 179).

Sardines in a Paper Box / Para hacer un plato de sardinas (1770)

Take one or two tercias of sardines, make a paper box for them and scatter it with a little parsley, some breadcrumbs and spices. Put the cleaned sardines in the open paper box with a little olive oil, sit it over hot embers, pour a little more oil over the sardines and sprinkle with salt. Close and cover the box with more hot embers, though there should be less above than below it, and you will have a very good dish.[18]

TROUT AND HAKE

Secrets of Trout Fishing

River fish were "stronger, fatter and tastier" when caught under a full moon, wrote Catalan prior Miquel Agustí in his *Book of the Secrets of*

Agriculture, published in 1617.[19] He recommended pouring poisonous potions into the river to make fish dozy and he gave half a dozen ways of making them. Other fishermen took short cuts by building dams to drain shallow rivers where fish could be scooped out from wet hollows. Little wonder that Aragonese brown trout, once famously plentiful, were disappearing by the nineteenth century. Stocks fell so low that in 1876 trout was imported from the New World to restock Aragon's rivers.[20] That brought a change: rainbow trout had arrived and now it is the region's most popular fish.

Poached Trout / Las Truchas

Trout are stupendous, a great treat. You need only water, salt and parsley stalks: be sure the trout are covered with the water. Once they are cooked, pour over a little citrus juice, dust them with pepper and serve them like this.

Using an earthenware or clay pot is a wonderfully easy way to keep water at a very gentle simmer for poaching fish. Bring the water to a boil in a kettle or pan, pour it into your pot, add salt and parsley stalks, adjust the heat so the water just quivers, slip in the trout, and poach till done. A half-pounder takes about 6 minutes, but check that it is cooked to your taste. Altamiras served his with salt, lemon, and black pepper; I like a little olive oil and some roasted red peppers on the side.

Trout in Lemon Sauce, and a Fish Soup / Truchas de Otro Modo

Take fat trout, gut and scale them. Wash and dry them well, and put them to cook in water with salt, olive oil, fried garlic and spices. When they are half-cooked, put them in fresh water seasoned with spices, simmer them till they are done and then dress them with an egg yolk and lemon sauce.

The first cooking water makes a delicious soup if you add hard-boiled eggs and a hazelnut sauce, and finish it off with little bits of candied citron.

Altamiras served poached trout with an egg and lemon sauce in this ingenious double recipe. Then he used the trout broth for a soup made zingy by candied citron, although you can also use lemon zest.[21] I like to skin and fillet the trout just before serving. The soup is good enough to make separately with a more flavorful mixed fish and shellfish broth.

4–6 cleaned trout, 4 cloves, 4 fried sliced garlic cloves

FOR THE SAUCE: a pinch of sugar, 2 tbsp lemon juice, 2 egg yolks, a few snipped chives, fennel leaves or parsley (optional).

Measure water to cover the fish in an earthenware dish, heat gently, and simmer with the cloves and fried garlic. Remove the cloves, add the trout and poach it, as in the previous recipe. Drain, skin and fillet it, and keep it hot. Reserve the fish broth. To make the sauce, have ready a small cooking bowl with the sugar dissolved in the lemon juice. Just before you are ready to serve the fish, set the bowl in a small pan in just boiling water, heat, whisk the egg yolks and then a large cupful of seasoned hot fish broth into the lemon juice; keep whisking without a pause, to give a smooth thickened sauce. Serve the sauce in a heated jug alongside the trout.

FISH SOUP WITH CANDIED LEMON ZEST: 1.4 l / 2½ pints fish or shellfish broth, 2 hard-boiled eggs, 2 tbsp hazelnuts, a few fresh breadcrumbs, 2 sliced garlic cloves fried in good olive oil, a squeeze of lemon juice, 3 tbsp plain or chopped candied lemon zest (see p. 235). Warm the broth. Blend the eggs, hazelnuts, breadcrumbs, and olive oil to a paste. Stir in a cupful of broth to give a thin cream and mix it back into the rest of the broth to give a soup. Squeeze in lemon juice. Put a teaspoonful of diced candied or plain lemon zest into a heated soup plate for each person and ladle the soup over it. I like to sprinkle this with chopped fennel.

Trout in a Green Sauce / Truchas en Guisado

Fry your trout in olive oil, or butter, which is even better for cooking fish, though we must all tailor our tastes to our pocket, or our gustos *to our* gustos. *Then chop fresh greens, parsley, mint, tender lettuce and sorrel when it is in season, pound these in a mortar as if you were making parsley sauce, add a little crumb from a loaf of bread you have soaked and squeezed dry, pound the bread with the greens and add sugar, spices, vinegar and enough water to give a thin sour-sweet sauce. Put the sauce on the fire, stirring it so your spoon moves the same way all the time, and add a little fried fine-chopped onion. Lay the trout in a copper dish, pour your sauce over them, let them cook and serve them hot.*

While I was working on *New Art* I had the luck to spend memorable days sitting at Gillian Riley's kitchen table talking about cookery, art, food, and writing. Food and art historian *extraordinaire*, Gillian already knew and loved the generous simplicity of Altamiras's cooking as well as his love of a good laugh. She began to make his recipes for everyday eating: his salt cod with tomato and orange and this trout with a green sauce, unusually cooked rather than raw, emerged as her favorites.[22] "Parsley, coriander, dill and mint all went in," she wrote to me one day, "With a few peas and some salad leaves together with one spring onion, some chopped garlic, freshly ground peppercorns, cinnamon, cloves, fennel and cardamom for spices, a pinch of salt and another of sugar." Altamiras surely improvised in the same way. Bear in mind you need to balance color and flavor: sorrel and mint turn murky green while spinach gives an emerald green sauce.

4–6 cleaned trout (whole or filleted), 60 g / 2 oz butter or olive oil
FOR THE SAUCE: 1 large chopped spring onion, 30 g / 1 oz butter or 3 tbsp olive oil, about 120 g / 4 oz finely shredded fresh herbs and salad leaves (see above for suggestions), lemon juice and zest to taste, pinches of sugar and spices, 2 tbsp fresh breadcrumbs.

First make the sauce. Put the finely shredded herbs and salad leaves in a large pan with the lemon juice, pinch of sugar, spices, and bread-crumbs. Warm through, stirring, till the greens wilt in their own juices, pour in enough hot water to make a sauce, pulping it with your spoon, and stir in the chopped spring onion sweated in the butter or olive oil. Season the trout, fry them in the butter or olive oil, lift them into an ovenproof dish, pour over the sauce, and bake in a warm oven till just done, about 10 minutes.

Trout, Ham, and Cabbage Toasts / Plato de Truchas y Yervas

Choose large trout. Scale and gut them, pull their flesh into little bits, and fry it with lean and fat cured ham. Have ready boiled white lettuce hearts, the best you can find, and fry some white bread in the skillet fat, then the lettuce too, but be sure it does not dry up. Make a bed of fried bread in a dish, lay the cabbage hearts and trout on top, add little bits of orange flesh and pepper, tuck fried bread sippets and fine-cut lean ham between the cabbage and trout. Serve this hot and it tastes even better if you can make it with butter instead of olive oil.

Now, Cooks and Brothers, I can already hear your quibble: how can I fry fish in melted butter or ham fat if I write here of cookery for lean days? This knotty question no doubt amuses you if it had not already occurred to you, but let me untie it here for you. True, I write of trout here alongside other fish and by its nature it may be eaten on meatless days, yet the dish above is also cooked as a treat on meat eating days. So you see, you may not tax my conscience, though I am a Cook, I cannot let you taste that pleasure, albeit trivial, for this poor cook's tastes and accounts follow Evangelical Law closely, as you shall note.

Writer Dionisio Pérez called this recipe "a very old Morisco dish"[23] in a posthumous anthology of his food journalism entitled *Classic Spanish Cookery*. He must have made the link between *New Art*'s recipes and the Morisco influences of the Valdejalón since it is an Altamiras original. Today this makes a great first course or *tapa*.

120 g / 4 oz butter, 120 ml / 4 fl oz olive oil, a large slice of country bread per person, 500 g / 15 oz blanched finely shredded green or white cabbage, 90 g / 3 oz streaky cured ham (Iberico if you can), 1 skinned trout fillet per person, juice of a lemon

Makes 8–12 toasts

Warm half the butter and olive oil in a large frying pan, fry the bread in it, and drain it on kitchen paper. Add a little more butter or oil to the pan, sweat the shredded cabbage, scoop it out, drain off and reserve any fat, and wipe the pan clean of any browned bits and pieces. Add the rest of the butter and oil to the pan, fry the chopped cured ham till crisp, then add the fish to the pan, and toss them together. Do not worry too much if the fish breaks up. To assemble the toasts make a bed of cabbage on each, top with the fried ham and fish, evenly divided between the toasts, and squeeze a little lemon juice over the top. Good with a chilled lemony white wine such as an Albariño.

Roast Hake / Luz Frito, o Merluza

On the subject of hake, or light, as we also call that fish, I would not leave you in the dark. So let me enlighten you here, though I shall assume you know hake, like other sea fish, comes salted. Lay it in running water as long as you need to wash out the salt, rinse it, cut it into pieces, dry them with a clean cloth, fry them, lay them in a glass dish and pour over a little olive oil fried with garlic. Chop four more raw garlic cloves, stir them into a little bitter orange juice with a dusting of pepper and a handful of fine-cut parsley, pour all this over your hake or light and cook it over hot embers, with more on the lid, and turn your fish so it sucks up the juices. This is very good and you may serve it with a hot hazelnut sauce. So now, when you come to cook hake, you can do it with great lucidity.

Fresh slices of hake are at their very best, I think, thick cut. Then, whichever way you poach or roast them, you can appreciate the fish's large smooth white flakes. For Altamiras, who could never resist a good pun, roast hake was also a great chance for a regional word game: it was called *merluza* in Castilian, but *luz* or *lluç*—also meaning light—in the dialects of the old Aragonese kingdoms. No prize for guessing which region enlightened the other here.

4–6 thick-cut hake slices, about 250 g / 8 oz each in weight, 8 tbsp olive oil, 1 sliced garlic clove

FOR THE BASTING JUICE: 3–4 cloves of sliced garlic, 4 peppercorns, 2 tbsp chopped parsley, the juice of 2 lemons, 2 tbsp water.

Preheat the oven (200°C, 400°F, gas mark 6). Put the hake slices in an ovenproof baking dish or roasting pan. Warm the olive oil with the sliced garlic and, when the garlic is golden, spoon both over the hake, turning the fish in the oil. Oven-roast for 5 minutes. Meanwhile pound the raw garlic cloves, peppercorns, and parsley, mix in the lemon juice and water, and spoon the basting juices over the hake. Roast till just done, for about another 3–4 minutes, and serve immediately. Hot new potatoes tossed with lemon zest and parsley are good with this.

TO PRESERVE OR PICKLE FISH

How rarely we pickle fish yet how delicious it can be.[24] Altamiras did his like Cordoba's anchovies in wine vinegar today, a dish designed to wake up tired taste buds; he added thyme, fennel, oregano, orange, and lemon for a subtle citric and herby marinade. Fried fish, though, he would have preserved in olive oil: it turns out this is why he had been so strict about frying fish unfloured. These both make delicious modern summer meals.

To Preserve Fried Fish in Olive Oil / Para Conservar Pescado

As you read in the Chapter where I gave you a recipe for fried salt cod this handbook does not allow fish to be floured before frying. Do not get annoyed with me that I dwell on what may seem trivial to you: I simply wish to spread

common sense unlike other Cooks, one of whom, when I told him not to flour fish, left it unfloured, so leaving this message engraved on his face: "I say one thing, but I do another." I do not take pleasure from telling you this story, but do so to warn you against Cooks or others you may come across who hide behind Carnival masks. So, then, preserve fish this way: fry it without flour, cool it, lay it in virgin olive oil and this way it shall keep for as long as you like. And take good note: fish that has been floured for frying spoils when it is preserved in olive oil.

Good fish for preserving in olive oil are firm-fleshed bream, grouper, trout, and albacore tuna. Salt them, fry them, lay them in a very clean dish, cover them with olive oil, and keep them chilled or cool. Bring the fish to room temperature before serving. This is fine hot-weather fast-food served with roasted red peppers, cheese in oil, and a basket of bread.

Fish Pickled in Adobo / Adobo para Pescado

Fry your fish without flouring it and make this adobo: *take bay leaves, crush garlic with thyme, fennel and oregano, infuse these in strong vinegar with some little bits of orange, cook them as a marinade, add the cooled fish and if it needs more salt, add it.*

Whitebait, anchovies, sardines, dogfish, and swordfish are all good pickled in an *adobo* with the cooking time adjusted to the fish's volume. Plan on two days for boned anchovies and three days for larger fish, but always try nipping a piece of flesh from the center every twelve hours so you end the marinading when the fish is just pickled, but not soft. Remove, dry well, and serve with a good fruity or grassy olive oil.

SHAD, LAMPREY, BARBEL, FROGS, SNAILS

Altamiras's final fish recipes were for local river lamprey and shad, frogs, and snails. The first of them, a pie with a tender olive-oil pastry, can be adapted to all kinds of fish and is one of my favorites.

A Fish Pie / La Saboga

Shad is good roasted like eel, or with a sauce, or baked in a pie. Make your pastry from flour, a little tepid water, olive oil, raw eggs, a little anise, aguardiente *and salt. Take your shad, scale and wash it, put pine kernels and parsley in its empty belly, dust it with pepper and salt, and you may add raisins, which are very good in this. Wrap the pastry around your shad, like a cone, carry it to the bread oven to bake and if you are cooking it for a meat-eating day, push bits of cured ham into gashes in the fish's flesh. You may serve this cold or hot or, on a lean day, pour a little olive oil flavoured with fried garlic over your shad or season it with raw garlic. Trust me in these matters for I speak from my own experience, unlike a certain floury friar who ran to the Unshoed Fathers, but found his questioning resolved against his wishes and in my favour.*

Altamiras made his shad pie the medieval way, with a whole fish,[25] but he replaced the older tough pastry crusts, designed to give an airless pre-serving box, with a soft and crumbly olive-oil dough. The recipe stood the test of time: it turns up in Alice B. Toklas's 1940s cookbook, given to the author by a Spanish friend. I like to make it with boned and skinned trout, hake, salmon, or butterflied sardines for a one-dish meal that is good served with a salad. It keeps well in the fridge for a day or two.

370 g / ¾-lb chunk of gutted, skinned, and boned salmon or hake, or equivalent weight of trout fillets or butterflied sardines, 12 chips of fatty cured ham, 100 g / 3½ oz toasted pine kernels, 3 tbsp snipped parsley leaves, 60g / 2 oz seeded and soaked Malaga or other raisins, a tablespoonful of onion *sofrito* (see p. 121)

FOR THE PASTRY: 275 g / 9 oz plain seasoned flour, 120 ml / 4 fl oz olive oil, 1 egg, 1 tsp dry anise spirit, 1½ tbsp aguardiente, chilled water to bind the pastry (about 2 tbsp), or 500 g / 1 lb readymade short-crust pastry.

Serves 4–6 for a first course.

Heat the oven (180°C, 350°F, gas mark 4). Sieve the flour with a pinch of salt and mix in the olive oil beaten with the egg, anis, and aguar-diente, adding 2 tablespoons chilled water to bind the dough. Knead then rest the wrapped pastry in the fridge for 30 minutes. Roll it out on a well-floured surface—the pastry is quite crumbly—and cut it into two pieces, one slightly larger than the other, to make the pie's lower and upper crusts. Check that the fish will fit on the larger piece with a rim all around for sealing the pie and that the smaller piece will cover it, like a hat. If not, roll the pastry out thinner and larger. Wipe the fish clean, season it, set it on the pastry, push the cured ham chips into slashes in the fish and scatter the pine kernels, parsley, and raisins over the top. Lay over the upper crust, seal the edges dampened with a little wine or water, crimp firmly to seal with an oiled fork (see p. 23), cut a steam hole in the top of the pie and bake for about 30 minutes, checking that the fish is cooked through with a knife pushed through the steamhole. This makes a good one-course meal with salad.

> "I think this said boat belongs to some river fishermen, for they catch the best shad in the world here."
>
> Sancho Panza to Don Quixote beside the Río Ebro,
> Miguel de Cervantes, *Don Quixote*, Part 2, 1615

River Lamprey / Lamprea de Rio

This fish is very like eel, it has ten or twelve airholes below the head and it is very bloody. To dress it, I wash it, cut it open, gut it, cut it into pieces, lay them in a big cooking vessel with fried garlic, pepper, saffron, cloves, cinnamon and pounded parsley, and put the lamprey to cook. The blood which runs out gives you a very good sauce.

Lamprey, or stonesucker, has been feasting food in Spain since Roman times. Today a few elderly lamprey swim in the Río Ebro's estuary,[26] but the big commercial catch comes from the Río Miño, in Galicia, where you can eat it in riverside restaurants during the spring season. Occasionally that lamprey makes its way to Madrid's wholesale market and from there to the capital's Galician restaurants. On the edge of the city, at El Torreón, I tracked down Benito Estévez, who cooks lamprey there to order, using a recipe from Arbo, his home-town on the Río Miño. First he marinades it overnight in blood, red wine, and olive oil then he slow-cooks it, adding onion, garlic, parsley, cloves, salt, and pepper. You can cook other meaty fish this way, too, for a special occasion. Serve with an intense red wine like Ribera Sacra, from Galicia, or a Catalan Priorato or Montsant.

Barbel Dressed with Olive Oil and Citrus / Barbo

Take a large barbel, scale it well, cut off its wings and tail, and give it a little boil, with salt. Serve it on a plate with fresh olive oil, a dusting of pepper, parsley and bitter orange. Many people like this fish, especially when they have little appetite.

Late in the winter the irrigation channels in the market gardens around La Almunia would be cleaned out by day workers, who would whoosh easy catches of small, bony barbel into buckets. For Altamiras it was a gift: enough fresh fish, however small and bony, to feed everyone a special lunch during Lent.[27] His simple finish—a few drops of bitter orange juice squeezed over the top, pepper, and parsley—is good for all kinds of white fish.

FROGS: FOOD AS PHYSICK

Frogs were medicinal food for anyone suffering from breathing problems, coughs and "a variety of other ailments," as Charles V's doctor, Luis Lobera, put it in his 1542 medical treatise, the *Banquet of Noble Gentlemen*,[28] but they were also thought good for healthy singers and preachers who needed plenty of lung power. Altamiras made them into pies and dumplings, and cooked them in garlic soup.

Fried Frog or Squid Pasties / Ranas en Pastelillos

Skin and wash your frogs and make pastry for them with a little cow's milk butter, hot water, salt and eggs, all in proportion. Then make the frogs' suits of pastry armour and be sure this is the first time they have worn it. Season them with salt and seedless raisins, prepare parsley, pepper, a little saffron, soaked pine kernels and a touch of raw garlic, stirred up together, then enclose them in their armour, fasten it tight, fry them in your skillet and serve them hot with sugar and cinnamon. This dish is for convalescents, and those without appetites.

Spaniards generally make *empanadillas* from ready-made discs of frying pastry, but the dough is not difficult to make yourself. Altamiras wittily sculpted his pasties just as court cooks did their grandiose pies of venison and boar.[29] Irreverently, he thought of his frogs as knights in armor. I find frozen frog's legs tasteless so I replace the flesh with squid, another watery creature cooked by friars in coastal kitchens.

1 heaped tbsp seedless raisins soaked in warm water, 2 tbsp olive oil, 1 onion, 1 finely chopped clove of garlic, 400 g / 13 oz chopped cleaned squid, a splash of dry white wine, 2 heaped tbsp finely chopped flat-leaf parsley, 1 heaped tbsp toasted pine kernels, a dozen crumbled saffron threads, a pinch of cinnamon

FOR THE PASTRY AND FRYING: 150 g / 5 oz flour, 15 g / ½ oz butter, 1 tbsp olive oil, ½ beaten egg, 75 ml / 3½ fl oz chilled water, a small panful of olive oil for shallow-frying.

Makes 8–12 pasties.

First make the pastry: warm the butter, olive oil, and water, remove from the heat as the liquid reaches boiling point, stir in the sieved seasoned flour all at once, beat well, then stir in the beaten egg. Knead the pastry lightly for 5 minutes on a floured surface then rest it, wrapped in the film in the fridge, for half an hour. Roll it out thinly on a well-floured surface, cut out eight to a dozen 12.5-cm / 5-in diameter discs with a bowl or glass, and chill these until you are ready to fry. To make the filling for the pasties, warm the olive oil, sweat the onion slowly in it, adding the garlic at the end, then the squid. Toss well, add the parsley, pine kernels, saffron, cinnamon and salt, splash in the wine, cover, and cook gently for 20 minutes. The squid should be tender, but not too soft. Stir the drained raisins into the filling and check the seasoning. Fill the pasties: lay a teaspoonful of squid filling in the center of each pastry disc, wet the rim, fold it over to make a half-crescent pasty, seal the dampened edges then crimp firmly with an oiled fork. Warm a finger's length of olive oil in a small deep frying pan till bubbling and drop in a little bit of pastry to test the temperature. When the pastry rises to the top it is ready for frying. Drop in one or two pasties, fry each for about 3 minutes, flipping them over when golden, lift them out to drain on kitchen paper, then drop in two more pasties. The oil should never be left empty as it fries. These are at their best eaten hot while the pastry is crisp with a glass of chilled white wine.

KITCHEN VISITORS

Sometimes Altamiras's recipes read like cookery classes. Here he writes about hygiene and, along the way, he gives us a glimpse of life in his kitchen, a busy workplace that must have echoed with the noise of knives chopping, pestles pounding, the friars washing up and visitors delivering wood, charcoal, olive oil, and other bulky food alms. There were unwanted visitors, too, like summer flies. Leafy tree branches were hung from the ceiling to attract them overnight and carried out in the morning. In winter the atmosphere would change: the cook would feed the kitchen hearth with logs and the friars would gather round to warm themselves.[30]

Frog Dumplings / Almondiguillas de Ranas

Take the frogs, remove the flesh from their bones, chop it with parsley and round it out with hard-boiled egg yolks. Then take breadcrumbs and a little cheese, but it should not speak too loud, bind everything with eggs, add salt and spices and make little dumplings, but do not touch these. You can use a mould or a little chocolate cup wetted every now and then in warm water, and then your dumplings will turn out perfectly, for I would not give any kind of cook, even the most punctilious nun, permission to touch them. Watch out for flies, too, for they will end up in your dumplings if you give them half a chance. So, you see, there are no flies on me and I hope I have not left you with a flea in your ear. Have hot broth to hand, among which fish or chickpea are best, bring it to the boil, throw in your dumplings, and they shall cook in no time. Serve them in their cooking broth thickened with egg yolks or hazelnuts, but be wary of serving too much sauce for that is the worst mistake a cook can make, especially in a fish dish.

Frog's Legs and Poached Eggs / Ranas con Huevos

Take a wide-mouthed cooking dish. Put water in it and warm it on the fire, add salt, parsley, fried garlic and spices, let them simmer. Throw in frogs' legs, crack in eggs too, let them spread and poach. Serve them like this. Some people think this dish is a great treat, and I am not surprised.

Unexpectedly this dish pops up in *A Recipe Book of Extremeño Cooking*, an excellent 1985 anthology of popular dishes.[31] Since the wording echoes Altamiras's original, we may guess his recipe became part of popular cookery wherever frogs were in plentiful supply from big rivers, like the Ebro and Tagus, or small water tanks. Friar Ángel, the cook at Santo Espíritu, near Valencia, remembers catching them not so long ago from a friary water tank to cook as a fiesta dish in Extremadura. Today imported farmed frogs are sold and these are tasteless.

Dijó la rana al mosquito	The frog said to the mosquito
Desde una tinaja	From a wine jar
Mejor es morir en el vino	I would rather die in wine
Que vivir en el agua.	Than live in wáter.

Francisco de Quevedo y Villegas,
"Vino," *Letrilla Burlesca V*, c. 1640

SNAILS

Snails have always been gourmet food in Spain.[32] In the seventeenth century, Juan de Pineda, the friary writer, had reckoned Valencians ate more snails than "Spain, Italy and France put together." Later, in Altamiras's lifetime, a 1720s census of Zaragoza discovered four dozen snail-gatherers working in the city, perhaps selling on to the Valencian market. Today the specialist snail stalls in Valencia's central market offer half a dozen varieties, ranging from big stripy *baquetas*, the paella snails, to little white *cabrillas*, their curl of flesh picked out with a pin for eating, usually as a tapa. Altamiras's recipe is good for all snails, once purged and cleaned.

Snails / Caracoles

Soak your snails, wash them with a handful of salt, put them in clean water, refreshing it two or three or as many times as you need. Boil the snails, skim off the foam that rises to the top, then throw in salt, thyme, bay leaves and a handful of oregano. When the snails are cooked, fry onion in your skillet, add the snails and let them cook together. These are very good, but even better served with a garlic and egg sauce.

The Gitanos are expert snail cooks, treating them with the care usually given to shellfish. In her book *Gitano Cooking* Matilde Amaya soaks snails in their cooking juices for a couple of days before eating them,[33] a good way to transform their flavor. Altamiras served his with *sofrito* to which you can add bay, thyme, and oregano. Make 500 ml / ¾ pint of onion *sofrito* (see p. 121) for half a kilo or one pound of snails in shell (about 4 to 6 dozen *baquetas*, for example). Parboil the snails according to producers' instructions then simmer them slowly in the *sofrito* for 45 minutes. Serve with the *ajo*, or garlic mayonnaise, below. The sweet, garlicky, earthy flavors are good with young red Mediterranean wines.

Garlic Mayonnaise / Ajo

Take a piece of bread, soak it in vinegared water and squeeze it dry. Pound garlic cloves, add a little pepper and salt, parsley and mint, pound all these well with the bread and add egg yolks. Take as many as you need for the quantity of ajo you want to make. Then take your oil pourer and drip oil, little by little, into your ajo, stirring one way, without pausing, till you have a thick paste, let it be a little salty. If your snails are for many people, put a little ajo *on each dish before you send them out. I warn you this is not for watery tastes, these are not good eaten with water.*

Gorgeously garlicky, unexpectedly minty, this garlic mayonnaise is bound by fresh breadcrumbs.[34] Its flavors improve, especially the mint, from one day to the next. Altamiras made it with the help of an olive-oil dripper, the narrow spouted pouring jug designed to let olive oil fall drop by drop into sauces and dressings. The design of these has hardly changed over the centuries and they remain invaluable kitchen gear.

2–4 garlic cloves, 2 large egg yolks at room temperature, a few drops of sherry vinegar, 30 g / 1 oz fresh breadcrumbs (optional), 200 ml / 7 fl oz of your best olive oil, a small handful of finely snipped fresh mint and flat-leaf parsley
Makes 250 ml / 8 fl oz sauce.
Pound the skinned garlic to a paste, put it in a glass or china bowl, add salt and pepper and stir in the egg yolks, a drop or two of sherry vinegar, and breadcrumbs. Set the bowl on a cloth so it does not move and start dripping in your olive oil, whisking all the time with the other hand till the mix catches to give a thick shiny emulsion. If it threatens to curdle, you can pull it back by whisking in a spoonful or two of hot just off-the-boil water. Finally stir in the snipped mint and parsley leaves and chill overnight, covered.

EGGS COOKED ALL KINDS OF WAYS

Eggs lay at the heart of friary eating. Altamiras cooked them in omelettes, whisked them up in a sweet foam, candied yolks in sugar syrup, and fried stuffed hard-boiled eggs. Elsewhere in the book he made custards, egg-topped bread soups and rices, and egg-thickened sauces. The friars were also famed for drinking raw eggs if they fell hungry while out on the road collecting alms. "When I'm fasting," declares Fray Antonio in Cervantes's play *The Blessed Ruffian*, "I feel no good, I'm weak, unpious and depressed." So saying, he begs two eggs and knocks them back from the shell.

Fried Stuffed Hard-Boiled Eggs / Huevos Rellenos

Make stuffed hardboiled eggs this way: halve them, take out the yolks, chop them up with a few green leaves and add breadcrumbs, spices, cinnamon, sugar and cracked and stirred eggs. Stir this to give a soft stuffing, fill your eggs with it, dip them in well-beaten egg and a little flour, fry them and serve them with sugar and cinnamon.

These stuffed eggs, very similar to earlier ones in Muslim cookbooks, are wonderful food for a crowd. I like them fried in a crunchy breadcrumb crust rather than the original deep-fried batter. You can add back in the earlier al-Andalus flavorings like onion and coriander juice if you want a flavor that is a little more pungent.[35]

6 hard-boiled large eggs, 2 tbsp chopped mixed fresh leaves and herbs (e.g., rocket, sorrel, fennel, mint, basil, chives, and flat-leaf parsley), 1 tsp fresh soft breadcrumbs, 1 tsp grated lemon zest, a few drops of olive oil
TO FRY: 3 tbsp plain flour, 1 beaten egg, 60 g / 2 oz fine dried breadcrumbs, olive oil for shallow-frying.
Halve the eggs widthways or lengthways, pop out the yolks, mash them with all the stuffing ingredients and season to taste. Stuff the whites and join the two halves of each egg. Don't worry if the stuffing overflows and the whites don't meet perfectly. Chill for an hour. Prepare platefuls of seasoned flour, beaten egg, and breadcrumbs. Roll the stuffed eggs in these to give a thick crumb crust, chill again for 20 minutes, then shallow-fry them in hot olive oil, rolling them over. They need 5 minutes frying in all. Drain them on kitchen paper and serve on a bed of green leaves, with *ajo* (see pp. 157–58) if you like.

Candied Egg Thread / Huevos Mexidos

To candy a couple of eggs put an ounce of sugar and the same of water in a cazuela over the fire. When your syrup is very hot, add your eggs, well beaten, and move them all the time with the iron you keep for this purpose till they set. Often these eggs are served to the sick.

Today Spanish patissiers sell sugared egg yolk thread as a decorative garnish. But Altamiras knew golden egg threads as food for the sick.[36] Perhaps that is why they were a friary and convent speciality, known to Mexican poetess and cook Juana de la Cruz too. If you want to try candying your own yolks, great as a garnish on a dark chocolate cake, you can use a modern chef's technique. Put the beaten yolks into a baby's bottle and press them in spirals on to the foam that rises to the top of a panful of simmering sugar syrup. When set, lift them into a bowlful of cold water, then on to kitchen paper to drain.

"And what shall I tell you, lady, of the natural secrets I have discovered by cooking? I see an egg holds together and fries in butter or oil, but on the contrary, it falls into shreds in a sugar syrup."

Sister Juana Inés de la Cruz,
Reply to Sor Filotea de la Cruz, 1691

How to Boil a Couple of Hundred Eggs / Huevos Passados por Agua

Some may find it frivolous I write about something that seems so easy, yet in truth it is not so. To cook a large quantity of eggs together, put a cauldron of water to boil, then lower in your fresh eggs in a basket.[37] In this way you may take them all out of the water at the same time too, because otherwise, if you want to boil a hundred pairs of eggs, you shall find some turn out hardboiled, some broken and others not even fit to drink.

Baked Eggs with Squash, Tomato, and Mint / Huevos en Abreviatura

Take squash, onion, tomato, parsley and mint. Fry them all and put them in a shallow, wide-mouthed cooking dish with a lid. Then stir your eggs very well, add salt to them, pour them over the fried squash and put the dish between hot embers till the eggs are golden. Afterwards cut this up like a large pie and serve it.

Do not stint on the mint in these eggs baked with squash and tomato: it lifts the whole dish.[38]

4 tbsp olive oil, 2 finely chopped onions, 370 g / 12 oz skinned and diced pumpkin, 2 skinned and chopped tomatoes, a generous handful of roughly snipped flat-leaf parsley and mint, 4 beaten eggs

Heat the oven to 150°C, 300°F, gas mark 2. Warm the olive oil in a frying pan, sweat the onions, add the pumpkin and tomatoes, toss till they soften, stir in the parsley and mint, season to taste. Turn into a lightly oiled baking dish, pour over the seasoned loosely beaten eggs, and oven-bake for a quarter of an hour. This makes a good quick lunch or supper.

EASTER EGGS

Eggs were off friary menus in Lent, but hens were laying then, so eggs were preserved by hard-boiling them or, if the shells were perfect, submerging them in urns of limed water.[39] Later the friars ate hard-boiled Easter eggs cooked in a nut sauce that looks as plain as their habits. Outside friary walls Easter eggs were laid on top of sugary flatbreads known as *culecas* or *monas*.

Hard-Boiled Eggs in Hazelnut Sauce / Huevos Duros

Take hard-boiled eggs, shell them and lay them in a dish. Bathe them in seasoned water, fry abundant onion, add parsley, mint and other spices, add a hazelnut sauce and give the dish a little boil. For the sauce moisten breadcrumb in vinegared water, pound hazelnuts with two cloves of garlic, and make your sauce with these and the seasoned water. Add some olive oil fried with garlic, and remember to take quantities of all these ingredients as fitting for your eggs.

We know these were an Easter dish thanks to Fray Sever de Olot, a Catalan friary cook who wrote a kitchen notebook in 1778, explaining at the foot of his recipes how they were eaten.[40]

4–6 shelled warm lightly hard-boiled eggs, 2 tbsp good olive oil, 1 chopped onion, 2 skinned and sliced garlic cloves, 30 g / 1 oz fresh breadcrumbs, 2 dozen small toasted skinned hazelnuts, 2 garlic cloves

FOR THE BROTH: 600 ml / 1 pint broth of water simmered with flat-leaf parsley and mint, a thumb's length of cinnamon stick, a couple of cloves, and a few drops of vinegar.

Put all the ingredients for the broth into a large pan and simmer for 15 minutes. Add the shelled hard-boiled eggs and warm them through very gently. Meanwhile warm the olive oil in a small frying pan and sweat the onion, adding the garlic towards the end so it does not burn, scoop into a bowl, add the breadcrumbs, nuts and garlic, blend till smooth, season to taste, and sharpen with a few drops of vinegar. Blend in spiced broth till you have a creamy sauce. Drain the hard-boiled eggs and pour the sauce over them.

Eggs Poached in Saffron Broth / Otros Diferentes

Pour seasoned water into a wide-mouthed shallow cooking dish, add parsley, mint, fried garlic, pepper and saffron, crack eggs into the water and poach them. If you have spring herbs and greens on hand then these eggs are very good.

This is classic Franciscan cooking: simple, with a throwaway beauty. For each person's soup bowlful of water I add 2 garlic cloves sweated in olive oil, celery leaves, and a few coarsely shredded spinach or rocket leaves. Simmer everything together in a large pan for 10 minutes, poach an egg for each person in the broth, add finely shredded mint leaves for the last minute or two of cooking, sprinkle with salt, and serve with crusty bread.

Egg Foam and Sponge Cakes / Huevos en Espuma

Take water, sugar and eggs in proportion, put them in a pot off the heat, then whisk them or beat them with your chocolate beater and put them on the fire, whisking as they warm and, as they boil, lift the foam on to a plate of sponge cakes, ladling it like chocolate.

Whisked as it cooks in a *baño maría*, this warm foam rises up light and bubbly, then settles as the bubbles become compact. Altamiras may have adapted it from a wine foam called *zampollón*. There is no reason why you cannot sneak back in a wine such as a Jerez PX dessert sherry for a sybaritic effect.[41]

1 large egg at room temperature, 1 tsp unrefined brown cane sugar, ½ sherry glass of cold water or PX sherry
Makes 750 ml / 1½ pints foam.
Put the egg, sugar, and water or wine into a 1.2 liter / 2 pint china bowl. Set it in a pan over a few inches of cold water, preferably sitting over the water without touching it. Put the pan over gentle heat and whisk without pausing. As the water comes to a boil, the foam will rise up, almost filling the bowl. Keep whisking all the time, about 15 minutes in all, by when the foam will settle. I like it served in stemmed glass dishes.

Chickpeas, Greens, and Eggs / Otros Huevos Duros

Cut hard-boiled eggs in half lengthways, slice them as you would an onion, fry fine-cut onion and, when it is well softened, add your eggs with a little chopped greenery and pounded chickpeas. Stir everything, season, add spices, and set this with more beaten eggs, and a little sharp citrus juice is very good in this.

Rocket, chard, borage, sorrel, mint, and parsley all work well as Altamiras's "greenery" in this ingenious double-egg omelette. First you hard boil eggs for slicing, then you bind them into an omelette with chickpeas and greens.

6 tbsp olive oil, 2 chopped onions, 300 g / 10 oz roughly mashed cooked chickpeas, 150 g / 5 oz shredded spinach or other greens, a squeeze of lemon juice, salt and pepper, 3 sliced hard-boiled eggs, 4 raw eggs
Serves 4–6 as a first course.
Heat a cool oven (150°C, 300°F, gas mark 2). Warm the olive oil in a heavy-bottomed frying pan, sweat the finely chopped onions in it till soft and golden, add the drained and mashed chickpeas, and shredded greens. When they have wilted, squeeze in the lemon juice and season to taste. Cook for another 5 minutes then cool. Mix in the lightly beaten raw eggs, adding an extra one if you need it to hold together the ingredients. Scoop into a lightly oiled 25 cm / 10 inch baking dish—a *cazuela* is ideal—arrange the hard-boiled egg slices on top, press them in lightly to submerge them, and oven-bake till just set, but slightly moist, for about 20 minutes.

Salt Cod Tortilla / Otros Huevos Diferentes

Take hake flesh, boned and soaked to wash away its salt, cut it into little bits as you would chop cured ham fat, and cook it with the eggs as an omelette. This is so good people will wonder if it is made with cured ham.

Today salt cod tortillas are a speciality of the Basque Country's cider houses.[42] I particularly like this one made with lots of lightly caramelized onions.

6 tbsp good olive oil, 3 sweet onions thinly sliced into rings or cut into julienne strips, 250 g / 4 oz (dry weight) soaked and flaked salt cod (see p. 238), 8 beaten eggs, cracked black pepper, 3 tbsp chopped flat-leaf parsley, 1–2 pickled hot green peppers
Serves 2 as a main course, 4–6 for tapas or a first course.
Gently warm the olive oil in a heavy-based frying pan, sweat the onions till soft and lightly browned, and scoop them into a large bowl, letting the frying oil drip back into the pan. Add the salt cod to the pan,

toss well in the oil, add it to the sweated onions. Cool to hand heat. Stir in the beaten eggs, season to taste, and leave the bowl to stand for half an hour. Pour the oil out of the pan, straining it, wipe the pan very clean, then pour back in 2–3 tablespoons of the oil. Warm it, running it around the frying pan, and pour in the omelette mixture, drawing in the cooked edges so the liquid egg runs out to the pan's rim to cook. When the omelette is set around the edges and underneath, but still slightly juicy on top, turn cooked side up on to a large plate then slide it back into the pan, the unfinished side down, to cook till just set, but juicy in the middle. Good with bread and salad.

"In the culinary arts the tortilla is the most difficult of all easy dishes."

Teodoro Bardaji, *Culinary Index*, 1915

Marzipan Eggs / Huevos Rellenos de Otro Modo

Empty fresh eggs of everything inside them: make holes as big as hazelnuts in the shells, empty out the eggs through the holes then make an almond paste, as soft as a bread dough, with yolks, broth, sugar, cinnamon and chopped almonds. Fill the egg shells through a small funnel with this paste, take care you do not dirty the shells, then cook these in a copper ladle. They are in very good taste, so much so that you may serve them even to a Provincial Visitor or Bishop &c.

If you make these marzipan-filled eggshells you will see why Altamiras considered them for entertaining the friars' most important guests: creamily rich, perfect food for a feast, they also raise a smile. The marzipan seems to have evolved from Toledo confectioner Miguel de Baeza's spiced almond paste, as soft as "fine bread dough," published in *The Four Books of the Art of Confectionery*, in 1592, which went on to become a classic.[43] The modern version below was re-created by Armando Jiménez Tejedor, whose restaurant, Las Viandas de Armando, overlooks the pine forests of the Avila countryside where he was born. A modest man, passionate about historical cooking, he led the team who re-created dishes from the monastery at San Escorial for a pioneering book published in the late 1980s. He told me that he thought the key to recipe recreation is an understanding of the cook's personality. However he did it, he pulled off this *trompe l'oeuil* dish almost effortlessly. Thank you Armando.

6 eggs, 500 ml / ¾ pint good broth (see pp. 105–6 and 135), 150 g / 5 oz cane sugar, 150 g / 5 oz skinned almonds, 2 pinches ground cinnamon

TO SERVE: pastry tartlets or an egg box.

Wash the eggs, cleaning them with a soft brush. Make a hole about the size of a hazelnut in the narrow end of each shell by pricking a series of little holes with a pointed tool like the tip of a corkscrew. Reserve the shell circles, as intact as possible. Pour out first the egg whites into one bowl, then the yolks into another. Cook the broth and sugar together in a large pan for 15 minutes, grind the almonds in a food processor and tip them into the broth syrup, add the cinnamon and the sieved egg yolks, stir well, and put back over gentle heat for another 10 minutes, stirring as the paste thickens. Remove from the heat and cool till easy to handle. Stand the empty egg shells, hole up, in an egg box and fill them with the cream, using a piping bag or teaspoon, pushing the filling in well to avoid trapped air bubbles. When the shells are full, cover the holes with the reserved shell circles. Now wrap the eggs in cooking film, twisting the plastic well to close at each end, and cook in gently simmering water (or more broth) in a covered pan for 15 minutes. Fish them out gently (the shells are fragile) and serve hot or cold. Armando thinks "they are good hot but delicious cold." I like to serve them, hole down, in egg cups with teaspoons to crack them open and eat like a boiled egg with a Jerez PX dessert wine.

MORE DISHES
FOR LEAN DAYS

BROTHS AND sops, sweet things and Lenten suppers: Altamiras wrote up all of these in his third chapter of lean day cookery, which showed how many delicious things, often vegetarian, could come from a simple larder of seasonal produce.

LEAN DAY BREAD SOUPS

Fish and Bread Soup / Sopa comun

Take trout broth and well-fried bread sops and a large lidded dish in which to make your soup. In it lay the toasted sops and on top of them chopped hard-boiled eggs, parsley, grated cheese, powdered cloves and cinnamon. Have ready some toasted hazelnuts, pound them with some garlic, pepper and saffron, dilute this with trout broth and boil it in a pot. Now soak the sops with the rest of the trout broth, give them a boil, take them off the fire, pour your hazelnut soup over them, then pour beaten eggs on top and cook this while sitting in hot embers with more in the lid (for by now, I'm assuming you have put on the lid). Cook till you have a golden crust and, if you like, add some little bits of another fish to this, for they make a very good addition.

Bread fried in olive oil lends a special aroma to this plain fish or shellfish broth thickened with cheese, parsley and, if you like, a hazelnut sauce. Throw in a few chunks of fresh fish just before the end of cooking time and you will have gourmet eating.[1]

1.4 liters / 2½ pints fish broth (see p. 147), 1 tbsp olive oil, 4–6 thin slices of bread fried in olive oil (see p. 234), 3 roughly chopped hard-boiled eggs, a small handful of scissor-snipped flat-leaf parsley, 120 g / 4 oz grated ewe's milk cheese, large pinches of powdered cloves and cinnamon, saffron infusion made with 2 dozen threads (see p. 102)

FOR THE HAZELNUT THICKENING: 3 dozen small skinned and toasted hazelnuts (see p. 178), 2 chopped garlic cloves, a small handful of fresh breadcrumbs.

Warm the fish broth in a large pan and check the seasoning. Turn on the oven to 170°C, 325°F, gas mark 3. Brush a warmed 2-liter / 3½-pint ovenproof casserole with olive oil. Make a bed of fried bread in the casserole, scatter the chopped hard-boiled eggs, parsley, grated cheese, and spices over it, pour on enough hot fish broth to soak the fried bread and put in the oven for a few minutes till it becomes spongy. Blend the thickening ingredients, add enough broth to give a thin cream, stir this back into the rest of the soup, add the saffron infusion and seasoning, pour this over the sops, and oven-bake for 15 minutes, adding fish chunks in the last few minutes if you like.

TOMATO AND BREAD SOUP: Friar Ángel at Santo Espíritu makes a tomato and bread soup. He fries up garlic, onion, and tomato in olive oil, layers this up with thinly sliced day-old bread, pours over warm broth and then heats this through gently—you can top it with eggs and cheese if you like, but they're not really needed.

Lenten Nut Bread Soup / Sopa de Quaresma

Cut large bread slices, lay them in a wide-mouthed cooking vessel and scatter over fine-cut parsley, a dusting of pepper and a little grated cheese, except in Lent or when it is forbidden. Then fry onion and garlic, spoon them over your bread and have prepared a pounded hazelnut or pine kernel thickening with garlic, pepper and saffron added to it. Add enough water to make a soup, warm it, stirring with a large wooden spoon, let the soup cook, pour a third over the bread, let it soak up the soup and put these sops on the fire. Give the rest of the thickened broth a little boil, pour it over the sops, let it spread evenly, then toast the sops under hot embers to give a golden crust.

Slowly sweated garlic and onion, pounded hazelnuts, saffron, parsley, and cheese give this vegetarian soup a big depth of flavor.

1.4 liters / 2½ pints hot water, 4 tbsp olive oil, 3 onions thinly sliced into rings, 1 bunch of wild green garlic or 4 fat garlic cloves, 3 thin slices of yesterday's bread, a small handful of snipped flat-leaf parsley, 2 chopped hard-boiled eggs, 90 g / 3 oz grated ewe's milk or other sharp mature cheese, a large pinch of pepper, saffron infusion made with 24 threads of saffron (see p. 102)

FOR THE HAZELNUT THICKENING: 4 dozen small skinned and toasted hazelnuts, 60 g / 2 oz pine kernels, 2 garlic cloves, a dozen threads of saffron.

Warm the oven (170°C, 325°F, gas mark 3). Heat the water. Warm the olive oil in a heavy-based frying pan, sweat the onion in it, adding the garlic towards the end. Meanwhile, brush a 1.6-liter / 2¾-pint flame-proof casserole with a little olive oil, make a bed of bread slices in it, scatter the parsley, chopped hard-boiled eggs and cheese evenly over the top then scoop the onion over the top of that. Blend the hazelnut thickening, add enough of the hot water and infusion to give a thin cream, pour it over the sops, wait until they are soaked through and swell with liquid, then pour the rest of the soup over them. Bake till bubbling.

A SHEPHERD'S BREADCRUMBS

"It's a poor man's dish," apologized the bell-ringer to his guest as he served up fried crumbs in Luis Buñuel's film *Tristana*. For centuries plain fried breadcrumbs were served as everyday food in homes around Spain though one is hard pushed to find a recipe for them in any cookbook.[2]

Served in the pan, they were placed in the center of the kitchen table, each person digging in with a wooden spoon. The friars, though, had their own bowlfuls, or *escudillas*, for Eiximenis, the friary philosopher, had warned, "it is impolite for several people to eat from the same dish, as the Saracens do." Usually the crumbs were fried up with garlic, but Altamiras replaced that here with onion, perhaps to make his *migas* "easy on the stomach" at breakfast time.[3]

Fried Breadcrumbs / Migas sin Ajos

You can make anything without garlic, but garlic is often the making of a good dish. So here is the way to make fried breadcrumbs without garlic taste good; cut your bread into little bits or crumbs, dampen them with water and salt, fry onion, add the crumbs to the onion, and toss them till they are toasted, and shred them with your spatula. To make a thicker pancake add more water and cook the crumbs like a tortilla, first on one side then the other, till both are well toasted. These crumbs are very tasty and easy on the stomach.

Fried breadcrumbs are delicious, but these days they are often served with egg, chorizo, or fish added to them. I prefer them plain, but they need a practiced hand to turn out well. Pedro Andrés Ballarín, a shepherd, is famed for those he serves at his family restaurant next to Santa María, a pilgrimage shrine at the heart of the Sierra de Rodanas. Altamiras probably knew the shrine, which is four hundred years old: he would have made the journey there with his family on foot or by cart. Pedro makes the dish exactly as his father taught him to do, although back then they fried the *migas* for breakfast before going out with the sheep. The bread must be dry, and never frozen, from a good country loaf; the crumbs should be cut as wafer-thin chips, not dice; the water to dampen them should be splashed over in drops; the crumbs are then left to sit overnight. The next day Pedro sweats a chopped onion and one or two chopped green peppers in olive oil, he turns the crumbs gently in the oil with the flavorings and shakes the pan over the heat for half an hour till the bread has turned gold, slightly crispy but still soft inside. Then—and this is a magical small twist to the recipe—he finely slices one or two raw garlic cloves over the top. If you want to try making these at home here are the guidelines: ¼ liter / ½ pint of water to dampen every kilo of crumbs, olive oil to cover the base of the pan, a medium onion, a small green pepper, a clove or two of garlic, and a sprinkling of salt. But I think this is a dish best searched out on the ground, for example, in Rodanas, and enjoyed with a sense of the kind of place that has thrown up such ingenious cooking.

VEGETARIAN BROTHS

Altamiras turned green vegetable, chickpea, and chard broths into lean-day soups.[4] Make them "well seasoned and hot," wrote the author of one 1650 Franciscan handbook, adding that the *hortelano* or kitchen-gardener should "always choose the best the kitchen garden offers the Community."[5]

Green Soup / Caldo

Make this soup from green vegetable broth, more mild than pungent. Put it in a pot and stir in a hazelnut thickening made with nuts, spices, a little bread, garlic and one or two beaten eggs. Add abundant fried onion, simmer your soup to let it absorb the flavours and let it sweat off the fire. Whisk a little of the soup with some eggs, stir well so no threads form, then beat this thickening back into your soup.

Green asparagus and a handful of spinach are a good pairing for a vivid green broth that can be left light in summer, flavored simply with the onion sweated in olive oil, or thickened in winter with egg, bread, and nuts. Croûtons, fried asparagus, and shredded spinach are good finishing touches.

1.4 liters / 2½ pints green vegetable broth (see pp. 234–35), a squeeze of lemon juice, 3 tbsp olive oil, 2 finely chopped onions, 2 beaten eggs (optional), a few shredded mint and parsley leaves

FOR THE HAZELNUT THICKENING: 4 dozen skinned toasted hazelnuts, 30 g / 1 oz fresh bread, a fat clove of garlic.

Heat the broth, squeeze in the lemon juice, and season to taste. Warm the olive oil, sweat the finely chopped onion, scoop into the broth, and simmer for 20 minutes. To thicken the soup, blend the nuts, bread and garlic with a ladleful of broth, and stir back into the soup.

Chickpea Broth / Caldo de Otro Modo

When you have cooked chickpeas, strain the broth into a pot to make soup. Warm it, add a hazelnut thickening and a handful of parsley, put the soup on the fire and, as it simmers, season it with spices. Then take your pot off the fire and put it into your haybasket and leave it there to sweat. When the soup is lukewarm stir a little into cracked eggs then stir them back into the soup. Dress your chickpeas and then you can serve this soup as an extra dish.

I like drinking chickpea broth as it comes, aromatized with lemon zest, spices, parsley, and blanched garlic, but you can also thicken it as Altamiras did with hazelnuts and eggs.

1.4 liters / 2½ pints chickpea broth (see p. 234), 1 head of unskinned garlic (optional), 3 tbsp snipped flat-leaf parsley, a little lemon zest

FOR THE HAZELNUT THICKENING: 2 dozen skinned toasted hazelnuts, 15 g / ½ oz bread (see p. 178), pinches of cloves and cinnamon.

Warm through the chickpea broth. Simmer the whole unskinned head of garlic in it for half an hour. Take it out and, when it has cooled to hand heat, pop out each clove, mash to a pulp, and blend back into the soup. If you want to add the thickening blend the ingredients together, stir them back into the soup with the parsley and lemon zest, check the seasoning, and simmer for 10 minutes.

Chard, Lettuce, and Sorrel Soup / Burete

We make this two ways in the Order of Saint Francis. The first way is with meat broth and the other, which I shall deal with here, is for lean days. Take green broth: chard broth is very good for this. Pour it into a pot, season it with spices, add parsley and a little mint, but be sparing with the mint and not just here, for it stands out in any dish. Boil lettuce, chop it with your chard stalks and a handful of kitchen-garden sorrel, add these to your soup with a skilletful of fried onion and a little cheese. Let your soup come to the boil, thicken it with breadcrumbs and when it has cooked, take it off the heat and leave it to sweat. For a sixteen-pint pot, say, take one and a half dozen eggs, whisk them into a little of the soup off the fire then pour this back into the pot, stirring so your egg does not form threads. This is so good that many people think it is made with meat.

Novelist, poetess, and food writer Emilia Pardo Bazán was the first modern writer to appreciate Altamiras's cooking, relishing its ancestral flavors, perhaps because she lived among writers, artists, and musicians who were turning back to old Spanish culture as a source of renewed inspiration for their own work. She wrote up this soup as a Franciscan speciality in 1913 in her book *The Old Spanish Kitchen*. In fact, the recipe may be much older than she thought: such crumb-thickened soups had been part of Muslim cookery.[6]

1.4 liters / 2½ pints vegetable broth or water, 3 tbsp olive oil, 2 chopped onions, 370 g / 12 oz thinly sliced chard stalk and 1 celery stalk, trimmed (optional), 200 g / 7 oz lettuce, 100 g / 3½ oz sorrel, 12 chopped mint leaves

TO SERVE: 90 g / 3 oz grated ewe's milk or other sharp cheese.

Heat the broth or water in a large pan and season it to taste. Warm the olive oil, sweat the chopped onions gently for a quarter of an hour, and scoop them into the broth. Simmer for 10 minutes, add the sliced chard and celery and a few minutes later throw in the washed lettuce, sorrel, and mint leaves. Cook for just long enough to let this greenery wilt. For a more filling soup, you can thicken the broth with fresh breadcrumbs, beaten eggs, and cheese though I prefer to serve the grated cheese separately so each person can stir it in themselves if they want.

FEAST-DAY SWEETS

So many small Spanish cakes and sweet things originated as celebratory food for saints' days. Today, in our age of affluence, they are more often sold in patisseries and indeed, even in Altamiras's day, some monasteries bought their sweet things.[7] But Altamiras made his own, frugal and simple: here he noted how to make deep-fried puffs sprinkled with anise, which are still made for Lent in Catalonia, and creamed rice with almond milk, a friary favorite, which, as a bonus, gave him the chance for one of his nun jokes. He fried his Lenten puffs the old Muslim way, in a big panful of bubbling olive oil instead of court cooks' lard.[8]

Deep-Fried Puffs / Buñuelos

Take a frying iron shaped like a little cup, the same width at the top and bottom and with a handle measuring one and a half feet, or at least the frying irons I know, those of locksmiths, are like this. Make a flour, egg and water batter that is more liquid than the one you use for wafers for mass. Now heat the frying iron in the fire, once it is hot lower it into a large pan of hot olive oil, then dip it in the batter, filling the iron, and lower it back into the oil, move it around till the puff loosens itself and rises and looks a little like those loaves we call bonnets, which puff out at the top as hats do. You may need to help them come away from the moulds with a cane. Then cut away uncooked dough inside them with scissors so you may fill them with fish or diced meat, lay them in a dish on paper, brush them with beaten egg and bake them, with more embers in the lid than below, till they are golden.

You may serve these sprinkled with sugar and cinnamon or plain with a little honey dissolved in hot water or anise poured over them and with the left-over batter you can make criss-cross lattices like those iron window-grilles that passers-by gaze through from the street: hold an olive-oil pourer full of batter high above the hot frying-pan and move it quickly back and forth and fry this lattice, then balance it on top of your puffs.

Today sugar, milk, and fat are added to give airier puffs, often called *bunuelos de viento*, which are filled with confectioners' cream, though I think it is hard to improve on the anise and honey glaze.

120 ml / 4 fl oz milk, 120 ml / 4 fl oz water, 2 tbsp dry anise liqueur, 15 g / ½ oz sugar, 125 g / just over 4 oz sieved plain flour, zest of ½ lemon, large pinch of cinnamon powder, olive oil for shallow frying

FOR THE HONEY AND ANISE GLAZE: 2 tbsp honey dissolved in 2 tbsp hot water, 1 tbsp anise.

Makes about 12–16 small puffs.

Put the milk, water, anise, and sugar in a pan and bring to the boil. Sieve the flour into a food processor bowl, or other large bowl, stir in the lemon zest, powdered cinnamon, and a pinch of salt. Pour in the boiling liquid and mix everything well, so there are no lumps, then incorporate the eggs, one by one. Scoop the dough into a bowl and chill for at least 30 minutes or until you are ready to make the puffs. Warm a thumb's depth of olive oil in a deep frying pan on the lowest heat till it is gently bubbling. Drop in a little bit of dough and when it rises to the top, surrounded by fizzy frying bubbles, start dropping in neat heaped teaspoonfuls of dough, which will rise, slowly puff up and fry till golden and crisp. If they don't turn themselves over, help them to do so. Allow about 5–7 minutes frying time for each, lifting them out as they are done to a rack sitting over kitchen paper. Cool. Before serving pour the honey and anise glaze over the puffs in a thin stream. You can also cut open these puffs, scoop out the dough inside and fill them, as you like.

OLIVE OIL

"Heat the frying iron in the fire, take it out hot and lower it into a large pan of hot olive oil. . . ." Altamiras had abundant olive oil for his lean day cooking. He used it for dressing vegetables, making sauces, even deep frying. Pressed from local Empeltre olives, a variety planted in the Ebro Valley since Roman times, it was sweet, almondy, golden, "light and gentle," as a farming census described it in the 1780s. Empeltre oils are still prized today, especially for cooking fish, dressing salads, making olive-oil pastries, and shallow or deep frying. Now they are sold as Bajo Aragon PDO oils and are widely exported. If you cannot find them, choose any other mild or delicate golden oil.

Creamed Rice with Almond Milk /
Arroz con Leche de Almendras

For every pound of almonds you need one of sugar, another of rice, six eggs and a little cinnamon. Throw the almonds into a small pot of boiling water, give them a little simmer then spread them out to dry on a wooden board. Skin them, lay them in cold water and take two ounces of pine kernels for each pound of almonds, for this will stop your milk turning brown. Pound the nuts, stir in cold water, warm this milk gently in a pot, sugar it and skim the foam off the top. Now take your rice, wash it in warm water, drain it and simmer it in fresh salted water. Infuse a grated cinnamon quill in hot water. Pour the cinnamon infusion into the rice with the almond milk, cook till the rice grains soften then take it off the fire. Stir the egg yolks into a little cold or lukewarm almond milk and stir it into the rice, but take care threads do not form. Serve this sprinkled with sugar and cinnamon and take note that when you add the almond milk, reserve a little so if your rice sets later and becomes too thick, then you can thin it.

When you have made your almond milk you will be left with dry dross fit only to throw away, though certain ladies, if I should call them such, are so piously poor they serve it stirred into their rice pudding. If you see this, but notice that guests turn a blind eye, do not take them for fools. Rather, some guests are diplomatically polite, and as I write I trust that certain nuns of refined manners will know only too well what I am saying.

Tradition in many monasteries and convents held that rice pudding and rice-flour blancmange were served on feast days like Sundays in Lent.[9] Often they were made with broken grains of rice given to the friars as alms by the rice mills.[10] Botín's desserts cook, María Peinada, helped me experiment with this recipe. We found the best results came from boiling the rice in salted water till firm before plumping it out gently rather than cooking it in warm almond milk. A little grated orange zest and a few drops of orange extract give the rice a satisfying citric aroma. Any surplus almond milk can be recycled as an iced drink (see pp. 220–21).

120 g / 4 oz Bomba or other quality round rice, 90 g / 3 oz sugar (or to taste), 120 ml / 4 fl oz cinnamon infusion (see p. 220), 1.4 l / 2½ pints home-made almond milk (see pp. 213–14), 3 egg yolks (optional), powdered cinnamon (optional)

FLAVORINGS (OPTIONAL): a few drops of orange extract and 1 tsp very finely grated orange zest.

Boil the rice in salted water for 15 minutes or until *al dente*. Drain and then dissolve the sugar in the cinnamon infusion, add to the rice, and simmer gently for 5 minutes. Lower the heat to a minimum, add 750 ml / 1½ pints almond milk, and cook very slowly with just the odd bubble rising, so the almond milk does not separate. Beat in the egg yolks and keep cooking gently till the rice thickens. Remove from the heat and leave to cool. The rice will keep sucking up the almond milk and by the time it is cold, it will be quite dry. At this point you can stir in more almond milk, enough to bathe the rice, and flavorings such as orange extract or orange flower water. Sprinkle a little powdered cinnamon over the top and serve.

Saffroned Rice with Fish and Vegetables / Otro Modo de Arroz

Wash rice well, put it in your cooking vessel and add flavourings: a handful of chopped parsley, pepper, saffron and olive oil warmed with garlic. Sweat your rice like this and when it is golden, add water, season it and leave it to cook. A little flaked fish is good in this, as are tomatoes, and if you like you can pour beaten eggs over it to make a golden crust under hot embers. Sugar and cinnamon are good sprinkled over the top too.

Matías Juan Ríco cooks at Casa Paqui, a renowned restaurant in Castalla in the mountainous hill country of Alicante. This was Morisco country, like the Valdejalón, and it keeps old rice dishes which, as in Aragon, start by the rice being tossed in olive oil before the cooking liquid is added.[11] Today fresh fish reaches these inland areas, but the old salt-cod rices are still sometimes made for their special flavor. Matías likes to choose and add the vegetables to this dish the old way, too, improvising around whatever comes to hand.

600 g / 1¼ lb vegetables (courgettes, asparagus, red peppers, mushrooms, green garlic, baby broad beans, as available), about 150 ml / 5 fl oz olive oil, 2 grated tomatoes, 2 cloves of chopped garlic, 400 g / 13 oz rice, about 1 liter / 1¾ pints very hot fish stock, a saffron infusion made with 2 dozen strands (see p. 102), salt, 500 g / 1 lb soaked best quality salt cod or firm-fleshed fresh fish, for example, monkfish, chopped fresh flat-leaf parsley

"Trim and dice your vegetables," wrote Matías. "Cover the bottom of a paella pan or a large earthenware *cazuela* with olive oil, add the grated tomato, cook it down, frying gently for 5 minutes, add the chopped garlic, then the rice, tossing it to seal it well, throw in the prepared vegetables, toss well, and pour over three-quarters of the hot seasoned fish broth and the saffron infusion. Check the seasoning, raise the flame so the rice boils fast for 15 minutes, remove from the heat, stir in the flaked salt cod or monkfish, cover and leave for 5 minutes till the rice is dry."

NUT CREAMS

These delicious almond and hazelnut creams date back to medieval times. Sadly they have disappeared today though Basque chefs have revived a walnut and milk cream called *intxaursalsa*.[12] Altamiras thickened his creams economically with bread, making them less rich, but they are still intensely sweet. An earthenware or clay dish gives the perfect low cooking temperature for making them.

Almond Cream / Almendrada

Throw your almonds into a ladleful of hot water in a pan, scald and drain them, then leave them lying in cold water before you skin them. I have given you these details for if you start your almonds in cold water then all the oil will run out when you pound them and you will achieve nothing more than a pharmacist. So pound the almonds and measure an ounce of sugar to every one and a half of almonds for each bowlful of cream, though we poor friars make do with an ounce of almonds and half an ounce of sugar. Count a dozen eggs for as many bowlfuls, as well as a little soaked bread or cornflour, add them, put the cream to cook on the fire and serve it with sugar and cinnamon on top.

If you do not have an earthenware or clay dish for making this, use a silicon bowl in a *baño maría*. The untoasted nuts and bread make for a pale cream, which is delicious served in small potfuls with macaroons, a red fruit purée, crème fraîche, and a chilled dessert wine.

90 g / 3 oz skinned almonds, 60 g / 2 oz sugar, 2 eggs, 30 g / 1 oz fresh breadcrumbs, about 200 ml / 7 fl oz water

Blend the almonds to a sticky cream with the sugar, eggs, and breadcrumbs. Scrape it into a heavy-based earthenware or clay pot, or a bowl in a bain marie, stirring well, and cook for about 10 minutes, adding enough water to give a thick cream. If you find lumps or egg threads, push the cream through a coarse sieve then divide it between little serving pots or ramekins and chill it.

Toasted Hazelnut Cream / Avellanada

For eight dishfuls of pudding take a pound of toasted hazelnuts. Prepare your nuts: pick off any bits of skin, lay the nuts in an earthenware dish, sprinkle them with a few drops of water and some fine salt, toss and drain. Toast them in a skillet, wrap them in a cloth, leave them to cool and rub off the skins in the cloth. Pound the nuts with toasted bread, moistened and squeezed dry, add enough water to make a thin cream and some sugar, as you see fit, then warm it till it rises in the pot like milk coming to the boil. The almond cream rises in the pot too, so you need a dish of water to hand to temper it, but take note, do not toast the breadcrumbs for the almond cream.

Toasting the nuts and the crumbs gives this eggless Lenten cream a lovely light praliny flavor. You can also use it as a base for an ice cream.

10 oz / 300 g skinned toasted hazelnuts, 3 tsp salt, a sprinkling of water, 30 g / 1 oz bread, 150 g / 5 oz unrefined brown cane sugar, 250 ml / 8 fl oz water

Put the hazelnuts in a heavy-based frying pan with the salt and a sprinkling of water and toast the nuts gently. Blend them with the toasted bread to a loose crumb mixture, mix in the water, little by little, to give a toffee-colored cream, dilute this to the thickness you like, scrape it into a heavy-based saucepan, stir in sugar to taste, warming to dissolve the sugar, pour into little pots or ramekins, and cool.

TWO CUSTARDS

Altamiras originally gave just one baked egg custard in *New Art*, but a new recipe appeared in the 1770 edition of the book (see opposite), the first that appeared after his death.[13] We may never know whether Altamiras wrote it himself or his publisher María Martí added it, but it is true to his cooking style, with its use of rustic kitchen tools. The milk was measured and poured from a wine flask and the sugar caramelized with a hot poker. I have included it here below Altamiras's first custard.

Baked Custard / Leche Assada

Take two cuartillos *of milk, perhaps a little more, and stir in half a pound of sugar and a dozen cracked and beaten eggs. Stir everything well then bake the custard in a dish between hot embers and it will come out tasting like cheesecake.*

Fill this dish right to the brim to get the crusty brown topping. I like to make it in small *cazuelas* and serve it alongside an apple or pear ragout (see p. 187).

> 500 ml / ¾ pint creamy milk, 200 g / 7 oz cane sugar, 5 eggs
> *Makes 1 liter / 1¾ pints custard.*
> Warm your oven (170°C, 325°F, gas mark 3). Whisk or blend the milk, sugar, and eggs in a large jug. Set a 1-liter / 1¾-pint baking dish in a roasting pan on a shelf in the middle of the oven. Pour in the custard till the dish is nearly full, then pour water around the dish to come half way up the sides. Push the pan into the final baking position and fill the dish to the brim with your custard. Bake for about 1 hour, till a knife stuck in the center comes out clean. Remember, the custard will firm up while cooling.

San José's Custard or Crema Catalana (1770) / Natillas

Take a wine flask full of milk or, if you have no milk, take a pound of raw almonds and make almond milk, as I have explained in my notes on almond blancmange. Then take six egg yolks, five ounces of sugar, an ounce and a half of rice flour, a cinnamon quill and a big bit of lemon zest. Put the yolks, flour and sugar in an earthenware casserole, stir with a wooden spoon, pour in the milk a little at a time, then put the pot over a gentle fire, and keep stirring. When you see this wants to boil, take it off the heat and pour it into a dish and let it cool, then afterwards put a little shovel or a poker in the fire and when it is good and hot, sprinkle the custard with sugar and burn it with the clean shovel or poker, a little at a time, till all the sugar is toasted, and then you will have a perfect custard.

We think of this dessert as Catalan cream, but in Altamiras's day it was a celebratory pudding made for San José. Today cream and egg yolks are added. I have adjusted the quantities and replaced the burnt sugar caramel on top with a liquid topping, an idea inspired by a recipe given by Fray Juan of Guadalupe. He won fame cooking at the Franciscans' hotel there for over twenty years and in 1996 he published a book of his favorite hundred recipes. I have changed the flavors of his topping, but kept to his original idea of a honey, saffron, and liqueur syrup rather than a brittle, teeth-cracking caramel.

750 ml / 1¼ pints milk, cinnamon quill, vanilla pod, curls of thinly pared lemon and orange zest, 8 egg yolks, 120 g / 4 oz cane sugar, 90 g / 3 oz rice flour, 1 tsp cornflour

FRAY JUAN OF GUADALUPE'S HONEY CARAMEL: 90 g / 3 oz cane sugar caramelized in 2 tbsp water, the finely grated zest of a lemon and orange, 2 tbsp of runny honey, a dash of liqueur, saffron, and cinnamon.

Warm the milk till just simmering with the cinnamon, vanilla, and citrus zests, infuse off the heat for 30 minutes, and reserve a cupful of the milk. Bring the rest back to a boil with the flavorings, then fish them out before you add the sugar, stirring till dissolved. Stir the rice flour into the reserved milk to make a cream and add it to the simmering milk, stirring all the time till the custard thickens smoothly. Finally take the pan off the heat stirring very well for another 5 minutes. Pour the cooked custard into one large dish, or small flat-bottomed serving dishes for each person, cool, and chill. Caramelize the sugar and water, adding a little extra water if you need, stir in the honey then the liqueur, saffron, and cinnamon. Just before serving pour it through a sieve into spirals on the top of the custard.

FOR A CHOCOLATE, COFFEE, OR TEA CUSTARD: You can add melted dark chocolate, a shot of expresso coffee, a strong cup of tea, or some cream to replace some of the milk.

COLLATIONS: SUPPER AT SUNDOWN

Lenten suppers, or collations, were born in late medieval times as minimal vegetarian snacks served at dusk with a drink of water. But as time went by they became artful small meals. French food philosopher Jean Anthelme Brillat Savarin looked back on the collations of his 1750s childhood in France as "masterpieces of a bygone age."[14] *New Art*'s were simpler, making the best of humble winter fruit and vegetables, but they were the ingenious high-point of Spanish collations. As papal rules for fasting relaxed over the following decades, they began to disappear from secular life.

Cabbage Custard / Col quaxada

Boil a head of cabbage in water with salt, drain and shred it. Take a little grated cheese, mint and parsley, chop them well, add fried onion and enough sugar to notice the sweetness, then stir in eggs. Turn your cabbage into a wide shallow cooking vessel, beat more eggs, pour them on top and leave the dish close to the fire, but not on it. Serve this sprinkled with sugar and cinnamon.

You can bake this in an oiled earthenware or clay dish, or pour it into a soufflé dish lined with oiled paper so you can turn it out on to a plate. Do not be tempted to overbake: it keeps firming up as it cools.[15]

about 1 kg / 2 lb trimmed chunks of green cabbage (pointed spring cabbage is good), 3 tbsp olive oil, 500 g / 1 lb onions, salt, 150 g / 6 oz grated ewe's milk or other mature cheese, a large handful of chopped fresh flat-leaf parsley and mint, 6 beaten eggs

Warm the oven (180°C, 350°F, gas mark 4). Simmer the cabbage chunks in salted boiling water, refresh them in cold water, drain, and squeeze very dry, first in your hands, then in a cloth. Shred with a sharp knife and put in a large mixing bowl. Warm the olive oil in a large frying pan, sweat the onion, add it to the cabbage with the cheese, parsley, mint, and five beaten eggs, season, toss, mix evenly, and pour it into an oiled ovenproof dish. Bake for 25 minutes or till a skewer comes out clean. The top should have a light golden brown crust. I like this served with a little fresh tomato *sofrito*.

Chard Fritters / Pencas de Acelgas en Pastelillos

Pick out your best chard stalks, simmer them in water with salt, chop them well, squeeze them dry in a linen cloth and put them in a basin. Stir in breadcrumbs, sugar and cinnamon to taste, then cracked and stirred eggs, and fry this batter to make fritters. Dip them in more beaten egg and fry them again, just like fish in batter in olive oil. These are very spongy and good served with a little sugar and cinnamon. Few people guess they are eating chard.

Made without the sugar, these fritters are a great vegetarian *tapa* served with Altamiras's garlic *ajo* (see p. 157). Fry them at the last moment for crispness. As with his stuffed eggs (see pp. 158–69), I replace the batter with breadcrumbs.

275 g / 9 oz fresh boiled or preserved chard stalks, 3 tbsp snipped flat-leaf parsley, 1 beaten egg, 6 tbsp fresh breadcrumbs, 1 tsp grated lemon zest

FOR FRYING: 1 tbsp plain flour, 1–2 egg yolks, fresh white bread-crumbs, olive oil for shallow frying.

Makes 18 fritters.

Mix the chopped chard stalks with all the other ingredients, season the mixture to taste, and chill for 2 hours. Prepare platefuls of flour, beaten egg yolk, and breadcrumbs for coating. Working quickly, while the mixture is still chilled, take large spoonfuls of batter, dip them in the yolk, coat them with the crumbs, and fry two or three at a time in bubbling hot olive oil till golden and crispy. Drain on kitchen paper and serve straight away.

SLOW-COOKED SQUASH AND ONIONS

Squash and onions were staple crops, especially before the potato was widely planted. The hard-skinned winter varieties would keep through the Lenten months strung up from the rafters of a cellar or granary while soft-skinned summer squash were cured in brine.[16] The number of recipes in *New Art* suggests their importance in the friars' everyday eating.

Squash Purée with Rice and Cheese / Escudilla de Calabaza

Skin a well-cured squash, cut it up in bits no bigger than walnut shells, boil them with salt, and when they are cooked pulp them with your wooden spoon. Add fried onion, pepper, saffron and grated cheese, have ready washed rice in proportion, add it to the pot and leave it to sweat off the fire.

In the early 1900s, a wave of books about cooking in Lent appeared in Spain. Some were written by chefs; all were aimed at the new reading market of middle-class women cooks. In came luxury dishes for lean days: lobster and oysters in creamy sauces, ornate cakes, and ice cream sundaes. Out went simple country dishes like those in which Altamiras excelled. Among these books *Fasting and Abstinence*, with recipes by Ignacio Domenech, a Catalan chef who had trained in Paris with Escoffier, became a classic. He did keep just one dish from *New Art* though, as so often, Altamiras did not get the credit he asked for. Here it is, as adapted by Domenech.[17]

3 tbsp olive oil, 1 roughly chopped onion, 500 g / 16 oz skinned and roughly chopped squash, bay leaf, a pinch of thyme, about 2 liters / 3½ pints of water, 60 g / 2 oz round-grain rice, a saffron infusion made from 1 dozen threads, 60 g / 2 oz grated ewe's milk or other sharp cheese, a few snipped parsley leaves

Warm the olive oil in a large frying pan, sweat the onion in it, throw in the squash and herbs and toss well, sweat together, pour in the water, season, and simmer for an hour. When the squash is very soft, blend it to a smooth purée, check the seasoning, add the rice and simmer for 25 minutes. Just before the end of cooking stir in the saffron infusion, cheese, and snipped parsley for green leafy flecks.

Roast Squash with Olive Oil and Lemon / Calabaza Assada

To make this dish well, pick a small squash, make two or three cuts in it and put it in a clay or earthen casserole with fresh olive oil, parsley, pepper, salt and a little sharp citrus juice or, when limes or lemons are not in season, add raw verjuice or bitter grapes. Pour in a little vinegar, sit your casserole in hot embers, with more in the lid on top of the casserole, and let the squash roast and the heat consumes their moisture. Take note, garlic does not improve this dish.

This pot-roasted squash is delicious served alongside fish or meat, mashed into the roasting juices.

500 g / 1 lb skinned squash, seeded and thinly sliced, juice of 1 lemon, 1 tsp wine vinegar, about 6 tbsp olive oil, snipped flat-leaf parsley

Warm a gentle oven (150°C, 300°F, gas mark 2). Lightly oil a large roasting pan, lay the sliced skinned squash in it, prick it with a fork and pour the lemon juice mixed with vinegar, olive oil, salt, and pepper over the top. Roast, covered, for about an hour or until tender.

Squash and Tomato Gratin with Mint / Calabaza en Otro Modo

Take tender squash, cut them into thin slices and lay these out over the bottom of a cooking vessel. Add pepper, salt and some tomatoes that you lay over hot embers, then skin and put more pumpkin slices on top, pour over fresh olive oil and put the pumpkins to bake, with hot embers below and in the lid, and, if you wish, throw on a few breadcrumbs, a little mint and some fine-cut onion. If you have no tomatoes, add dried verjuice. When you cook your pumpkin do not hurry it. Then serve this. It makes a good Lenten supper for passing travellers, but do not serve it too often or it may annoy people.

Kitchen-garden squash and tomatoes are a natural flavor match, but Altamiras warned friary cooks not to serve them too often, perhaps because guests would be offended by what might seem humble food.[18]

about 6 tbsp olive oil, 500 g / 1 lb squash, skinned, seeded, and thinly sliced, salt and pepper, 4 skinned tomatoes, 8 tbsp fresh bread-crumbs, chopped fresh mint leaves

Warm your oven (180°C, 350°F, gas mark 4). Rub a little of the oil over a roasting pan or ovenproof dish. Make a bed of overlapping squash slices in it, season, lay sliced tomatoes on top, repeat the layering and seasoning and finish with tomatoes. Pour the rest of the olive oil over the top, sprinkle over the breadcrumbs and mint, and oven bake for about half an hour or until the squash is very tender. Keep an eye on the crumb crust and cover the dish if it begins to burn.

Squash Ragout / Calabaza Reogada

Cut your squash up into fair-sized pieces, put them in a pot on the fire with a skilletful of fried onion, pounded garlic, pepper, salt and tomatoes. Stir so the squash cooks slowly. A handful of parsley and mint are good in this, if you want to add them. There are other people who like squash plain, that is, boiled with salt and served with a little fresh olive oil and pepper, for distinguished taste may return to simple things, and though some may say I am a flatterer, there is no disputing taste.

Altamiras notes two recipes here: the first, for squash, onion, and tomato ragout, and the second, for boiled pumpkin with olive oil, which, he hinted, was a favorite dish of people in high places. He went no further, probably because his patrons preferred to keep a low profile.

3 tbsp olive oil, 1 skinned and grated onion, 3 chopped garlic cloves, 4 grated tomatoes, 750 g / 1½ lb skinned squash, a small handful of snipped fresh parsley and mint

Warm the olive oil, stir in the onion, sweat it till soft, add the chopped garlic, soften it, then stir in the grated tomatoes. Season and add a pinch of sugar unless your tomatoes are very sweet. Cover and cook gently to give a thick reduced *sofrito* (see p. 121). Dice the squash, add it, cover and braise, turning it till it is soft. This is good served as a winter lunch with *patatas a la panadera* (see p. 237) and a green salad.

BORONIA: Andalusia has a delicious dish, *boronia*, based on the same combination of pumpkin and tomato spiced with cumin and seasoned with garlic, lemon juice, and salt.

Squash in White Wine / Calabaza en Otra Forma

Take squash before they grow too large, cut them in slices as thick as your cutting finger, scald them, drain them on a board, dredge them with a little flour, fry them in your skillet and, when they are well browned, put them one by one in a cooking vessel, with white wine and cinnamon, and give them a quick simmer. These you will find better than those served up by Bishops, and I think them in better taste.

Altamiras's final squash recipe ended jokily with a wink at some kind of friendly rivalry he must have felt with the Bishops' cooks at the nearby cathedral.[19]

600 g / 1¼ lb squash, skinned and thinly sliced, 2–3 tbsp plain flour, 3–4 tbsp olive oil, a bottle of fruity white wine, a shard of cinnamon

Simmer the squash in salted water for 3 minutes, drain and dry, dust with seasoned flour, brown in olive oil, pour over the wine, add pinches of cinnamon and salt, and cook for 5–10 minutes till soft.

Braised Onion Wedges / Cebolla Reogada

Skin onions, cut each one into four wedges and put these to fry gently in your skillet with a little salt. When they are half-done, put them in a large pot to braise, add a little pepper, throw in a handful of breadcrumbs, toss everything well and take the onions to table. If you are cooking a lot, throw in more breadcrumbs, and if you still cannot face onions when cooked like this, I can do no more to help you, for this is the best way I know to cook them.

In the rich soils of the Ebro valley, onions grew sweet and juicy, as big as a fist. Altamiras probably cooked the next two recipes with these though all onions turn out well pot-roasted this way. I like to use crispy fried breadcrumbs thrown over them at the last minute for a special crunch.[20]

6 tbsp olive oil, 4–6 large sweet onions, skinned and quartered, 175 ml / 6 fl oz fried breadcrumbs, 4 tbsp olive oil

Warm the oven to 180°C, 350°F, gas mark 4. Choose a flameproof dish where the quartered onion wedges fit comfortably. Warm the oil, set the onions on their backs in it, brown them gently then put the pot in the oven, spooning over the oil. Cover the dish and pot-roast for 45 minutes, opening up from time to time to baste the onions with the oil. When they are done, take them out and leave them to rest till you are ready to eat, then sprinkle them with the fried breadcrumbs. These are good served on their own as a first course.

Onions with a Fresh Herb Stuffing / Cebollas rellenas

Cut out the hearts of your onions, leaving their outer layers untouched. Boil the hearts in water with salt, chop them, cook them in olive oil or cow's milk butter in your skillet, add parsley, mint and boiled lettuce hearts, all chopped and stirred up with the onion. Add beaten eggs, stir everything well, cook till the eggs are done and turn this mixture on to a wooden board. Chop it again, add cheese, breadcrumbs, raw eggs and spices or sugar for a sweet stuffing, in which case you should add no spices or cheese. Stuff your onions, cook them in chickpea broth, if you have any, for it is the best in this dish, and finish this with a pine kernel or hazelnut sauce.

Choose evenly sized, chubby onions for stuffing. I bake them before hollowing them out, then chop up the softened central flesh to make the stuffing.

4–6 chubby unskinned whole onions, each weighing 150–200 g / 5–7 oz, 150 ml / ¼ pint vegetable or chickpea broth (see p. 234)

FOR THE STUFFING: 60 g / 2 oz grated ewe's milk or other sharp mature cheese, 2 tbsp fresh breadcrumbs, 2 tbsp butter or olive oil, 2 eggs, 60 g / 2 oz shredded lettuce heart, 3 tbsp snipped flat-leaf parsley, 1 beaten egg.

Warm the oven (180°C, 350°F, gas mark 4). Wipe the onions' skin clean, rub them with olive oil, wrap them in cooking foil, and bake for 30 minutes. Remove, cool, cut off the tops and roots, but leave the bases intact. Cut a hole at the top of the onions to scoop out a large central hollow, leaving the outer layers intact. Chop the flesh you have scooped out and mix in the cheese and breadcrumbs. Warm the butter or olive oil, scramble the eggs in it with the lettuce and parsley, stir in the onions, and season to taste. Set the onions in an oiled baking dish, spoon the stuffing into the hollows, pour over the chickpea or a vegetable broth and oven-bake for 20–30 minutes. You can reduce the broth or thicken it for a sauce (see p. 27). I like these served warm in a pool of the broth with a little olive oil poured over the top.

FRIARY FRUIT

In the countryside the friars kept their own walled or fenced fruit orchards, often with a lock on the gate. But in the cities they bought fruit and so, through the kitchen accounts of San Diego, in Zaragoza, where Altamiras cooked, we know what filled their summer fruit bowls: first came cherries, then peaches, plums, and grapes. By the end of winter, though, often only apples were left and so they became everyday eating in Lent.[21] For Altamiras, though, they brought other things to mind: forbidden fruit, women, romance.

Apple and Red Wine Ragout / Camuesa Reogada

Do not condemn me as a cowed man for, hard-pressed as I may be, I have the nerve to pick a pippin for you, skin it then cut out its heart. Let me tell you how to do that. Cut your apple into little bits, and this is no great feat for it has lost its heart, and put the bits in a pot with sugar, cinnamon and a little white wine, sipping first as you need to check the wine is not sour. Take note, I have not written for nuns here for fear they might be shocked. Now put your pippins to cook on a gentle fire.

Altamiras's apples, or *camuesas*, were squat green and red pippins, but any good apples, the tarter the better, or cooking pears, work well in this compôte. You also need three-quarters of a bottle of sweet wine: white Moscatel or Marsala work well as does red Mavrodaphne. Simmer it with cinnamon and thinly pared orange and lemon zest. Leave to infuse, slice the skinned apples or pears, top up with water, bring to a simmer with the wine and cook till just soft. Scoop into a dish, add the honey, simmer a little longer, cool and chill. This keeps well in a covered glass dish in the fridge.

Baked Apples with Cane Sugar / Camuesas assadas

Cut up your pippins: slice into the top of each one, turn it upside down, cut into the bottom and, when you have halved the pippin like this, quarter it and quickly cut out the heart from each with the tip of your knife, as if you were stitching. Fill the hollows left behind with sugar and cinnamon, recompose your apples as if you had never opened them up then bake them. You may also stuff them whole if you like, they are even better then, but harder to prepare. One person spent three years cooking with me and could not learn how; he was his own excuse.

These baked apples are good served warm while their volcanic cores of bubbling melted cinnamon sugar are still soft. Spanish cooks often add brandy, or you can mix in butter for a liquid toffee.

Warm the oven (180°C, 350°F, gas mark 4). Mix 3 tsp cane sugar for each apple with a small slug of brandy and a large pinch of cinnamon. Cut a hollow cup at the core of each apple, working with a knife or potato peeler from the stalk end and making sure you leave the base of the fruit intact. Stand the apples in a lightly buttered or oiled dish, spoon in the filling, and bake for 35–45 minutes. Good hot or cold.

CHAPTER IV

ON VEGETABLES, PULSES, AND OTHER DISHES

"**E**VERY MOVING thing that lives shall be food to you," ran the book of Genesis. "I have given you all things, even as the green herbs." In Altamiras's day *yerbas*, or green vegetables, were little better than weeds to many cooks, but for the friars they were a divine gift. "This is the friars' main source of sustenance," commented one handbook, "and so we often say the kitchen-garden is like a butcher's shop for us."[1] Alongside vegetables of all kinds, old and new, there grew herbs, scented flowers for the church, fruit trees, and often a discreet tobacco plant or two. In small friaries like San Lorenzo, in La Almunia, the cooks doubled up as gardeners, so Altamiras may have harvested his own vegetables. Sowing followed saints' days. In Aragon broad beans, planted early in winter, were the first harvest of the year, but chard, which survived frost and drought, resprouting annually, was the classic refectory vegetable, nicknamed *matafrailes* or friarkiller, because it was dished up so often. Here Altamiras fried it two ways.

Chard Fried Two Ways / Acelgas

There is much to say of this vegetable here; I shall give you a couple of popular ways to cook it. Take large tender stalks, strip off their threads, cut them into little bits, give them a quick boil with salt, drain them on a board, make a flour and egg batter for them, just as you would for salt cod, dip the chard stalks in the batter, fry them and serve them with sugar and cinnamon.

These are very good, but costly for the poor. For them, after the stalks are boiled with salt, add fried garlic and a handful of flour browned in the same oil: they are lighter like this and not at all bad done this way.

One summer evening I joined the members of La Almunia's gastronomic society for a few glasses of wine and delicious pan-fried chicken livers. The next morning Miguel Angel Mosteo Achutegui, the society's president and cook, and Santiago Cabello, writer, photographer, cook, and society member, met me to discuss which of Altamiras's dishes the gastronomic society would like to cook for the book. This was the dish they chose: humble, healthy greens, emblematic of the town's kitchen gardens.

Often a big head of chard gives two dishes: the leaves are cooked one way, the stalks another. Here is Miguel Angel's recipe for the leaves. Having cut them off the stalks, wash them, shred them, and simmer them in salted water with two peeled and chunked potatoes for 20 minutes. Drain well in a colander. Warm a glassful of olive oil in a large frying pan, sweat half a dozen whole skinned garlic cloves in it and add the potato and chard. Toss well so everything is coated with the oil. This is lovely homely food, a good first course or light meal.

The stems, or *pencas*, usually make up a third of the total weight of a head of chard. Altamiras fried them just as modern chefs do in vegetable tempura though his batter would probably have given a thicker crust. They are very good in tempura: wash, dry, and cut the stalks into short lengths (see p. 236). Blanche silver chard stalks for just 20 or 30 seconds, and red chard stalks for 2 minutes. Make the tempura batter. Dip the stalks in it, shallow-fry them in lots of lightly bubbling olive oil, drain them on kitchen paper, and serve hot and crispy. The textures and flavors go well with fish.

GREENS: SPRING TO SUMMER

In the Ebro Valley's kitchen gardens spring and summer greens follow winter chard. Altamiras dressed each one with an aromatized olive oil. These may have been dishes local to La Almunia where sweet olive oil abounded and had long been used to flavor Jewish and Morisco dishes made with locally grown kitchen garden produce.

Broad Beans / Habas verdes

After you have given these a little boil in salted water cut open the pods and add olive oil warmed with garlic. Make a toasted hazelnut sauce: pound the nuts with a bit of bread soaked in water and vinegar, squeeze it dry, add pepper, enough eggs and seasoned water. Pour this over your broad beans, give them another boil, but do not let them stick and burn, and let me add: all kinds of leaves and stalks are good scalded so they lose some of their greenness.

If you grow broad beans yourself, try picking them when the whole pods are no bigger than your little finger: cook them whole, pod and all. Otherwise try serving Altamiras's hazelnut sauce with fresh, frozen, or preserved podded beans.[2]

4 tbsp olive oil, 3 sliced cloves of garlic, 2 kg / 4 lb fresh broad beans in pod (or preserved or frozen equivalent of shucked fresh, preserved, or frozen beans), about 370 g / 3/4 lb

FOR THE HAZELNUT SAUCE: 1 dozen toasted skinned hazelnuts (see p. 178), ½ slice bread, few drops of wine vinegar, 120 ml / 4 fl oz water, salt, and pepper to taste.

Blanche the broad beans for 5 minutes in salted water, drain them, and put them into a flameproof serving dish or pot. Warm the olive oil with the sliced garlic till it is golden, season, pour it over the beans and keep them hot. Blend the toasted hazelnuts, bread, vinegar, and water to a paste, dilute with hot water to give a creamy sauce, season to taste, pour the beans, toss, and cook together for 10 minutes. This makes a good first course or side dish for ham or chicken.

Artichokes in Onion Oil / Algarchofas Mondadas

Put a pot of water to warm on the fire and have ready the artichokes, their tough outer leaves pulled off. When the water boils, scald the artichokes, and cook them, then lay them in an earthenware casserole, pour over broth with salt and a dusting of pepper. Fry onion in olive oil, lift it out of the skillet, brown a handful of flour in the oil left behind, add the onion oil to your artichokes then add more broth, so if you turn everything in the cazuela with your spoon you have a little sauce. This is the best way for lean days. But if you cook these on meat-eating days and can add a little streaky ham, with lean and fat in it, they are better still, even though I say so myself.

Vegetables are no longer Lenten penance. Today well-cooked artichokes are thought of as luxuries. Altamiras added olive oil flavored with onion, which gives a very subtle pungency to this forgotten but comforting and subtle dish typical of the way vegetables' flavors are left to speak clearly in the Basque country and Aragon.

1.5 kg / 3 lb baby artichokes, 4 tbsp olive oil, 2 finely chopped onions, 2 sliced cloves of garlic, 200 g / 7 oz diced jamón, 2–3 tsp flour, ½ glass of white wine, about 750 ml / 1¼ pints vegetable broth (see pp. 234–35) or water

Prepare baby artichokes whole, but larger ones as halves, removing all the tough leaves then any choke (see p. 70). Rub the artichokes over with a cut lemon and leave them in cold water with a few parsley stalks floating in it. Warm the olive oil in a large flat-bottomed flameproof frying pan or casserole, add the finely chopped onion and garlic, sweat them slowly together for about 15 minutes. Pour the pan's contents through a sieve, pressing out every drop of oil. Put the oil back in the pan, add the cured ham, and sweat it till the fat runs opaque. Sprinkle in the flour and cook, stirring, to give a little golden roux. Scoop in the artichokes, toss them, add the wine, toss again, then add the vegetable broth or water. Salt carefully, lower the heat and cook for about 30–45 minutes, though this will depend on the age of your artichokes.

Spinach with Raisins and Pine Kernels / Espinacas

Wash the leaves, put them in a pot with salt and a little oil and let them cook slowly in the water yielded by the spinach, no more. Drain and dress them. Warm olive oil, fry garlic in it, take raisins, be sure you pull off their stalks, and lay them in the oil till they swell up. Pour this on the spinach, throw in a handful of soaked pine kernels and a dusting of pepper. Stir well, chop the leaves in the dish where you have cooked them with your wooden spatula for the sake of cleanliness. If you want you may boil the spinach before dressing it, but it is not as good.

Altamiras spread a hidden sweetness through his version of a classic Spanish and Italian dish by plumping up his raisins in the olive oil. It lends a delicious original twist to a recipe still widely cooked today, especially in Catalonia. Another good version was given by an Augustinian cook, Antonio Salsete, who rounded off his recipe, "And remember the proverb 'like olive oil on spinach,' for the leaves should be dry but oily."[3]

4 tbsp best-quality olive oil plus a trickle for cooking the spinach, 3–4 sliced skinned fat garlic cloves, a small handful of soaked and seeded raisins (see p. 237), 1 kg / 2 lb washed spinach leaves, 60 g / 2 oz toasted pine kernels

Warm the olive oil in a small pan with the sliced garlic, fry it gently till golden, add the raisins, remove from the heat, and leave to sit overnight, if possible, or for at least 4 hours so the raisins swell up in the oil. Put the spinach in a large pot with the washing water that clings to the leaves, add a trickle of olive oil and salt, clamp on a lid, and put over very low heat so the leaves wilt. Drain them, cool to hand heat, squeeze dry the leaves, chop them with knives or kitchen scissors, arrange them on a serving dish, pour over the garlic oil and raisins, scatter over the toasted pine kernels, and sprinkle with salt flakes.

Asparagus Revuelto / Esparragos

Cut your asparagus into little bits and put the most tender ones to soak. Then boil water, scald the asparagus, put it in fresh water, boil it with salt and when it is done season it with fresh olive oil, cloves, cinnamon and a little saffron. If you like you can turn the asparagus stalks into a pie dish and crack eggs over the top, and the egg and asparagus cooked together this way are very good.

Cordoba's taste-making ninth-century caliph Ziryab promoted the foraging of thin-stemmed green asparagus, or sprue. The taste stuck, especially on Spain's great wheat plains where wild asparagus, or *trigueros*, flourished.[4] Today these *revueltos* are popular all around Spain, but now they are made with cultivated green asparagus. The spices Altamiras added with his olive oil give an unexpected twist to a familiar dish.

about 700 g / 1½ lb green asparagus, 3 tbsp olive oil, a dozen saffron stigmas, coarsely grated cinnamon and a tiny pinch of powdered cloves to taste, 4 eggs

Serves 4–6 as a first course.

Snap the washed asparagus into small bite-sized pieces, working down from the tips, until you reach the thicker-skinned lower stalks. Discard everything below the point from which they do not snap cleanly and easily. Wash the tender bits in cold water in a colander, let them drip dry, but no more. Warm the olive oil in a large heavy-based frying pan, tip in the asparagus all at once and toss gently for about 2½ minutes till the asparagus turns bright green. Add the saffron, the coarsely grated cinnamon, a little pinch of powdered cloves, and a larger one of salt. Keep tossing the asparagus till it is *al dente*, pour in the loosely beaten eggs, scramble quickly and turn on to warm plates. I like to serve this with triangles of bread fried in olive oil.

Los de abril para mi,	April's asparagus is for me.
Los de mayo para mi amo,	In May it is for the landlord,
Los de junio pa' ninguno,	In June it is good for nobody
Y los de julio para el burro.	And in July it is for my mule.

Spanish proverb

Green Beans / Judias Verdes

Wash your beans, boil them with a little salt and when they are done season them: have ready onion, chopped and fried, add it to the beans with a little salt and a dusting of pepper, and stir them two or three times so they receive the flavourings.

Just south of San Cristóbal lies the spectacular Río Grío valley, once famed for its green bean crop. San Cristóbal's friars collected food alms in the villages strung along the winding valley so Altamiras would have had an ample supply to cook in Lent and through the summer.[5] As the Grío has dwindled to a stream, so, too, the bean crop has shrunk and now local varieties have been lost. Altamiras's recipe for them is ingeniously simple and good. For every kilo of trimmed, blanched, and drained flat, runner or haricot green beans, sweat two large finely chopped sweet onions in a small cupful of olive oil and toss with the well-drained beans. This is delicious served hot, at room temperature, or as a cold salad.

La Virgen les dice:	The Virgin says to them:
?Que quieres lograr?	What are your wants?
Un chorrito d'agua	Just a little water,
Pa poder regar.	They say, for our plants.

Processional drought song, Jalón Valley[6]

Peas in Their Pods / Guisantes Verdes

Take tender peas. Clean them, nip off the stalks' ruffs, scald them, give them a little boil with salt and set them aside. Turn them on to a plate and serve with fresh olive oil and a dusting of pepper. This seems to me the best way to dress peas for rich and poor alike.

FUNGHI AND ROOTS

Wild funghi and roots were considered humble food with one exception, black winter truffles, long prized by Spanish cooks, who called them *criadillas de tierra*, or earth testicles. Later, confusingly, the same name was given to other roots, first brown summer truffles and then New World potatoes.[7] The same recipes were used for all these different roots and so it was that Altamiras gave one of the first dishes for potatoes, tacked on to an older formula for truffles.

Braised Wild Mushrooms / Setas de Monte

Wild mushrooms are usually washed well, so there is no taste of soil. If yours are dried leave them to soak overnight, squeeze them dry, simmer them with a little salt then, when they are cooked, drain them and fry them in olive oil. Half-way through add some chopped onion, then put them in a cazuela, *make a hazelnut sauce, throw in a handful of parsley, mint and a dusting of pepper, and let all this simmer together briefly. These are very good, but if the sauce does not please you, then you can eat them with the fried onion.*

La Almunia's sierras still give spring and autumn morels, and thistle mushrooms flourish on the wheat plains below. Cooked like this they make a wonderful stew infused with fresh mint and parsley (see p. 10). You can also prepare this dish more economically with field mushrooms and a few added dried funghi with their soaking liquid. Start the stew by chopping an onion finely and sweating it gently in olive oil. Add the cleaned and thickly sliced mushrooms, cook them gently, with a tightly clamped lid over the top, shaking occasionally and, when softened, stir in plenty of scissor-snipped fresh parsley and mint.

Earth Testicles: Truffles, Terfezia, and Potatoes / Criadillas de Tierra

This vegetable is a great treat and it grows underground like potatoes. Skin and soak the roots in bits in cold water: scald them, then simmer them, and when they are cooked keep their broth. Turn them into a clay or earthen casserole, add warm olive oil fried with garlic, and compose a little sauce with some of the broth and all kinds of spices, and leave this to boil. If broth remains, you may use it for cooking, as you would meat broth, for it tastes just as good, and, indeed, you may wonder whether it is meat or fish broth.

Potatoes may be cooked the same way yet let me warn you, if you eat too many you will find yourself so airy and full of strong wind you could blow a ship to see the Papa, or Pope, and, if you cannot, it's only because your wind's so gusty it has ripped your ship's sails and it's too costly to get them repaired for it will set you back more than the cost of a few potatoes.

When Spanish chroniclers wrote home from the New World, they called potatoes *criadillas de tierra*, a name readers would recognize, although Spanish colonists called them *papas*, as they were known in Peru, and they kept that name in Madrid's markets where they sold well to returned colonists. However, they failed to impress most other people. "I must confess," wrote Aragonese botanist Bernardo de Cienfuegos after trying them in the 1620s, "I find them insipid and tasteless unless helped along by a tasty little sauce or hot spice or citrus fruit." Perhaps that paleness of flavor helps to explain why they remained for so long a subsistence crop, untaxed, handily stored in the earth till needed and very often fed to livestock along with carrots and turnips. Only in the 1780s in Aragon, and even later elsewhere, were there potato planting campaigns to help feed the hungry.[8] Altamiras clearly knew *papas*—he would have talked to friars who had cooked them in the New World and probably brought them back for experimental planting in Spain—but he was sceptical, not because of the old-fashioned suspicion that they might "provoke lust and incite Venus," as reported by Cienfuegos, but by the idea they would give a strong tailwind. The recipe he gave for them here went on to become very popular in the nineteenth century, when it was known as *caldo de crillas*, or testy broth.

750 g / 1½ lb peeled waxy potatoes, 4 tbsp olive oil, 3–4 sliced garlic cloves, about 475 ml / 16 fl oz vegetable or meat broth (see p. 234), large pinches of ground nutmeg, cinnamon, and cloves

Simmer the potatoes in salted water for 10 minutes, dry, drain, and chunk them. Warm the olive oil in a heavy-based frying pan, fry the sliced garlic in it, then toss the potatoes quickly in the oil till sealed and golden. Pour over broth to cover, spice, and season to taste, and cook till the potatoes are done. Remove the potatoes to keep warm while you reduce the broth to a little sauce. I like these potatoes as a first course or served with roast chicken or turkey, lamb, beef, and game.

POOR MAN'S TRUFFLES: You can also cook this with *turmas de agua* or Jerusalem artichokes and with Spain's so-called desert or brown-skinned truffles, *Terfezia*. Fresh in early summer, when they appear in speciality greengrocers, they are good wood-grilled to bring out the best of the aromatic skin around the pink-veined flesh. By contrast the preserved ones, skinned in jars and sold as a gourmet speciality, are quite tasteless.

GOD'S ACRE: THE MUSLIM LEGACY

In Zaragoza the friars grew their vegetables in two square acres of rich river soil where Muslim farmers had first planted carrots, sorrel, artichokes, spinach, and aubergines. All these were thirsty vegetables whose cultivation depended on the Muslims' ingenious culture of irrigation. Waterwheels, river dams, and sluice-gates helped to channel water precisely in sparing quantities to the vegetables, grown in deep furrows. The friars inherited these irrigation systems and also the skills of manuring, pruning, grafting, and seed selection taught by Morisco farmers to their neighbors. "Seeds shall be kept separately, with labels saying what each one is, better in clay pots than squash skins, and covered to keep well so they cannot be eaten by rats and ants," ran one friary handbook.[9] Skilled growers developed their own varieties, for example, of the aubergine or eggplant, the Muslim favorite: there were the small, white round varieties that looked like eggs; others long and thin, streaked white and green; yet others bulbous and purplish, like those we know today.[10]

Roast Aubergines / Berengenas assadas

Skin the aubergines, boil them with salt, cut them in pieces and lay them in a dish that is wide, but not deep. On a meat-eating day these are good cooked with a skilletful of streaky ham: roast the aubergines sitting in hot embers, with more in the lid above, and when they are roast, infuse them with lime juice and a dusting of pepper. Here is another note for lean or meatless days: flavour the aubergines with warm olive oil fried with garlic, pound some peppercorns, garlic, parsley and salt and, as you turn the aubergines, let olive oil drip on to them from a handful of feathers like morning dew: they are tasty like this too.

This dish is not among the two dozen or more recipes given in al-Andalus's cookery treatises, but the flavors—olive oil, lime, and garlic—and charcoal-roasting, easy in a small brazier, are typical of popular Spanish Muslim and Morisco cooking.

2 large trimmed and washed aubergines, each weighing 370 g / 12 oz, 6 tbsp olive oil, 3 thinly sliced garlic cloves

Warm your oven (220°C, 425°F, gas mark 7). Cook the aubergines in salted boiling water for 5–7 minutes, drain them, rinse them in cold water, squeeze them dry, scoop out the flesh, chop it, discarding the seeds. Put the flesh in an oiled ovenproof dish, pulp it, warm the olive oil with the sliced garlic, tip it over the aubergine pulp, oven roast for 20 minutes and finally squeeze over the lime juice.

WITH JAMÓN OR PANCETTA: Warm 125 g / 4 oz diced jamón or pancetta gently in a frying pan so the fat runs out without scorching, tip the ham and liquid fat over the aubergines, toss well, check for seasoning, cover and roast, finally squeezing over a little lime juice.

> "I have found neither word nor news of these written by ancient authors in either Greek or Latin, nor by modern authors, nor doctors, except the Moors."
>
> Alonso de Herrera on aubergines, *General Agriculture*, 1513

CLOSE TO HOME

Turnips, borage, cardoon, and thistle mushrooms were local vegetables for Altamiras. We might think of them as the tastes of terroir, but for him they were simply close to hand, easily available, and inexpensive. He opened a group of recipes for them with humble turnips. "I am their enemy," the court cook Martínez Montiño had written. Too lowly, perhaps, for him: no problem for a friary kitchen.[11] The ingenious recipe, once again with aromatized olive oil, is a great way to cook all sorts of roots.

Turnips in Onion Oil / Nabos

Aragon's best turnips grow in Maynar, a Place in the Community of Daroca. These are good to eat, and rogues to skin, as hard as the back of a spoon. Clean them well, wash them once or twice, soak them so no soil clings to them, scald them and boil them with salt, and, when they are cooked, drain them and dress them: fry fine-cut onion in good olive oil, lift the onion out of the oil, throw in a little flour to brown in the oil, add it to the turnips with a dusting of pepper, sit them over gentle heat, turn them once or twice, and they cook splendidly done like this.

The onion you fried in the oil is good with eggs, or to dress beans or chickpeas, but with it you need to add more olive oil. It is good to invent uses for leftovers, for often they serve for something else, and we friars who follow Christ's example after he fed five thousand men with gathered-up leftovers must make the best use of everything we have.

Altamiras's smooth-fleshed turnips from Mainar, a village close to La Almunia, kept their fame right through to the 1950s, cooked in *cocido* one-pot stews, but they died out as varieties with bigger yields came in.[12] No matter—this recipe is good for all kinds of dry fibrous roots: I look for organic ones whenever possible.

120 ml / 4 fl oz olive oil, ½ large chopped onion, 750 g / 1½ lb hard-fleshed turnips, yams, celeriac, swede or soft potatoes, 2 tbsp of seasoned flour

Make the onion oil. Warm the oil, sweat the onion in it slowly till soft then strain through a fine sieve into a bowl, pushing out the oil with a wooden spoon. Skin your roots, cut them into cubes about 5-cm / 2-in square, put them in a non-stick roasting tin or earthenware dish, pour over just enough of the olive oil to coat them. Toss and season the roots then roast till golden, anything from 45 minutes to 1¼ hours, depending on which you are cooking. Turn them into a hot serving dish and finish off with the oil.

Fried Borage / Borrajas Rebozadas

This vegetable may not look appetising to plump people who enjoy rich foods, but many others like it served this way, as written below. Take tender borage stalks, cut them up to make into lengths the width of four fingers, wash them

well, boil them with salt and, when they are done, drain them on a clean wooden board. Make a light batter with eggs and a little flour, as you would for salt cod, dip the borage in it, then fry the bits, one by one, in your skillet, and serve them sprinkled with sugar and cinnamon. This is a good dish, but if you are served borage as plainly as we humble poor eat it, boiled with salt and a streak of olive oil, then you will find your appetite struck down as if you had been hit by lightning.

Wild borage flowers were used by Muslim healers of the Ebro Valley to make medicinal jams and cordials,[13] but later cooks began to harvest young leaves and stalks. The stalks are watery, almost transparently glassy green; the broth is delicate. Today borage is still an everyday vegetable in Aragon though it is tricky to track down elsewhere. It is an easy vegetable to grow yourself, but bear in mind you need to deprickle the stalks with a small brush wearing rubber gloves. Fry the stalks and leaves like chard (see p. 190) and add the broth to soup, as the Aragonese do. They also drink it as a health tonic.

Borage Soup / Caldo de Borrajas

Take good olive oil, fry fine-cut onion in it, lift it out with a skimming spoon when it is done and pour the oil into your borage broth. Make a hazelnut thickening: pound toasted hazelnuts, a little bit of bread, soaked and squeezed dry, peppercorns, saffron, cloves, cinnamon and a clove of garlic. Stir this into the broth, let it cook a little, add salt if need be, take it off the fire. Whisk as many eggs as you see fit with a little vinegar, add them to the broth when it is tepid so the eggs do not cook to threads. Sweat the soup off the fire. This is mild and good, indeed, so good people may ask if it is a meat broth, and remember, a broth may be worth more than what you made it from, just as a collar may be worth more than the dog who wears it, and borage broth is so good that those who drink it never lead a dog's life.

Most modern borage soups are made with natural vegetable thickenings, like potatoes and carrots, but this one, softly spiced, is rounded out by Altamiras's nut *picada* and beaten eggs. The modern recipe comes from José Carlos Martín, the chef of La Almunia's restaurant, El Patio de Goya, whose family has borage broth at home at least once a week. He has brought to the recipe his taste for a very subtle refined broth.

13 oz / 400 g borage stalks left in iced water, 1.4 liters / 2½ pints mineral water seasoned to taste, 200 ml / 7 fl oz olive oil, 1 large chopped onion, 2 eggs

FOR THE HAZELNUT THICKENING: 18 small toasted skinned hazelnuts, a large pinch of saffron threads, 1 fat garlic clove, 2 cloves, a small handful of white breadcrumbs with the crusts off, pinch of cinnamon, pinch of black pepper.

Cook the borage in the water with the salt for just 4 minutes. Drain, reserving a few trimmed stalk lengths for each serving of soup. Make the onion oil: sweat the onion in the oil and sieve it. Make the hazelnut thickening: pound together or blend all the ingredients with a ladleful of the broth and blend to a cream. Add the oil and cream to the broth, adjust the seasoning, and simmer for 20 minutes. You should have quite a liquid soup. Just before serving lower the heat and beat in two egg yolks thinned first with a cupful of broth.

Cardoon with Hazelnut Sauce / Cardos de la Huerta

Clean your cardoons well. Strip off their threads and membranes, cut them up, lay them in cold water so the flesh does not blacken, scald them, then boil them with salt, rinse them in a second pot of warm water with salt. Pound pine kernels or hazelnuts with peppercorns, garlic and moistened breadcrumbs, thin this paste with the seasoned rinsing water to make a sauce, add it to the cardoon with fresh olive oil, and give it a quick simmer. If you have no sauce, just add olive oil warmed with garlic.

Spanish cardoon has long been famed for its quality. In *La Cuisinière Bourgeoise*, a best-selling French cookbook published the year after *New Art*, the author Menon wrote of "cardons d'Espagne."[14] For centuries the Ebro valley has been its growing heartland and you can still find it cooked there in many different ways. Some people think of it as a vegetable best enjoyed in restaurants: cleaning and preparing it take time and skill. But when I went to meet Mariano Lechal and Mari Carmen Edo of the Hostal Castellote (see p. 74) to try their carnival dumplings, I discovered they still cook cardoon more or less exactly the way Altamiras did. This is a lovely recipe, showing off the silky texture and subtle artichoke flavor of cardoon against a rich hazelnut sauce. Here, then, is Castellote Christmas Eve cardoon, served before roast lamb or pork stuffed with almonds and raisins—a fine feast.

2 kg / 4 lb fresh cardoon stalks or two 370 g / 12 oz jars of preserved cardoon (see p. 235)

FOR THE HAZELNUT OR ALMOND SAUCE: 120 g / 4 oz toasted skinned almonds, hazelnuts, or pine kernels, 60 g / 2 oz toasted bread, 1 skinned garlic clove, 250 ml / 8 fl oz hot water, 200 ml / 7 fl oz sweet golden olive oil, 15 g / ½ oz sweet pimenton red pepper.

Slice fresh cardoon heads vertically down the center and throw out the tough central stems and bitter white leaves attached to them. Soak the remaining stalks, which you are going to cook, in ice-cold water. Cut across the base of each one, pull off the rib threads, and peel off the stalks' membranes. Cut the stalks into 5-cm / 1-inch lengths, leave them in water with lemon juice to avoid blackening, then scald them twice for about 5 minutes each time. The first scalding takes away the bitterness. The second one, in salted water, begins to cook the cardoon. Reserve a cupful of the second cooking liquid. Pound the toasted nuts and bread. Warm the olive oil, fry the sliced garlic clove till golden, add the pimentón when the garlic is done so it does not scorch, then add the pounded bread and nuts and cooking broth. Pour this sauce over the cardoon, warm it through, check the seasoning, and cook for 15–35 minutes. This last cooking time varies a lot with the age of the cardoon so keep a close watch on it to see when it is done.

Thistle Mushroom Pasties / Setas de Cardo

Thistle mushrooms are our best funghi. When you have washed them well and scalded them with salt and squeezed them dry, fry them with onions. Make a dough, as I have told you elsewhere, and a paste of hazelnuts pounded with a clove of garlic, spices, and eggs. Your dough should be firm: make pasties from it, filled with the mushrooms and nut paste, and fry them in your skillet. These are a very good extra dish and some people prefer them to partridges; but I would pick the birds, and I do not think I would err in my choice.

Freckly fat-necked thistle mushrooms were Altamiras's favorite wild fungi. They sprouted on the roots of thistles in the wheat fields close to La Almunia so perhaps he foraged them himself when he was a child. When cooked they reveal a special deep chestnut-like sweetness.[15] Often oyster mushrooms are sold under the same name: they are closely related but quite different to eat. Fresh field mushrooms are a better alternative.

2 tbsp olive oil, 1 skinned and chopped onion, 300 g / 10 oz cleaned and chopped thistle or field mushrooms

FOR THE HAZELNUT FILLING: 60 g / 2 oz small toasted skinned hazelnuts, 30g / 1 oz fresh breadcrumbs, 1 egg, a large pinch of cinnamon, 2–3 tbsp water.

FOR THE PASTRY AND FRYING: a double quantity of frying pastry (see p. 155), made with 300 g / 10 oz plain flour, and small panful of olive oil for shallow-frying.

Makes 2 dozen pasties.

Warm the olive oil, sweat the onion, add the mushrooms, season, toss them in the oil, and cool. Blend the hazelnuts to a paste with the other filling ingredients and season to taste. Roll out the pastry. Cut out 12.5-cm / 5-inch circles with a cutter or drinking glass. Place a dob of hazelnut paste off-center on each circle, then a teaspoonful of mushrooms on top, leaving an ample rim around the edge for sealing. Run a wet finger around the edge, fold over each circle to make a half-moon pasty, or *empanadilla*, press the edges together, crimp with a fork, shallow-fry the pasties in bubbling hot olive oil, drain on kitchen paper, and serve hot or cold as a tapa or first course.

HOT SALADS: KNOWING AND REMEMBERING

Knowing and remembering went hand in hand, taught the great Franciscan Mallorcan philosopher Ramón Llull. That idea shaped Altamiras's idea of cookery: he mixed up old and new dishes without favoring fashion. Here he took four old vegetable dishes, or hot salads, updating them to his own tastes. If you take out some of their sweetness, they make original modern eating with unexpected flavors and textures.

Potatoes and Greens in Saffron Sauce / Criadillas de Tierra de Otro Modo

I thought it a good idea to give you one of the many other ways to cook earth testicles. Pick the largest ones, boil them with salt and once they are peeled, cook them slowly in good olive oil with fried onion. Have ready chickpea broth with spices, a little saffron and well chopped greenery, put your earth testicles in this, season them with salt then set them with egg yolks and a little lemon juice or vinegar.

I have eaten a very good simplified country version of this dish in Galicia; the eggs are hard-boiled in their shells with the potatoes, then peeled and cut into the stew. Altamiras added his egg yolks raw, as in the original court recipe, originally designed for truffles.[16]

750 g / 1 ½ lb scrubbed waxy potatoes, 4 tbsp olive oil, 1 small chopped onion, 250 ml / 8 fl oz hot chickpea or vegetable broth (see p. 234), a saffron infusion made with 2 dozen strands (see p. 102), 120 g / 4 oz spinach, watercress or rocket, juice of ½ lemon, 2 egg yolks
Serves 4–6 as a first course.

Cut the potatoes in half, or into even pieces, and bring them to a boil in salted water. Simmer for 5 minutes, drain, dry well, and cool. Skin them if you like, and cut them into even bite-sized chunks. Warm the olive oil in a frying pan, sweat the onion in it, add the potato chunks, toss well till glossy with oil, then add the hot chickpea or vegetable broth. Simmer gently till nearly done, about 15 minutes, stir in the saffron infusion, and seasoning to taste. Put the shredded spinach on top, cover it with a lid, and allow to wilt, then stir in. Whisk the raw egg yolks and lemon juice (see p. 13), stir in, and simmer briefly till the sauce thickens. The tart citric sauce goes beautifully with plain grilled fish and a glass of dry white wine.

Aubergines with Cheese / Berengenas Rellenas

Cut them in half, boil them in salted water, drain them, and carve the flesh from their hearts so they are hollow like walnut shells. Chop some of the flesh, fry a little onion in good olive oil, add it to the flesh with a little mint and raw eggs. Cook this over a warm fire, stir till the eggs are dry, turn it all into a clay or earthen dish, and add eggs as you see fit, a few breadcrumbs, a little cheese, spices, cinnamon and powdered sugar. Fill your aubergine halves with this mix, have ready a light flour and egg batter, dip them in it, fry them in your skillet and serve them with sugar and cinnamon.

This very old aubergine dish inspired Baltasar de Álcazar to come up with a legendary ode to his lover and his favorite foods, which he put on an equal footing. Altamiras would have known the older honeyed recipes well, though his version was considerably less sweet.[17] I have left out the sugar and the fried finish, but kept in the mint. This is a great vegetarian tapa, by the way.

2–3 large aubergines, each weighing around 370 g / 12 oz, 2 tbsp olive oil, 1 finely chopped skinned onion, 60 g / 2 oz grated ewe's milk or other sharp cheese, 1 tbsp dried breadcrumbs, 2 eggs, 1 tbsp finely chopped mint, large pinch powdered cinnamon

Cut the aubergines in half lengthways, including the stem. Blanche them for 10–15 minutes till soft, drain them, cool, discard any aubergine seeds, and scrape out the cooked flesh to leave each aubergine half like a boat, with a thin fleshy layer inside the skin. Keep warm. Sweat the onion in the olive oil, stir in the chopped aubergine flesh, then the cheese, breadcrumbs, mint, and cinnamon, and season to taste. Finally add the beaten eggs and cook for another 5 minutes. Pile the filling into the aubergine skins and warm through in the oven. If you like you can finish this off with a little extra cheese.

Tres cosas me tienen preso,	Three things have captured
De amores de corazón,	My heart's love and they are these,
La bella Inés, el jamon,	The beautiful Inès, cured ham
Y berenjenas con queso.	And aubergines with cheese.

Baltasar de Alcázar (1530–1606)

Hot Curly Endive Salad / Chicorias, y Escarola

Trim your chicory, wash it, scald it, simmer it with salt and drain it. Keep the cooking water, which is good for hypochondriacs, dress the chicory with olive oil and fried garlic. Curly endive, washed well, is cooked the same way. Dress it with fresh olive oil and with powdered sugar on top.

Raw curly endive is still dressed this way in southern Spain, and cooked endive is also good served like this.[18] Boil a crisp head of curly endive, its tatty outer leaves removed. Fry 4 cloves of thinly sliced garlic in olive oil. Drain the endive, squeeze it dry, chop it, and dress it with the garlic oil. I like to throw in a few pomegranate seeds. This is a good salad to follow rich or fatty dishes.

Carrots with Honey and Wine Vinegar / Zanahorias

This is a simple food, apt for beasts. But you may like carrots. If so boil them with salt, slice them, put them in a cazuela *with fried onion, season them with spices and salt, add hot water till they are covered, sweeten them with*

sugar or honey and add vinegar, so they are very sweet yet sour. Fry a little flour, brown it well, thin it with the carrot's broth and it will thicken with just a little boil, and in this way a brutish food becomes rational sustenance, though it is unrewarding and of little substance.

Altamiras may have disliked *zanahorias*, or orange carrots, because he had eaten the crisp sweet purple carrots, called *carlotas*, which are still grown in Mediterranean kitchen gardens today, or it may be that, like many cooks, he thought of turnips, potatoes, and carrots as animal fodder. I cook this with young Chantenay carrots: they are excellent with ham or garlicky pot-roast lamb.[19]

1 kg / 2 lb carrots, trimmed and thinly skinned (Chantenays are good), pinches of sugar and salt, about 2 tbsp honey and the same of white wine vinegar (plus a little more to hand), 1 skinned and finely chopped onion, 3 tbsp good olive oil

Cover the carrots with water, add pinches of sugar and salt, simmer gently, and cook till tender. Now drain the carrots, reserving the broth, boil it down to about 370 ml /12 fl oz, and strain it. Choose a flameproof casserole, ideally a *cazuela*, warm the oil in it, sweat the onion till sweet and soft, add the carrots, pour over the broth, stir in the honey and vinegar— go carefully, tasting the balance—check the seasoning, and simmer for 5–10 minutes. The cooking liquid reduces to a syrupy broth. Serve with a grassy sprinkling of chives. Pistachios are also good crumbled over the top.

> "'Vegetables indeed!' the Cebre priest's housekeeper would have cried, laughing from the heart, with her ribcage too, 'Vegetables on the patron saint's feastday! They'll do for the pigs.'"
>
> Emilia Pardo Bazán, *The House of Ulloa*, 1886

VARIOUS DISHES

CONVENT BEANS AND CHICKPEAS

One day I phoned Sister María Isabel Lora, a Dominican nun, author of the best-selling book, *The Nuns' Cooking Pot*. I had noticed that it includes sixteen recipes for bean stews and that in these Sister María, like Altamiras, rarely soaks her beans. She cooks in a closed convent in Daroca, just an hour's drive south from Altamiras's home town, and while she knew nothing of *New Art*, she had learned from her mother to avoid soaking beans because the fermentation it provokes makes them indigestible. The only problem, of course, is that you need to cook the beans for much longer, probably the reason why this method has disappeared from modern home cooking, but is kept alive by convent and friary cooks.

Sor María Isabel Lora's and Juan Altamiras's Beans / Potage de Judias Secas

Take cleaned beans, wash them and put them to cook, take care they boil quickly, and drain off this first water. Add fresh water and, when the beans are cooked, dress them with fried onion, garlic pounded with pepper, saffron and mint, and, if you want a thicker sauce, throw in a handful of grated breadcrumbs and a little cheese. These beans are also good with a little cooked rice.

Sor María Isabel's method is ideal for beans no more than a year old. White beans and black-eyed peas, such as Spanish *carrillas, judías de la virgen*, and *habichuelas* (see also p. 237 for other alternatives), are the most popular in Aragon, but you can cook any red or black beans this way too. An earthenware or clay pot is ideal for the cooking since it effortlessly helps to keep the very low simmer, around 50–60°C / 140°F, which helps the beans' pectins thicken the broth. Here, then, is Sister Maria Isabel's master bean method. Altamiras's flavorings follow.

400 g / 13 oz dried beans, 1 head of garlic, 2 small thyme sprigs, 2 bay leaves, 100 ml / 3½ fl oz olive oil
Makes 1.5 litres / 3 pints.
Cover the beans with plenty of cold water (use mineral water if you do not have good tap water) and bring to a fast boil. Strain after 5 minutes. Put the beans in a large pot, ideally a *cazuela* or *puchero*, cover with fresh cold water, add the garlic, herbs, and olive oil, bring to a boil, lower the heat, and simmer for 1–1½ hours, till soft. The time will depend on the type of bean and its freshness. Season to taste and finish in any of the following ways.

Other Bowls of Beans: With Fresh Herbs, Saffron Broth, or Olive Oil / Otro Modo de Guisar Judias

When you have boiled your beans, drain off their broth, add fresh olive oil, pepper, a handful of parsley and mint, and put these over a gentle fire, stirring once or twice, and do not forget to add salt to them, or you may leave the beans in their broth and season them with salt and saffron, or you may drain and dress them with olive oil and pepper, but not with vinegar. Let those who like it add it to their own bowl of beans.

Here are a trio of ideas for meatless beans. One: drain and toss them with olive oil, fresh parsley, mint, and seasoning. Two: leave them soupy and add a saffron infusion. Three: toss them with olive oil and pepper and serve them with wine vinegar on the table. Some people like sherry vinegar instead, but be wary and add it drop by drop. The fact that Altamiras gave so many flavorings suggests well how often the friars must have been eating these beans.[20] Here are his ideas given in the master recipe.

WITH ONION, GARLIC, MINT, AND SAFFRON: 2 large onions, 4 tbsp olive oil, 3 garlic cloves, a handful of snipped mint, an infusion made with 3 dozen threads of saffron (see p. 102). Sweat the chopped onions in the olive oil and scoop them into the beans with the chopped garlic, mint, salt, pepper, and saffron. Simmer for 10 minutes.

WITH CHEESE AND BREADCRUMBS: Allow a handful of fresh breadcrumbs and 90 g / 3 oz mature ewe's milk cheese for 1.5 liters / 3 pints cooked beans. Stir them in at the end of cooking.

WITH RICE: For beans and rice allow 120 g / 4 oz rice plus 150 ml / 5 fl oz extra water. Add them about 25 minutes before the beans are done and keep simmering.

Dried Broad or Fava Beans with Rice, Saffron, and Mint / Abas Secas

Take good clean dried broad beans, the worms already picked out, then, before you cook them, scald them and skim off the foam that rises to the top for the little worms that linger will rise with it. In cold weather pound some garlic for your beans, but if those who are going to eat them do not like garlic or spices, adapt yourself to their tastes because you can dress beans well without them. Pound the garlic with peppercorns, saffron and sprigs of mint, and wash them into the beans with hot water. Add one handful of rice for every four of beans, stir well and put the beans to sweat gently off the fire, stirring from time to time with your big wooden spoon.

Dried broad beans are plain to the eye, but when well cooked they have a seductive velvety-smooth sweetness within their runkled brown jackets. In Valencia they are considered gourmet eating and are served as a tapa with spicy-hot unthickened cooking juices. But they are also good cooked in this more filling dish.[21]

500 g / 1lb dried broad beans (around six or seven handfuls), 1 onion spiked with 2 cloves and 1 bay leaf, 90 g / 3 oz Bomba or other paella rice, 2–3 garlic cloves, snipped mint leaves, a saffron infusion made with 3 dozen threads (see p. 102)
Makes 1.75 litres / 3¼ pints.
Soak the broad beans overnight in plenty of water. Drain them, cover them generously with fresh water, throw in the clove-spiked onion and bay leaf and simmer, covered, for 1¾–2 hours, topping up the water if need be. When the beans are softened but firm add the finely chopped garlic and seasoning to taste, plus the rice. Top up the water level, simmer gently for 10 minutes, and stir in the mint and saffron infusion gently for 20 minutes.

CHICKPEAS AND PEAS

Chickpeas, the most universal Spanish pulse, grow with little water, a blessing in dryland areas. They may be casseroled in dozens of ways or toasted whole or puréed, but there is one dish, Lenten *potaje*, that holds a special place in Spaniards' hearts. Is it nostalgia or its soothing character as spoonfood that makes it so appealing even to those who never fast in Lent? The best modern *potaje* I know comes from Dolo Campayo Sánchez; she is one of the rare home cooks who has always used Altamiras's key technique for making it with unsoaked raw salt cod. By the way, Altamiras was the first cookery author to publish a recipe for this classic *potaje*, now prepared by avant garde chefs and home cooks.

Chickpeas, Four Ways / Garbanzos Comunes

If you have chard or spinach broth, soak the chickpeas in it, or, if not, then use saltcod broth. Once they are soaked, washed and scalded, boil them with a little fresh olive oil then, when they are done, add fried onion and spices pounded with a few garlic cloves. Season them with salt and to thicken them, if you want, add one-sixth of their volume in rice.

For a high table, you can add a thickening of hazelnuts and eggs, or, for the poor, you can pound a big spoonful of chickpeas with egg yolks, and then put the whites to good use in an omelette, which, made with one egg and a couple of whites, will not disappoint. I note all this here because you will come across strange people who ask you to account even for an egg, and this I tell you from my own experience.

Hard dry salt cod heads and a few bulbs of garlic added to a pot of chickpeas turn out well, though this depends on the fish heads. If they are rotten you will be warned by their whiffy smell from time to time, and this I hope you learn to notice by experience before the heads are too far gone. If guests turn up then you can make these chickpeas go further with greens, well pounded or chopped. Your pot will grow that way, but take care with your conscience.

Dolo Campayo grew up in the years of hunger that followed the Spanish Civil War in the Sierra de Ayna in southern Castile. The rural *cocina pobre* of her childhood, largely forgotten today, ingeniously made the most of every ingredient and had its own dishes and techniques. For example, like Altamiras, she has always cooked her chickpeas with dry salt cod heads, the fishy equivalent of a hambone. A poor cut they may be, but they give an incomparably deep briny flavor. However, Dolo does throw in other modern additions—potatoes, sweet red pepper, and pimentón paprika—which round out the chickpeas well.

500 g / 1 1lb chickpeas, 150–200 g / 5–7 oz dry salt cod heads, 2 bay leaves, 2 handfuls of spinach or chard (about 120 g / 4 oz), 3 tbsp olive oil, 2 chopped onions, 2 potatoes, 1 large sweet red pepper, and 1 level tsp sweet pimentón paprika (optional)

Makes 1.2 litres / 2 pints beans; serves 4–6 as a first course.

Wash the chickpeas. Soak them overnight in tepid (not cold) water or in Altamiras's green or salt cod broth. Drain. Scald them briefly in boiling water, skim off the foam, drain them, and put them back in the pot. Cover with fresh water, add the salt cod and bay leaves, bring to a gentle simmer, and cook for 1–1½ hours until tender. Meanwhile wilt the spinach or boil the chard, drain it, cool, and squeeze dry. Warm the olive oil, sweat the onion, add the peeled chunked potatoes, chopped red pepper and pimentón, toss well and, when the chickpeas are done, add the spinach. Check the seasoning and cook for 5–7 minutes.

CHICKPEAS FOR THE HIGH TABLE: For every 600 ml / 1 pint of chickpeas blend a dozen skinned hazelnuts with 250 ml / 8 fl oz water and 2 whole eggs and stir into the cooked chickpeas. This gives a satisfyingly smooth white sauce. Simmer slowly without boiling.

CHICKPEAS FOR THE POOR: For every 600 ml / 1 pint of cooked chickpeas and broth, blend 2 egg yolks with a cupful of chickpeas and a little black pepper. Stir into the chickpeas to give a sunny yellow stew. Again, simmer but do not boil, to finish.

Dried Green Peas / Guisantes secos

Our best dried peas come from France. Make sure they are good and clean, soak them like chickpeas, or in warm water and salt, scald them, then boil them fast in fresh water, like all vegetables and pulses, and if you know they are very hard add a little fresh olive oil to soften them. Dress these like chickpeas, in winter with olive oil, fried onion and garlic cloves. Add spices, too, and a little rice if the stew is not thick enough.

Altamiras's dried peas probably came from France, brought south over the Pyrenees by the merchants who sold cured ham and lard in Aragonese cities.[22] The flavorings—onion, olive oil, garlic, and spices—make an interestingly different dish today, good served alongside ham, pork, or game.

2 chopped leeks, large bunch of mint, 1.7 liters / 3 pints water, 370 g / 12 oz split peas

FOR THE REFRITO: 4 tbsp olive oil, 1 large onion, 2 fat garlic cloves, snipped mint leaves.

Put the chopped leeks and bunch of mint into the water and simmer, tightly covered, for 30 minutes. Strain into a large earthenware pot or pan where you will cook the peas. Top up with extra water as needed to make 1.4 liters / 2½ pints. Add the peas, bring to a boil, and simmer for about 45 minutes, stirring occasionally so they cook evenly. Meanwhile warm the olive oil, add the onion and sweat it slowly, adding the finely chopped garlic and mint for the last few minutes of cooking time. Scoop this *refrito*, as the Spanish call it, into the dried pea stew, check the seasoning, and keep simmering them for 10–20 minutes till the peas are soft in the center but just holding some shape. Serve these as a soupy first course with fried or toasted bread triangles, or as a thick purée, good with sausages, boiled ham, roast chicken, or game.

ALMONDS

In Spain's almond growing country, where blossom splashes Mediterranean hillsides pink and white in springtime, almonds are eaten green while they are still young, a little bigger than a thumbnail, and are popped out of their skins to eat with a few grains of salt. Sometimes they are also eaten raw off the tree, like a long-haired peach. When you bite into one, the unexpected taste, fruity and satisfyingly sharp, like a lemon or a punchy plum, explains why they have been thought of as a delicacy.

Green Almonds / Almendras Verdes

Pick your almonds green before the nuts set, scrub them with a coarse cloth to take off their furry down, and then they will be a fine thing, ready to boil with salt. Once they are cooked, drain them, fry fine chopped onion and cook together with the almonds. Bathe them with broth, add spices, cinnamon and a little sugar, simmer them quickly, give them just a couple of boils and add a little chopped greenery. Serve them like this, without any egg thickening.

Once I experimentally harvested a bagful of green almonds in Alicante and cooked them this way for Kiké, a Madrid friend. Unexpectedly, he finished the lot. In Altamiras's time they were often preserved in sugar or honey syrup,[23] but this recipe is also good unsugared.

For 2 dozen green almonds in their shell (about 150 g / 5 oz) you need about 4 tbsp of fruity olive oil, 1 onion, ½ tsp salt, large pinches of nutmeg and cinnamon, 175 ml / 6 fl oz vegetable stock, 2 heaped tbsp chopped fresh flat-leaf parsley, rocket, or mint

Brush off the almonds' down as well as you can. Cut off the stalks and scars, boil the almonds for 10 minutes in salted water, drain, and dry well with a cloth. Warm the olive oil, sweat the onion, and when it has softened add the almonds, cover with a lid, toss well, add the nutmeg, cinnamon, and vegetable stock, and simmer for 10 minutes. Serve as a first course.

El día de San Juan, madre,	On St. John's day, mother,
Cuaja la almendra y la nuez.	Almonds and walnuts set inside their shells
También cuajan los amores	Not only that, the love of those
De los que se quieren bien.	Who truly long for each other sets like nuts.

Old Spanish country poem, celebrating St. John's day

Almond Milk Blancmange for Lent and Holy Week / Escudilla de Angel para Cuaresma, y a los Eclesiásticos Servira para Semana Santa

To make this you need a pound of sugar and another of almonds for every one of rice. Wash it in tepid water, drain it between tablecloths, and when it is dry grind it and pass it through a flour sieve. If you make this rice flour a day early, spread it on a board so it does not ferment. Now make your almond milk. Bring a jugful of water to the boil and, when it boils, add the almonds, scald them quickly, skin them and lay them in cold water. Drain them well, grind them and make your milk with them, strain it through a clean napkin, pour it into a pot and warm it gently with the sugar. Dissolve the rice flour in a little of the almond milk, break up the lumps, and put everything together in the pot where you will make your blancmange over a slow flame. Stir all the time with your big wooden spoon, and stir quicker as you see the blancmange thickening, and when it is nearly done check it does not taste of rice flour. Have ready an infusion made with an ounce of cinnamon, stir it into the blancmange and, for twenty small bowlfuls you need six ounces of sugar and a quarter of powdered cinnamon to serve alongside it.

This rice-flour blancmange or *menjar blanc* from Reus, in southern Catalonia, is still cooked in Holy Week. I have adapted the recipe, lightening it and adding almond extract to stand in for the one or two bitter almonds that Spanish cooks add to soups, milks, and puddings to give a more intense flavor.[24] I like this chilled with a swirl of fruit purée, tuiles, and a dessert wine. Among fruit purées try spiced pear, raspberry, or peach.

200 g / 7 oz sugar, 90 g / 3 oz rice flour, 30 g / 1 oz cornflour
FOR THE ALMOND MILK: 250 g / ½ lb skinned almonds, 1.4 liters / 2½ pints cold water, a few drops of almond extract.

Make the almond milk: grind the almonds in a food processor, adding water little by little to make a thick cream, then dilute with the rest of the water to a liquid milk. Leave soaking for 6 hours, regrind, filter (see p. 214) and add a few drops of almond extract, to taste. Reserve two cupfuls: dissolve the rice flour in one, the cornflour in the other. Put the rest of the almond milk into a very clean earthenware pot or stainless steel pan, begin to warm gently, and stir in the rice cream. When it begins to simmer, stir in the cornflour cream. Keep stirring as the blancmange

ALMOND MILK

"Make your almond milk." Altamiras made almond milk for lean-day dishes like rice pudding and blancmange. He blanched his almonds quickly in hot water to skin them then lay them in cold water to soften, adding pine kernels to keep the milk white. Today it is easy to make almond milk in a food processor. Leave the almonds ground with water to sit for 6 hours before filtering through a clean cloth, well rinsed so there is no soapy flavor. In Spain one or two bitter almonds are added to round out the flavor: instead you can add a few drops of almond extract. The milk will keep in the fridge, covered tightly, for two days. When heated it separates easily, so warm it through gently or add a thickening flour to bind it before heating (see p. 213).

thickens, lower the heat if you see it is beginning to stick, pour it into a glass or earthenware dish, cool to room temperature, cover with film to stop a skin forming, and chill.

Cinnamon Toasts / Tostadas de Pan con Manteca

Cut slices from a good loaf and toast the bread on the fire. Warm lard in your skillet, sprinkle your toast with water, shake it dry then fry it, lift it out, dust it with powdered sugar and cinnamon, put it on a plate and eat it hot. And take note if these toasts seem vulgar to you: many cooks do not know how to make them, and with this brief news, they will have no need to ask, and besides often there is nobody to ask.

Sometimes dipped in egg before frying, these cinnamon toasts were called *panatela* in hospitals where they were served as breakfast for the sick. Perhaps Altamiras made them for sick friars and travelers.[25]

COUNTRY PRESERVES

The home-made preserves in Altamiras's larder included sausages, lard, ham, and pickled fish. In summer pumpkin was brined, in winter apples were stewed for a compote. Here he explained how to preserve tomatoes and olives, the year's most important fruit harvest. In the Spanish Mediterranean today most olives are pressed for oil, but some are picked a few weeks earlier, just as they turn purple, for brining as table olives. At Santo Espíritu de Monte the friars prepare their own olives, gashing or cracking them, as Altamiras described, then leaving them to soak in fresh water, changed every day, till they have just the right pungency. Friar Ángel generally counts on eight days to soak the olives in water before laying them down in a garlic and oregano marinade. You can also use these marinades for improving bought brined or dry-salted olives.

Tomatoes Preserved in Olive Oil / Para Conservar Tomates

Preserve them in olive oil before they are fully ripe and you can keep them all year, as if newly harvested, but you must pick them before the sun rises; and there are many uses for the oil you preserve them in.

Altamiras's tomato preserving was an experimental affair. Later friary cooks, like Joan Bagués, who cooked for over thirty years in Gerona hospital, sun-dried their tomatoes or made relishes. Bagués gave one "to animate the appetite" in his 1787 recipe notebook. After wood grilling the tomatoes and pulping the flesh he mixed it with finely chopped garlic, salt and pepper, parsley, onion, and vinegar for a cold relish or with cumin, oregano, and broth for a hot sauce.[26]

Olive Marinades / Adobo de Aceytunas

Pick the olives from the tree when one or two have turned purple, which is a sign they are as fat as they can grow. Cut four or five gashes in each one, steep them in fresh water, turning them every couple of days till they sink to the bottom. Prepare a large nine-pint pitcher of brine where you can steep the olives: put them in the pitcher or another vessel, add lemon slices, strew bay and olive leaves and fennel stalks over the top, then pour over brine. Take cinnamon and cloves, half their volume in pepper and a little saffron, and let all these infuse in it.

Prepare your olives a few at a time, for the lemons turn the marinade bitter after just a few days, and when they are all eaten, prepare more in the same way, and keep doing this through the year, for olives steeped in plain brine keep well, but only if well covered with the brine, for otherwise their flesh softens.

Here is a second easier way to preserve them. Take newly harvested olives, plump and perfect, put them in a glazed vessel, cover them with water and add plenty of salt for flavour. If you leave these olives untouched, they will keep all year. Crack small or marked ones and when you want to eat them make a marinade. Boil water with fennel, thyme, bay leaves, orange skins and pounded heads of garlic, and plenty of salt for a good flavour.

But be aware these olives do not keep for much longer than a month, so if you wish to keep them longer, put them in water with salt, a handful of fennel, a couple of thyme plants and some orange skins, all strewn on top, marinate them like this, then you can keep them for two or three months. But before marinating cracked olives this way they should have been steeped and the water refreshed and changed every nine days till they lose their vitality and green pungency.

SPICED MARINADE: For 500 g / 1 lb olives take a brine made of 500 g / 1 lb salt and 2 liters / 64 fl oz mineral water. Add a sliced well-scrubbed lemon, 3 bay leaves, a cinnamon quill, and 6 cloves pounded with a few peppercorns and a dozen saffron threads (see p. 238). Pour the marinade over the olives in a non-reactive jar, cover, and keep in a cool place for up to three weeks, fishing out the lemon after the first 48 hours.

HERBY CITRIC MARINADE: Rub a small handful of dried fennel stalks and seeds and thyme sprigs between your hands into the brine, add torn bay leaves, the finely chopped pithless zest of half an orange and, if you like, some sliced raw garlic.

Pues tienes que saber que estoy	You need to know I'm
cogiendo olivas	picking olives
Y tu tienes que echarme	And for me you have to add
Un huevo a las migas.	A fried egg to the crumbs.

Olive-picking song, Valdejalón[27]

Friend and cook, you now have a short but adequate account of dishes for meat-eating and lean days, and I hope its contents and the way I speak may please you, for it would give me singular pleasure. It is impossible to please everyone, I know, though not so hard to leave some content, and so those who wish may take away the refreshments which follow.

AN ADDITION

ICED DRINKS
AND OTHER ADVICE

TODAY SAN CRISTÓBAL'S kitchen shows no trace of any imprint left by Altamiras. There is no blackened hearth and the church has toppled down into rubble over the wine bodega. But a short walk beyond the spring, up the path that leads to the top of the sierra, you will find the friary's snow-well, almost exactly as Altamiras knew it, perfectly intact under its domed roof. You can gaze into its dark depths where the friars trod down the snow they harvested during the winter months. Canes lined the well's floor and straw was layered between every few feet of snow to make it easy to cut into blocks.[1] When the well was full the mouth, shadowed by the roof, was sealed up till spring came. As the weather grew warm, blocks were cut and carried down to the infirmary and kitchen. Visitors were served snow-water, a monastic tradition,[2] but Altamiras also put the ice to good use in slushy iced drinks, which he called *aguas* and we know as *granizadas*. These are the first recipes for them in a Spanish cookbook.

Lemon Granizada / Aguas de Limón

For a dozen glasses you need twelve ounces of sugar and one lemon. Pare the lemon half a day before you make your iced water, crush the zest in a china or metal mortar, stir it into your measured water and put it in your ice-box. Leave it till it is good and lemony, strain it, sharpen it with lemon juice then sweeten it, and go gently with the sugar, for you may need less than I mention. Now sieve the lemon water through a thick cloth and freeze it in your icebox. For this have ready three pounds of snow. Put a layer of fine snow mixed with lots of salt at the bottom, then put lumps of ice as big as eggs mixed with more salt on top. Stir the water round from time to time with an oak spatula, for otherwise the ice settles and freezes solid on the sides and bottom of the ice-box. When the moment comes to serve this, take it out of the box, have ready a spoon, a very clean one you keep just for this, and follow this rule for all the other waters.

Altamiras's lemon *granizada* may have been medicinal since it emphasized tangy lemon zest like earlier fruit waters made in al-Andalus. But what was medicinal might also be pleasurable: we know, from the purchase of snow and lemons that the friars of San Diego and their guests drank this iced lemon on the eve of the Virgen del Pilar, Zaragoza's most important fiesta.

2 big juicy organic or unwaxed lemons, 1 liter / 2 pints of still mineral water, about 100 g / 3½ oz cane sugar (or more if you have a sweet tooth)

Makes 6 large glasses, or about 1.25 l / 2¼ pints.

Pare off the lemon zest, making sure you keep no pith, and whizz it with 250 ml / 8 fl oz water to give a pale yellow water. Chill overnight. Dissolve the sugar in a small panful of the remaining water, simmer briefly, and leave to cool. Pour the syrup and lemon water into a non-stick silicon or plastic container, ideally a round one, sieve in the lemon juice and freeze, drawing the iced fringes into the liquid center every hour till you have an even slush, about 4 hours. If you are in a hurry you can use a non-stick metal container, breaking up the ice crystals more often. Just before serving, blend the *granizada* again and pour into freezer-cooled glasses or goblets. Today a little pomegranate or strawberry syrup or red wine may be dripped in for a sunset effect.

> *"Quien quiere agua, agua mas fría que la nieve?"*
> "Who wants water, water colder than snow?"
>
> Peregil the waterman's street cry,
> *Tales of the Alhambra*, Washington Irving, 1832

Cinnamon Granizada / Agua de Canela

For cinnamon water, you need the same amount of sugar as I noted for lemon water and three-quarters of an ounce of cinnamon infused the day before: simmer this in fresh water in a clean pot, cover it for half an hour so its vapours do not escape, then sit the pot in a box of sand or hay. The following day, come the time to ice the water, put the cinnamon infusion and sugar dissolved in a cazuela *together in your ice-box or, if your sugar is coarse, grind it up first, then pass all this through a thick cloth: use the same method as the first water.*

Guillermo Castellat of Los Alpes, one of my favorite ice-cream parlors in Madrid, makes a wonderful dark pink, aromatic cinnamon ice cream. His grandfather, Pietro Marchi, came to Spain from Tuscany in the 1930s with just one recipe for ice cream, vanilla, noted on a scrap of paper. Today his team offers a rolling menu of around two dozen sorbets, ice creams, and iced drinks, their character given by quality natural ingredients. For example, Guillermo uses Malagasy cinnamon left in a cold infusion for a full day and night to extract its full color and aroma. Here he has given two versions of Altamiras's recipe: made with and without a sorbetière. This is less sweet, by the way, than the courtly cinnamon water, which came to Madrid from France.[3]

1 liter / 2 pints of still mineral water, 100 g / 3 oz plus a teaspoon of sugar (or additional sugar to taste, if you like), 80 g / a scant 3 oz glucose, 1 pounded cinnamon quill, grated zest of ½ orange
Makes 6 large glasses, or about 1.25 l / 2¼ pints.
Warm the water with the sugar, glucose, and cinnamon, bring briefly to the boil, take off the heat, and add the orange zest. Infuse, chilled, for 24 hours, strain, and pour the cinnamon syrup into a non-stick plastic or silicon container, preferably round. Freeze (see previous recipe). Guillermo suggests serving dark chocolate or lemon biscuits with this.
CINNAMON SORBET: For this recipe you do need an ice-cream maker or sorbetière maker, glucose, and xantana gum: measurements are 1.75 liters / 3¼ pints still mineral water, 2 cinnamon quills, 250 g / 8 oz sugar, 250 g / 8 oz glucose, 15 g / ½ oz xantana gum, grated zest of 2 oranges, 3 saffron threads. Warm the water with the cinnamon, whizz while still hot (being careful not to break the blender, notes Guillermo), add the sugar mixed with the glucose and the xantana, bring to a boil, remove from the heat and, while still very hot, add the

CINNAMON

"For cinnamon water . . . you need three-quarters of an ounce of cinnamon infused the day before." Altamiras infused whole cinnamon sticks or quills overnight to extract their full color and flavor; he mixed powdered or grated cinnamon with sugar and sprinkled it generously over his rice puddings, blancmanges, fresh cheese, and Lenten suppers (see pp. 186–88); he added pinches to braised or stewed dishes. Cinnamon's intensity of flavor and aroma will depend on its provenance: the best comes from Sri Lanka, Indonesia, or Malagasy. It is worth paying a little extra for this and avoiding Caribbean cassia, which is often sold as cinnamon, but is a different and less perfumed spice.

saffron and orange zest. Chill in the freezer for half an hour, then in the fridge for a day, covered, and make your sorbet.

Almond Granizada / Leche de Almendras

For a dozen glasses, use one pound of sugar and twelve ounces of almonds. Skin the almonds in cold water so the milk stays white, then grind the almonds, and when they are finely ground, stir them into the twelve glasses of water. Dissolve the sugar then strain the sugar water, and strain the almond milk in the same way, till no almonds are left in it, wringing out your straining cloth and throwing away the useless dross, then make your drink, preparing the snow as I have said.

Home-made almond *granizada*, often with nutty chunks in it, can still be found occasionally at cold drink kiosks around the Mediterranean coast. It is easily made at home, with or without the nut chunks, and a touch of lemon zest.

1½ pints of still mineral water, 200 g / 7 oz skinned untoasted almonds, about 3 tbsp sugar, a curl of lemon zest, a cinnamon stick
Makes 6 large glasses, or about 1.25 l / 2¼ pints.

Reserve 150 ml / 5 fl oz water. Add the rest slowly to the almonds in a food processor to make a thick cream that you then slowly dilute. Leave for 30 minutes for the flavor to develop. Warm the reserved water with the sugar, lemon zest and cinnamon, simmer for a minute or two and leave to infuse for a quarter of an hour. Filter the almond milk through a clean well-rinsed tea-towel into a large bowl, squeezing out the final milk between your hands, add the strained lemon syrup, stir well and freeze, preferably in a silicon container, for 4 hours, stirring in the ice from the edges from time to time and blending to a slush before serving (see p. 218).

Dawn Water / Agua de Aurora

For a dozen glasses, add a pound of sugar; six glasses should be of almond milk and the other six of cinnamon water. Mix these with the sugar, stir, put it all well stirred in the ice-box, then put in the snow, as for other waters.

This blend of almond milk and cinnamon water is very sweet, but it is an amazing reviver on hot days. Mix even quantities of the two waters, sugar to taste and chill.

FRESH MILK AND CHEESE

Fresh milk was a seasonal luxury. Altamiras used it to make blancmange, custard, iced milk, and fresh curds. Probably he learned how to make curds with fresh sheep's and goat's milk in childhood, but as a friary cook at San Cristóbal he had cow's milk, perhaps from the herd of cattle that grazed at Alfamén.

Iced Milk / Leche Helada

Fresh cow's milk is the best. For every glassful an ounce of sugar is needed together with three-quarters of an ounce of infused cinnamon for a dozen glasses of milk. Dissolve the sugar in the cinnamon water, strain this, pour it all with the milk into the ice box till it is a little more than half-full, then pack the snow around it, as you do for the other waters. Have ready a whisk as broad as your finger, with rounded spokes like a dome, and go to work like a chocolate maker, whisking. When you see the milk stick to the walls of your ice-box, loosen it with your big wooden spoon, so that in the end all the milk is iced, then scoop this out, fill glasses to the brim with it and serve them with a little spoon to drink from.

Frothy *leche helada*, a very old drink in Spain,[4] is still made in ice-cream parlors and from it you can make *leche merengada*, or meringued milk, stirred up with egg white frothed with icing sugar. It's one of the most popular summer coolers right along the Mediterranean coast.

1 liter / 2 pints cow's or goat's milk, 2 level tbsp cane sugar, long strip of lemon zest, cinnamon stick
Makes about 1 l / 1¾ pints.
Warm the milk with the other ingredients in a large saucepan, simmer for 10 minutes, turn off the heat, and leave to set. Chill in the fridge then in the freezer in a plastic or silicon container to infuse with the cinnamon and lemon, scooping the slushy sides into the center. Just before serving, remove the lemon and cinnamon, and whizz the milk to a frothy slush.

How to Make Fresh Curd Cheese / Modo de Hacer Requesones

Put your milk in a clean pot used for nothing else, stir in a little rennet, in proportion to the milk, put it on the fire and, as curds form, lift them out with a clean round spatula, put them in a little basket so they drain, and when you wish to serve this, or just before, lay a skimmer with big holes on the cheese, pressing it down a little, and what comes will be like pine kernels. As you make them put them on plates and serve them with powdered sugar and cinnamon, and some people say they look like worms. Wild thistle flowers or dried artichokes, pounded in a metal mortar, then dissolved in milk sieved to take the seed tufts, make good rennet.

Quite why Altamiras made cheese the Jewish way, with thistle-rennet, we do not know, but probably the technique had become mainstream long before he was born, especially in rural areas where thistles were easily at hand. This vegetarian rennet is still a distinctive ingredient of Spanish cheese-making, giving fresh cheeses a special honeyed sweetness and sheep's milk *tortas* their spoonable stickiness. Almost certainly this was a fiesta dish.[5] For a modern fast-food version of the finished dessert rub

Spanish *requesón* (or Italian ricotta) through a large-holed spatula into a mound on a large plate, sift icing sugar over the top and then grate over cinnamon, but coarsely, so every spoonful has a sweet aromatic bite.

> *La edad es algo que no es importante a menos que usted sea un queso.*
> Age is something that is not important unless you happen to be a cheese.
>
> Luis Buñuel

DRIED FRUIT

Dried Peaches, Apricots, or Prunes in White Wine / Para remojar Orejones, ò Cascabeles

Soak the dried apricots or prunes in lukewarm water the day before you serve them. Leave them like that till nightfall, drain them well, bathe them in white wine till they are covered, serve them with sugar and cinnamon, and if you soak them in wine alone, they will be even better.

Today Altamiras's homeland is famed as peach-growing country. The orchards spread east from Alcañiz and surround Calanda, the birthplace of Luis Buñuel, which is home to a craft preserving company that prepares hand-cut apricots or peaches, nicknamed *orejones*—or ears[6]—in wine syrup. Altamiras may have made his fruit compote as a Christmas Eve dish.

250 g / 8 oz dried peaches or apricots, mixed with a few raisins if you like, about 500 ml / ¾ pint mineral water, 1 bottle of white Moscatel wine or fruity Mediterranean red wine (e.g., Bobal or Monastrell), sugar to taste, 1 cinnamon stick, a little aguardiente or eau-de-vie

Wash the dried fruit. Put it in a glass or china bowl, cover with the mineral water at room temperature and soak for 6 hours. Drain, reserving the soaking water. Return the fruit to the bowl, cover with wine, and soak overnight. The following day drain the fruit, warm the soaking wine and water in a pan with the sugar, cinnamon, and *aguardiente*, and reduce to give just enough syrup to cover the fruit, adding extra wine if needed. Leave to steep with the washed cinnamon stick for at least a day. Serve with crisp almond biscuits and, if you like, whipped cream or crème fraîche.

KITCHEN REMEDIES

Friary remedies can seem like indulgent treats to modern eyes: medical treatises recommend sponge cakes, iced drinks, sweet wine, tobacco, tea, coffee, and drinking chocolate.[7] In his 1713 handbook Diego Bercebal, who took care of the sick at San Francisco, Zaragoza's largest friary, gave this memorable triple-cocoa formula for chocolate whipped up into a frothy drink: "take equal parts of cocoa from Caracas and the Islands, exalt it with a little Guajaca cocoa; and do not be sparing with cinnamon, for it is reviving and balsamic, of mild aroma and flavour." Altamiras may have thought of all the sweet recipes in this chapter as medicinal; he rounded them off with two ointments.

To Heal Cuts / Para Curar Cortaduras

I would share this recipe with you, friend and cook, for while it may seem to step outside the subject of my handbook or other such kitchen books, and you should know it is not mine, you may, very easily, by mishap or bad luck, need it, since you work among knives and handle them, so may cut yourself some time, and then anyone may use this remedy. So if you cut yourself, find a plant called the Milan grape, which is like a mass of pine kernels and grows on the rooftops. Pound it in a mortar, press out its juice, put it in a flask, leave it in the sun and the liquid will become like olive oil. Apply cloths soaked in this liquid to your wounds, and you will soon be healed.

A Mediterranean survivor, the Milan grape, known usually as cat's grape (*Sedum album*) or stonecrop, has round leaves like miniature grapes, pale green in color, which give a liquid that André Laguna, Spain's classic modern herbalist, thought close to miraculous for healing cuts. It puts down its roots wherever droplets of rain gather in tiny quantities between roof tiles or on stone walls. Altamiras pressed out the juice, let it sit in the sun, reduced it to a thick oily liquid, and kept it for accidents with kitchen knives.

For Those Who Burn or Scald Themselves / Para Los Que se Quemen, o Escalden

If boiling water splashes on the fire's embers and scalds you, lay the burnt skin in a ceramic dish of virgin vinegar, let it soak it for some time and in that way no blister shall form. Others take a pounded onion and rub it over their scalded skin, but if a blister forms and becomes an ulcer, put a little pot of water on the fire, but two fingers short of being full, add white wax in pellets, or any other kind, warm this, take it off as soon as the water boils. Have ready a little olive oil in a vessel, and pour the wax into it, little by little, and take care so only the wax falls, though it matters little if some water drips in, and as you pour the wax, stir with a little stick till the ointment sets. Spread it on the ulcer every morning, and you will be cured in just a few days.

This pomade, a little like the famous Morisco healers' beeswax ointment called *basilicón*, made with olive oil and pine resin,[8] can be re-created with beeswax pellets or, even better, beekeepers' brown wax.

6 tbsp of best organic extra-virgin olive oil, 60 g / 2 oz bees' wax, 500 ml / 1 pint water (this measure is not too important) in which to melt the wax

Have ready a 1-liter / 2-pint glass or china bowl and a wooden spoon. Pour the olive oil into the bowl, making sure it completely covers the bottom, and sit it on a board, wrapping a tea-towel around the bottom so it will not move when you are stirring. Warm the water and wax gently in a small saucepan and as the wax melts and floats, carefully pour it into the oil, beating with the wooden spoon. If a little water trickles in with the wax, do not worry. It quickly separates out and you can easily pour it off. Scoop the pomade into a clean lidded jar.

THE WELL-TEMPERED SKILLET

To Temper a Skillet and Make a Rolled Omelette / Para Templar Sartenes

Nothing tarnishes a cook's name like badly fried eggs, and often the problem lies in skillets that are not well-tempered. This is the way to temper them: wash them well, put them on the fire, rub them all over with a piece of ham rind, and like this they are quickly tempered. Other times you can make a skillet good and hot, sprinkle the outside of the base with vinegar; or, if you are in a hurry, throw in two eggshell halves of beaten egg over the fire, for their smoke usually tempers well. But heed me about the ham fat, it is the surest way.

Make your rolled omelette like this: add a little olive oil to the skillet, sit it over hot embers, at the same time beat the eggs, and when the oil is very

hot, add them, let them set. Roll up the omelette with your small fire shovel, turn it without burning it, and it should be soft enough that it breaks easily if you pick it up by one end, and it will look like a rope. On that thought I end this handbook for otherwise it may unravel endlessly.

Now, friend and cook, you have what you need to set about your work, as I have learnt from experience and practise: bear in mind that here I am not talking to first-class Cooks, for I suppose they are better taught then I may ever be, but to apprentice cooks. So, amend my errors and correct what does not please you, pardon what is missing, forgive my style, learn what interests you and hold silence on what you do not need, for, you see, I have simply wanted to give you pleasure in everything, and I submit all this to your correction; and stay with God, who keeps us in friendship and grace.[9]

Barcin. Die 19 Aprilis 1767
REIMPRIMATUR
MATHEU V.G. & Off.
Barcelona, y Abril 20, de 1767
REIMPRIMASE
De Irabien

AFTERWORD

FRAY ÁNGEL had begun cooking recipes from *New Art* at Santo Espíritu del Monte as my work on this book was drawing to a close. During my research I had discovered much about *New Art* and Juan Altamiras, or Raimundo Gómez, the man who wrote it. I had tracked how his recipes had passed from one generation to the next.[1] I had discovered much of his life and times. Yet the ending of Altamiras's life remained elusive until, by chance, I found his death noted at Santa Catalina, Cariñena, the wine town east of La Almunia, between 1770 and 1772. I decided to search for the friary ruins when I had a chance. Roberto del Val, a botanist who knew the country-side like the back of his hand, offered to help me. We drove east from Cariñena and turned down a track through undulating vineyards until the ruins appeared on a hilltop. One façade of the church stood and the ice well was intact, but the tombs in the church floor had been dug up long before. Walking around the edge of the ruins, now surrounded by almond groves, one could feel the peace a countryman might seek for a resting place. To the southwest the views stretched over the plains to La Almunia, where a squat flat-topped mound rose up from the plains. Roberto pulled out a copy of a local map from the 1920s. On it he showed me the mound's name: the Cerro de Altamira. We drove there, clambered up the scrabbly slopes and looked down: here below us on all sides was the world Altamiras had known, wide-horizoned sierras and plains, green and dun, speckled by river-towns and villages, built on the edge of an old kingdom[2]; a place of transit, a land of many communities, once of three great faiths, where received ideas from the outer world might be quietly challenged by everyday local ways. In these long perspectives of time and place, back-lit by a pale sun, there seemed to lie an ending, but also a beginning.[3]

COOKING WITH ALTAMIRAS

GUIDELINES AND GLOSSARY

"On publishing a cookbook, it seems natural to say I have no pretensions of mastering this science and art. I am, very simply, a modest *aficionada*."

Emilia Pardo Bazán, *The Old Spanish Kitchen*, 1913

W HEN I began this book I planned to give cooking notes for just a few dishes, but, encouraged by friends who came to eat them, I ended up cooking my way through the book. As I did so I discovered the truth of British chef Mark Hix's remark on historic recipes—so much lies in the spaces between the words. That is exciting, but it can be costly. So finally, after friends who ate Altamiras's dishes also wanted to cook them, I decided to give fuller guidelines and these general notes.

INGREDIENTS AND FLAVORS

Altamiras's larder products are easy-going. He knew his readers cooked with various flours, breads, fats, and milks, and you can, too, unless his recipes say otherwise. A few distinctively Spanish ingredients, like *jamón* or air-dried ham, and salt cod or *bacalao*, may be tricky to find elsewhere so alternatives are given in the glossary and the recipes. Cane sugar gives his dishes a deep rounded sweetness; in savory dishes I have sometimes replaced the sugar with sweet ingredients more familiar to us today, like wine or onion *sofrito*, for example. Quality spices make a world of difference.

Most of the fresh seasonal produce in the recipes—game, ewe's milk cheeses, mutton or hogget lamb, home-made sausages and river fish—may be tracked down at farmers' markets, whole-beast butchers, poulterers, speciality, or ethnic food shops. Unusual vegetables like borage, cardoon, and heritage tomatoes may be grown from seed, now available through the Internet. Cooking with fresh organic produce often transforms the dishes and I am sure brings us closer to his original flavors and textures. But since it can be expensive, or unavailable, I have not specified it.

Salt and pepper do not appear in the ingredients lists since tastes vary so much—often people eat no salt at all—but they appear in the method as a reminder when to add them.

OLD AND NEW EQUIPMENT

Two bits of Altamiras's cooking equipment remain invaluable.

One is an earthenware or clay cooking pot. In fact Altamiras had various pots: flat-bottomed *cazuelas*, little *cazuelitas*, deep fat-bellied *ollas* and jugged *pucheros*. All these, made of earthenware or clay, spread heat slowly but evenly, giving effects very different to cooking in a metal pot. They allow you to slow-cook at a low simmer over direct heat, as many Spanish cooks did till well into the twentieth century, and you can also oven braise or pot-roast, fry, sizzle, or poach fish in them. If you seal the rim between the pot and the lid with flour and water dough or oiled paper the temperature inside rises, but is moist, ideal for long braising.

Altamiras's pots, like most in Spain today, were glazed inside (you can also use unglazed clay pots). When you buy them, look for a label guaranteeing a lead-free glaze: it is a vital guarantee. Choose your first pot according to the kind of dishes you want to cook in it. A *cazuela* is good for many uses. Pots from other food cultures may stand in well: a French *cocotte*, for example, is not so different from an *olla*. To cook over direct heat you need to set your pots on a flame-tamer or heat-diffuser, rather like a metal mat. In the oven, place them on a silicon rack to keep the heat even. If you enjoy cooking in these pots then it is worth buying two or three, keeping one for sweet dishes only. For tempering, see p. 237.

A pestle and mortar are also invaluable. I crush, bash, and powder peppercorns, spices, sea salt, and herbs in a large glazed earthenware mortar with a wooden pestle and I keep two smaller sets for special uses: a wooden one for garlic and a glazed white pottery one for saffron (see p. 102). I grind nuts in a food processor and make sauces, creams, pulps, and purées with a hand-held blender.

Among modern kitchen gear, I think Altamiras would have enjoyed using a skimmer jug for defatting his broths, a spice infuser, and microplane grater for extracting the best from his cinnamon, extra-strong foil for make roasting envelopes (see pp. 99, 106–7), and cooking parchment or paper for making lids.

MODERN MEALS

When you first cook Altamiras's dishes many of them look plain, but it is easy to give them a simple natural beauty. You can curve a stem of flat-leafed parsley around the edge of a dish, snip pale celery leaves over the top or add a flash of color with roasted red peppers, shiny black olives, or golden hard-boiled egg yolks. Try thinly pared orange zest, a swirl of sieved red berry purée, or a few pomegranate seeds on blancmanges and rice puddings. Altamiras's trompe l'oeuil dishes—his marzipan-stuffed eggshells, cheese worms, pies shaped like knights in armor, and pastry window railings (see pp. 154–55, 164–65, 173–74, 222)—can inspire other ideas.

Cook *New Art*'s dishes as eighteenth-century meals or drop them into everyday modern eating. For example, his vegetable dishes, beans, and chickpeas, usually first courses in Spain, are very good as one-dish meals with salad, bread, and cheese, or combined in a vegetarian spread. They are also easily adapted; the dishes which contain nuts or raw egg yolks may usually be cooked without them; many of his sweet dishes have the advantage of being gluten free.

One final thought: Altamiras rarely comments on the temperature at which to serve dishes, but his flavors sing out well when warm rather than piping hot. Perhaps they were meant to be eaten that way?

TECHNIQUES AND METHODS

Altamiras's cooking techniques, like braising meat in its own fat, slowly sweating onion sofrito, cooking salt cod, soaking saffron, and making slushy iced drinks are easily mastered. All are explained in the text and glossary.

Occasionally I have updated older cooking methods, as Altamiras did. For example, sometimes he browned meat by wood-grilling before braising it (see p. 10). How wonderful the undertow of smoky flavor would be! But on the other hand, how many people nowadays can light a wood grill or barbecue on an everyday basis? In such cases I have opted to make recipes as accessible as possible, though if you want to follow the original methods they are there. For health reasons I have removed some of his raw egg thickenings from stews.

WEIGHTS, MEASURES, TEMPERATURES

Altamiras gave a few weights, the Castilian ones imposed on Aragon around the time of his birth: his *libra*, or pound, was 16 *onzas* or ounces; his *cuartillo*, or pint, just over 16 fluid ounces; his *cantaro*, or two gallons, 16 pints.

But he wrote that he would have liked to give more guidance on measures, so I have done so in the familiar modern way, as quantities for 4–6 people, except for meat-loafs and pies, for which I have given a weight or dimension. Where possible I have left measurements simple. Tablespoonfuls (15 ml) and teaspoonfuls (5 ml) are level. A glass of wine is 100 ml / 3½ fl oz. A bottle of wine is 750 ml / 1¼ pints; half a bottle of wine is 375 ml /12 fl oz.; pints are European (or Imperial).

I have also added guideline oven temperatures though these need adapting to each kitchen. Fan oven temperatures, for example, should be lowered by 10–20°C, 25°F, gas mark ½–1.

Likewise, you need to adjust them if you are cooking in earthenware rather than metal pots, allowing around 30 minutes to 1 hour extra for oven braised or pot-roasted dishes. Altamiras was probably braising over charcoal embers at just over boiling point, around 110°C / 200°F. But most home cooks today braise or casserole in the oven, often at higher temperatures (e.g., 180°C, 350°F, gas mark 4) for quicker cooking times or at newer lower temperatures (70°C, 150°F, gas mark ¼) for slower cooking. The choice is yours.

METRIC, IMPERIAL, AND BASIC AMERICAN VOLUME EQUIVALENTS

These are guidelines to the conversions given for weights and measures in the recipes.

g / ml	oz / fl oz
15	½
25	¾
30	1
45	1½
60	2
75	2½
90	3
100	3½
120	4 (4 oz: ¼ lb)
150	5
175	6
200	7
250	8 (8 oz: ½ lb; 8 fl oz 1 US cup)
275	9
300	10 (10 fl oz: ½ UK pint)
340	11
370	12 (12 oz: ¾ lb)
400	13
430	14
460	15
500	16 (16 oz: 1 lb /16 fl oz: ¾ UK pt or 2 US cups)
600	20 (20 oz: 1¼ lb / 20 fl oz: 1 UK pt or 1¼ US pt)
750	24 (750 g: 1½ lb / 750 ml: 1¼ UK pts or 3 US cups)
850	1¾ lb

g / kg	lb
1kg	2 lb
1.15 kg	2½ lb
1.5 kg	3 lb
1.6 kg	3¼ lb
1.85 kg	3¾ lb
2 kg	4 lb
2.3 kg	5 lb

ml	fl oz / pts / cups
250 ml	8 fl oz / 1 US cup
300 ml	10 fl oz / ½ UK pt
370 ml	12 fl oz
475 ml	16 fl oz / 2 US cups
600 ml	20 fl oz / 1 UK pt
750 ml	24 fl oz / 3 US cups
1 l	32 fl oz / 4 US cups
1.4 l	45 fl oz / 5½ cups
2.8 l	80 fl oz / 11 cups

A COOK'S GLOSSARY

Adobo (*marinade or pickle*): For tenderizing, preserving, or flavoring meat, fish, or olives.

Aguardiente (*grape spirit*): Literally "burning water," the Spanish equivalent of French *eau-de-vie* and *marc*: in the eighteenth century it was a medicine, popular drink, and cookery ingredient.

Anis: Aniseed-flavored aguardiente.

Bacalao: See Salt cod.

Bread, breadcrumbs, and sops (*pan, migas, sopas*): Everyday bread was baked with whole wheat, rye, barley, or mixed grain flour (all called *pan moreno*) though on the wheat plains fine white flour was used too. **BREADCRUMBS:** Best from day-old or dry bread, sometimes knife-cut (see p. 170), but more often finely or coarsely grated. **TOASTED BREAD:** Sometimes dry-toasted, others fried in olive oil. Fried bread is especially good in soups: it holds its texture. Oven-toasting works well for dry toast or crumbs. Bought croûtons are a good short-cut for toast-thickened sauces.

Broths (*caldos*): **CHICKPEA BROTH:** Blanche, refresh, and simmer 500 g /1 lb chickpeas with prepared carrots, onions, and a whole head of garlic in 1.4 l / 2½ pints of water. Salt the broth towards the end of cooking. **HEN (OR CHICKEN) BROTH:** At its best made with a hen (see pp. 105–6, 135). **MEAT BROTH:** See pp. 28–29, 74–75 for a rich broth. **GREEN VEGETABLE BROTH:** Simmer 2–3 celery or cardoon stalks, 200 g / 7 oz Swiss chard leaves and stalks, and 3 green garlic shoots or spring onion tops in 1.4 l /2½ pints of salted water for 30 minutes. **SAFFRON BROTH**: See p. 25.

Butter (*mantequilla*): Altamiras liked cooking fish in butter (see p. 147). You can use unsalted or salted butter.

Candied citrus zest (*acitrón*): Buy or make it at home: blanche thinly pared zest batons or curls in water for 5 minutes, and drop them into a syrup made with 120 g / 4 oz sugar and 120 ml / 4 fl oz water. Simmer for 5–7 minutes and drain on kitchen paper.

Capers (*alcaparras*): Rinse then soak brined or dry-salted capers in cold water for 4–5 hours so they are slightly salty but still firm.

Cardoon (*cardo*): Preserved cardoon is widely available and eaten in Spain. A good stand-in when fresh is not available.

Cheese (*queso*): Altamiras cooked with mature goat's or ewe's milk cheeses. Manchego or Parmesan, suggested by court cook Diego Granado in his 1614 cookbook, work well.

Cinnamon (*canela*): See p. 220.

Citrus fruit (*agrias*): Lemons and Seville oranges (see p. 144) are the most widely available of Altamiras's citrus fruit; he also knew citrons and bergamots.

Cooking papers (*papel de estraza*): Cooking parchment or grease-proof paper stand in well for Altamiras's coarse paper, like butcher's paper, but made of rag.

Cured ham (*jamón*): See p. 72. Diced *jamón*, streaky or lean, can be replaced by *pancetta* or *lardons*. Probably Altamiras's hams came from acorn-grazed pigs, close to today's Ibérico hams. Their diced offcuts, bones, fat, and soft lard are all good value if you can find them. A smoked hock bone replaces a *jamón* bone well.

Eggs (*huevos*): The recipes have been cooked with medium eggs (size 3–4, 55–65 g), but size is not always important. Some raw egg thickenings have been removed.

Frying (*freir*): Altamiras used just one word for six different frying techniques: to toss and lightly brown in hot oil (*saltear*), warm gently in oil (*rehogar*), sweat slowly (*sofreir*), fry to brown and seal (*sellar*), coat and deep-fry (*freir*), and render (*fundir*). **A SPANISH FRYING BATTER:** Blend and chill 90 g / 3 oz sieved plain flour, a pinch of salt, 1 raw egg yolk, 30 ml / 1 tbsp raw olive oil, and 150 ml / 5 fl oz iced water. Dip foods without flouring. **TEMPURA BATTER:** Mix with a fork 1 egg, 90 g / 3 oz plain flour, 50 g / 2 oz cornflour, and 200 ml / 7 fl oz iced water just before using. Dip without flouring. **BREADED CRUST:** Dip or roll foods in seasoned plain flour, then beaten egg yolks, and finally breadcrumbs (see p. 236). Fry them in very hot olive oil (strain to reuse for frying similar foods).

Garlic (*ajo*): Cooked in different ways for varying flavor effects, mild to pungent: whole in its skin, as bulbs or cloves, or skinned and chopped or sliced (e.g., to warm with olive oil to flavor it) or pounded. **GREEN GARLIC** (*ajo verde*): Sold fresh in Spain, like spring onions. Fresh wild green garlic stands in well.

Herbs (*hierbas*): Fresh parsley, mint, sage, bay leaf, thyme, oregano, and fennel were Altamiras's herbs.

Jamón: See Cured ham.

Longaniza: See Sausages.

Nuts: ALMONDS: Look for varieties: Marconas, with their high oil content, make the best marzipan; sweet Pestañas are ideal for almond milk; snap-dry Larguetas are good for thickening pastes. See p. 214 for making almond milk. **HAZELNUTS (FILBERTS):** Look for small dry-farmed nuts. **PINE KERNELS (PINE NUTS):** Soaked and used soft and white in *New Art*, or you can toast them.

Ollas: See Pots.

Pastry (*masas*): Puff or short crust doughs stand in well for Altamiras's baked butter and olive oil pastries (see p. 59–60 and 152). **FRIED EMPANADILLA PASTRY:** See p. 155.

Pepper (*pimienta*): Peppercorns gave their name to medieval Aragonese pepper stews, called *pebres* or *prebes* (see pp. 11–12). Later, home-made *pimentón*, or ground red pepper, replaced pricy peppercorns in regions like Valencia.

Picada (*a chopped flavoring or thickening paste*): Altamiras's hazelnut paste is close to modern Catalan almond, hazelnut, and sometimes pine kernel *picadas*, used in sauces like *romesco*.

Pluck (*asadurilla*): Lamb and kid's pluck (heart, liver, and lungs) is popular in Spain though melts (or spleen, see p. 14) are no longer sold.

Potatoes (*patatas*): Widely grown from the 1770s in Aragon, they accompany many of Altamiras's dishes well. **PATATAS A LA PANADERA:** These thinly sliced potatoes are roasted with flavorings rather than cooked in liquid and emerge with a dry, golden brown, crunchy crust. Warm the oven (180°C, 350°F, gas mark 4). Butter or oil an earthenware dish or roasting tin, scatter over half a finely sliced onion, layer 1 kg / 2 lb of washed, peeled, and thinly sliced potatoes on top, sprinkling a finely chopped garlic clove, salt to taste, and a few very finely chopped parsley leaves between each layer. Pour over the top 2 tbsp olive oil, 1 tbsp fresh lemon juice, and 2 tbsp white wine, cover with tinfoil, bake for an hour, remove, repeat the basting with liquid, and bake uncovered till the potatoes are cooked in the middle, and crispy brown on top, about 1¼ hours.

Pots (*cazuelas, ollas*): New pots need soaking overnight in water; dry and rub inside and out with garlic (some people use olive oil), fill them with water, and put over gentle heat, raising it slowly to boil the water briefly.

Poussins (*coquelets*): Recipes have been cooked with European 500–750 g / 1–1½ lb poussins.

Pulses (*legumbres*): **HARICOT BEANS** (*alubias, judias*): Look for new-season or shrink-wrapped beans for the best velvety texture. Quality Spanish beans include brown-eyed *judías de la virgen* (from Aragon, probably what Altamiras cooked), white *alubias blancas*, pink-speckled *alubias de canela*, black *alubias de Tolosa*, and red Leonese *alubias rojas*. **CHICKPEAS** (*garbanzos*): Leonese Pedrosillanos, small and thin-skinned, are especially sweet and nutty.

Raisins (*uvas pasas*): Grapy-sweet, fleshy Malaga raisins are ideal, but hard to find; smaller sultanas are an alternative. Soak in warm water for an hour before removing the pips.

Rice (*arroz*): Altamiras's rice was round-grained like Bomba, today's premium paella rice, which remains firm while soaking up to four times its volume in liquid. Other paella or risotto rices stand in well.

Roasts (*asados*): Altamiras pot-roasted meat and vegetables over hot embers; he roasted turkeys in the bread oven and he spit-roasted paper-wrapped smaller birds in front of the fire. You can pot-roast in an earthenware or clay pot over gentle heat or roast birds on a rack in the oven.

Saffron (*azafrán*): See p. 102. Look for dust-free orangy and red stigmas; organic stigmas are smaller but give intense color and aroma. Boiling saffron flattens its flavor; add it to simmering liquids for no more than 10 minutes at the end of cooking, or after removing from the heat.

Salt cod (*abadejo, bacalao*): See p. 117. Allow 150–200 g / 5–7 oz modern dried salt cod fillet, about 180–250 g / 6½–8 oz soaked weight, for each main course serving. For convenience, soak dry salt cod when you buy it, then freeze it ready for use, or buy it pre-soaked, as it is now in France. Spanish cuts include fillets and strips (*tiras*); the thin-fleshed tail (*cola*) rich in plasma; pieces (*migas*) for dumplings, omelettes, and rices; the head (*cabeza*). **SOAKING:** Put the well-rinsed dry salt cod in a colander immersed in a large bowl of cold water. Fillet strips need about 24 hours soaking, thin fillet portions 36 hours, thick portions 48 hours; pieces 6 hours; change the water for each 2–3 times. Check cod is desalted by tasting a small bit nicked raw out of the center. **HOME-SALTING:** This gives fresh cod a simple briny flavor. Lay evenly sized fillets on a bed of salt in a china or glass dish, cover with more salt, chill for 12 hours. Rinse and soak for 12 hours, changing the water twice.

Salt tuna (*atún salado, mojama, tonyina de sorra*): See p. 141.

Sausages (*longaniza, salchicha*): Aragonese *longaniza* sausage is sweetly spiced with nutmeg, cinnamon, aniseed, cloves, and garlic. Good pure pork chipolatas can stand in for fresh *longaniza* or unspiced *salchicha*.

Sofritos: See p. 121.

Sugar (*azúcar*): Look for cane sugar, refined or unrefined, or dried cane juice (*panatela*).

Tomatoes (*tomates*): Altamiras's small furrowed tomatoes were probably as sweet as fruit, like similar old-fashioned Mediterranean varieties today. Cherry tomatoes stand in well.

Tortilla (*unrolled omelette, thick or thin*): Best known with potato, but can be flavored in many ways (see pp. 30–31, 163–64).

Verjuice (*agraz*): An acidic seasoning, either liquid or granulated, made with lightly fermented sour grape juice. Widely used in medieval times and enjoying a revival today for its fruity edge. In Navarre it is made with Garnacha and Mazuela grapes.

Wine (*vino*): See p. 56. On the whole white *afrutados*, or fruity wines, work well in the recipes. **SWEET WINES:** You can cook with Spanish Moscatel or Pedro Ximénez, or, if not available, with Marsala from Sicily, or Mavrodaphne from Greece, diluting each appropriately.

NOTES

Introduction

1. As models for this "fictive" introduction I have used Marcelin Defourneaux's 1966 imaginary "Letter from a Journey in Spain" in his *Daily Life in Spain in the Golden Age*, trans. Newton Branch (Stanford: Stanford University Press, 1971), Foreword, 13–27, and Carlo Ginzburg's analysis of building "true history on the fictitious" in *Threads and Traces: True, False, Fictive*, trans. Anne C. Tedeschi and John Tedeschi (Los Angeles: University of California Press, 2012), 72–82. The principal sources are archival, printed Franciscan books on the rules governing Franciscan life, and evidence on the ground today. On censors' sensitivity to erotic references and "attacks" on reputation, Marcelin Defourneaux, *Inquisición y censura de libros en la España del siglo XVIII*, trans. Diego González (Madrid: Taurus, 1973), 32, 50.

2. San Francisco was Madrid's only Observant friary in 1745; it was also the provincial house for Castile and home of the Comisario de las Indias, a crown post created in 1581 to coordinate Franciscan mission work in the New World.

3. After the flood on 2 June 1731 the townspeople "went to other places . . . and the friary gave many days of habitation, day and night, to many families." Juan Generes Regled, *Libro de Bautizos, Difuntos y Matrimonios*, 5 July 1731, Registry of Baptisms, Deaths and Marriages, APLA.

4. Altamiras was baptized "Raimundo, son of Jacinto Gómez y Catalina del Val, godmother Dña Blassa Ortiz" in La Almunia on 12 February 1709 (*Libro de Bautizos*, APLA) and he took vows as a lay friar (*Disposición de El Colegio de San Diego de Zaragoza*, 1770–1772, ex-cat, ACPV). His family's comfortable social and economic position is revealed by his parents' marriage agreement (*Capitulaciones matrimoniales*, Libro notario Crisólogo Pascual, 1693. 46v to

49r. Signature 456, Archivo de Protocolos Notariales, AMLA). Félix de Latassa y Ortín identifies him as a cook at the Colegio de San Diego, a Franciscan university college in Zaragoza in his *Biblioteca nueva de los escritores aragoneses*, 1798–1801, Vol. V, 150. We know he was cooking in Madrid in 1745 (Juan Altimiras, *Nuevo Arte de Cocina*, Madrid: Juan de Soto 1760, f. 5) and find him at San Diego, age 55, in 1764, as *portero* (*Disposición*, 1764. Ex-cat, ACPV). He may have cooked in a patron's home in Madrid for up to ten years (see note 17) or, after publishing his book, he may have returned to Aragon to cook in a kitchen at a large friary, like San Francisco in Zaragoza. San Cristóbal, the friary in the sierra near La Almunia, is the only one he mentions in the book so he may have studied as a novice there rather than in La Almunia.

5. Gonzalo Anés y Álvarez de Castrillón, *Las Crisis agrarias en la España moderna*, (Madrid: Taurus, 1970), 428–31. One Italian Jeronimo monk wrote of his journey from Catalonia to Zaragoza in 1755, "*ne vous semblerait-il pas . . . que je voyage dans les deserts de l'Afrique?*"; "would not it seem to you . . . that I am travelling in the deserts of Africa?" Norberto Caimo, *Voyage d'Espagne, fait en l'année 1755*, transl. P. de Barnabite Livoy (Costard, Paris, 1772), 87. On economic decline, Rosa María Blasco Martinez, *Zaragoza en el siglo XVIII 1700–1770* (Zaragoza: Librería General, 1977), 105, 117, 122–23.

6. Bourbon centralization: Norman Davies, *Vanished Kingdoms, The History of Half-Forgotten Europe* (Allen Lane, London, 2011), 221–23. The unification also meant that for the first time Aragonese friars could be sent to the New World. Agustín Boadas Llavat, "Ética y Vino: San Júnipero Serra, Los Franciscanos y California," in *Aportaciones al diccionario biográfico franciscano de España, Portugal, IberoAmérica y Filippinas* (Córdoba: ADEF, 2014), 57–65.

7. On the eighteenth-century city, Blasco Martínez, *Zaragoza*, 1977, 12–24 the city, 120 San Diego, 136–39 cultural life. Also, John Crow, *The Root and The Flower: An Interpretation of Spain and the Spanish People* (Berkeley: University of California Press, 2005), 175. Robert Hughes, *Goya* (New York: Alfred A. Knopf, 2003), 29–33. Ignacio Jordán de Asso, *Historia de la Economía Política de Aragón* (Zaragoza: Estación de Estudios Pirenáicos, 1947), 234.

8. This description draws on the illustration in Altimiras, *Nuevo Arte*, 1760, ff. 34–35; the kitchen inventory in *Disposicion*, 1764, ACPV: Ángel Luis Schlatter Navarro, *La Embajada Keicho y Espartiñas. Nuevas Aportaciones a Una Estrecha Relación* (Espartinas: Ayto de Espartinas, 2014), 182–96. The lattice-fronted cupboards, called *alacenas*, were often set into walls. Fragments of friary ceramics have been found at San Cristóbal, Alpartir, and Santa Catalina, Cariñena. A fine collection of *mudéjar* craftwork may be seen in Teruel's Museo Provincial and is the subject of Tobed's Sala Mudéjar.

9. The Franciscans' eating calendar: NA, *Estatutos Generales para la familia Cismontaña*, (Madrid: n.p., 1705), 26–27 and "Exposición del Señor Papa Clemente Quinto" on following local fast-days.

10. On the porosity of La Almunia to Jewish culture, see Encarnación Marin Padilla, "Los judíos de La Almunia de Dona Godina, villa aragonesa de señorio, en La Zaragoza mitad del siglo XV," Sefarad, 1, 1991, 51–84. I am also indebted to José Manuel Mosteo Achategui for information on Morisco businesses in La Almunia he has found in papers in Ricla archives on property ownership and debts. Morisco culture was in resistance from 1520, but wherever its communities made up a majority of the population, as in the Jalón valley, it shaped everyday life up to and long after the 1610 expulsion. Clay Stalls, "The Dilemma of Conquered Muslims under Christian rule: the Aragonese Solution," Ch. 6 in *Possessing the Land, Aragon's Expansion into Islam's Ebro Frontier Under Alfonso el Batller 1104–34* (Leiden: Brill, 1995). The expulsion: James Casey, *Early Modern Spain, A Social History* (London: Routledge, 1999), 226. Spanish-Morisco irrigation culture and farming in the New World: William Dunmire, *Gardens of New Spain: How Mediterranean Plants and Food Changed America* (Austin: University of Texas Press, 2004), 13, 16, 150.

11. Zaragoza's exceptional libraries were destroyed during Napoleon's 1808–1809 siege of the city. Caimo, *Voyage*, 104; Hughes, *Goya*, 55, 58. The inventory of the Cariñena friars' library survives: *Tierra de Conventos: Santa Catalina del Monte y San Cristóbal de Cariñena*, ed. Encarna Jarque Martínez (Zaragoza: Institución Fernando el Católico, 2010), 79–80. Fray Juan de San Antonio gives clues about the books Altamiras could have borrowed within Franciscan walls (he recommends Ramón Llull, Lope de Vega and Cervantes) in his *Bibliotecha Universal Franciscana* (Madrid: n.p., 1732), Vol. X, 8. On friary book-borrowing NA, *Estatutos*, 23. Altamiras's modern ideas on hygiene, which have intrigued food historians, echo those in novices' handbooks. Francisco Velázquez, *Doctrina para la educación y crianza de los novicios y nuevos profesos* (Valencia: Viuda de Juan Guasch, 1650), 118–20. He also had access to farming guides (Velázquez, *Doctrina*, Chap. 11, 121). Fernando Serrano Larráyoz has shown Altamiras's notebook predates other monastery recipe collections once thought to be his sources: "Confitería y cocina conventual en la Navarra del siglo XVIII," *Revista Príncipe de Viana* 243 (2008), 148–86. More likely, his ability to leap from medieval to modern came from the relative freedom, or looseness of authority, in friary kitchens. In other religious orders cooks were obliged to stick rigorously to established dishes: improvization and creativity was forbidden. Gregorio Sánchez Meco, *El Arte de la Cozina en los Tiempos de Felipe II* (San Lorenzo del Escorial: Egatorre, 1998), 205. Altamiras was also freer than court cooks, who were obliged to follow etiquette and social convention.

12. In 1745, Spain's twenty-five Franciscan Provinces included Mexico, the Yucatan, Mechoacan, Guatemala, Nicaragua, Zachetecas, Jalisco, Florida, Peru, and, in Asia, India, the Philippines, and Malacca. The friars also worked in Muslim cultures, including Morocco and the Holy Land. Altamiras would have talked to returning missionaries at San Cristóbal, where they rested, and

San Diego. Famed eighteenth-century Aragonese missionaries included José de Parras (1728–1784), who explored Buenos Aires, Paraguay, and Uruguay, and Francisco Hermenegildo Garcés (1738–1781), who discovered the inland route from Mexico to Lower California.

13. Altamiras lacked the approval of "a Learned monk" and his superiors' license to publish, both of which were rigorously required by a Franciscan friar. NA, *Estatutos,* 43, 45. Consulting the friars at San Francisco was Don Pascual's only way of ensuring that it was correct for him to issue the license.

14. The influence of French cooking at the Madrid court began when the Spanish crown passed to the Bourbons in 1700, but it was not until the appointment of Matheo Hervé as head of Madrid's palace kitchens in 1746 that it held sway. María del Carmen Simón Palmer, *La Cocina de palacio 1561–1931,* (Madrid: Castalia, 1997), 103, 168.

15. On 6 July 1745 the Supreme Council of Castile approved *New Art's* proofs. They were prefaced by a dedication to San Diego de Alcalà, venerated as a healer in Madrid, and an "Aprobación," or "Approval" by Francisco Ardit, a court cook specializing in Holy Week dishes. Altamiras, *Nuevo Arte,* 1760, ff. 2–5. Contratos Francisco Ardit, Caja 1340; Exp 8, 9. Archivo Personal, Archivo General, Palacio Real de Madrid, Colección Real. Altamiras did not commission Ardit and may not have known him. We do not know whether Altamiras thought he was a good cook.

16. Velázquez, *Doctrina,* 1650, 103: *"el oficio de mayor confiança que ay en un Convento es el del Portero"*; "the office of greatest trust in a Friary is that of the Porter." Gómez may have won patrons' trust through his contact with them while he was a cook.

17. I am indebted to friary academics (OFMs) Thomas Herbst and Cayetano Sánchez Fuertes for their suggestions about how *New Art* was published in the context of Franciscan publishing tradition. Given that there is no mention of a printer's, bookseller's, or friary Syndic's financing at the front of the book, a patron almost certainly covered the costs. Probably this also explains why the book was published in Madrid, not Zaragoza, and why Altamiras, although a friar in the Province of Aragon, is cited as having been in Madrid, as "a resident in this Court, and a cook in it" in 1745. (Altimiras, *New Art,* 1760, paratexts, f. 5.) He may have taken his pen-name because his patron was able to guarantee a secular publishing licence. The idea that he cooked in his patron's home while organizing the book's publication would tie in with other examples: Fray Luis de San José, an Ávila friar and healer, lived in and worked from a noble's palace in Madrid from the 1720s to 1737 at his superiors' request.

18. Influential Aragonese figures in Madrid who may have helped the book on its way in 1745 included Ignacio de Luzán, poet, who had negotiated the Zaragoza Inquisition with the help of religious orders there; Blas de Antonio Nasarre, director of the Royal Library, and Joaquín Pignatelli, tenth Count of

Fuentes, whose family had founded San Diego in Zaragoza in 1601. He is the most likely patron of the book; his father-in-law, the Duke of Mirándola, Chief Steward and Head of the Royal Household for over a decade, was responsible for hiring kitchen staff, including Francisco Ardit, who wrote the required "Approval" of *New Art* (see note 15). Others who may have helped were Francisco de Bardaji y Villareal, an Aragonese lawyer in the Royal Council, and Don Antonio Dara y Vives, Noble of Aragon and benefactor of San Diego, who held a position in the Inquisition.

19. The 1763–1766 crisis was reflected in San Diego's accounts: in 1767 outgoings doubled income (£2,003 to £993.00). *Cabreo del Colegio de Diego, Zaragoza*, 1767, L. 18781 (1878L), Clero Secular Regular, Archivo Historico Nacional, Madrid (AHN). It is significant that Charles III issued pardons for all eleven death sentences resulting from the 1766 Zaragoza bread riots, or *motín de broqueleros*. The suppression of the Spanish Jesuits just weeks before the 1767 edition of *New Art* was printed may also have encouraged a new edition since it was clear the friars would need many new trained cooks in missions, especially in the New World: their numbers there rose from 300 to 1,000 between 1740 and 1780. Boadas Llavat, "Ética y Vino," 57–65.

20. All Barcelona editions had used the spelling Altamiras, but the 1767 edition is the first Castilian one to use it. Only from 1763–1764, after publishing reforms, did authors have the right to decide spellings. Until then typesetters decided them and paid for the cost of corrections; it would have been natural for Joseph Gonzalez de la Cuesta, who set *New Art* in 1745, to have changed Gómez's pen-name to Altimiras, a Castilian surname known at court. Francisco Javier Burgos Rincón, *Imprenta y Cultura del libro en la Barcelona del seteciento* (PhD diss.: Universitat Autónoma de Barcelona, 1993), 350. Fermín de los Reyes Gómez, "La Estructura formal del libro antiguo español" in *Paratesto* 7 (2010); 37, 41–42. Mercedes Agulló y Cobo, *La Imprenta y comercio de libros en Madrid, siglos XVI–XVIII* (PhD diss.: Universidad Complutense de Madrid, 1981–2001), 72–73. Application to publish and request for price *Nuevo Arte de Cocina*, 5 July and 17 August 1745, Expedientes de impression 1745–1760, Consejos, 50641, AHN. For Altimiras as a court surname: Will, María de Austría, 1603, Caja 83, Exp. 12; Caja 66, Exp, 50, Archivo Monasterio Descalzas Reales, Colección Real, Patrimonio Nacional (CRPN).

Prologue

1. Practical skills were excluded from Franciscan novices' studies to avoid distracting them. Velázquez, *Doctrina*, 3.

2. This anecdote is probably true: women were allowed to enter the cloister and church for mass on special occasions. NA, *Estatutos*, 34–35.

3. Although San Diego (c. 1463) is generally remembered for his work feeding the poor, he was also revered as a miraculous healer at the Madrid court, which would explain why *New Art* was dedicated to him rather than San Pascual Bailón, the Aragonese patron saint of cooks.

4. Juan de Soto, the printer of the 1760 Madrid edition of *New Art*, added an illustration of this board at the beginning of the book. Altimiras, *New Art*, 1760, f. 33.

Book One: Introduction

1. The ceramicists who specialized in treating clay to withstand heat and making cookery pots from it were called *maestros de las ollas* (pot masters) or *olleros*. Hence Almonacid's nickname *"de las ollas."* The 1610 expulsion of the Moriscos from Aragon left many pottery quarters deserted, but in the Jalón Valley production continued at Tobed (tableware), Sestrica (oil and wine urns), and Alpartir (cooking pots). On continuities see Manuel Monterde y López de Ansó, *Ensayo para la descripción geografica, física y civil del corregimiento de Calatayud* (1788) (Calatayud: Centro de Estudios Bilbilitanos-Institución Fernando el Católico, 1999), 24, 88. The continuity of shapes, decoration, and styles after the Morisco expulsion is beautifully shown at the Museo de Teruel. On New World mission pots see Bonnie G. McEwan, *Spanish Missions of La Florida* (Gainesville: University Press of Florida, 1993), 81.

2. The kitchen tools mentioned here are listed in *New Art*. Many appear in San Diego's kitchen inventories. *Disposición*. Ex-cat, ACPV. For example, the cost of mending cracked pots by stitching them with iron and renewing the tin linings of copper cauldrons is noted. Other tools, like carving knives and forks, were kept in the refectory. Velázquez, *Doctrina*, 118.

3. Jose María Busca Isusi, *Antología gastronomica de José María Busca Isusi* (Hondarrabia: Euskal Gastronomi Akademia, 1993), 121–22.

4. Dunmire, *Gardens*, 155, 302. John C. Super and Thomas C. Wright, *Food, Politics and Society in Latin America* (Lincoln: University of Nebraska Press, 1985), 7, 13.

5. Pigs appear in the Convento de San Diego's inventories, but not every year. *Disposición*, 1753. Ex-cat, ACPV. Pig-killing costs at San Diego were noted in the kitchen accounts, but these never included hired help: *Libro de gastos ordinarios*, 13th–21st December, 1794. L. 18781 (1878L), AHNM. Schlatter Navarro, *La Embajada Keicho*, 197.

6. "The history of the sheep and wool economy is in a way the capsule history of the Spanish economy." Crow, 2005, 125. Rural Spanish friaries occasionally kept flocks: Schlatter Navarro 2014, 197. In the New World (Arizona, Texas, and California) Spaniards and Indians living on mission settlements ate mutton. Dunmire, 2004, 302.

Book One: Chapter I

1. Gallants were city dwellers and, by suggestion, sophisticated in taste. Crow, *Root and Flower*, 131.

2. Poet and playwright Pedro Calderón de la Barca (1600–1681) had called *estofado* "the prince of stews" in his satirical sketch entitled *"Los Guisados,"* or "The Stews," c. 1650. Altamiras was, then, opening with a flourish.

3. Ibn Razin al-Tugabi, *Relieves de las mesas, acerca de las delicias de la comida y los diferentes platos* (Gijón: Trea, 2007), 159. In 1732 *estofado* was defined as meat cooked with watered wine, or water and a little vinegar, plus seasoning and spices, *"tapandole de manera que no exhale xugo ni vapor,"* "covering it in such a way that it exhales no juices or steam." Real Academia Española, *Diccionario de Autoridades* (Madrid: Gredos, 1976), Vol. 2, 693. Such braising, like the tough meat it tenderized over slow-burning charcoal or wood fires, continued well into the twentieth century. Nancy Johnstone, who lived in Catalonia during the Spanish Civil War, wrote in her memoir *Hotel in Spain*, "braising meat in oil over charcoal in a closed dish was a delicious way of coping with the wiry Catalan sheep" (London: Faber and Faber, 1937), 100, 313.

4. Altamiras was fully aware that he was favoring friary and popular tastes over culinary fashions. Francisco Martinez Montiño had written in *Arte de Cocina, pastelería, vizcochería y conservería* (Valencia, Librerías Paris-Valencia, 1997), 83–84: *"porque la canela no ha de entrar en cosa que no llevé dulce"*; "cinnamon should not appear in things which do not carry sweetness." The friars also cooked with coriander: Schlatter-Navarro, *Embajada Keicho*, 194. In humble home kitchens the peppercorns in his recipes would often have been swopped for home-grown red peppers, sometimes called Spanish peppers (*pimientos españoles*). Eloy Terrón, *España, Encrucijada de Culturas Alimentarias* (Madrid: Ministerio de Agricultura, Pesca y Alimentación, 1992), 215.

5. Luis Irizar and Manuel Martínez Llopis, *Las Cocinas de España* (Madrid: Alianza Editorial, 1990), 209. Mexican *gigote*: Xavier Domingo, *De la Olla al Mole* (Instituto de Cooperación Iberoamericana: Madrid, 1984), 150. Catalan friary cook Joan Bagües added prunes, young pumpkin, and boiled wild mushrooms, renaming the dish *picadillo*. *Llibreta del Hermano Joan Bagués del Hospital Civil de Gerona*, c. 1775, recipe 5. Ms 47, University Library, Special Collections (Cookery), Leeds (ULSCL). Another modern name is *carn trinxada o a la castellana*: N.A., *La Cuynera Catalana* (Barcelona: Germans Torres, 1835), 57.

6. Ruperto de Nola, *Libro de Guisados*, ed. Dionisio Pérez and José María Pisa Villarroya (Huesca: La Val de Onsera, 1994), 147–48, 205; Diego Granado, *Libro del Arte de cozina* (Barcelona: Pagès, 1991), 335. Today *pebre* (or *prebe*) is the name for a peppery Galician sauce with red *pimentón* and black pepper, olive oil, garlic, and salt. Johnstone, *Hotel*, 313.

7. Usually *lampreados* were dishes of fried or roast meat cooked in wine or water with added sugar or honey and spices. *Diccionario*, Vol. 3, O Ñ, 356. Domingo Hernández de Maceras, *La alimentación en la España del Siglo de Oro*, ed. and intro. by María de los Ángeles Pérez Samper (Huesca: La Val de Onsera, 1998), 87–88, 200. Johnstone, *Hotel*, 323.

8. This quick anthology of ideas for ragouts shows off Altamiras's wide-ranging tastes and knowledge. Among written sources may be Nola, *Libro*, 125–66; Granado, *Libro*, 49. He may have learned how to make flour thickenings from French farmworkers: Pilar Orna Almarza, "La Población de la Almunia de Doña Godina en la primera mitad del siglo XVIII" in *Las Gentes en La Almunia y Comarca, ADOR 5* (La Almunia, 2000), 153–65.

9. Gilles and Laurent Laurendon, *Cocina Monacal, Las Recetas mejor guardadas de una deliciosa tradición* (Barcelona: Hachette, 2011), 142–56.

10. The authors of Spain's Golden Age comedies rebelled against the rules of court theater and language in favor of everyday language as spoken on the street, modern themes, plots drawing on the past, and short formats designed to keep a popular audience's attention. Lope de Vega—or Félix Lope de Vega y Carpio—was considered the master of the genre. His verse manifesto in its defense, *Arte Nuevo de hacer comedias en este tiempo* (1609), was hugely successful, hotly debated for several centuries, and seems to have provided Altamiras with a model for his own book.

11. Dario Vidal Listerri, *Flor de Cardo Azul, la gastronomía tradicional de Teruel* (Teruel: Instituto de Estudios Turolenses, 2003), 66–67.

12. The crusts' ingredients changed as *costradas* and braziers moved sideways to humble kitchens. Simón Palmer, *Cocina*, 166. Emilia Pardo Bazán, *La Cocina española antigua* (Poniente, Madrid, 1981), 16–17. One legacy of brazier cookery is a dish made today: Elche's *arroz con costra*, a rice with pork ribs and sausages topped by a thick unsweetened egg custard, still occasionally prepared over then under a brazier of glowing charcoal.

13. David M. Gitlitz and Linda K. Davidson, *A Drizzle of Honey. The Lives and Recipes of Spain's Secret Jews* (New York: St. Martin's Press, 1999), 180–81. Franciscan kitchens may have been a main conduit through which Jewish and Muslim cookery entered modern Spain's culinary mainstream, particularly in the so-called Morisco parishes. Casey, *Early Modern Spain*, 223, 226, 233. There is no indication that local dishes with Jewish or Muslim origins would have been forbidden in their kitchens.

14. Garlic as a medicinal remedy: Luis Lobera de Ávila, *El banquete de nobles caballeros* (Donostia: R&B, 1996), 145–47. In popular and friary cooking: "*cada uno lo mezcla [perejil] . . . a su gusto, lo mas ordinario es pimienta y ajo*"; "each person mixes it [parsley] . . . to their taste, ordinarily with pepper and garlic." Juan de Pineda, *Diálogos familiares de la agricultura Cristiana*, ed. Juan Meseguer Fernandez (Madrid: Atlas, 1964), Vol. 2, 62. Garlic was preserved

through the year kept in straw, smoked, or cured in brine. Miquel Agustí, *Libro de los secretos de agricultura, casa de campo y pastoral. Traducido de lengua catalán en castellano* (Barcelona: Juan Piferrer, 1722), 69. *Libro de gasto,* San Diego. August 1794, L.18840, AHN.

15. Ibn Razin al-Tugabi described meatballs as *"bolitas con la carne del tamaño que quieras, grandes or pequeñas"*—"small balls with the meat shaped the size you want, large or little"—in *Relieves,* 189. He used doughnut molds to shape them. Later court meatballs were usually smaller *almondiguillas.* Martinez Montiño, *Arte,* 85–87, 91. The song "One Meatball," 1940, by Hy Zaret and Louis Singer of Tin Pan Alley drew on older lyrics about the poor ordering food among wealthier diners in restaurants. The 1940s version became a classic of the American folk revival.

16. Capuchin stuffed peaches for the feast of St. Francis, 1819: María José Martí García, "Productos Americanos en la Mesa Conventual" in *La Mediterrània, àrea de convergència de sistemes alimentaris (segles V–XVIII),* ed. Miquel Barceló, Antoni Riera Melis (Palma de Mallorca, Institut de Estudis Balears, 1996), 437. Stuffed apples during the Spanish Civil War: Ignacio Doménech, *Cocina de Recursos (Deseo mi comida),* ed. M. I. Arrieta Gallastegui (Gijón: Trea, 2011), 128.

17. Sour pomegranate juice in meat stews: Ibn Razin al-Tugabi, *Relieves,* 165. Sweet pomegranate juice in *chile en nogada*: Raymond Sokolov, *Why We Eat What We Eat* (New York: Touchstone, 1993), 37.

18. In 1772 the Barcelona Junt de Comercio (Board of Trade) discussed potatoes and described them *"cultivandose en la mancha baxo el nombre improprio de batatas manchegas o de irlanda y empleados regularmente en guisados y tortillas"*; "cultivated in la mancha [sic] under the unsuitable name of Manchego or Irish sweet potatoes and used regularly in stews and omelettes." See Fernando Serrano Larráyoz, "Confitería y cocina conventual Navarra del siglo XVIII. Notas y precisiones sobre el 'Recetario de Marcilla' y el 'Cocinero Religioso' de Antonio Salsete." *Revista Principe de Viana* 243 (2008), 167.

19. Martinez Montiño, *Arte,* 500. Granado, *Libro,* 43, 44. José Vicente Lasierra Rigal, *La Cocina Aragonesa* (Zaragoza: Everest, 1987), 167.

20. Spanish cooks' recipes for brains are best known from the fry-up of eggs and sheep's offal called *duelos y quebrantos,* quoted by Cervantes in Don Quixote. There has been a long debate about this dish and its origins: see Carolyn A. Nadeau, *Food Matters. Alonso Quijano's Diet and the Discourse of Food in Early Spain* (Toronto: University of Toronto Press, 2016), 105–109. However, the most likely origin is given by Francisco Javier Alonso Madera and Carlos García, as a dish cooked "on Saint Peter's day when shepherds and flock owners ate together to agree prices" in their book *La Mancha y El Queso Manchego* (Tarancón: Consejería de Agricultura: Junta de Comunidades de Castilla La Mancha, 1986), 44.

Book One: Chapter II

1. Luis Buñuel, *My Last Breath* (London: Vintage, 2003), 8.

2. On a possible Swiss monastic origin for crème caramel, José María Gorrotxategi Pikasarri in *Historia de la confitería y repostería vasca* (Vitoria Gasteiz: Sendoa, 1987), Vol. 1, 264–65.

3. N.A., *Estatutos*, 27–28, and Velázquez, *Doctrina*, 64–65. Capuchin etiquette: María de los Ángeles Pérez Samper, *Mesas y cocina en la España del siglo XVIII* (Gijón: Trea, 2011), 10, 251, 258–59.

4. Aprons, or *delantales*, and *alpargatas* appear in kitchen accounts. *Disposición* 1774, kitchen inventory. Ex-cat, ACPV. On the etymology of *sopas*, Joan Corominas, *Diccionario Etimológico de la Lengua Castellana* (Madrid: Gredos, 1990), 543.

5. Antonio Salsete gives ten rules for making bread soups in *El Cocinero Religioso instruido en aprestar las comidas de Carne, Pescado, Yerbas y Potages a su comunidad*, intro. Victor Manuel Sarobe Pueyo (Pamplona: Gobierno de Navarra, 1990), Vol. 1, 60. Rafael Montal Montesa, *El Pan y su influencia en Aragón* (Institución Fernando el Católico, 1997), 79. Antxon Urrusolo, *La Cocina del monasterio, Recetas para el cuerpo y alma* (Barcelona: Plaza & Janes, 2009), 44.

6. Martinez Montiño, *Arte*, 47. He added a rich chicken-fat topping.

7. On courtly soups' architecture, Ben Rogers, *Beef and Liberty* (London: Vintage, 2003), 33. For a Spanish court recipe Martinez Montiño, *Arte*, 42. Comfits and dragées in Carnival cooking, Simon Palmer, *La Cocina del palacio*, 26. A soup *"i pot presentarse à un general"*—you can serve to a general—appears in N.A., *Cuynera Catalana*, 19.

8. Bartolomeo Murillo's 1746 painting of a Seville Observant Franciscan kitchen, entitled *The Angels' Kitchen*, now hanging in the Musée du Louvre, shows plain white *escudillas* laid out on a kitchen table, as does an undated portrait of San Pascual Bailón, the Aragonese patron saint of cooks, in the friary at Villareal. The blue and white ceramic fragments found at San Cristóbal and Santa Catalina, Cariñena, may be eighteenth century.

9. Emilia Pardo Bazán, *Cocina española*, 15. Probably the recipe jumped over friary walls to become *borreta*, a popular Alicantino soupy vegetable stew. Francisco G. Seijo Alonso, *Gastronomía de la Provincia de Alicante* (Alicante: Instituto de Estudios Alicantinos, 1973), 136–42.

10. Nola, *Libro*, 141.

11. Terrón, *España, Encrucijada*, 281–88. In 1739 *carne de sabado* was defined as *"los extremos, despojos y grossura de las carnes"* or "extremities, innards and fat of meats" by the Real Academía's *Diccionario* (Madrid: Gredos), Vol. 3: S–Z, 1.

12. A modern offal *pepitoria*: Lasierra Rigal, *La Cocina aragonesa*, 154–56.

13. A modern recipe for blood: Francisco G. Seijo Alonso, *Gastronomía de la Provincia de Alicante* (Alicante: Editorial Villa, 1977), 92

14. Carolina Ibor Monesma, *Músicas y palabras en Vadejalón* (La Almunia de Doña Godina: Tintaura, 2012), 41, note. Thanks to Santiago Cabello for the gift of the book. On friary calf-fattening, *Libro, San Diego*, Kitchen Accounts, 13 May and October 1794, L. 18840, AHNM. Schlatter Navarro, *Embajada Keicho*, 201. Today's feasting food calendar: Esperanza Almansa Cervera, *La Cocina Bilbitana* (Barcelona: Marrà Produccions Editorial, 2004), 21–26.

15. The Spanish taste for veal: N.A., *Cuynera Catalana*, 73.

16. Agustí, *Libro*, 19. Schlatter Navarro, *Embajada Keicho*, 200. Rabbit as gourmet food: Pérez, *La Cocina*, 121–24. Lasierra Rigal, *Cocina Aragonesa*, 154–55. Vidal Llisterri, *Flor de Cardo*, 29–31.

17. Casey, *Early Modern Spain*, 245. Antonio Pisa Benito, "Apoteosis del Carnaval" in *Cuadernos de Gastronomía* 19 (1994), 18–25. Antolinez de Piedrabuena, *Carnestolendas de Zaragoza, en sus tres días*, intro Luis García-Abrines Calvo (Zaragoza: Institución Fernando El Católico, 2005).

18. Roast lamb's heads at funerals, Fray Sever d'Olot, *Libro del Arte de Cocinar*, ed. Jaume Barrachina (Barcelona: Palacio de Pereleda, 1982), 323. Lasierra Rigal, *Cocina Aragonesa*, 167. Vidal Llisterri, *Flor de Cardo*, 81.

19. Alejandro Dumas, *Cocina Española* (Madrid: Seteco, 1982), 45, 93, 123. Monterde y López de Anso, *Ensayo*, 188. However, in 1845 Richard Ford called Spanish hare "the glory of edible quadrupeds" in his *Handbook for Travellers in Spain, Parts I and II of the 3rd edition* (1845) and suggested Spaniards appreciated them as tavern food (London: Centaur Press, 1966), Vol. 1, 98.

20. Juan Altamiras, *Nuevo Arte de Cocina, Sacado de la Escuela de la Experiencia Economica. Añadido en esta ultima impresión* (Barcelona: Joseph Bro, 1770), 132. Antoni Dalmau, *Plats casolans de cuina catalana, recull de receptes populars* (Barcelona: Milla, 1969), 100–101.

21. "*Si has de dar varios Platillos el de masa se sirve entre los guisos, el ultimo es el asado con la ensalada.*" "If you have to serve various small dishes the one made with pastry is served between stews, the last one is the roast served with salad." Salsete, *El Cocinero Religioso*, Vol. 2, 142. Cooking in the warmth of a cooling bread oven: Martinez Montiño, *Arte*, 408. The friars' oven: Rafael Montal Montesa, *El Pan y su influencia en Aragón* (Zaragoza: Institución Fernando el Católico, 1997), 74.

22. Joan Santanach, ed., *The Book of Sent Soví, Medieval recipes from Catalonia*, transl. Robin M. Vozelgang (Woodbridge: Suffolk, 2006), 115 (Llet malcuit). Almost all later cooks dropped the toasted breadcrumbs and lost the crunch: Sever d'Olot, *Libro*, 39.

23. Juan de Pineda quotes the imagery of Franciscans as nightingales in *Diálogos*, 274. As minstrels or troubadours, John Crow, *The Root*, 130, and Norman Davies, *Vanished Kingdoms*, 171–74.

Book One: Chapter III

1. In 1913 Emilia Pardo Bazán wrote: *"siendo mas frecuente asarlo en marmite que en asador"*; "it being more frequent to roast in a casserole than on a spit," *Cocina Española*, 103. Prices: Sánchez Meco, *El Arte de la Cozinha*, 323. In a typical year outside economic crisis the friars fattened 12 kids and 8 calves, but only 1 lamb. *El Libro de gasto ordinario*, 1794, L. 18840, AHN.

2. Frances Eiximenis, *L'Art de manger, boire et server à table*, transl. Patrick Gifrau, pref. Pierre Torrès (Perpignan: Les Éditions de la Merci, 2011), 59. Santanach (ed.), *Sent Soví*, 101–102. Richard Ford describes the range of Spanish bread well, from "close grained and caky *candela*" to black rye or barley bread, *"pan de munición,"* Ford, *Handbook*, II, 80.

3. Miguel de Cervantes Saavedra, *Segunda Parte del Ingenioso Cavallero Don Quixote de La Mancha* (Madrid: Cátedra, 2011), VIII, XLIX, 519, 741, 750. Both the relevant scenes were set in Aragon.

4. Calf's feet were four times more expensive than lamb's or sheep's feet. Sánchez Meco, *Arte de la Cozina*, 323. Javier de Sagastizabal, ed., *La Cocina monacal. Los secretos culinarios de las monjas clarisas*, coord. Hermanas Ana María y Ester (Barcelona: Planeta, 2005), 214.

5. Lasierra Rigal, *La Cocina Aragonesa*, 174. Juan Bosco Gracía Aldaz, ed., *Somos lo que comemos* (La Almunia de Doña Godina: IES Ramón y Cajal, 2001), 36. Rosa Loreto López and Ana Benitez Muro, *Un bocado para los ángeles. La cocina conventual novohispana* (Mexico DF: Clio, 2000), 64.

6. On the rice and coconut dishes that have come down to us today, Raymond Sokolov, *Why We Eat What We Eat* (New York: Threshold, 1993), 67. Thanks to Ángel Oñero for cooking me Columbian Arricoa, the starting point of my research here. On the early New World preference for almond and coconut milk: John C. Super and Thomas C. Wright, eds., *Food, Politics and Society in Latin America* (Lincoln: University of Nebraska Press, 1985), 12, footnote.

7. Edouard de Pomiane, *Cooking with Pomiane* (London: Serif Books, 2009), 162.

8. San Diego had its own granary and received wheat as alms. *Disposición*, Repairs 1758, Inventory 1764. Ex-cat, ACPV. Baked loaves as alms: Fra Francesc Roger, *Art de la Cuina. Llibre de cuina menorqui del segle XVIII*, ed. Andreu Vidal Mascaró (Mahón: Vidal, 1993), 30. Recycling crumbs today: Almansa Cervera et al., *La Cocina*, 117.

9. Vidal Llisterri, *Flor de Cardo*, 91.

10. Late medieval flour noodles, Ruperto de Nola, *Libro*, 55.

11. A modern recipe, Lasierra Rigal, *La Cocina Aragonesa*, 168.

12. Dionisio Pérez (Post-Thebussem), *La cocina clásica española* (Huesca: La Val de Onsera, 1929), 178. Altamiras's clear culinary distinction between meat from heifers and dairy cows was echoed by a later friary cook, Joan Bagües,

who distinguished between the meat of "*Bo o vaca*," beef or cow. *Llibreta, Joan Bagués*, c. 1775, Recipe 36, ULSCL.

13. Norman Davies, *Vanished Kingdoms*, 191.

14. Ford, *Handbook*, II, 92, 114. In 1755 Norberto Caimo, an Italian Jeronimo monk, described Aragonese inns as "*les plus indignés cabarets que l'on puisse imaginer où des loups affamés se trouveroient fort mal et encore plus les honnêtes gens.*" "the most undignified cabarets imaginable where hungry wolves feed very badly and honest people even worse." *Voyage d'Espagne, fait en l'année 1755* (Paris: Costard, 1772), 83.

15. Monterde y López de Anso, *Ensayo*, VIII, 11, 88.

Book One: Chapter IV

1. Hughes, *Goya*, 32. Ford, *Handbook*, Vol. 1, 98: he wrote, "the peasants, who are sad poachers, will constantly hail traders from the field with offers of partridges, rabbits, melons, hares." Franciscan cooks, Francesc Roger and Joan Bagues, also omitted large game from their recipe notebooks.

2. Quail was highly considered in al-Andalus. "It has an excellent taste and chemo of great quality; recommended as much for healthy people as convalescents," Abu Marwan, *Kitab Al-Agdiya*, ed., trans. and intro. by Expiración García Sánchez (Madrid: CSIC/Instituto de Cooperación con El Mundo Árabe, 1992), 53. On egg and flour or crumb crusts in Muslim game recipes, Nadeau, *Food Matters*, 114–15. For Goya's letters to Zapater, Francisco de Goya, *Cartas a Martín Zapater*, ed. Mercedes Águeda and Xavier de Salas (Tres Cantos: Istus, 2003).

3. Bernardino de Sahagún, *A General History of the things of New Spain: Florentine Codex* (1540–1585), ed. and trans. by Arthur J. Andersen and Charles E. Dibble (Salt Lake City: School of American Research, 1982), Bk 10, 85; Bk 11, 53. (Altamiras would not have read the book, but he would have heard the same news by word-of-mouth.) On New World turkey: Xavier Domingo, *De la Olla al Molé* (Barcelona: Instituto de Cooperación Iberoamericana, 1984), 60. Dunmire, *Gardens*, 176, 181, 234–38. The peacock recipe: Nola, *Libro*, 62, 82. Turkey's arrival in Europe, Maguelonne Toussaint-Samat, *History of Food* (Oxford: Basil Blackwell, 1992), 343.

4. On partridge recipes, Pérez, *La Cocina*, 115–19. Manuel Martínez Llopis questioned Escoffier's provenance of partridges "a la Alcántara" mainly on the basis of its luxurious ingredients, especially the Port wine (personal communication, Madrid, 1998).

5. The original reads "*gâtées par la quantité de poivre dont on les avait assaisonnées,*" "spoiled by the amount of pepper with which they'd been seasoned." Caimo, *Voyage*, 73.

6. Pardo Bazán, *Cocina Española*, 84. Desalting dry salted fish over a fire, Dumas, *Cocina*, 92. Juan Ruiz, Arcipreste de Hito, *Libro de Buen Amor*, ed. Alberto Blecua (Madrid: Cátedra, 2003), 351.

7. Jorge Puyó Navarro, *Notas de la Vida de Un Pastor* (Ansó: n.p., 1967), 83.

8. Gabriel Alonso de Herrera, *Agricultura General,* intro. Eloy Terrón (Madrid: Ministerio de Agricultura, Pesca y Alimentación, 1996), 357. There were between two and six dozen hens at San Diego at any one time. *Disposicion, San Diego,* Inventories 1758, 1764. Ex-cat, ACPV. See also note 18.

9. A modern liver-thickened sauce: Vidal Llisterri, *Flor de Cardo,* 76.

10. An alternative modern recipe using different offcuts: Sánchez Meco, *El Arte de la Cozina,* 319.

11. Domingo Rodrigues, *Arte de Cozinha,* 43. His pigeons' sauce was flavored with flour "toasted till well darkened."

12. Agustí, *Libro,* 381. Herrera, *Agricultura,* 345–46. Asso, *Historia,* 86. Altamiras adapted his recipe from Martínez Montiño, *Arte,* 15, 43.

13. On spirits as an everyday drink, Pilar Orna Almarza, "La Población de La Almunia de Doña Godina en la primera mitad del siglo XVIII," in *Las Gentes en La Almunia y Comarca,* ADOR 5 (La Almunia: Centro de Estudios Almunienses, 2000), 156. Monterde y López de Anso, *Ensayo,* 25.

14. María de los Ángeles Pérez Samper considers Altamiras's silence on the historical and social contexts of recipes unique: "Cataluña y Europa a la Mesa," in *Cuadernos de Historia Moderna,* 1998, Vol. 35, 16–17.

15. Alfredo Mateos Paramio and Juan Carlos Villaverde Amieva, coords. and eds., *Memoria de los Moriscos, Escritos y relatos de una diaspora cultural* (Madrid: Sociedad Estatal de Conmemoraciones Culturales, 2010), 181–83. As this exhibition catalog shows very well, the Morisco cures are a tiny element of a much larger Aragonese literary tradition known as *la literatura aljamiada,* made of up stories, legends, and other texts handwritten on pergamine scrolls found pasted into the walls of old houses in Morisco villages. One of the biggest finds was made in Almonacid. This exhibition catalog gives a good picture of this: the medicinal recipes reveal the deep knowledge of wild ingredients in popular Morisco culture. In most cookbooks "Morisco" has been a shorthand for almondy flavors, added spices—for example, cumin and caraway—and green tangy leaves like fresh coriander. Nola, *Libro,* 101–102; Martinez Montiño, *Arte de Cocina,* 63; Rodrigues, *Arte,* 12, 25, 187. Ignacio Doménech Puigcercos and F. Marti, *Ayunos y Abstinencias, Cocina de Cuaresma,* intro. Dolors Llopart (Barcelona: Altafulla, 1982), 266. Dionisio Pérez reprinted one trout recipe from *New Art* (without citing the source). He called it Morisco: *La Cocina clásica,* 59.

16. Agustí, *Libro,* 387. Squab are still kept in the Jalón Valley, but traditionally in lofts rather than pigeon houses. For country pigeon recipes, Alfredo Juderías, *Cocina de Pueblo* (Madrid: Editorial Seteco, 1983), 192–93.

17. Nola, *Libro,* 94, 152. José Manuel Porquet Gombau, *Comer en Huesca* (Huesca: La Val de Onsera & Diputación Provincial de Huesca, 1989), 78. Joan de Bagües: *"como se pot fer una panada al ast"*—"how to make a pie on the spit."

Llibreta, Joan Bagués, recipe 29, MS 47, ULSCL.

18. San Lorenzo friary in La Almunia received hens and eggs every year from Mesones village to thank the friars for attending the dying during an outbreak of the plague in 1694. Francisco Zaragoza Ayarza, *El Convento de San Lorenzo de la Villa de La Almunia* (La Almunia de Doña Godina: Excmo Ayuntamiento de La Almunia de Doña Godina, 2002), 38.

19. Porquet Gombau, *La Cocina,* 77, 149.

20. Martinez Montiño, *Arte de Cocina,* 161.

21. Irving, *Tales,* 17.

22. Elena de Pizzi quotes Miguel de Cervantes Saavedra, *El Licenciado Vidriera,* 1613, in her book *Los Moriscos que no se fueron,* 1991, 182. She uses Cervantes's comment as an example of knowing but protective references to Moriscos leading itinerant anonymous lives in order to stay in Spain after the expulsion.

23. *New Art* supports Rachel Laudan's fascinating argument that medicinal knowledge drove culinary change in the 17th–18th centuries, though not in predictable ways. "A Kind of Chemistry," in *Petits Propos Culinaires,* 62 (1999), 8–22. The friars no longer dispensed on the Spanish mainland, but they ran infirmaries and hospices. See, for example, Luis Miguel García Simón, "Franciscanos y Clarisas en Cariñena: Los Conventos de Santa Catalina y San Cristóbal," *Tierra de Conventos,* 32. They also grew simples, kitchen-garden medicinal plants. Outside Spain they ran dispensaries, most famously in Jerusalem, and in large expanses of the New World they were the only medical practitioners. For a detailed overview of Franciscan medical ideas, mixing alchemy with observational medicine, see Diego de Bercebal, *Recetario medicinal espagírico* (Zaragoza: Diego de Larumbe, 1713). Bercebal had been infirmarian at San Francisco. Among medicinal foods he listed cinnamon, 58; onion and honey, 102; tea, coffee, and chocolate, 165.

24. Mechanical as opposed to hand-turned spits appear relatively late in Spain: for example, in 1821 in the Basque Country. Busca Isusi, *Antología,* 153.

25. Herrera, *Agricultura,* 395.

26. In contrast to the friars, the nuns hired sausage makers. *Cuentas de Santa Clara,* kitchen accounts, December 1744, L. 18600. Clero Secular Regular; Franciscanas Menores Observantes; CSIC, AHNM. The friars' pig-killing costs are clearly spelled out in *Libro, San Diego.* December 13–21, 1794, spices and a sausage needle, L. 18840. AHNM. Pig bladders were dried and stretched over pumpkins or earthenware pots to make drums.

Book Two: Introduction

1. Velázquez, *Doctrina,* 118, ". . . *encenderà la lumbre, pondrá la olla al fuego. . . .*"; he will light the hearth, put the pot to heat on the fire.

2. N.A., *Estatutos Generales,* 26–28, Pope Clement V had also laid down that "*la guardia de aquellos ayunos à los quales por común constitución de la Iglesia son obligados los otros cristianos*": "the fasting to which other Christians are

bound by the shared church constitution"; in other words, Spanish fast-days. Details of Capuchin fasting: Vaquerín Aparacio, *Vida*, 267–74.

3. Doménech and Martí, *Ayunos*, II-xx–xxi.

4. At San Diego cocoa first appeared in kitchen and general accounts after the Papacy relaxed fasting rules: *Disposición*, Inventory 1788. Ex-cat, ACPV. But Altamiras was skilled with a chocolate beater (see p. 157). In his lifetime, supplies may have reached the friaries as gifts or payments. *Cuentas de Santa Clara*, April 1744, L.18600, AHNM. The nuns account for gifts of chocolate to the friars: 11 lb to their confessor for Lent, the same to his "companion" and 6½ lb to a preacher. On Jeronimo chocolate-drinking, Zarco Cuevas, *Discursos*, 49–53. In Capuchin friaries, Vaquerín Aparacio, *Vida*, 261–66.

5. Juan de Pineda, *Diálogos familiares de la agricultura cristiana*, ed. Juan Meseguer Fernández (Madrid: Atlas, 1964), Vol. 5, 47. The Capuchin Rule of St. Bernard also rejected "daintiness in food" (clause 137).

6. N.A., *Estatutos*, 26–28. "... *que los Frayles no anden comiendo a escondidas, ni buscando desordenamente lo que han menester para vivir*" / "that the Friars should not eat in secret nor search in a disorderly way for sustenance to live."

7. Pineda, *Diálogos*, Vol. 5, 47. For him wine was "*como el beber vino, que es beber y comer*," / "drinking wine is drinking and eating"; that is, it provides much-needed calories. Eiximenis, *L'Art*, 12–19. Ch. 15. He details how to serve, taste, and drink wine, as well as types of wine. As served in hospitals: Asunción Fernández Doctor, *El Hospital Real y General de Ntra Señora de Gracia de Zaragoza en el siglo XVIII* (Zaragoza: Institución Fernando el Católico, 2000), 239.

8. Olive oil was fundamental to the friars' cookery. In 1733, a letter to a patron who had failed to send alms of olive oil to San Diego ran, "*Y por hallarse dicho Colegio con necesidad urgente, suplica dicho Guardian a V.S. Altma por amor de Díos, mande despachar el Libramiento, para que perciba dicha limosna*" / "And since the Colegio now finds itself in urgent need, the Guardian begs you for the love of God to order the Delivery to be sent, so we receive the alms." *Carta del Padre Guardian de San Diego*. Letter from Guardian of San Diego. 17 May, 1733. Caja 98. 2/2 (caja 7054). Archivo Historico. Archivo Municipal del Ayuntamiento de Zaragoza.

9. Velázquez, *Doctrina*, 1650, 72. "*Quitados los platos y escudillas cogera uno la fruta en una cesta.*" / "Once the plates and bowls are cleared away, one of the friars shall fetch the fruit in a basket."

10. Iceboxes were sufficiently valuable that they were kept in the refectory. *Disposición*, Inventory and purchases, 1756, "*1 caja de madera con cercillos de hierro pa una garapiñera*" / "a wooden box with iron hoops for an icebox." Excat. ACPV.

11. "... *los muchos años hace, que voy tostandome entre las cocinas mas Fuertes de esta Corte* ..." / "the many years that I have spent toasting myself in the

Greatest kitchens of this Court." Francisco Ardit, "Aprobación" in Altimiras, *Nuevo Arte* (Madrid: Juan de Soto, 1760), ff. 4–5.

Book Two: Chapter I

1. Simón Palmer, *Cocina*, 173–74. Lenten salt-cod: Pérez Samper, *Mesas*, 276–77. In *Discursos leidos ante la Real Academia de la Historia en la recepción pública de R.P. Fr Julián Zarco Cuevas* (El Escorial, 1930), Julian Zarco-Bacas y Cuevas mentions portion sizes in the El Escorial Jeronimo kitchen: 250 g / 8 oz to students and 370 g / 12 oz to farmworkers in 1749, 39–53. In poorer kitchens: Martí García, "Los Productos Américanos en la Mesa Conventual," in *La Mediterrànea*, ed. Barceló and Riera, 511.

2. Salted conger: Nola, *Libro*, 176. Martinez Montiño, *Arte*, 504 (for stockfish, *estocafix*). Granado, *Libro*, 206.

3. Clearly defined by Covarrubias: "*Abadejo: pescado que se trae seco para la gente común: dicho así, a diferencia de algún otro que llamarían abad, como han puesto otros nombres los pescadores de obispo y fraile. Por otro nombre se dice bacalao.*" "*Abadejo*: a fish brought dried for the common people: so-called, differently to another that some name abbot, and the fishermen have given other names, bishop and friar. It [*abadejo*] is also called by another name, *bacalao*." The second fish, called abbot, is probably ling or haddock. Covarrubias, *Tesoro*, 25.

4. Pérez, *La cocina*, 77.

5. On Mediterranean Spain's taste for "golden" cured salt cod from Terranova landed at Mediterranean ports like Alicante and Barcelona in the 18th century, see Lorena Gallart Jornet and Isabel Escriche Roberto, *La salazón de pescado, una tradición en la dieta mediterránea* (Valencia: Servicio de Publicaciones, Universidad Politecnica de Valencia, 2005), 59–72. On the different processes for salting and drying salt cods: J. M. Zaldumbide, *El Bacalao recetario de la PYSBE* (Donostia: Ttarttala, 1992), 269.

6. Fergus Henderson, *Nose to Tail Eating: A Kind of British Cooking* (London: Bloomsbury, 2007), 154–55.

7. José Antonio de Hebrera y Esmir, *Crónica de la Provincia Franciscana de Aragón, Partes primera y Segunda* (Madrid: Cisneros, 1991), Bk II, XLV, 507. Velázquez, *Doctrina*, 1650, 120. According to Agustín Bodas Lllavat, OFM, the friar portrayed by Bartolomeo Murillo in his 1646 painting *The Angel's Kitchen* is Sant Salvador de la Horta, who failed to cook a meal for a Viceroy. "Ética y Vino. San Júnipero Serra, Los Franciscanos y California," in *Aportaciones al diccionario biográfico franciscano de España, Portugal, Ibero América y Filippinas* (Cordoba: ed. AHEF, 2013), 62.

8. Cofradia Extremeña de Gastronomia, *Recetario Cocina Extremeña* (Badajoz: Universitas Editorial, 1985), 106–107. Jaume Fabregas, *Traditional Catalan Cooking*, transl. Paul Martín (Barcelona: La Magrana, 1997), 196–97.

Carmen Sánchez's recipe: Ángel Muro, *Diccionario de cocina*. Intro. by Manuel Martínez Llopis (Donostia: R&B Ediciones, 1996), Vol. I, 261.

9. Popular Easter salt cod dishes were designed to make use of every bit of the whole fish. Almansa Cervera, *La Cocina*, 24. Sagastiazabal, *La Cocina*, 91.

10. "*Aquest plat procedeix del monestir de Poblet.*" Antoni Dalmau, *Plats caso-lans de cuina catalana, recull de receptes populars* (Barcelona: Milla, 1969), 68. Other salt-cod and honey dishes: Almansa Cervera *et al*, *La Cocina*, 96.

11. Some Basque writers believe garlic needs to be present for the juices to emulsify. Busca Isusi, *Antología*, 55.

12. For a brief but well-documented account of the tomato's arrival in Spanish kitchens, see Janet Long-Solís, "El Tomate, De hierba silvestre de las Américas a denominador común en las cocinas mediterráneas," in Antonio Garrido Aranda (ed.), *Los sabores de España y América, cultura y alimentación* (Huesca: La Val de Onsera, 1995), 222–53. Raw tomato sauces, like those served with *cocidos*, had been made in Spain since at least the mid-seventeenth century. Agustín Moreto, a Madrid-born playwright, referred to a *puchero* or stew served with a spicy tomato sauce, "*su salsa picante de tomates,*" in *El Entremés con Mariquita* (c. 1650), line 153. Two recipes, one for a raw and the other for a cooked sauce, appeared in Juan de la Mata, *Arte de Repostería* (1747), (Burgos: Ediciones La Olmeda, 1992), 165. Quite why Altamiras innovated by using tomatoes as a seasoning rather than the main ingredient of a sauce we do not know, unless it was to spread the flavor of a limited supply through as many dishes as possible.

13. Cadiz's fish soup with bitter orange juice is called *caldillo de perro*.

14. A 1567 papal ban on clerics', monks', and friars' attendance at bullfights was so unpopular that Philip II negotiated its reversal in 1596. A Franciscan friar, Antonio de Córdoba, wrote a treatise that is said to have contributed to the reversal. On the Franciscans and bullfighting in general: Daniel Vaquerín Aparacio, *Vida, Espiritualidad y Proyeccion Social de los Franciscanos Descalzos en la España Ilustrada* (PhD diss., Universidad Complutense de Madrid, 2004), 267–74. Zaragoza's bullring opened in 1764. The money was raised by Ramón Pignatelli, Goya's patron, a canon of the cathedral; all income from bullfights went to charity.

15. Francesc Eiximenis laid down the main lines of Franciscan thought on food and drink in "Como usar bé de beure e menjar," a section of the third volume of his encyclopedia *Lo Crestía*, c. 1384 (Eiximenis, *L'Art de manger*, 2011). Scholarly and well-traveled, Eiximenis suggested the superiority of Catalan food and wine culture.

16. *Instrucció breu i útil per los cuiners principians segons lo estil dels Carmelitas*, Francesc del Santísim Sagrament, c. 1800. Biblioteca de Catalunya, TOP MS 47. The "Warning" (*Aviso*) is an interesting indicator of *New Art*'s influence.

Book Two: Chapter II

1. River eel was preferred. Sever d'Olot, *Libro*, 63–64. N.A., *La Cuynera*, 57.

2. Monterde y López de Anso, *Ensayo*, 17. On eel-fishing rights as payment for work, Fausto Moya Maluenda, "Las acequias de Michén, Nueva, Vieja y el Río Mediano," in *ADOR X, El agua en La Almunia y Comarca*, 1999, 24–25. Lasierra Rigal, *La Cocina*, 133.

3. Vicente Blasco Ibáñez, *Cañas y Barro* (Madrid: Alianza Editorial, 2009), 192. The Albufera fishermen's cooperative in El Palmar still sells wild eels, but they are now only a little larger than farmed ones.

4. The rice fields near Zuera: Asso, *Historia*, 76.

5. A nut thickening for *all-i-pebre*: Fabregas, *Traditional Catalan*, 190–91.

6. Sturgeon swam up the River Guadalquivir well beyond Seville. In the nineteenth century a small craft caviare industry was set up at Coria, further upstream. From that time on, stocks dropped steadily until the last native sturgeon was caught in 1956. Sturgeon also swam in the River Guadiana, but Covarrubias wrote in his 1611 dictionary that "*solo . . . los principes y poderosos*," "only princes and powerful people," could acquire it. *Tesoro*, 943.

7. Sturgeon, though not a native species, is farmed organically at Ríofrio at the foot of the Granadan sierras: the flesh is cooked, vacuum packed, and sold to chefs.

8. The marinade comes from Martinez Montiño. He served the fish on a bread trencher or roll emptied of its crumb. *Arte*, 272. Granado, *Libro*, 287–88.

9. None of Spain's old-fashioned sugared fish dishes survive today although sweet trout millefeuilles, called Nicanores de Bonar, invented in the 1880s, are still popular.

10. Sturgeon, "*le llaman algunos lobo de rio. Su carne es muy regalada, y algunos con Huerta le tienen por el Asturión.*" "some call it the river wolf, its flesh is a great treat, and some with kitchen gardens keep it as sturgeon." Real Academia Española, *Diccionario Nacional de Autoridades* (Madrid: Gredos, 1976), S-Z 144.

11. Fabregas, *Traditional Catalan Cooking*, 122. Soaking salt tuna, Granado, *Libro*, 252.

12. Nola, *Libro*, 177.

13. Sever d'Olot, *Libro*, 62. The northern preference for white tuna (*bonito del norte*) and Mediterranean taste for blue-fin tuna (*atún*) still persists.

14. Sever d'Olot, *Libro*, 63. Joan Bagües made it with "*tonyina de la negra y un tall de sorra bien dessalat*"; "tuna cut from the dark flesh and a length of well soaked and desalted *sorra.*" *Llibreta, Tractat de Peix*, no 11, MS 47, ULSCL.

15. Busca Isusi, *Antologia*, 58, on bream's brief winter season as an oily blue fish, 177, 182, 189–90.

16. Santanach (ed.), *Sent Soví*, 193. Fray Joan Bagües thought of this as a traveler's dish, "*fret pot portar maltes lleguas*"; "apt to carry many leagues." *Llibreta, Tractat de Peix*, no. 23, MS 47, ULSCL.

17. On 24th December, 1 lb fresh salmon cost the friars the same as 3½ lb fresh hake or 3 lb fresh red bream. *Libro, San Diego*, December 31, 1793 and 1794, L. 18840, AHNM.

18. Altamiras, *Nuevo Arte*, 171.

19. Agustí, *Libro*, 475.

20. Trout farmed at the Monasterio de la Piedra, Nueválos, Soria, was used for the 1876 restocking of the river.

21. Candied citron: Mata, *Arte*, 45.

22. Gillian Riley, *The Oxford Companion to Food* (Oxford: Oxford University Press, 2007), 476–77. Altamiras may have cooked his green sauce for hygiene rather than culinary reasons.

23. Pérez, *La cocina*, 59. Lasierra Rigal, *Cocina Aragonesa*, 55–59.

24. A visitor to Seville's Carthusian monastery in 1633 noted among the foods served, "*el atún adobado que llaman pavonado, muy costoso y muy suave*"; "the tuna in adobe they call *pavonado*, very costly and very mild." Carlos Serra y Pickman, *La Cartuja de Santa María de las Cuevas, conferencia leida ante la Academía de Bellas Letras* (Sevilla: R. Blanco, 1929).

25. Nola, *Libro*, 66, 160. Granado, *Libro*, 184, 283, 299.

26. The lampreys in the Río Ebro's estuary, protected from fishermen, include fish estimated as over a hundred years old. Joan Bagües gave several recipes for them: *Llibreta, Tractat de Peix*, nos. 33–35, MS 47, ULSCL.

27. Lasierra Rigal, *La Cocina*, 135. Granado, *Libro*, 240.

28. Lobera de Ávila, *El banquete*, 81.

29. Frog pies (*pasteles de ranas*) are cited as part of a 1589 *merienda*, or buffet, prepared by Madrid's palace kitchens for nuns. Simón Palmer, *La Cocina*, 140–41.

30. N.A., *Estatutos*, "Silencio," 14. A Franciscan kitchen: Velázquez, *Doctrina*, 118–20.

31. Cofradía Extremeña de Gastronomía, *Recetario*, 219.

32. Pineda, *Diálogos*, Vol. 1, 320. In the Jalón Valley snails were eaten with garlic *ajo* to celebrate San Juan. Ibor Monesma, *Músicas*, 81–83, 215, 238. Many people in Aragon still head into the countryside after rain to forage snails that come out to graze on rosemary, fennel, and other herbs.

33. Almansa Cervera, *La Cocina*, 239.

34. The recipe for Altamiras's *ajo* is similar to French *beurre de Provence* cited by Hervé This as the first egg emulsion in print in François Marin's *Les Dons de Comus, Ou Les Délices de la Table*, 1739, quoted in *Cours de gastronomie moléculaire, no 2: les precisions culinaires* (Paris-Versailles: Éditions Quae/Belin, 2010), 84.

35. Lucie Bolens, *La Cocina andaluza, un arte de vivir, Siglos XI–XIII* (Madrid: Edaf, 1991), 186. Ibn Razin al-Tugabi, *Relieves*, 2007, 253.

36. Martinez Montiño, *Arte*, 325. Like Altamiras, he candies only the yolks, but calls the recipe "eggs." Fernández Doctor, *El Hospital Real*, 241. The Basque equivalent were *huevos mol*. Gorrotxategi Pikassari, *Historia*, 265–67.

37. On "fresh" and "ordinary" eggs, Simón Palmer, *La Cocina*, 51. On ways of keeping fresh raw eggs: Gorrotxategi Pikassari, *Historia*, 265–67.

38. On *abreviatura*, Covarrubias, *Tesoro*, 30.

39. Eggs for the sick in Lent: Pineda, *Diálogos*, Vol. 5, 47. Hardboiled eggs on Easter *culeca* breads: Ibor Monesma, *Músicas*, 83.

40. Sever d'Olot, *Libro*, 65.

41. Possibly adapted from *zampollón*, a wine foam. Mata, *Arte*, 121. The friars were given sponge cakes: *Cuentas de Santa Clara, Calatayud, 1739–71*. August and December 1744, L. 18600, AHN. Nuns' fame for cake-making: Martinez Montiño, *Arte de Cocina*, 67. Small sponge cakes in paper cases, *soletillas*, are a Calatayud speciality. Almansa Cervera, *Cocina*, 20.

42. Zaldumbide, *El Bacalao*, 163.

43. For an early soft marzipan recipe, Miguel de Baeza, *Los quatro libros del arte de la confitería, compuestos por Miguel de Baeza, confitero, vecino y natural de la imperial ciudad de Toledo* (Alcalà de Henares: Juan Gracián, 1592), 71–72. For a 1607 recipe for candied egg threads with soft marzipan, Hernández de Maceras, *La alimentación*, 105.

Book Two: Chapter III

1. A modern recipe is given by Antxon Urrusola, *La Cocina del Monasterio* (Barcelona: Plaza & Janes, 2009), 44.

2. "*Cada día, antes de abandonar sus aposentos, procede a machacar una pizca de ajo, lo frie en aceite con migas de pan, como son fuera un pudin hecho a toda prisa y se ingiere de una sentada.*" "Each day, before leaving their lodgings, they [Spaniards] proceed to pound a little bit of garlic, fry it in olive oil with breadcrumbs, as if it were a pudding made in great haste, and eat it at one sitting." John Mishen, 1627, quoted by Andrés Gómez-Flores, *Historia de la cocina de Albacete y sus mejoras recetas* (Albacete: Los Libros del Sur, 1997), 189. Lasierra Rigal, *La Cocina*, 98–101.

3. Eiximenis, *L'Art*. Ch. 41.

4. Almost certainly these vegetable broths are also the base of Altamiras's soups for the poor. "Gone are the days when two or three thousand bowlfuls of soup were served at the door of one or another friary in Salamanca, Valencia or Valladolid. Those were happy times for the students." G. d'Alaux, 1838, quoted by Vicente de la Fuente, *La sopa de los conventos ó sea Tratado de economía política en estilo jocó-serio, 1868,* ed. Álvaro Capalvo (IFC: Zaragoza, 2013), 58, footnote.

5. Velázquez, *Doctrina*, 121.

6. Pardo Bazán, *La Cocina*, 25. Seijo Alonso, *Gastronomía*, 25 (note on *borreta*, probably evolved from *burete*), 136–42. On Muslim breadcrumb-thickened soups: Cofradía Extremeña de Gastronomía, *Recetario*, 23; Ibn Razn al-Tugabi, *Relieves*, 80 (footnote), 81–99.

7. The Cistercians of the Monasterio de la Piedra bought sponges, turrón, and *bolados* (fondants) for Christmas. *Libro de gastos ordinarios*, Monasterio de Ntra Sra de Piedra de Nuevalos, 69. L. 18677, Clero Secular Regular; Cistercienses. CSIC, Archivo Historico Nacional.

8. Martinez Montiño, *Arte*, 198–203. Court cooks either fried puffs in boiling pork lard or made them from a lard-enriched batter, presumably to mark a distance from earlier Muslim recipes.

9. "*En los días de celebración del Prior, y algunos mas, se da a cada monje una tacita de arroz con leche*"; "on the Prior's celebratory days, and a few more, a little cup of rice pudding is given to each monk." They included Sundays in Lent and the seven following Fridays. Zarco-Bacas y Cuevas, *Discursos*, 49–53. The anecdote about eating with nuns may have come from personal experience since we know the friars did eat with nuns after preaching to or giving them confession. N.A., *Estatutos*, "De los Monasterios de Monjas," 39. *Cuentas, Santa Clara*, March–August 1744 and October 1749, L. 18600, AHNM. One payment is glossed, "*a la comunidad de Nuestro Padre de San Francisco por Benir a la fiesta*"; ". . . to the community of Our Father of San Francisco for Coming to the fiesta."

10. Broken rice: Fray Angel Martín OFM, personal communication on his time as a friar at Pego, Alicante. Interview Colegio San Antonio de Padua, Carcaixent, July, 2012. On the frequency of jokes against nuns: Casey, *Early Modern Spain*, 124.

11. N.A. *La Cuynera*, Arros a la Caputxina, 4. Lasierra Rigal, *La Cocina*, 5–7, 11. Carnival rice with an egg crust, Pérez Samper, *Mesas*, 113.

12. On the Muslim origins of these nut creams, Serrano Larráyoz, "Confitería y cocina," 2008, 142–43. On medieval creams Gorrotxategi Pikassari, *Historia*, 49. As food for the sick, Nola, *Libro*, 119–20, and Lobera de Ávila, *El banquete*, 121. Pérez Samper, *Mesas*, 63. The ingredients appear together in San Diego's kitchen accounts in the days just before the feast-day of San Francisco. *Libro, San Diego*. October 3–4, 1794–1795, L. 18840, AHNM.

13. A modern recipe: Josep Lladanosa i Giró, *El Gran Libro de la Cocina Catalana* (Barcelona: Peninsula, 1992), 609.

14. Brillat-Savarin, Jean-Anthelme. *The Physiology of Taste: Or Meditations on Transcendental Gastronomy. The Philosopher in the Kitchen*. Transl. Anne Drayton (London: Penguin Books, 1970), 231–36. On sugar as a medicinal food, Fernando Serrano Larráyoz, "Confitería," 128. On Lenten eating Pérez Samper, *Mesas*, 275–88, and Domenech and Martí, *Ayunos*, Intro., xvii. Collations were also served to travelers: N.A., *Estatutos*, 29.

15. Granado, *Libro*, 150.

16. Lobera de Ávila, *El banquete*, 135. Agustí described young squash as being quartered, blanched, and kept in salt with vinegar, or, if pumpkins were picked young and green they might be hung from the rafters on strings or in nets, *Libro*, 73. Hernández de Maceras, *Libro*, 39.

17. Domenech and Martí, *Ayunos*, 181. Sever d'Olot, *Libro*, 48.

18. Their shared New World origins. See Book 2, Chapter X, note x.

19. The original Spanish pun reads: *"assi es la Calabaza menos mala que la que dan los obispos à sus subditos, pero mas gustosa."*

20. On onions as medicinal food for the eyes and symbolizing charity: Pineda, *Diálogos*, Vol. 1, 190. Ebro Valley onions are now grown under PDO regulations at Fuentes de Ebro, a river town east of Zaragoza which had a dense Morisco population.

21. Friary fruit: *Libro, San Diego*, April–October 1794, L. 18840, AHNM. On the friars padlocking friary orchards: Velázquez, *Doctrina*, 121. On fruit in general, Asso, *Historia*, 68 (peach-growing); Lobera de Ávila, *El banquete*, 179 (apples and health); Dunmire, *Gardens*, 125, 175–76, 190–91, 209 (New World). Novitiates' handbooks reveal an intended symbolism in friary fruit arrangements: Velázquez, *Doctrina*, 116. Hence, painters were reflecting not creating these. William B. Jordan and Peter Cherry, *Spanish Still-Life from Velázquez to Goya* (London: National Gallery, 1995), 20, 119, 161.

Book Two: Chapter IV

1. Genesis 9:3. To put the number of Altamiras's vegetable recipes in context, De Nola (c. 1529) offered 13 among 274 recipes (about one-twentieth) c. 1529; Martinez Montiño (1611) offered 40 among 500 recipes (about one-fifteenth); Altamiras offered 44 out of 220 (about one-fifth). Velázquez, Cap 11, "Del oficio del Hortelano," in *Doctrina*, p. 121; Vaquerín Aparicio, *Vida*, 259–61; Dunmire, *Gardens*, 2004, 125, 140, 175. Serrano Larráyoz, "Confitería," 142–43.

2. A similar modern sauce is given by Sor María Isabel Lora in *El Puchero de Las Monjas* (Barcelona: Martínez Roca, 2002), 266.

3. Salsete, *El Cocinero Religioso*, Vol. 2, 106. Santanach, *Sent Soví*, 127. Granado, *Libro*, 260.

4. Ibn Razin al-Tugabi, *Relieves*, 157. Sever d'Olot, *Libro*, 55. Vidal Llisterri, *Flor de Cardo*, 55. On eighteenth-century farmers' aversion to asparagus-growing, Asso, *Historia*, 69.

5. Bean growing in the Grío valley: Monterde y López de Anso, *Ensayo*, 15, 88. As Holy Week food Ibor Monesma, *Músicas*, 81. The local variety, for which seeds were kept by a few local people, are now being replanted in kitchen gardens.

6. Ibor Monesma, *Músicas*, 239. Bunuel tells a story of similar prayers for water in his childhood in Calanda (*My Last Breath*, 8).

7. Calling black truffles, desert truffles, and potatoes by the same name, *criadilla de tierra*, led to much confusion. Covarrubias says it originated for black truffles, "*Este nombre dieron melindrosos o melindrosas a las turmas de tierra . . .,*" "This name was given by *melindrosos* or *melindrosas* to black truffles," but he also quoted Dioschorides, who wrote, "*suelense cavar por la primavera*"—"they are usually dug up in the spring," the season for desert not black truffles and Andrés Laguna, "*carecen de todo sabor*"—"they lack all flavor," suggesting desert truffles or potatoes. *Tesoro*, 370. Eloy Terrón mentions further confusion with the name *patacas*, originally given to sweet potatoes in Andalusia.

8. On the spread of potato-planting: Terrón, *España, Encrucijada*, 98–105, 115–39. Bernardo de Cienfuegos is quoted by Javier López Linaje in *De Papa a patata. La difusión española del tubérculo andino* (Madrid: Ministerio de Agricultura, Pesca y Alimentación, 1991), 73. He also discusses the spread of potato planting up the Ebro Valley from the mid-eighteenth century, *De Papa*, 93. On the idea that agricultural crises in the 1740s, 1768–1772 and 1811–1812 were the trigger for the potato's acceptance: María de los Ángeles Pérez Samper, "La integración de los productos Americanos en los esistemas alimentarios mediterráneos," in *La Mediterrània, àrea de convergència de sistemes alimentaris (segles V-XVIII),* eds. Miquel Barceló and Antoni Riera Melis (Palma de Mallorca: Institut de Estudis Balears), 97, 128. Serrano Larráyoz, "Confitería y Cocina," 167.

9. The friars' kitchen garden, the largest in Zaragoza, appears in a 1798 plan: Asso, *Historia*, 408–409. Ibn Luyun summed up Muslim farming skills in his key *Tratado de Agricultura*, 1248. "*Los cuatro elementos que forman la agricultura: tierra, agua, abonos y trabajo.*" "The four elements that make up agriculture: land, water, manure, and work." On manuring as part of farming culture in La Almunia de Doña Godina, Francisco Zaragoza Ayarza, *Las Ordinaciones de La Almunia de Doña Godina* (1610), (Zaragoza: Institución Fernando el Católico, 2004), 74–77.

10. Miguel de Cervantes famously described Spanish Muslims as "aubergine eaters" in *Segunda Parte del Ingenioso Cavalero Don Quixote de La Mancha*, Ch. XXVII, 649. Ibn Razin al-Tugabi, *Relieves*, 268–77; 22 dishes. The variety giving small, round, white fruit reminiscent of eggs is depicted in the Valencian tiled kitchen in Madrid's Museo de Artes Decorativos.

11. Martínez Montiño, *Arte*, 259. Sever d'Olot, *Libro*, on the turnip as Capuchin eating because "*satesface pronto,*" "it satisfies quickly," 50.

12. On Mainar turnips, Lasierra Rigal, *La Cocina Aragonesa*, 102–103. Locals say the original turnips were lost in the 1980s although one small local grower is trying to plant them now.

13. Gorrotxategi Pikasarri, *Historia*, 48.

14. Menon, the best-selling French cookery author, called cardoon *cardons d'Espagne* in *La Cuisinière Bourgeoise, Suivie de l'Office,* first published in 1746

(Angers: Maine, 1803), 264. Altamiras called it *"cardo de la huerta"* to distinguish it from wild *cardo*, which gives a vegetarian cheese-making rennet.

15. Lasierra Rigal, *La Cocina Aragonesa*, 185. Granado, *Libro*, 317.

16. Martinez Montiño, *Arte*, 295. Granado, *Libro*, 110.

17. Nola, *Libro*, 129 (*cazuela moji*). Granado, *Libro*, 262–63. Busca Isusi, *Antología*, 1993. Pérez, *La Cocina clásica*, 101–106.

18. Ibn-Razin al-Tugabi, *Relieves*, 271. Altamiras gave no raw salads; Salsete did, writing 50 years later in *El Cocinero Religioso*, Bk. 2, 104.

19. Martinez Montiño, *Arte*, 96–98.

20. Monterde y López de Ansó referred to beans as *"alimento común y ordinario de las gentes,"* "a common and ordinary food of the people," *Ensayo*, 15. An anonymous Catalan author also wrote in 1830 that they were "a principal part of cookery, mainly for the poor." N.A., *Manual de Cuinar amb tota perfecció / Nuevo Manual de Guisar Toda Perfección* (c. 1830), pres. y prol. Luis Ripoll (Barcelona: Cossetània Edicions, 1977), 89. Super and Wright point out the difficulty of tracking the history of beans in certain food cultures in which they were so abundant that they never became a food commodity. *Food, Politics and Society*, 4. In Aragón: Asso, *Historia*, 15–16. Modern recipes: Porquet Gambau, *Comer en Huesca*, 16, Lasierra Rigal, *La Cocina aragonesa*, 33, Sor María Isabel Lora, *El Puchero*, 125.

21. Busca Isusi, *Antología*, 125. Cooking dried broad bean recipes with fresh beans: Lasierra Rigal, *La Cocina aragonesa*, 117.

22. French dried peas: *Disposición*, Inventory 1761. Ex-cat, ACPV.

23. Green almonds in syrup, Baeza, *Los quatro libros*, 52.

24. Catalan *menjar blanc* still keeps its medieval rice flour thickening while most European blancmanges had switched to arrowroot, corn flour, or potato flour by the eighteenth century. C. Anne Wilson, *Food and Drink in Britain from the Stone Age to Recent Times* (London: Constable, 1973), 226. Flor Díaz Viñas, *La España dulce* (Madrid: Ciclo, 1989), 175. Sagastizabal, ed., *La Cocina monacal*, 15.

25. Fernández Doctor, *El Hospital Real*, 240. Her quantities for *panatela* are 2 oz bread, ½ egg, ½ oz sugar.

26. Later friary recipes for preserving tomatoes: Salsete, *El Cocinero Religioso*, Bk. 2, 133. Sever d'Olot, *Libro*, 77.

27. Olive growing: Asso, *Historia*, 68. Mata, *Arte*, 160–61. Song: Ibor Monesma, *Músicas*, 239.

An Addition

1. Alberto Bayod Camarero and José Antonio Benavente Serrano, *Neveras y pozos de nieve o hielo en el Bajo Aragón: el uso y comercio de la nieve durante la Edad Moderna* (Alcañiz: Al-Quannis, 1999). On Jalón Valley snow wells: José Luis López Casamayor, "Almonacid de la Sierra, Monumentos de Interés,"

in *ADOR 7. Arte, Arquitectura Civil en La Almunia y Comarca;* 1996: 126, 131–61. Marcelin Defourneaux, *Daily Life in Spain in the Golden Age,* transl. Newton Branch (Stanford: Stanford University Press, 1979) 65.

2. Gorrotxategi Pikassari, *Historia,* 1987 (Vol. 1, 318).

3. Cinnamon water at the Madrid court, Simón Palmer, *La Cocina,* 59. An aristocratic recipe with more cinnamon and sugar, Gorrotxategi Pikassari, *Historia,* 1987 (Vol. 1, 318).

4. Jaime Fabregas, *Traditional Catalan,* 323.

5. Fresh white cheese was made for San Juan (June 21st) in the Jalón Valley. Ibores Monesma, *Músicas,* 215, 238.

6. The peaches and plums are cut into strips before drying and curve into "ears." On *cascabel* plums, Busca Isusi, *Antología,* 270. On raisins, Schlatter Navarro, *La Embajada Keicho,* 195.

7. On other medicinal foods, see note p. 255n23.

8. Morisco *basilicón* was made with pine resin, beeswax and olive oil. Villaverde Amieva and Paramio, *Memoria de los Moriscos,* 181–83.

9. Martinez Montiño, *Arte,* 340.

Afterword

1. Handwritten friary kitchen notebooks inspired by *New Art* began to appear soon after it was published. Among them were *Arte de cuina* by Francesc Roger, a Franciscan lay friar in Ciutadella, Menorca, c. 1750–1764; *Común Modo de Guisar,* a Jesuit recipe collection dated by Serrano Larráyoz to c. 1754; the mid-1770s *Libreta* by Joan de Bagués, a Franciscan cook in Gerona's civil hospital; *Libro del Arte de Cocinar,* by Sever d'Olot, a Catalan Franciscan friary cook, who wrote in 1787, and *El Cocinero Religioso* by Antonio Salsete, an Agustinian writing in Pamplona in the late eighteenth or early nineteenth century (Serrano Larráyoz, 2008). All these authors drew on Altamiras in the way they structured their recipes and in the dishes themselves. In the nineteenth century, Francesc Santissim de Sagrament, an Unshoed Carmelite, handwrote a recipe collection openly critical of Altamiras. *New Art* was also influential outside Spain: the Portuguese author Lucas Rigaud published *A Nova Arte de Cozinha* in 1780 and in Mexico Jeronimo de San Pelayo, a missionary, wrote a handbook. Taken as a group, these books set a new model: each cook grouped their own dishes, often using local ingredients, around a shared core repertoire. Later nineteenth-century Spanish cookbooks handed on many of the recipes in *New Art,* but they were rarely credited. N.A., *La Cuynera Catalana* (1835), written for housewives, took on board 81 of his dishes, acknowledged by the authors simply as recipes by *"Autors que millor han escrit,"* the authors who have written best. Ángel Muro's *Diccionario* (1892), a two-volume reference work written for professional cooks, absorbed practically the entire book. Why, then, did Altamiras remain in print?

Small and cheap, the book gave recipes that were useful in every area of inland Spain and could be prepared in the simplest kitchens. Only in the twentieth century, as artists and intellectuals began to turn back to elements of disappearing Spanish culture, did Emilia Pardo Bazán, writing in 1913, credit Altamiras as the author of dishes, recipe by recipe, as he had requested in his prologue.

2. Tony Judt defined the edge as "the place where countries, communities, allegiances, affinities and roots bump uncomfortably up against one another—where cosmopolitanism is not so much an identity as the normal condition of life." *The Memory Chalet* (London: Vintage, 2011), 206.

3. Raimundo Gómez would have known the Cerro de Altamira as the best panoramic view around the Val de Jalón and his parents may have owned farmland near there. The 365° view from the top of this low flat-topped hill standing up above the plains would have defined the horizons of the world he knew before he went to Zaragoza: in this way his pen-name defined his cookery.

BIBLIOGRAPHY

ARCHIVE SOURCES
(with abbreviations)

Archivo Curia Provincial de los Franciscanos, Provincia de Valencia (ACPV)

Disposición de El Colegio de San Diego de Zaragoza (*Disposición*). Inventories, cost of works, lists of deceased. 1754–1798. Excat. Archivo Curia Provincial, Nuestra Señora de los Ángeles (Valencia).

Archivo Historico Nacional, Madrid (AHNM)

Cabreo del Colegio de Diego [*sic*]*, Zaragoza* (*Cabreo, San Diego*). General accounts. 1752–1767. Clero Secular Regular; Franciscanos Menores Observantes. L. 1871 (1878L). CSIC, Archivo Historico Nacional.

Libro de Gastos Ordinarios, que se hizó siendo Guardian el R.P. Fr. Francisco Fernandez, año 1793 (*Libro, San Diego*). Kitchen accounts. 1793–1798. Clero Secular Regular; Franciscanos Menores Observantes; L. 18840. CSIC, Archivo Historico Nacional.

Cuentas de Santa Clara, Calatayud (*Cuentas, Santa Clara*). General and kitchen accounts. 1739–1771. Clero Secular Regular; Franciscanas Menores Observantes; L. 18600. CSIC, Archivo Historico Nacional.

Expedientes de impresión (*Expedientes*). Licences to publish: applications and approvals. 1745–1760. Consejos; 5064. CSIC, Archivo Historico Nacional.

Archivo Municipal, La Almunia de Doña Godina (AMLA)

Capitulaciones de matrimonio (*Capitulaciones*). Marriage capitulations. 1693. Libro notario Crisólogo Pascual, 456, 46v. a 49r. Archivo de Protocolos Notariales. Ayuntamiento de La Almunia de Doña Godina, Archivo Municipal.

Archivo Municipal del Ayuntamiento de Zaragoza (AMZ)

Carta del Padre Guardián de San Diego (*Carta*). Letter from Guardian of San Diego. 1733. Archivo Historico; Caja 98. 2/2 (caja 7054). Ayuntamiento de Zaragoza, Archivo Municipal.

Archivo Parroquial, La Almunia de Doña Godina (APLA)

Libro de Bautizos, Difuntos y Matrimonios 1691–1739 (*Libro de Bautizos*). Book of Baptisms, Deaths and Marriages. Ex-cat. Registers of Baptisms, Deaths and Marriages. Archidiócesis de Zaragoza, Archivo Parroquial La Almunia de Doña Godina, Nuestra Señora de Asunción.

Colección Real, Archivo General (CRAG)

Testamento de María de Austria (*Testamento*). Will. 1603. Archivo Monasterio Descalzas Reales; Caja 83, Exp.12; Caja 66, Exp. 50. Patrimonio Nacional. Colección Real, Palacio Real de Madrid.

Contratos Francisco Ardit (*Contratos Ardit*). Court cooks' contracts. 1745, 1758. Archivo Personal; Archivo General; Caja 1340; Exp. 8, 9. Patrimonio Nacional. Colección Real, Palacio Real de Madrid.

The University Library, Special Collections (Cookery), Leeds (ULSCL)

Llibreta del Hermano Joan Bagués del Hospital Civil de Gerona (*Llibreta Joan Bagués*). Kitchen notebook. c. 1775. Special Collections (Cookery), MS 47. University of Leeds, The University Library.

ARTICLES AND GENERAL BOOKS

Abad Zardoya, Carmen. *La casa y los objetos. Espacio doméstico y cultura material en la Zaragoza de la primera mitad del XVIII.* Zaragoza: Delegación del Gobierno en Aragón y Caja de Ahorros de la Inmaculada, 2005.

Aguilar Piñal, Francisco. *Bibliografía de autores del siglo XVIII.* Madrid: Consejo Superior de Investigaciones Científicas, 1981–2001.

Agulló y Cobo, Mercedes. *La Imprenta y comercio de libros en Madrid, siglos XVI–VXIII.* Madrid: Universidad Complutense de Madrid, 1981–2001.

Agustí, Miquel. *Libro de los secretos de agricultura, casa de campo y pastoril. Traducido de lengua catalán en castellano.* Barcelona: Juan Piferrer, 1722 (1617).

Andreu Lorent, Concepción, "El 2 de junio de 1.731 en La Almunia de Doña Godina, 'La Ruina,'" in *ADOR 2 (La Fiesta)*, 1996: 127–39.

Andreu Lorente, Concepción, María Pilar Latorre, María Carmen Potoc. "Evolución del plano de La Almunia," in *ADOR 1 (El Territorio)*, 1996: 21–53.

Anes, Gonzalo. *Las Crisis agrarias en la España moderna.* Madrid: Taurus, 1970.

Asociación Cultural Barbacana de Calatoroa, "La Mezquita Aljama Mudéjar de Calatorao, Zaragoza," in *ADOR 17 (Construcciones significativas en Valdejalón)*, 2012: 105–12.

Asso, Ignacio Jordán de. *Historia de la Economia Politica de Aragon* (1798). Zaragoza: Estación de Estudios Pirenáicos, 1947.

Bayod Camarero, Alberto, and José Antonio Benavente Serrano. *Neveras y pozos de nieve o hielo en el Bajo Aragón: el uso y comercio de la nieve durante la Edad Moderna.* Alcañiz: Al-Quannis,1999.

Bercebal, Diego. *Recetario medicinal espagírico.* Zaragoza: Diego de Larumbe, 1713.

Bernal, Chesús, and Francho Nagora, eds. *Diccionario Aragonés.* Zaragoza: Revista Cultural Aragonesa y Consello d'a Fabla Aragonesa, 1999.

Blasco Ibáñez, Vicente. *Reeds and Mud* (1902). Translated by Isaac Goldberg. New York: Dutton, 1928.

Blasco Martínez, Rosa María. "Datos para la historia de un gremio zaragozano," in *Cuadernos de historia Jerónimo Zurita,* 23–24 (1970–1971): 7–122.

Blasco Martinez, Rosa María. *Zaragoza en el siglo XVIII 1700–1770.* Zaragoza: Librería General, 1977.

Boadas Llavat, Agustín, "Ética y Vino: San Júnipero Serra: Los Franciscanos y California," in *Aportaciones al diccionario biográfico franciscano de España, Portugal, IberoAmérica y Filipinas.* Cordoba: Adef, 2014.

Brenan, Gerald. *South from Granada.* London: Hamish Hamilton, 1957.

Brillat-Savarin, Jean-Anthelme. *The Physiology of Taste: Or Meditations on Transcendental Gastronomy. The Philosopher in the Kitchen* (1825). Translated by Anne Drayton. London: Penguin Books, 1970.

Buñuel, Luis. *My Last Breath*. Translated by Abigail Israel. London: Vintage, 2003.

Burgos Rincón, Francisco Javier. *Imprenta y cultura del libro en la Barcelona del seteciento* (PhD diss., Universitat Autónoma de Barcelona, 1993).

Busca Isusi, José María. *Antología gastronomica de José María Busca Isusi*. Hondarrabia: Euskal Gastronomi Akademia, 1993.

Caimo, Norberto. *Voyage d'Espagne, fait en l'année 1755*. Translated by P. de Barnabite Livoy. Paris: Costard, 1772.

Casey, James. *Early Modern Spain, A Social History*. London: Routledge, 1999.

Cervantes Saavedra, Miguel de. *Segunda Parte del Ingenioso Cavalero Don Quixote de La Mancha* (1605/1615), ed. Allen, John Jay. Madrid: Cátedra, 2011.

Cervantes Saavedra, Miguel de. *Los baños de Árgel, El rufián dichoso* (nd). Madrid: Allianza, Madrid, 1998.

Covarrubias, Sebastián de, *Tesoro de la Lengua Castellana o Española* (1611). Madrid: Castalia, 1994.

Crow, John A. *The Root and the Flower: An Interpretation of Spain and the Spanish People*. Berkeley: University of California Press, 2005.

Cruz, Sor Juan Inés de la. *Carta a Sor Filotea de la Cruz* (1691). Mexico DF: Universidad Nacional Autonoma de Mexico, 2004.

Davidson, Alan. Edited by Jane Davidson, Tom Jaine, Helen Saberi. *The Oxford Companion to Food*, Oxford: Oxford University Press, 2006.

Defourneaux, Marcelin. *Inquisición y censura de libros a la España del siglo XVIII*. Translated by Diego González. Madrid: Taurus, 1973.

Defourneaux, Marcelin. *Daily Life in Spain in the Golden Age*. Translated by Newton Branch. Stanford: Stanford University Press, 1971.

Delibes, Miguel. *Viejas historias de Castilla la Vieja*. Barcelona: Destino, 1964.

Dunmire, William. *Gardens of New Spain: How Mediterranean Plants and Foods Changed America*. Austin: University of Texas Press, 2004.

Eiximenis, Francesc. *L'Art de manger, boire et servir à table* (1384). Translated by Patrick Gifrau. Preface by Pierrre Torrès. Perpignan: Les Éditions de la Merci, 2011.

Elliot, John H. *History in the Making*. Yale: Yale University Press, 2012.

José Estarán Molinero, "El Ciclo festivo de invierno en La Almunia," in *ADOR 9. Tradiciones y Leyendas de Valdejalón*, 2004: 13–20.

Fernández-Colomé, J. Victor, and Àlex Farnos, *Els esturions* (*el cas del rui Ebre*). Tarragona: Generalitat de Catalunya, 1999.

Fernández Doctor, Asunción. *El Hospital Real y General de Ntra Señora de Gracia de Zaragoza en el siglo XVIII*. Zaragoza: Institución Fernando el Catolico, 2000.

Font Quer, Pío. *Plantas medicinales, El Dioscórides Renovado*. Barcelona: Peninsula, 1999.

Ford, Richard. *A Handbook for Travellers in Spain, Parts I and II of the 3rd edition*. London: John Murray, 1855.

Gallart Jornet, Lorena, and Isabel Escriche Roberto. *La salazón de pescado, una tradición en la dieta mediterránea.* Valencia: Servicio de Publicaciones, Universidad Politecnica de Valencia, 2005.

García Serrano, José Luis, "Trabajos y oficios en la Edad Moderna," in *ADOR 8 Trabajos y Oficios en Valdejalón,* 2008: 23–36.

Gamoneda, Antonio. *Blues Castellano.* Madrid: Bartleby, 2007.

Garrido Aranda, Antonio. *Los sabores de España y América, cultura y alimentación.* Huesca: La Val de Onsera, 1995.

Ginzburg, Carlo. *The Cheese and the Worms, The Cosmos of a Sixteenth-Century Miller.* Translated by John and Anne Tedeschi. Baltimore: Johns Hopkins University Press, 1992.

Gómez de Valenzuela, Manuel. *La vida cotidiana en Aragón durante la Alta Edad Media.* Zaragoza: Librería General, 1980.

Gorrotxtegi Pikasarri, José María. *Historia de la confitería y repostería vasca.* Vitoria-Gasteiz: Sendoa, 1987.

Greene, Graham. *Monsignor Quixote.* London: Vintage, 2000.

Harvey, L. P. *Islamic Spain 1250 to 1500.* Chicago: University of Chicago Press, 1990.

Hayward, Vicky. "Celebrating with Altamiras: the Spirit of Fiesta Food," in *Petits Propos Culinaires,* 97 (2012): 45–57.

Hebrera y Esmir, José Antonio de. *Crónica de la Provincia Franciscana de Aragón, Partes Primera y Segunda* (1703). Coordinated by Antolín Abad García. Madrid: Cisneros, 1991.

Herrera, Gabriel Alonso de. *Agricultura General* (1513). Introduction by Eloy Terrón. Ministerio de Agricultura, Pesca y Alimentación, 1996.

Hughes, Robert. *Goya.* New York: Alfred A. Knopf, 2003.

Ibor Monesma, Carolina. *Músicas y palabras en Valdejalón.* La Almunia de Doña Godina: Tintaura, 2012.

Irving, Washington. *Tales of the Alhambra* (1851). Las Vegas: Lits, 2010.

Jaque Martínez, Encarna, ed. *Tierra de Conventos: Santa Catalina del Monte y San Cristóbal de Cariñena* (*siglos XV–XIX*). Zaragoza: Institución Fernando el Católico, 2010.

Lasierra Rigal, José Vicente. *La Cocina Aragonesa.* Zaragoza: Everest, 1987.

Latassa y Ortín, Félix de. *Biblioteca nueva de los escritores aragoneses.* Pamplona: Joaquín de Domingo, 1798–1801.

Lobera de Ávila, Luis. *El banquete de nobles caballeros.* Donostia: R&B, 1996 (1542).

Lomas Cortés, Manuel. *La expulsión de los moriscos del Reino de Aragón. Politica y administración de una deportación* (*1609–11*). Teruel: CEM. 2008.

Lópe de Vega y Carpío, Félix. *Arte nuevo de hacer comedias* (1609). Ed. Garcia Santo-Tomás, Enrique. Madrid: Cátedra, 2006.

López Linaje, Javier, ed. *De Papa a patata. La difusión española del tubérculo andino.* Madrid: Ministerio de Agricultura, Pesca y Alimentación, 1991.

Marín Padilla, Encarnación, "Los Judíos de La Almunia de Doña Godina," in *Sefarad*, L 2. 1991: 299–337.

Martín, Ángel. *Franciscanos de Aragon*. Carcaixent y Valencia: http://www.ofmvl.org. 1995–2013.

Martínez Llopis, Manuel. *Historia de la gastronomía española*. Huesca: Val de Onsera, 1995.

Montal Montesa, Rafael. *El Pan y su influencia en Aragón*. Zaragoza: Institución Fernando el Católico, 1997.

Monterde y López de Anso, Manuel. *Ensayo para la descripción geogafica, física y civil del corregimiento de Calatayud* (1788). Translated & introduction by José María Sánchez Molledo. Calatayud: Centro de Estudios Bilbilitanos— Institución Fernando el Católico, 1999.

N.A. *Diccionario de Autoridades*. Madrid: Real Academia Española, 1726–1739.

N.A. *Estatutos Generales de Barcelona para la familia Cismontaña de la regular Observancia de Nuestro Padre de San Francisco*. Madrid, n.p., 1705 (1621).

Fausto Moya Maluenda, "Las acequias de Michén, Nueva, Vieja y el Río Mediano," in *ADOR X, El agua en La Almunia y Comarca*. La Almunia de Doña Godina: Centro de Estudios Almunienses, 1999.

Peiró Arroyo, Antonio. "La Crisis de 1763–66 en Zaragoza y el 'Motín del Pan.'" *Cuadernos Aragoneses de Economia* 6 (1981–1982): 235–50.

Pérez, Dionisio (Post-Thebussem). *Guía del buen comer español. Inventario y loa de la cociina clásica española y sus regiones*. Madrid: Patronato Nacional de Turismo, 1929.

Pérez Samper, María de los Ángeles. *Mesas y cocinas en la España del siglo XVIII*. Gijón: Trea, 2011.

Pezzi, Elena. *Los Moriscos que no se fueron*. Almería: Cajal, 1991.

Pineda, Juan de. *Diálogos familiares de la agricultura cristiana* (1589). Ed. Meseguer Fernández, Juan. Madrid: Atlas, 1964.

Puyó Navarro, Jorge. *Notas de la Vida de un Pastor*. Ansó: n.p., 1967.

Real Academia Española, *Diccionario de Autoridades* (1723–1739). Madrid: Gredos, 1976.

Reyes Gómez, Fermín de los. "La Estructura formal del libro antiguo español." *Paratesto 7* (2010): 9–59.

Riley, Gillian. "Sor Juana in the Kitchen" (Paper presented at the *London Symposium of Food*, London, 1974).

Robson, Michael. *The Franciscans in the Middle Ages*. Woodbridge: Boydell. 2006.

Ruiz, Juan, Arcipreste de Hito. *Libro de Buen Amor*. Edited by Alberto Blecua. Madrid: Cátedra, 2003.

Sahagún, Bernadino de. *A General History of the things of New Spain: Florentine Codex* (1540–1585). Edited and translated by Arthur J. Andersen, and Charles E. Dibble. Salt Lake City: School of American Research, 1982.

San Antonio, Juan de. *Bibliotecha Universal Franciscana I y II*. Madrid: n.p., 1732.

Sánchez Tobajas, Inmaculada. *Identificación de los moriscos de Calatorao en el momento de la expulsión, apellidos calatorenses 1572–1620*. Calatorao: Asociación Iniciativa Cultural Barbacana de Calatorao, 2009.

Schlatter Navarro, Ángel Luis. *La Embajada Keicho y Espartiñas. Nuevas Aportaçiones a Una Estrecha Relación*. Espartinas: Ayuntamiento de Espartinas, 2014.

Serra y Pickman, Carlos. *La Cartuja de Santa María de las Cuevas, conferencia leida ante la Academía de Bellas Letras*. Sevilla: R. Blanco, 1929.

Serrano Larráyoz, Fernando. "Confitería y cocina conventual Navarra del siglo XVIII. Notas y precisiones sobre el 'Recetario de Marcilla' y el 'Cocinero Religioso' de Antonio Salsete." *Revista Principe de Viana*, 243 (2008): 148–86.

Simón Palmer, María del Carmen. *La Cocina de palacio 1561–1931*. Madrid: Castalia, 1997.

Simón Palmer, María del Carmen. *Bibliografía de la gastronomía y alimentación en España*. Gijon: Trea, 2003.

Super, John C., and Thomas C. Wright, eds. *Food, Politics and Society in Latin America*. Lincoln: University of Nebraska Press, 1985.

Terrón, Eloy. *España, Encrucijada de Culturas Alimentarias*. Madrid: Ministerio de Agricultura, Pesca y Alimentación, 1992.

Vaquerín Aparicio, Daniel. *Vida, Espiritualidad y Proyeccion Social de los Franciscanos Descalzos en la España Ilustrada* (PhD diss., Universidad Complutense de Madrid, 2004).

Vela i Aulesa, Carles, "La col.lació, un àpat medieval, poc conegut," in *La Mediterrània, àrea de convergència de sistemes alimentaris (segles V–XVIII)*. Edited by Miquel Barceló, and Antoni Riera Melis. Palma de Mallorca: Institut de Estudis Balears, 1996: 669–86.

Velázquez, Francisco. *Doctrina para la educación y criança de los novicios y nuevos professos, que toman el abito en la S. Provincia de S. Juan Bautista de Frayles Menores Descalços de la Regular Observancia de N. Serafico P.S. Francisco*. Valencia: Impr. Viuda de Juan Guasch, 1650.

Villaverde Amieva, Juan Carlos. "Recetas médicas," in *Memoria de los Moriscos, Escritos y relatos de una diáspora cultural*. Coordinadores y editores Alfredo Mateos Paramio and Juan Carlos Villavierde Amieva, 181–83. Madrid: Sociedad Estatal de Conmemoraciones Culturales, 2010.

Zarco-Bacas y Cuevas, Julián. *Discursos leidos ante la Real Academia de la Historia en la recepción pública de R.P. Fr Julián Zarco Cuevas*. San Lorenzo del Escorial: Imprenta del Real Monasterio, 1930.

COOKBOOKS

Aduriz, Andoni Luis, Edorta Agirre, Santos Bregañas, and David de Jorge, eds. *Bacalao*. Barcelona: Monteagud, 2004.

Almansa Cervera, Esperanza. *La Cocina Bilbilitana*. Barcelona: Marrè Produccions editorial, 2004.

Altamiras, Juan. *Nuevo Arte de Cocina, Sacado de la Escuela de la Experiencia Economica*. Barcelona: Imprenta de Maria Angela Martí Viuda, 1767.

Ibid. (1767). Fuenlabrada: Medici, 1981.

Ibid. (1758). Edited by José María Pisa Villaroya. Huesca: La Val de Onsera,1994.

Ibid. *Nuevo Arte de Cocina, Sacado de la Escuela de la Experiencia Economica. Añadido en esta ultima impresión*. Barcelona: Joseph Bro, 1770.

Altimiras, Juan. *Nuevo Arte de Cocina, Sacado de la Escuela de la Experiencia Economica*. Madrid: Juan de Soto, 1760.

Altimiras, Juan. *Novísimo Arte de Cocina, selecta colección de las mas recientes fórmulas de las cocinas española, francesa, italiana y americana*. Barcelona: Parsifal, 1905.

Amaya, Matilde, and Eva Celada. *La Cocina gitana de Matilde Amaya*. Madrid: Belacqua, 2002.

Baeza, Miguel de. *Los quatro libros del arte de la confitería, compuestos por Miguel de Baeza, confitero, vecino y natural de la imperial cuidad de Toledo*. Alcalà de Henares: Juan Gracián, 1592.

Barrera, Juan Luis. OFM. *100 recetas de Fray Juan de Guadalupe*. Madrid: PPC, 1996.

Bosco Gracia Aldaz, Juan, ed. *Somos lo que comemos*. La Almunia de Doña Godina: IES Ramón y Cajal, 2001.

Dalmau, Antoni R. *200 Plats casolans de cuina catalana, recull de receptes populars*. Barcelona: Milla, 1969.

Díaz Viñas, Flor. *La España dulce*. Madrid: Ciclo,1989.

Doménech Puigcercos, Ignacio, and F. Marti. *Ayunos y Abstinencias, Cocina de Cuaresma*. Introduction by Dolors Llopart. Barcelona: Altafulla, 1982.

Domingo, Xavier. *De la olla al mole*. Instituto de cooperación Iberoamericana: Madrid, 1984.

Dumas, Alejandro. *Cocina Española*. Madrid: Seteco, 1982.

Gitlitz, David M., and Linda K. Davidson. *A Drizzle of Honey, The Lives and Recipes of Spain's Secret Jews*. New York: St. Martin's Press, 1999.

Gómez-Flores, Andrés. *Historia de la cocina de Albacete y sus mejoras recetas*. Albacete: Los Libros del Sur, 1997.

Granado, Diego. *Libro del arte de cozina* (1614). Barcelona: Pagès Editorial, 1991.

Hernández de Maceras, Domingo. *La alimentación en la España del Siglo de Oro. Libro del arte de cozina* (1607). Edited and introduction by María de los Ángeles Pérez Samper. Huesca: La Val de Onsera, 1998.

Ibn Razin al-Tugabi. *Relieves de las mesas, acerca de las delicias de la comida y los diferentes platos* (c. 1277). Translated and edited by Manuela Marín. Gijón: Trea, 2007.

Lasierra Rigal, José Vicente. *La Cocina aragonesa*. Zaragoza: Everest, 1987.

Lora, Sor. María Isabel. *El Puchero de las Monjas*. Barcelona: Martínez Roca, 2002.

Loreto López, Rosa, and Ana Benítez Muro. *Un bocado para los ángeles. La cocina conventual novohispana*. Mexico DF: Clio, 2000.

Mata, Juan de la. *Arte de Repostería* (1747). Burgos: Ediciones La Olmeda, 1992).

McGee, Harold. *Keys to Good Cooking, A Guide to Making the Best of Foods and Recipes*. London-New York: Penguin Press, 2010.

Martinez Montiño, Francisco. *Arte de Cocina, pastelería, vizcochería y conservería* (1611). Valencia: Librerías París-Valencia, 1997.

Muro, Ángel. *Diccionario de cocina* (1892). Introduction by Manuel Martínez Llopís. Donostia: R&B Ediciones, 1996.

N.A. *La Cocina de Los Jesuitas, Común Modo de Guisar, Que Observaban en Las Casas de Los Regulares de La Compañía de Jesús* (1756, 1818). Dos Hermanas: S.L. Portada, 1994.

N.A. *La Cuynera Catalana*. Barcelona: Imprenta dels Germans Torres, 1835.

Nola, Ruperto de. *Libro de Guisados* (1529). Edited by Dionisio Pérez and José María Pisa Villarroya. Huesca: La Val de Onsera, 1994.

Pardo Bazán, Emilia. *La Cocina española antigua* (1913). Madrid: Poniente,1981.

Porquet Gombau, José Manuel. *Comer en Huesca*. Huesca: La Val de Onsera & Diputación Provincial de Huesca, 1989.

Pérez, Dionisio (Post-Thebussem). *La cocina clásica española*. Huesca: La Val de Onsera, 1994.

Ripoll, Luis. *Manual de Cuinar amb tota perfecció / Nuevo Manual de Guisar Toda Perfección* (c. 1830). Barcelona: Cossetània Edicions, 1977.

Rodrigues, Domingo. *Arte de Cozinha* (1732). Valladolid: Maxtor, 2009.

Roger, Francesc Fra. *Art de la cuina. Llibre de cuina menorquina del segle XVIII*. Edited by Andreu Vidal Mascaró. Mahón: Vidal, 1993.

Sagastizabal, Javier de. ed. *La Cocina monacal. Los secretos culinarios de las monjas clarisas*. Coordinadores Hermanas Ana María y Ester. Barcelona: Planeta, 2005.

Salsete, Antonio. *El Cocinero Religioso instruido en aprestar las comidas de Carne, Pescado, Yerbas y Potages a su comunidad*. Introduction by Victor Manuel Sarobe Pueyo. Pamplona: Gobierno de Navarra, 1990.

Sánchez Meco, Gregorio. *El Arte de la Cozina en los Tiempos de Felipe II*. Recipes by Armando Jiménez Tejedor. San Lorenzo del Escorial: Egatorrre, 1988.

Santanach, Joan, ed. *The Book of Sent Soví, Medieval recipes from Catalonia*. Translated by Robin M. Vogelzang. Woodbridge: Tamesis, 2008.

Scappi, Bartolomeo. *Del Arte de Cocinar, Obra del Maestro Bartolomeo Scappi, Cocinero Privado del Papa Pio V* (1570). Translated and introduction by Rafaello Dal Col and Juan Luis Gutiérrez Granado. Gijón: Trea, 2004.

Sever d'Olot, Fray. *Libro del Arte de Cocinar*. Edited by Jaume Barrachina. Introduction by Xavier Domingo. Barcelona: Palacio de Perelada, 1982 (1787).

Thibaut-Comelade, Eliane. *La Cuisine Catalane*. Paris: Jacques Lanore, 1991.

Toklas, Alice B. *The Alice B. Toklas Cookbook*. London: Serif, 1994 (1954).

Urrusola, Antxon. *La Cocina del monasterio. Recetas para el cuerpo y alma*. Barcelona: Plaza & Janes, 2009.

Vidal Llisterri, Dario. *Flor de Cardo Azul, la gastronomía tradicional de Teruel*. Teruel: Instituto de Estudios Turolenses, 2003.

Zaldumbide, J. M. *El Bacalao recetario de la PYSBE*. Donostia: Ttarttala, 1992.

GENERAL INDEX

(braised dishes and stews), 7–9; fat, hens' ovary, 103; fish, pickled, 150–51; fish, river, 131–37, 145–49, 151–54; frogs, 151–53, 154–55; frugal, 113–15; fruit, 25, 187–88, 217–18; fruit, dried, 223; for a funeral, 53; funghi, 195, 196–97; game, 5, 18, 79–85; garlic, 11, 17, 21, 169–70, 248n14; "gilded hens," 98–99; green almonds, 212; green beans, 194; hake, 149–50; ham, cured, 51–52, 78–79, 110; hares, 54–55; honey, 123–24; lampreys, 12–13, 153; lungs, 76–77; morels, 195; mushrooms, 195, 202–3; mutton, 4–5, 19; nut creams, 177–78; offal (variety meats), 44–47; olive oil, 114–15, 174; olives, 215–16; onions, 25–26, 182, 186–87; oranges, bitter, 143–44; partridges, 84–85; peaches, 223; peas, dried, 211–12; pigeons, 97–98; pomegranates, 28–29; poultry, 4, 81, 89; preserves, 150–51, 214–15; rabbits, 49–50; red beans, 207; red bream, 142–44; rice, 68–69, 132, 175–77; saffron, 102, 238; salmon, 136, 144–45; salt tuna, 139, 141–42; for Saturday, 44–47; sea bass, 138; shad, 131, 151–53; sheep's tails, 31; snails, 152–54, 157; squash, 27, 182–85; sturgeon, 134–37; sweets, feast-day, 173–80, 212–14, 216, 217–23; tavern food, 54, 78; truffles, 195–97; tuna, 139–42; turkey, wild, 83–84; turnips, 199; vegetables, 180–87, 189–206; white beans, 206–8; wolf-fish family, 138
Ford, Richard, 54, 78
Franciscans, ix, xiii, xxii, 54; Christmas, 88; cookery, x, xv–xvi, xx, 3–5, 50, 113–15; everyday life, xviii, xxi–xxii; singing, 59; travellers, xx, 243n12, 78–80
friaries: bells, 35; breadcrumbs in, 73; chocolate in, 224, 256n4; Christmas, 87–88; feast days, 45, 57–61, 213; kitchen gardens, 189, 197; kitchens, xv, xviii, 155, 172, 217; meatless eating, 113–15; monasteries, 114, 124, 167, 169; olive oil, importance of, 256n8; ovens, 57; table manners, 36; wine, 54–55. See also specific friary names
frying oil, recycling, 129
Fuentes, Joaquín Pignatelli, Count of, 40

Galicia, 79
Gallego, Río, 132
Gallegos, Diego, 134, 135–36
Gitanos, 157
Gitlitz, David, A Drizzle of Honey, 18
Gómez, Catalina, xvi
Gómez, Jacinto, xvi
Gómez, Raimundo. See Altamiras, Juan
Gómez Flores, Andrés, A History of Cooking in Albacete and its Best Recipes, 86
Gonzalez, Carlos, 58
Goya, Francisco de, xvii, 38, 50–51, 80
Goya, José de, xvii
Granado, Diego, 235
Grío, Río, 194
Guadalquivir, Río, 134
Guadalupe, Fray Juan de, 180

hen coops, 89
Herrera, Gabriel Alonso de, General Agriculture, 89, 100, 107
Hita, Archpriest of, Book of Good Love, 87
Holy Week. See Easter.
Hospital de la Sangre, Seville, 126
Hostal Castellote, 74, 201–2
humors, 105
hunting, 81, 83, 85, 94–95
hygiene, xxiv, 36

ice churning bucket (garrapiñera) ingredients, 229–30, 234–39
Inquisition, xv, xxi, 20

xxi; patron, 40; prologue, xv, xx–xxii; publication, ix–x, xxi; success, ix

New World, 69, 83, 195–96; cattle ranching, 68; Franciscan travelers, xx; potatoes, 195–96; rice dishes, 68–69; salt cod, 117; tomatoes, 126; trout, 145–46; turkeys, 83, 88–89

Nola, Ruperto de, *Libre del coch*, xx, 84

Nuestra Señora de Los Ángeles, Valencia, 42, 88

nuns, 97, 108, 156; cooking, 45–46, 71, 97, 156, 206–7

oil, recycling, 129

Oliveras, Juan, xxi

Olot, Fray Sever de, 51, 53

ovens, 57, 232

Pages, Carme, xii

Pardo Bazán, Emilia, 87, 166; *The House of Ulloa*, 206; *The Old Spanish Kitchen*, 229

Peinada, María, 175

Pérez, Dionisio, 117; *Guide to Good Spanish Eating*, 77; *Spanish Cookery*, 148–49

Pérez, Fray Francisco, xvi

Pérez Palmer, Juan, 64

Peris, Vicent, 139, 141–42

pestles and mortars, 230–31

Philip V, King, xvii

pig-killing, xx, 4, 107–10

Pignatelli, Ramón, 40

Pineda, Juan de, xx, 114, 157

Pomiane, Edouard de 71

Poor Clares, 45, 97

Porquet, José Manuel, *Cooking in Huesca*, 39

potatoes, 195–97, 203–4; confusion with truffles, 264n7; potato planting 264n8; tortillas, 10, 249n18

pots, xx, 3, 230–31, 246n1; clay, 3, 9, 232, 237; earthenware pots, 3, 9, 230; *olla* (cooking pot), 3, 230–31

proverbs, 75, 76, 130, 192–93

Puxmija, Clara de, 20

Puyó Navarro, Jorge, 88

Pyrenees, 77

quail, 81–83; in al-Andalus cookbooks 253n2

Quevedo, Francisco de, 156

A Recipe Book of Extremeño Cooking, 156

rennet, thistle, 222–23

Reus, 213–14

Rico, Matías Juan, 176

Riley, Gillian, 147–48

Rodriguez, Domingues, *Arte de Cocina*, xx

Rodríguez, Jaime, x

Romans, 69, 174

Ruzafa, 42

Sánchez, Carmen, 118–19

Sánchez, Don Pascual, xv–xvi, xxi

Sahagún, Fray Bernardino de, *General History of the Things of New Spain*, 83

St. Francis, xx, 57

saints' days, 45

Salsete, Antonio, 192–93

salt cod, 117–18, 122, 125, 129; Spanish names for 257n3

San Antonio de Padua, Durango, 97

San Cristóbal, Alpartir, ix, xvi, 3, 31, 89, 113, 129

San Diego, California, xvii

San Diego, Zaragoza, xvii, xxi, 13, 40, 47, 131

San Francisco, California, xxii

San Francisco, Madrid, xv, xxi

San Francisco, Zaragoza, xviii, 224

San Lorenzo, La Almunia, xvi, xviii

San Lorenzo de El Escorial, 114

San Sebastian (Donostia), 124–26

Santa Clara convent, Tudela, 45

Santa María de Casbas, 98–99

Santamaría, Santi, 10

Sâo Pedro de Alcántara, Lisbon, 84–85

Saracens, 169

Sarobe Pueyo, Vicente, 54
Serra, Juniper, xxii
sheep, 4–5, 19, 29, 31
Sicily, xvii
Sierra de Ayna, 210
Sierra de Rodanas, 170
simples, 13–14
snow well, ix, 217, 265–66n1
spices, 9–10, 25, 230. *See also* food, cinnamon; food, saffron.
Sri Lanka, 220
stonecrop, 224

table manners, 36, 40, 169
techniques, 232; artichoke preparation, 70; braising, sealed, 8–9, 77–78, 85–86; custards, baked and boiled, 178–80; dried beans, cooked unsoaked, 206–9; *escabeche*, 143; fat, removing from soups and stews, 17, 19, 36–38; frying, 129–30, 230, 236; garlic, 21; *granizadas* and sorbets, 217–22; marinading and pickling, 135, 150–51, 216; pastry–making, 59–60, 152, 155; poaching fish in a clay pot, 146; rendering Iberico ham fat, 72; roasting (and pot–roasting), 52–4, 65–6, 83–4, 86–7, 88–9, 101–02, 106–07, 131–2, 138, 145, 183, 197–98; saffron, 102; salt fish, salting and soaking,141–42, 238; *sofrito*, 121; stuffings, 24–28, 92, 98, 183; tortilla omelettes, 19–20, 159, 163–64; thickenings for sauces (egg, fish gelatin, liver, roux), 13, 14, 15–16, 24, 37, 46, 147–48, 201; toasting flour, 93
Tejedor, Armando, 164–65
Terron, Eloy, 44
Thibaut Comelade, Éliane, *Catalan Cuisine*, 49

thistle mushrooms, 202–3
thistle rennet, 222–23
Toklas, Alice B., 152
tomatoes, 10, 11, 17–18, 89–90, 126–27, 128–29, 215; history and taste for in Spain, 126–27, 258n12
travelers, 78–80, 95–96
trout fishing, 145–46
Tudela, 45–46
Al-Tuğībī, Ibn Razīn, *Matters of the Table*, 92

Valdejalón. *See* Jalón Valley
Valencia, 42, 88, 131, 133; broad beans, 209; court city, xvii; cured fish, 139; eel dishes, 131, 133; restaurants, 64, 124; snails, 157
Vega, Lope de, xx; *New Art of Writing Comedies*, 16–17
Las Viandas de Armando, Avila, 164–65
Vidal Llisterri, Darío, *Blue Thistle Flower*, 53
Villa de Zueras, 132
Virgen del Pilar, Zaragoza, 218
Voltaire, François Marie Arouet de, xvii

water, irrigation systems, 191
wayfarers, 95
weights and measures, 232–34

El Zafrana, 102
Zaragoza, ix, xvi, xvii; bread riots, xxii; iced drinks, 217–21; irrigation systems, xix–xx, 197; pilgrims, 95; Río Ebro, 131; snails, 157
Ziryab, caliph, 193
Zouhai, Noreddine Lamaghaizi, 63, 123–24

RECIPE INDEX

wine, 77–78; flattened meatballs, 79–80; fricassee with garlic, 10–11; meatballs, 23–24; stuffed vegetables, 24–28. *See also* calf's cheeks; calf's liver; feet; ox's cheeks; veal

black pudding with onion, 109

blancmange: almond blancmange for Lent and Holy Week, 213–14; angel's blancmange, 42–44

blood: black pudding with onion, 109; fried blood, 47

borage: borage soup, 200–1; fried borage, 199–200

braised dishes. *See* stews and braised dishes

brandy: baked apples with cane sugar, 188

bread, 234; carnival dumplings, 73–75; cinnamon toasts, 214; country ham, artichoke and bread soup, 38–39; fish and bread soup, 167–68; game, sausage and bread soup for a grandee, 40–41; green soup with meat, 41–42; Lenten nut bread soup, 168–69; salt cod dumplings, 122–23; spiced bread sauce, 16; trout, ham and cabbage toasts, 148–49

breadcrumbs, 234; baked salt cod and breadcrumb pie, 114–15; braised onion wedges, 185–86; breadcrumb noodles, 75–76; crumb custard, 58–59; egg and breadcrumbs for frying, 236; fish cakes, 137; fried breadcrumbs, 169–70; fried stuffed hard–boiled eggs, 158–59; little chicken dumplings, 102–3; quail in a breadcrumb jacket, 81–82

bream, red: red bream orange *escabeche*, 143–44; roasted red bream, 142–43

brik pastry: pluck pie, 64

broad (fava) beans, 191; dried broad beans with rice, saffron, and mint, 208

broths, 234–35; broth custards, 35–36; chicken or hen essence for the infirm, 105–6; chickpea broth, 171–72; green vegetable broth, 234–35; meat broth, 36–38

butter, 235

butternut squash: squash and honey soup, 44; stuffed squash, 27

cabbage: cabbage custard, 181; carnival dumplings, 73–75; trout, ham and cabbage toasts, 148–49

calf's cheeks, braised, 60–61

calf's liver: Aragonese cheese and liver soup, 39–40; country ham, artichoke, and bread soup, 38–39; game, sausage and bread soup 40–41

candied egg thread, 159–60

candied citrus zest, 235; fish soup with candied lemon zest, 147

capers, 235; fricassee with garlic, 10–11; rabbit casserole with peppercorns, capers, and lime, 49

caramel: artichokes in caramel glaze, 71–72; custard, 179–80; Fray Juan de Guadalupe's honey and sugar caramel, 180

cardoons, 198; cardoon with hazelnut sauce, 201–2; roast turkey with cardoons and lettuce, 88–89

carnival dumplings, 73–75

carrots with honey and wine vinegar, 205–6

carters' chicken with poor men's sauce, 104

casseroles. *See* stews and braised dishes

chard: chard, fried two ways, 189–90; chard fritters, 181–82; chard, lettuce and sorrel soup, 172–73

cheese, 235; Aragonese cheese and liver soup, 39–40; aubergines with cheese, 204–5; breadcrumb noodles, 75–76; cabbage custard, 181; carnival dumplings, 73–75; country ham, artichoke and bread soup, 38–39; fish and bread soup, 167–68; fresh curd cheese, 222–23; green soup with meat, 41–42; lamb's feet with tomato, cheese and pine kernel sauce, 32–33; Lenten nut bread soup, 168–69; meatballs, 23–24; onions with a fresh herb stuffing, 186; squash purée with rice and cheese, 182–83

chicken: carnival dumplings, 73–75; carters' chicken with poor men's sauce, 104; chicken or hen with sorrel or wild greens, 96–97; chicken pies, 99–100; chicken with liver and wine gravy, 90–91; gilded cinnamoned chicken, 98–99; lamb, artichoke and chicken pie, 22–23; little chicken dumplings, 102–3; roast chicken, 89–90; saffroned roast chicken, 101–2; stuffed cucumbers, 28. *See also* poussins

chicken livers: chicken liver *pepitoria*, 91–92; chicken with liver and wine gravy, 90–91

chickpeas: carnival dumplings, 73–75; chicken or hen essence for the infirm, 105–6; chickpea broth, 135, 171–72, 234; chickpeas four ways 209–10; chickpeas for the high table, 210–11; chickpeas for the poor, 211; chickpeas, greens and eggs, 162–63

chorizo: carnival dumplings, 73–78

cinnamon, 220; angel's blancmange, 42–44; cinnamon *granizada*, 219–20; cinnamon infusions, 220; cinnamon sorbet, 219–20; cinnamon toasts, 214; dawn water, 221; gilded cinnamoned chicken, 98–99

cod: fresh, 118. *See also* salt cod

coffee: angel's blancmange, 42–44

cooking papers, 235

costradas. See meatloaves

country ham, artichoke, and bread soup, 38–39

couscous: barley and almond milk cream, 66–67

cow, or beef, in white wine, 77–78

creams, nut, 177–78

curd cheese, 222

custards, 178; baked custard, 179; broth custards, 35–36; cabbage custard, 181; crumb custard, 58–59

dawn water, 221

deep-fried puffs, 173–74

drinks: almond *granizada*, 220–21; cinnamon *granizada*, 219–20; dawn water, 221; iced milk, 221; lemon *granizada*, 217–18. *See also* milk

drunk poussins, 100–1

duck: duck for wayfarers, 95–96; duck with quince sauce, 94–95

dumplings: carnival dumplings, 73–75; frog dumplings, 156; little chicken dumplings, 102–3; salt cod dumplings, 122–23

eel: eel in hazelnut sauce, 133; rice with eel, 132; roast or griddled eel, 131–32

eggs, 154, 229; baked custard, 179; baked eggs with squash, tomato and mint, 160; boiling a couple of hundred eggs, 160; broth custards, 35–36; cabbage custard, 179; candied egg thread, 159–60; chickpeas for the high table, 210–11; chickpeas for the poor, 211; chickpeas, greens and eggs, 162–63; crumb custard, 58–59; custard, 178; egg foam, 162; eggs poached in saffron broth, 162; fish and bread soup, 167–68; fricassee with garlic or *aguardiente*, 10–11; fricassee with pine kernels and capers, 10–11; fried stuffed hard-boiled eggs, 158–59; frog's legs and poached eggs, 156; hard-boiled eggs in hazelnut sauce, 161; lamb and pepper stew, 11–12; lamb *costrada* with spiced omelettes, 19–20; lamb or mutton ragout with bread sauce, 14–16; lamb tortillas, 30–31; marzipan eggs, 164–65; pluck pie, 63–65; rolled omelettes, 225–26; salt cod tortilla, 163; thickening stews, 13

empanadas (pies): lamb, artichoke, and chicken pie, 22–23; thistle mushroom pasties, 202–3; squid pasties, 154–55. *See also* pies

endive: hot curly endive salad, 205

fava beans. *See* broad beans

feet: calf's feet fritters, 67–68; lamb's feet with tomato, cheese, and pine kernel sauce, 32–33; pig's trotters, 45–46

filo pastry: pluck pie, 63–65

fish: fish and bread soup, 167–68; fish cakes, 137; fish pickled in *adobo*, 151; a fish pie, 151–53; to preserve fried fish in olive oil, 150–51. *See also general index; specific type*

fowl. *See specific type*

fricassees: fricassee with aguardiente, 11; fricassee with garlic, 10–11; fricassee with jamón, 11

fritters: calf's feet fritters, 67–68; chard fritters, 181–82

frogs: frog dumplings, 156; frog's legs and poached eggs, 156; little frog pasties, 154

fruit. *See specific type*

frying, 129–30, 236

game: game, sausage, and bread soup, 40. *See also specific type*

garlic, 236; beans with onion, garlic, mint and saffron, 207–8; carnival dumplings, 73–75; fried breadcrumbs, 169–70, 186; garlic gravy, 16; garlic mayonnaise, 157–58; green, 24, 236; lamb tortillas with roasted garlic and thyme, 30–31; salt cod with garlic and parsley sauce, 121–22; Sor María Isabel Lora's beans, 207; spinach with raisins and pine kernels, 192–93

gilded cinnamoned chicken, 98–99

goat. *See* kid

goat's milk: angel's blancmange, 42–44

granizada: almond *granizada*, 220–21; cinnamon *granizada*, 219–20; lemon *granizada*, 217–18;

gratins: *patatas a la panadera* (baker's potatoes), 237; squash and tomato gratin with mint, 183–84

gravy: almond milk gravy, 80; garlic gravy, 16; liver and wine gravy, 90–91; spiced roux, 14–15

green almonds, 212

green beans, 194

green garlic, 24, 236

green mutton, 16–17

green sauce: salt cod in a green sauce, 124–26; trout in a green sauce, 147–48

green soup, 170–71

green soup with meat, 41–42

green vegetable broth, 234–35

greens: chickpeas, greens, and eggs, 163; potatoes and greens in saffron sauce 203–4. *See also specific type*

hake, 149–50

ham (cured), 71; beef *salpicón*, 68; carnival dumplings, 73–75; a fish pie, 151–53; a ham in spiced white wine, 78–79; ham rashers, three ways, 151–52; lamb's head with ham, garlic and parsley, 53–54; trout, ham and cabbage toasts, 148–49. *See also* jamón

hare in white wine, 54–55

hazelnuts, 236; borage soup, 200–1; braised lamb with pomegranate juice, 28–29; broad beans, 191; cardoon with hazelnut sauce, 201–2; chicken liver *pepitoria*, 91–92; chickpea broth, 171–72, 234; chickpeas for the high table, 210; country ham, artichoke and bread soup, 38–39; eel or monkfish in hazelnut sauce, 133; fish and bread soup, 167–68; green soup, 170–71; hard-boiled eggs in hazelnut sauce, 161; hazelnut sauce, 16; kid's *pepitoria*, 46–47; lamb or mutton ragoût with hazelnut sauce, 14–16; lamb's head with hazelnut sauce, 54; Lenten nut bread soup, 168–69; meat broth, 36–38; meatballs, 23–24; *picadas*, 237; rabbit in hazelnut sauce, 49–50; stuffed poussins with spiced lamb stuffing and hazelnut sauce, 92; thistle mushroom pasties, 202–3; toasted hazelnut cream, 178

herbs: herby citric marinade, 216; trout in a green sauce, 147–48. *See also specific type*

honey: carrots with honey and wine vinegar, 205–6; Fray Juan de Guadalupe's honey and sugar caramel, 180; salt cod and honey, 123–24; squash and honey soup, 44

iced milk, 221

infusions: cinnamon, 219, 220; saffron, 102

jamón (cured ham), 72; artichoke hearts fried with cured ham, 71; artichokes in caramel glaze, 71–72; carnival dumplings, 73–75; country ham, artichoke and bread soup, 38–39; flattened meatballs, 79–80; fricassee with jamón, 11; game, sausage and bread soup for a grandee, 40–41; pot-roast artichokes, 73; roast chicken, 89–90

kid: kid *pepitoria,* 46; pluck pie, 63–65; pot-roast kid, 65–66

lamb: braised lamb or mutton with lemon, 8–9; braised lamb with pomegranate juice, 28–29; carnival dumplings, 73–75; chicken or hen essence for the infirm, 105–6; fricassee with aguardiente, 11; fricassee with garlic, 10–11; fricassee with jamón,

11; green mutton, 16–17; lamb and pepper stew, 11–12; lamb and sausage loaf with pine kernels, 21–22; lamb, artichoke and chicken pie, 22–23; lamb braised with garlic, pepper and tomato, 17–18; lamb *costrada* with spiced omelettes, 19–20; lamb or mutton ragout, 14; lamb or mutton ragout with sage, bay, and red wine, 16; lamb or mutton stew, 7–8; lamb ribs, 31–32; lamb tortillas, 30; lamb tortillas with roasted garlic and thyme, 30–31; lampreyed lamb, 12–13; pot-roast lamb, 65–66. *See also* mutton

lamb offal and stuffings: lamb's brains, 32; lamb's feet with tomato, cheese, and pine kernel sauce, 32–33; lamb's testicles, 65; lungs in hot vinaigrette 76–77; meatballs, 23–24; pluck pie 63–65; roast squab or pigeonneaux with spiced meat stuffing, 97–98; stuffed artichokes, 70–71; stuffed poussins with spiced lamb stuffing and hazelnut sauce, 92; stuffed vegetables, 24–28

lamb's head: lamb's head with ham, garlic and parsley, 53–54; lamb's head with hazelnut sauce, 54

lamb's liver: country ham, artichoke, and bread soup, 38–39; game, sausage, and bread soup for a grandee, 40–41; lamb's *pepitoria* 46

lampreyed lamb, 12–13

lard, 101, 110

lemon: braised lamb or mutton with lemon, 8–9; candied citrus zest, 235; fish soup with candied lemon zest, 147; lemon *granizada*, 217–18; roast squash with olive oil and lemon, 183; roast turkey with soursweet lemon sauce, 81–82; trout in lemon sauce, 146–47

Lenten nut bread soup, 168–69

lettuces: chard, lettuce and sorrel soup, 172–73; chicken or rabbit pies,

99–100; green mutton, 16–17; lettuce packages, 27; onions with a fresh herb stuffing, 186–87; roast turkey with cardoons and lettuce, 88–89; stuffed lettuces, 26–27

limes: rabbit casserole with peppercorns, capers, and lime, 49; salt cod with lime, 119–20

liver: Aragonese cheese and liver soup, 39–40; chicken liver *pepitoria*, 91; chicken with liver and wine gravy, 90–91; country ham, artichoke and bread soup, 38–39; game, sausage, and bread soup, 40–41; kid *pepitoria*, 46

longaniza sausages, 52, 109; lamb and sausage loaf with pine kernels, 21–22

marinades: clove and herb marinade for fish, 135; herby citric marinade for olives, 216; spiced marinade for olives, 216

marzipan: marzipan eggs, 164–65; sweet tongued pastries, 59–60

mayonnaise, garlic, 157–58

meat: broth custards, 35–36; meat broth, 36–38. *See also specific type*

meatballs, 23–24; flattened meatballs, 79–80

meatloaves: lamb and sausage loaf with pine kernels, 21–22; lamb *costrada* with spiced omelettes, 19–20

medicinal remedies: bees' wax for burns, 224; stonecrop to heal cuts, 224–25

milk: angel's blancmange, 42–43; baked custard, 179; crumb custard, 56–57; boiled custard, 179–80; fresh curd cheese, 222–23; iced milk, 221–22; squash and honey soup, 44. *See also* almond milk

mint: baked eggs with squash, tomato, and mint, 160; beans with onion, garlic, mint, and saffron, 208; dried broad beans with rice, saffron and mint, 208–9; lamb or mutton ragout with parsley and mint, 14–15;

squash and tomato gratin with mint, 183–84

monkfish in hazelnut sauce, 133

mushrooms: braised wild mushrooms, 195; thistle mushroom pasties, 202–3

mutton, 19; braised lamb or mutton with lemon, 8–9; lamb and pepper stew, 11–12; lamb or mutton ragout, 14; lamb or mutton ragout with sage, bay, and red wine, 16; lamb or mutton stew, 7–8; mutton steaks in white wine, 29–30; roast mutton with cloves, 106–7; stuffed vegetables, 24–28. *See also* lamb

noodles, breadcrumb, 75–76

nuts: nut creams, 177–78; toasting, 178. *See also* almonds; hazelnuts

offal: green soup with meat, 41–42; offal sausages, 109; pluck, 63–65. *See also* feet; heads; liver

olive marinades, 216

olive oil, 174; barbel dressed with olive oil and citrus, 154; for burns, 224–25; to preserve fried fish in olive oil, 150–51; tomatoes preserved in olive oil, 128

omelettes: lamb *costrada* with spiced omelettes, 19–20; rolled omelettes, 225–26

onions: artichokes in caramel glaze, 71–72; beans with onion, garlic, mint, and saffron, 208; black pudding with onion, 109; braised onion wedges, 185–86; cabbage custard, 181; fried blood, 47; lamb or mutton stew, 11–12; Lenten nut bread soup, 168–69; onion *sofrito*, 120–21; onions with a fresh herb stuffing, 186–87; salmon and onion *sofrito*, 144–45; salt cod and onion *sofrito*, 120–21; salt cod tortilla, 163–64; snails with onion *sofrito*, 157; stuffed onions, 25–26; tuna and onion in white wine, 139–40; turnips in onion oil, 199

oranges (bitter), 144; barbel dressed with olive oil and citrus, 154; cinnamon *granizada,* 219; cinnamon sorbet, 219–20; herby citric marinade for olives, 216; red bream or snapper in orange *escabeche,* 143–44; salt cod with tomato and orange, 126–27

organ meats. *See specific type*

ox's (or calf's) cheeks, braised, 60–61

paper box, sardines in a, 145

papers for cooking, 235

parsley, 10; ham rashers with parsley, olive oil and verjuice, 51–52; lamb or mutton ragout with parsley and mint, 14–15; onions with a fresh herb stuffing, 186–87; salt cod with garlic and parsley sauce, 121–22

partridge: partridge casseroled in wine, 85; partridge in pepper sauce, 86; partridges with sardines, 86–87

pastries, savory and sweet: deep-fried puffs, 173–74; sweet tongued pasties, 59–60; thistle mushroom pasties, 202–3

pastry: frying pastry, 155; olive-oil piecrust, 152

peaches: dried peaches in white wine, 223

peas, dried green, 211

peas in their pods, 195

pepitoria: chicken liver *pepitoria,* 91–92; lamb's or kid's *pepitoria,* 46

peppercorns, 236–37; fried salt cod in pepper sauce, 129–30; lamb and pepper stew, 11–12; lamb braised with garlic, pepper and tomato, 17–18; partridges in pepper sauce, 86; rabbit casserole with peppercorns, capers and lime, 49

peppers (bell): chickpeas, four ways, 209–11; fried breadcrumbs, 169–70; tuna *salpicón,* 141–42

picadas, 237

pickles: fish pickled in *adobo,* 151

pies: baked salt cod and breadcrumb pie, 118–19; chicken or rabbit pies, 99–100; a fish pie, 151–53; lamb, artichoke and chicken pie, 22–23; little squid pasties, 154–55; pluck pie, 63–65; thistle mushroom pasties, 202–3. *See also empanadas*

pigeons: roast squab or pigeonneaux with spiced meat stuffing, 97–98

pig's trotters, 45–46

pine kernels: a fish pie, 151–53; fricassee with garlic, 10–11; lamb and sausage loaf with pine kernels, 21–22; lamb's feet with tomato, cheese, and pine kernel sauce, 32–33; little squid pasties, 154–55; meatballs, 23–24; rice in stock and pine kernel milk, 68–69; spinach with raisins and pine kernels, 192–93

pluck, 14, 237; pluck pie, 63–65

pomegranates: braised lamb with pomegranate juice, 28–29; dawn water, 221

poor men's sauce, 104

pork: carnival dumplings, 73–75; dressing a pig, 108–10; lard, 110; *longaniza* sausages, 109; meatballs, 23–24; offal sausages, 109; pork sausages or loin in white wine, 52; roast squab or pigeonneaux with spiced meat stuffing, 97–98; roast suckling pig with rice, 57–58; salting cuts, 110; scratchings sweetbread, 110; stuffed vegetables, 24–28

pot-roast artichokes, 73

pot-roast lamb or kid, 65–66

pot-roast rose veal, 48

potatoes, 196–97; *patatas a la panadera* (baker's potato gratin), 237; potatoes and greens in saffron sauce, 203–4

pots, 3, 230–31

poussins, 237; drunk poussins, 100–1; poussins with wine and saffron,

93–94; stuffed poussins with spiced lamb stuffing and hazelnut sauce, 92

preserves: fish pickled in *adobo*, 151; fried fish in olive oil, 150–51; tomatoes in olive oil, 128

prunes: dried prunes in white wine, 223

puffs, deep-fried, 173–74

pulses, 206–9. *See also* beans; chickpeas

pumpkin: baked eggs with squash, tomato, and mint, 160. *See also* squash

quail: quail casseroled in wine, 82–83; quail in a breadcrumb jacket, 81–82

quince paste: game, sausage, and bread soup for a grandee, 40–41

quinces, 94; duck with quince sauce 94–95

rabbit: rabbit casserole with peppercorns, capers, and lime, 47; rabbit in hazelnut sauce, 49–50; rabbit pies, 99–100

ragouts, 13; apple ragout, 187; lamb or mutton ragout, 14–16; squash ragout, 184–85

raisins, 237; a fish pie, 151–53; honey sauce, 124; little squid pasties, 154–55; spinach with raisins and pine kernels, 192–93; tuna fishcakes with raisins, 140–41

red bream. *See* bream, red

rice, 238; angel's blancmange, 42–44; beans with rice, 208–9; creamed rice with almond milk, 175–76; dried broad or fava beans with rice, saffron and mint, 208–9; rice in stock and pine kernel milk, 68–69; rice with eel, 132; roast suckling pig with rice, 57–58; saffroned rice with fish and vegetables, 176–77; squash purée with rice and cheese, 182–83

rice flour: almond blancmange for Lent and Holy Week, 213–14

rocket: potatoes and greens in saffron sauce, 203–4

saffron, 238; angel's blancmange, 42–44; beans with onion, garlic, mint and saffron, 208; dried broad (or fava) beans with rice, saffron and mint, 208; eggs poached in saffron broth, 162; lampreyed lamb, 12–13; potatoes and greens in saffron sauce, 203–4; poussins with wine and saffron, 93; saffron broth, 102; saffron infusion, 105–6; saffroned rice with fish and vegetables, 176–77; saffroned roast chicken, 101–2

salads, hot: aubergines with cheese, 204–5; carrots with honey and wine vinegar, 205–6; hot curly endive salad, 205; potatoes and greens in saffron sauce, 203–4

salmon: a fish pie, 151–53; salmon and onion *sofrito*, 144–45

salpicón: beef *salpicón*, 68; tuna *salpicón*, 141–42

salt: salting cuts of pork, 110; tuna *salpicón*, 141–42

salt cod, 117–18; chickpeas, four ways, 209–11; fried salt cod in pepper sauce, 129–30; saffroned rice with fish and vegetables, 176–77; salt cod and breadcrumb pie, 118–19; salt cod with honey sauce, 119; salt cod and onion *sofrito*, 120–21; salt cod dumplings, 123–24; salt cod in a green sauce, 124–26; salt cod tortilla, 163–64; salt cod with garlic and parsley sauce, 121–22; salt cod with lime, 119; salt cod confit with tomato, 128–29; salt cod with tomato and orange, 126–27; salting cod, 238; soaking dried salt cod, 238

sardines: a fish pie, 151–53; partridges with salted sardines, 86–87; sardines in a paper box, 145

sauces: almond milk gravy, 80; garlic and parsley sauce, 122; garlic gravy, 16; hazelnut sauce, 15–16, 47–8, 90, 128, 156–57, 195; honey sauce, 124;

liver and wine gravy, 90–91; pepper sauce, 129–30; poor men's sauce, 104; quince sauce, 92–93; spiced bread sauce, 14; spiced roux, 15; tomato and orange sauce, 126–27; tomato, cheese, and pine kernel sauce, 33

sausages, 238; carnival dumplings, 73–75; game, sausage, and bread soup for a grandee, 40–41; lamb and sausage loaf with pine kernels, 21–22; *longaniza* sausages, 52, 109; offal sausages, 109; pork sausages or loin in white wine, 52

scratchings sweetbread, 110

sea bass, roast, 138

shad, 151–53

sherry: egg foam, 162

snails, 157

snapper: roasted snapper, 142–43; snapper in orange *escabeche*, 143–44

sofrito, 238; onion *sofrito*, 120–21

sorbet, cinnamon, 219–20

sorrel: chard, lettuce and sorrel soup, 172–73; chicken or hen with sorrel or wild greens, 96–97

soups, 36–42, 44; Aragonese cheese and liver soup, 39–40; borage soup, 200–201; chard, lettuce and sorrel soup, 172–73; chickpea broth, 171–72; country ham, artichoke, and bread soup, 38–39; fish and bread soup, 167–68; fish soup with candied lemon zest, 147; game, sausage and bread soup, 40–41; green soup, 170–71; green soup with meat, 41–42; Lenten nut bread soup, 168–69; meat broth, 36–38; squash and honey soup, 44

spiced roux, 14–15

spinach: chickpeas, four ways, 209–11; chickpeas, greens, and eggs, 162–63; green soup, 170–71; potatoes and greens in saffron sauce, 203–4; spinach with raisins and pine kernels, 192–93

squabs: roast squab or pigeonneaux with spiced meat stuffing, 97–98

squash: roast squash with olive oil and lemon, 183; squash and honey soup, 44; squash and tomato gratin with mint, 183–84; squash in white wine, 185; squash purée with rice and cheese, 182–83; squash ragout, 184; stuffed squash, 127. *See also* pumpkin

squid pasties, 154–55

stews and braised dishes: braised lamb or mutton with lemon, 8–9; braised lamb with pomegranate juice, 28–29; braised veal, 55–57; cow, or beef in white wine, 77–78; fricassee with aguardiente, 11; fricassee with garlic, 10; fricassee with jamón, 11; green mutton, 16–17; hare in white wine, 54–55; lamb and pepper stew, 11–12; lamb braised with garlic, pepper and tomato, 17–18; lamb or mutton ragout, 14; lamb or mutton stew, 7; lampreyed lamb, 12–13; partridge casseroled in wine, 85; pot-roast rose veal, 48; quail casseroled in wine, 82–83; rabbit casserole with peppercorns, capers, and lime, 49; rabbit in hazelnut sauce, 49–50; thickening with eggs, 12

stuffed cucumbers, 28

stuffed vegetables, 24–28

sturgeon: poached sturgeon, 134; sturgeon fishballs, 135–36; sturgeon with an egg crust, 136; wood-grilled sturgeon, 134

suckling roast pig with rice, 57–58

sugar, 238

sweetbread, scratchings, 110

tempura batter, 236

thistle mushroom pasties, 202–3

toasts: cinnamon toasts, 214; trout, ham, and cabbage toasts, 148–49

tomatoes, 126; baked eggs with squash, tomato, and mint, 160; lamb and pepper stew, 11–12; lamb braised with garlic, pepper, and tomato, 17–18; lamb's feet with tomato, cheese, and pine kernel sauce, 32–33; roast chicken, 89–90; salt cod confit with tomato, 128–29; salt cod with tomato and orange, 126–27; squash and tomato gratin with mint, 183–84; squash ragout, 184–85; sundried tomato skin, 135–36; tomatoes preserved in olive oil, 128

tongues: sweet tongued pastries, 59–60

tortilla: lamb tortillas, 30–31; lamb tortillas with roasted garlic and thyme, 31; salt cod tortilla, 163–64

trout: a fish pie, 151–53; poached trout, 146; trout, ham and cabbage toasts, 148–49; trout in a green sauce, 147–48; trout in lemon sauce, 146–47

truffles, 195–97

tuna: tuna and onion in white wine, 139–40; tuna fishcakes with raisins, 140–41; tuna *salpicón,* 141–42

turkey: roast turkey with cardoons and lettuce, 88–89; roast turkey with soursweet lemon sauce, 83–84

turnips in onion oil, 199

veal: braised veal, 55–57; pot–roast rose veal, 48; roast squab or pigeonneaux with spiced meat stuffing, 97–98; veal steaks in white wine, 29–30

vegetables: saffroned rice with fish and vegetables, 176–77; stuffed vegetables, 24–28. *See also specific type*

venison: fricassee with garlic, 10

verjuice, 239; ham rashers with parsley, olive oil and verjuice, 51–52

vinegar: carrots with honey and wine vinegar, 205–6; fish pickled in *adobo,* 151; red bream or snapper in orange *escabeche,* 143–44

wine, 56, 239; apple and wine ragout, 187; braised calf's or ox cheeks, 60–61; chicken with liver and wine gravy, 90–91; cow, or beef in white wine, 77–78; dried peaches or apricots in white wine, 223; drunk poussins, 100–1; a ham in spiced white wine, 78–79; hare in white wine, 54–55; lamb or mutton ragout with sage, bay and red wine, 14–16; mutton or veal steaks in white wine, 29–30; partridge casseroled in wine, 85; pork sausages or loin in white wine, 52; poussins with wine and saffron, 93; quail casseroled in wine, 82; roast turkey with cardoons and lettuce, 88–89; saffron broth, 105–6; squash in white wine, 185; tuna and onion in white wine, 139–40

wood-grilled: lamb chops or ribs, 131–32; sturgeon 134–35